# The

## A Reader

# AFRICANS

This book was developed for general use in African studies courses and as the text for a telecourse. THE AFRICANS telecourse consists of nine one-hour public television programs, a study guide, and a faculty guide. The series was produced by WETA-TV, Washington, D.C., and the BBC with major funding provided by the Annenberg/CPB Project. Additional funding comes from the National Endowment for the Humanities, the Public Broadcasting Service, and the Corporation for Public Broadcasting. Project director and executive producer of THE AFRICANS is Charles Hobson, Senior Vice President – Special Projects, WETA-TV.

For further information on telecourse licensing, purchase of pre-recorded video-cassettes, and print materials, contact:

 **The Annenberg/CPB Collection**

1213 Wilmette Avenue
Wilmette, IL 60091
1-800 LEARNER (532-7637)
(In Illinois 312-256-3200)

# The AFRICANS
## A Reader

Senior Editor
## Ali A. Mazrui

Managing Editor
## Toby Kleban Levine

Coordinating Editors

Tracy Burke Carrier

Frieda Lindfield Werden

PRAEGER

New York
Westport, Connecticut
London

**Library of Congress Cataloging in Publication Data**

Main entry under title:

The Africans : a reader.

Text developed as a companion volume to the public
television series, The Africans, co-produced by the
British Broadcasting Corporation and WETA/TV,
Washington, D.C.
Includes bibliographies and index.
1. Africa-Civilization   I. Mazrui, Ali Al'Amin.
II. Levine, Toby Kleban.   III. Africans (Television
program)
DT14.A3745        1986        960        85-28166
ISBN 0-275-92066-6 (alk. paper)
ISBN 0-275-92073-9 (pbk. : alk. paper)
ISBN 0-275-92074-7 (SG)

Cover Illustration by Mark English

Library of Congress Catalog Card Number: 85-28166
ISBN: 0-275-92073-9

First published in 1986

Praeger Publishers, 521 Fifth Avenue, New York, NY 10175
A division of Greenwood Press, Inc.

Printed in the United States of America

The paper used in this book complies with the Permanent
Paper Standard issued by the National Information Standards
Organization (Z39.48-1984).

10 9 8 7 6 5 4 3 2

# Political map of Africa

# Contents

**Chapter 2: The Triple Heritage of Lifestyles    60**
Elliott P. Skinner

**Chapter 3: New Gods    82**
Lamin Sanneh

**Chapter 4: Exploitation    108**
Robert I. Rotberg

**Chapter 5: New Conflicts    133**
Pearl T. Robinson

**Chapter 6: In Search of Stability:**
**Independence and Experimentation     156**
Fred M. Hayward

*Readings*

**Chapter 7: A Garden of Eden in Decay?     189**
Victor Olorunsola, with the assistance of Dan Muhwezi

*Readings*

**Chapter 8: A Conflict of Cultures     212**
Elliott P. Skinner
Gwendolyn Mikell

*Readings*

**Chapter 9: Africa in the World     233**
Victor T. Le Vine

*Readings*

# List of Maps and Tables

# Foreword

*The Africans: A Reader* is an important part of a major international television project that has been developed over a period of five years. The prime-time public television series, *The Africans*, is hosted and has been developed by Ali A. Mazrui. It represents an unparalleled degree of joint development for its co-producers, the British Broadcasting Corporation and WETA/TV, the public television station in Washington, D.C. The entire project includes a nine-hour television series that will premiere on PBS during the Fall 1986 season, a companion book for general viewers by Ali A. Mazrui, a viewer's guide, a 13-week college course syllabus, a study guide, a faculty guide, a record album, and this text. It is expected that *The Africans* will reach audiences throughout the world, not just during its initial broadcast season, but for many years to come through rebroadcast, nonbroadcast uses, and adoption into college curricula.

Our purpose in producing *The Africans* has been to present Africa through the eyes of an African. Much of the complexity and glory of the continent, its history, and its people are unknown to Western audiences whose view of Africa has often been influenced by texts that emphasize colonization and news reports that are dominated by views of famine, coups, tribal conflicts, and bureaucratic corruption and bungling.

Ali Mazrui offers a different vision. Born in a British colony in Kenya and educated in British and U.S. schools, Mazrui is an internationally recognized scholar, author, and lecturer. In *The Africans* Mazrui examines historical themes that clarify the present reality and explores what he views as the triple heritage of Africa—its indigenous, Western, and Islamic legacies.

*The Africans: A Reader* introduces students to other voices on Africa to complement Mazrui's vision. Here you will see a collection of scholarly articles on a broad range of subjects from history to literature, from political science to anthropology. The text has been organized by Professor Mazrui and telecourse director Toby Kleban Levine to support 13 weeks of undergraduate instruction. Part I, Indigenous Africa, introduces students to one part of the triple heritage. Part II, Examining the Triple Heritage, nine chapters that correspond to the nine programs in the television series, looks at the conflicts and syntheses that have resulted from the coexistence of three major heritages in

Africa. Parts III and IV, Africa Is One and The Cultural Diaspora, consider Africa's relationship with and contributions to the wider world. In most cases, chapters include an introductory essay and a selection of short primary source readings. The text may be used as one element of a complete telecourse, supported by a study guide and a faculty guide, or may be used alone in African studies or related courses.

As producers of *The Africans*, we have put our best efforts into visualizing Ali Mazrui's themes and ideas. We have undertaken production on three continents. We have endured hardships entailed in filming in some of the more difficult parts of the world. Some 20 countries have been visited, and enormous logistical difficulties have been overcome. With the completion of the series, we will have filmed more than 5,000 scenes, logged hundreds of hours of film, and traveled on every kind of transport imaginable.

While we have struggled as producers, it is teamwork that has been the key to *The Africans*. This reader and the television series that it complements are a testament to what can be achieved when scholars and media producers join forces. The experience of working with Ali Mazrui, with his brilliant insights, was a powerful one. We are deeply grateful also to *The Africans* Advisory Committee, many of whom have written articles for this text, and to a group of scholars throughout the world who contributed their knowledge and insight to the production of *The Africans*.

We would like to take this opportunity also to express our gratitude to the organizations whose support made this project possible: The Annenberg/CPB Project, the National Endowment for the Humanities, the Public Broadcasting Service, and the Corporation for Public Broadcasting.

We hope this volume will enhance your appreciation and understanding of the television series, and that it will make you aware of the grandeur of the people and the politics of Africa.

Charles Hobson, WETA-TV
David Harrison, BBC
Executive Producers, *The Africans*
August 1985

# Preface

Three civilizations have helped to shape contemporary Africa: Africa's rich indigenous inheritance, Islamic culture, and the impact of Western traditions and lifestyles. The interplay of these three civilizations is what *The Africans* is all about.

Even before Islam came to Africa there was an older triple heritage on the continent: an interplay between African culture, Semitic culture, and the legacy of Greece and Rome. This ancient triple heritage is best illustrated in Ethiopia, where Christianity has flourished since the fourth century, where the impact of Judaism is captured in local versions of the legend of Solomon and Sheba, and where the Greco-Roman legacy is manifest in both social traditions and brick and mortar.

This ancient triple heritage (African, Semitic, and Greco-Roman) underwent a change in time. The Semitic element (which was once both Hebraic and Arabian) narrowed to become mainly Islamic. On the other hand, the Greco-Roman legacy expanded to become the impact of modern Western civilization as a whole on African life and culture. If Ethiopia is the best illustration of the ancient triple heritage, Nigeria in the 20th century is the best illustration of the new triple heritage.

But what is the African strand in these legacies? What indigenous civilization did Africa have before the arrival of Islam and the West? There are two major schools of thought among African historians. One school of interpretation emphasizes that Africa had indeed produced great kings, grand empires, and elaborate technological skills before colonization. The evidence ranges from the remains of Great Zimbabwe to the bronze culture of West Africa. Indeed, ancient Egypt was itself an African miracle and, in part, a "Negro" civilization. Because this school of historical perspective prefers to emphasize the glorious moments in Africa's history and the grand civilizations it produced, we may call it the perspective of *romantic gloriana*.

In contrast to this approach, there is the perspective of *romantic primitivism*. Here the idea is not to emphasize past grandeur but to validate simplicity and give respectability to nontechnical traditions. This historical perspective takes pride in precisely those traditions which European arrogance would seem to despise.

Romantic gloriana looks to the pyramids as a validation of Africa's dignity, takes pride in the ruins of ancient Zimbabwe, and turns to the ancient empires of Ghana, Mali, and Malawi for official names of modern republics. Romantic primitivism seeks solace in stateless societies, finds dignity in village life, and discerns full cultural validity in the traditions and beliefs of the people. *The Africans* aspires to do justice to both of these contrasting aspects of Africa—the great and the simple, the complex and the basic, the grandeur of scale and the dignity of diminution.

What both types of African society have shared is a nearness to nature. For centuries the continent has had abundant animal life and vegetation; and the indigenous religions have fused God, man, and nature. Islam and Western Christianity have challenged this fusion. Only man is supposed to have been created in the image of God, contrary to indigenous African beliefs that the image of God takes many forms. According to Islam and Western Christianity, among God's creatures only man is close to the sacred, in possession of a soul, and destined for spiritual immortality. This is contrary to indigenous religions which allow other creatures to share in sanctity and sometimes endow mountains and springs with a holiness of their own.

The coming of Islam and especially of Westernism have disrupted the Africans' ancient relationship with nature. The impact of the West has been particularly harmful. Capitalism and the cash economy have resulted in the rape or prostitution of Africa's environment, often by Africans themselves. Under the impact of the profit motive, which came with the West, Africans no longer hold nature in awe; they hold it in avarice and greed. Traditionally, Christianity has neither sacred nor profane animals; Islamic doctrine includes profane animals but not sacred ones. Indigenous African religion has always had room for both the sacred and the profane. By taking the animal kingdom outside the realm of moral worth, the Western impact on Africa has reduced animals to their economic worth.

In the final analysis, Africa's triple heritage is a social complexity rather than merely an ecological doctrine. The triple heritage is about man's relationship not only with nature, not only with God, but with himself. And, it is about women. Has Africa's triple heritage complicated the role of women in society or has it improved prospects for the female of the species? Islam gives women more economic rights, such as the right to inherit land, than they enjoy under some indigenous laws. On the other hand, Islam gives women narrower economic roles, for instance around activities such as cultivating the land or marketing the produce, than women pursue under indigenous traditions. There is a conflict here between formal rights, which are better protected by Islam, and practical roles, which are discouraged by Islam.

A similar dilemma can be detected in the West's impact on Africa. Uneducated or non-Westernized African women in the countryside are often at the core of agricultural production. But with Western education women move from the productive sector to the service sector. They learn a European language and other verbal and literary skills only to leave the soil in favor of the office, the hoe in favor of the white collar. Western education turns African women into clerks and secretaries instead of cultivators. This is a case of functional marginalization. It may be true that the West's impact upon Africa has raised the legal status of women, but it has narrowed the economic functions of women. Women's rights are better protected in the post-colonial era, but the role of women is less fundamental in the society than it was before. In short, the African woman is confronted with expanding rights and a shrinking role in the post-colonial state.

In the political arena and the economic domain, Africa's triple heritage is at the center of conflicts not only between indigenous and imported cultures but also between tradition and modernity. And the triple heritage has affected other basic conflicts within the African condition: tensions between city and countryside, between soldiers and politicians, between the elite and the masses, between ethnic groups and social classes, between the religious and the secular, and between a longing for autonomy and the shackles of dependency.

Given the African predicament, there is a search for a new way of understanding its problems and a quest for a new science to solve them. Western economists have in the past focused on theories of economic growth and development. In the case of post-colonial Africa, should we be looking for a theory of economic decay? Western aid donors have increasingly turned their consciences to those African countries which have always been poverty-stricken (the least developed) and may always remain seriously deprived. But a country like Ghana was once well endowed and has since declined. Is it more deserving or less? Is Ghana's worsening underdevelopment and relentless decay a warning signal for Africa as a whole?

In *The Africans* the problem of societal decay will be measured by diminishing productivity, declining stability, and the erosion of public morality. Dependency theories do not really explain decay. Taiwan and Singapore may be very dependent, but unlike Ghana, Uganda, and Zaire, they are booming rather than decaying. So why is Africa faced with the danger of decay? *The Africans* will confront that question in both a local and a global context.

*The Africans* aspires to approach Africa from these different perspectives in an effort to explain the historical complexities of the continent and the bewildering realities of its contemporary condition. It will seek to catch a glimpse of the soul of a continent—a soul which is presently split three ways and is in search of its own inner peace.

Ali A. Mazrui, D. Phil. (Oxon)
Research Professor, University of Jos (Nigeria)
Professor, The University of Michigan (U.S.A.)

# PART I

## INDIGENOUS AFRICA

### Christopher Davis-Roberts

*Indigenous*, the *Oxford English Dictionary* tells us, means "born or produced naturally in a land or region; native, or belonging naturally *to* (the soil, region, etc.)." The definition is clear, and we are all familiar with it; but in the context of Africa, the term often loses its true meaning and instead comes to imply something undeveloped or incomplete. This implication may take a number of forms, some obvious, some subtle. It appears, for example, in the idea that the indigenous is opposed to the modern, and that modernization would have to result in the elimination of indigenous culture. It is implicit in the characterization of indigenous Africa as ancient or traditional, suggesting that it has survived the centuries without undergoing change. Even when we speak positively of indigenous Africa as purer than Western culture, simpler and more organic in its approach to human life, we reveal a conception of the world in which life for "us" is fundamentally different from life for "them," due to the simplicity of "their" experience of life's events. We perceive the indigenous as present in their lives, but not our own. These pre-formed and often unconscious ideas we bring to the experience of indigenous Africa require careful thought, for they can cause us to view the facts about Africa in certain limited, pre-conditioned ways.

The organizing theme of this book is the concept that contemporary Africa has been formed by a triple heritage: the indigenous, the Islamic, and the Western traditions. This idea describes a social and historical reality, but also serves as a means by which our minds can grasp and our memories retain something of the abundance of information and flood of sensations involved in African experience. Taken from a certain point of view, the triple heritage might seem to be the story of how two foreign or externally derived traditions set to work on the cultural raw material of pre-existing, indigenous Africa. Seen in that way, the protagonists of the historical drama would seem to be Islam and Christianity—the familiar Arab and European cultures— while indigenous Africa serves as a setting or background against which their activity takes place. Underlying that view there is the additional assumption that Islam, Christianity, and indigenous African culture can be regarded as distinct or separable entities. However, much of what will be discussed in the chapters that follow will demonstrate that indigenous Africa thoroughly permeates the other two traditions. From this perspective, the indigenous constitutes the cultural medium or code in terms of which the "alien" forms have been domesticated. If Islam and Christianity tie Africa to other parts of the globe, it is by means of indigenous culture that they in turn are transformed into something specifically African. They themselves have become something "produced naturally in a land or region."

Approaching indigenous Africa on the level of sociological fact reveals still another ambiguity in our use of the term. Although many African societies are distinguishable by only slight cultural variations, there are over 2,000 named African societal groupings in all. Languages on the continent can be divided into four main families (Afroasiatic, spoken in North Africa and the Horn; Nilo-Saharan; Niger-Congo, spoken in western, central, eastern, and parts of southern sub-Saharan Africa; and Khiosan, spoken in southern Africa); and each of these language groups differs from the others as much as the Indo-European language family differs from the Sino-Tibetan. Within those larger families, there are perhaps as many as 1,000 African languages that differ from each other as much as English differs from German. (Vaughn, 1977:9) When we take into consideration the changes that history has wrought even within individual societies, it becomes clear that the word most characteristic of indigenous Africa is *difference*. One is struck by the generality and artificiality of a classification which would put this world of human experience into a single word. There is not one indigenous Africa; there are thousands.

It is in the domain of lived experience that the idea of the indigenous becomes most ambiguous of all. We recognize something as belonging naturally to ourselves or our region primarily when we come in contact with objects, beliefs, or practices that are exotic or foreign to what we know. In a sense, the indigenous does not exist *as such* in individual lives but comes into being in interactions—at the interfaces between one worldview and another. When an American comes to live in a rural African village, for example, much conversation is devoted to both the similarities and differences between the two cultures, and to the characteristics of other cultures in Africa and elsewhere in the world. In contemporary Africa, as elsewhere, people have a clear idea of what is indigenous to their own particular setting, and of what beliefs and practices are particularly African. What tends to strike the observer as indigenously African, however, are those aspects of people's responses or explanations that make sense when they occur, but which could never have been imagined in advance by an outsider. It is not so much that life events are different, but that there is a momentary difference in responses to these events. With explanation, the difference is finally resolved as understanding, sympathy, sameness. At such a moment, we must come to grips with our own cultural limitations—our own indigenousness to another, different cultural tradition. When we arrive at renewed understanding, we ourselves have been changed. Not only have we become aware of our own cultural pre-conditioning, we have also gained a sense of the universality of life's problems. At this moment, the indigenous disappears altogether, and there are only human beings.

The readings which follow have been selected to be evocative of themes and approaches to life that are indigenously African.

**REFERENCE**

Vaughn, James H. 1977. "Environment, Population and Tribal Society," in *Africa*, edited by Phyllis M. Martin and Patrick O'Meara. Bloomington: Indiana University Press, pp. 9–24.

---

## Reading I.1

Africa is present in Western life. In the percussive styles and improvisatory drive that underlie popular music, and in the forms which heavily influenced modern art, Africa has given shape to everything we understand as "modern" and "urban"—everything that makes us feel that life is endless possibility. Yet this very sense of familiarity can obscure the real differences between ourselves and Africa, and so keep us from discovering the identities—the universals—which Africa articulates in her own unique and quite specific ways.

In the reading that follows, John Miller Chernoff considers African social values through a discussion of musical performances. It is not just the sound, but also appropriate participation which makes a musical performance an important event. Learning to participate shapes a person's sensibility, creates his or her personhood, and brings identity into being.

## John Miller Chernoff, *African Rhythm and African Sensibility*

At an African musical event, we are concerned with sound and movement, space and time, the deepest modalities of perception. Foremost is the dynamic tension of the multiple rhythms and the cohesive power of their relationship. Founded on a sense of time and presence, the art of improvisation involves the subtle perfection of this rhythmic form through precision of performance, complexity of organization, and control of gestural timing. The act of creation is above all purposeful, never random, and the goal is balance and a fulfilling interdependence. As they display style and involvement, people make their music socially effective, transforming the dynamic power of the rhythms into a focus for character and community. We are even quite close to a metaphysics of rhythm if we remember that sensing the whole in a system of multiple rhythms depends on comprehending, or "hearing," as Africans say, the beat that is never sounded. At the convergence of essence and form stands the master drummer, not creating new rhythms but giving order and organization to those already there. Every place, a drummer once told me, has its own rhythms which give it character; going there, one must find a rhythm that fits, and improvise on it. On the man's drum was painted the popular slogan, "God's Time is the Best." In applying a musical metaphor to social situations, this drummer asserted that his musical sensibility could serve him well as a basis for participation in African social life....

African affinity for polymetric musical forms indicates that, in the most fundamental sense, the African sensibility is profoundly pluralistic. One of the most patronizing Western biases regarding people in societies we call "traditional" is the notion that the events of their lives are nestled in and determined by the ready-made patterns of a culture they uncritically accept. Indeed, the idea of a traditional "sensibility" sometimes arouses in us a kind of romantic nostalgia, as if people in traditional societies live in a world of continuously meaningful experiences. Actually, life in African societies seems, possibly even more than in our own, to be marked by a discontinuity of experience in the encounters and status dramas of daily life. Just as a participant at an African musical event is unlikely to stay within one rhythmic perspective, so do Africans maintain a flexible and complicated orientation toward themselves and their lives. Relying on their sense of appropriateness, they may participate equally in what we might think of as exclusive kinds of identities, perhaps being both nationalistic and tribalistic, Animist and Christian or Muslim, traditional and Westernized.... In African cities, one can find magnified almost all the factors which various social analyses have said are the source of our contemporary anxiety: rapid change, congestion and noise, unemployment and poverty, uprootedness and family dispersion. Without suggesting that the situation is good, one at least notices that it does not seem as debilitating on the human level as it could be. In this disorganized and potentially alienating world, the adaptability and strength of an African's sense of community and personal identity reside in the aesthetic and ethical sensibility which we have seen both expressed and cultivated in one of its aspects, music. As such, the values in an African musical event represent not an integrity from which we are moving away but rather an integrity which, with understanding, we might approach. It is a felicitous orientation in a world of many forms.

---

## Reading I.2

The multiple aspects of social reality are complemented by the multiple layers of metaphysical reality—ways of addressing the problems posed to people by their life experience itself. Westerners have often dismissed as mere superstition ideas that provide the means for addressing some of life's deepest mysteries. The following discussion by Edward Evans Evans-Pritchard demonstrates how members of one African society view the relationship between chance and fate. These people, the Azande of Zaire and the Sudan, use the concept of witchcraft to explain unique events, which are more fascinating to them than is the general and universal.

---

## Edward Evans Evans-Pritchard, *Witchcraft, Oracles and Magic among the Azande*

My old friend Ongosi was many years ago injured by an elephant while out hunting, and his prince, Basongoda, consulted the oracles to discover who had bewitched him. We must distinguish here between the elephant and its prowess, on the one hand, and the fact that a particular elephant injured a particular man, on the other hand. The Supreme Being, not witchcraft, created elephants and gave them tusks and a trunk and huge legs so that they are able to pierce men and fling them sky high and reduce them to pulp by kneeling on them. But whenever men and elephants come across one another in the bush these dreadful things do not happen. They are rare events. Why, then, should this particular man on this one occasion in a life crowded with similar situations in which he and his friends emerged scatheless have been gored by this particular beast? Why he and not someone else? Why on this occasion and not on other occasions? Why by this elephant and not by other elephants? It is the particular and variable conditions of an event and not the general and universal conditions that witchcraft explains. Fire is hot, but it is not hot owing to witchcraft, for that is its nature. It is a universal quality of fire to burn, but it is not a universal quality of fire to burn *you*. This may never happen; or once in a lifetime, and then only if you have been bewitched.

In Zandeland sometimes an old granary collapses. There is nothing remarkable in this. Every Zande knows that termites eat the supports in course of time and that even the hardest woods decay after years of service. Now a granary is the summerhouse of a Zande homestead and people sit beneath it in the heat of the day and chat or play the African hole-game or work at some craft. Consequently it may happen that there are people sitting beneath the granary when it collapses and they are injured, for it is a heavy structure made of beams and clay and may be stored with eleusine as well. Now why should these particular people have been sitting under this particular granary at the particular moment when it collapsed? That it should collapse is easily intelligible, but why should it have collapsed at the particular moment when these particular people were sitting beneath it? Through years it might have collapsed, so why should it fall just when certain people sought its kindly shelter? We say that the granary collapsed because its supports were eaten away by termites. That is the cause that explains the collapse of the granary. We also say that people were sitting under it at the time because it was in the heat of the day and they thought that it would be a comfortable place to talk and work. This is the cause of people being under the granary at the time it collapsed. To our minds the only relationship between these two independently caused facts is their coincidence in time and space. We have no explanation of why the two chains of causation intersected at a certain time and in a certain place, for there is no interdependence between them.

Zande philosophy can supply the missing link. The Zande knows that the supports were undermined by termites and that people were sitting beneath the granary in order to escape the heat and glare of the sun. But he knows besides why these two events occurred at a precisely similar moment in time and space. It was due to the action of witchcraft. If there had been no witchcraft people would have been sitting under the granary and it would not have fallen on them, or it would have collapsed but the people would not have been sheltering under it at the time. Witchcraft explains the coincidence of these two happenings.

---

## Reading I.3

African cultural forms provide the means for people to think clearly and deeply about human character. These excerpts from a discussion by Victor Turner give examples of how the Ndembu of Zambia define good and bad character, and how character affects the outcome of social events. Ideas of personality underlie Ndembu divination techniques, which can be used for determining the necessary actions for responsible management of illness. The figurine of *Chamutang'a* described is one of the two *tupyona* figures typically found in diviners' baskets and used by them in divination trances.

---

## Victor Turner, *Revelation and Divination in Ndembu Ritual*

The ... *Chamutang'a* ... represents a man sitting huddled up with chin on hands and elbows on knees. *Chamutang'a* means an irresolute, changeable person. One informant told me a little tale to bring out the meaning of the term. "Once there was a sick man in a certain village. One of his relatives said to the others, 'Let's go to another village to divine for our relative who is very ill.' They answered, 'Oh but we haven't enough money to pay a diviner.' Some days passed, but the patient grew worse. So another relative said, 'Please let's go today to divine for our kinsman, for he seems very, very ill.' The others said, 'Why not ask those two men over there to go with you? For our part we haven't enough money, and besides we're tired today for we drank a lot of beer yesterday and anyway we've just come from working in our gardens. We can't possibly go today. We're exhausted.' Time passed, and still the man grew worse. At last some women asked the patient's relatives, 'What about paying the sick man a visit? After all you do live in the same village.' They replied, 'Oh, is he really ill? Yes, I think we'd better have a look at him.' They entered his hut. They found him on the point of death and cried, 'Oh dear, he must be dead. Well, we can't do anything more for him now.' A few days later the patient really was dead. Now when that matter was taken to a diviner, he divined and saw *Chamutang'a* on top, and said, 'This matter was never properly settled by the patient's relatives. That is why he died.' He went on to find out who the actual sorcerer was. The sorcerer was dealt with, but those hesitating people had their share of the guilt even though they weren't sorcerers or witches themselves. In this case *Chamutang'a* stood for prevaricating people [*antu adilabeka*]."

\* \* \*

A sinner (*mukwansbidi*) is defined as "one who has ill feeling for other people [*mukwansbidi watiyang'a kutama nawakwawu antu*]." *Ku-tama*, "to be bad, evil, unpleasant, ugly," is linked with the symbolism of blackness, darkness, death, sterility, and night in Ndembu ritual. It is the opposite of *kuwaba*, "to be good, morally upright, pleasant, beautiful." It is also linked with witchcraft/sorcery, theft, adulterous lust, and murder. *Ku-tama* is associated with "secret things" (*yiswamu*), with the concealment of thoughts or possessions from others. What is good, for Ndembu, is the open, the public, the unconcealed, the sincere. A man is said to be good when he performs his duties from "the liver," not from calculated policy, concealing malice beneath outward politeness. A man is bad when there is a marked inconsistency or disparity between his public behavior and his private thoughts and feelings. The former is outwardly correct, but it conceals malice and envy. Thus the hypocrite is the real sinner, "the whited sepulchre." We find in the diviner's basket a representation of the weeping hypocrite (*Katwambimbi*) and several references to the duplicity of bad people, the witches and sorcerers.

---

### Reading I.4

If religion creates a map of the world whereby humans find their place and determine their responsibilities, the inverse is also true: it is by virtue of the vividness of human relations that rites and ritual actions shape people's experience of reality. In the next three readings, we consider how a society shapes its members and itself through ritual or symbolic means.

In divination and religion we may see symbols as objects, or as means of reflecting upon human relationships; but there is also a respect in which the capacity of ritual to change, indeed to create, a human being is dynamically real. The ordeal of initiation permanently transfigures young men and women. It changes them into adults in the domain of social life, and it teaches them adult responsibilities by means of symbols. Victor Turner has examined transfiguration and symbols as they relate to initiation among the Bemba of Zambia. Here he is discussing the process whereby girls are transformed into women.

---

## Victor Turner, *The Forest of Symbols*

The passivity of neophytes to their instructors, their malleability, which is increased by submission to ordeal, their reduction to a uniform condition, are signs of the process whereby they are ground down to be fashioned anew and endowed with additional powers to cope with their new station in life. Dr. [Audrey] Richards, in her superb study of Bemba girls' puberty rites, *Chisungu*, has told us that Bemba speak of "growing a girl" when they mean initiating her (1956, 121). This term, "to grow" well expresses how many peoples think of transition rites. We are inclined, as sociologists, to reify our abstractions (it is indeed a device which helps us to understand many kinds of social interconnection) and to talk about persons "moving through structural positions in a hierarchical frame" and the like. Not so the Bemba and the Shilluk of the Sudan who see the status or condition embodied or incarnate, if you like, in the person. To "grow" a girl into a woman is to effect an ontological transformation; it is not merely to convey an unchanging substance from one position to another by a quasi-mechanical force. Howitt saw Kuringals in Australia and I have seen Ndembu in Africa drive away grown-up men before a circumcision ceremony because they had not been initiated. Among Ndembu, men were also chased off because they had only been circumcised at the Mission Hospital and had not undergone the full bush seclusion according to the orthodox Ndembu rite. These biologically mature men had not been "made men" by the proper ritual procedures. It is the ritual and the esoteric teaching which grows girls and makes men. It is the ritual, too, which among Shilluk makes a prince into a king or, among Luvale, a cultivator into a hunter....

When one examines the masks, costumes, figurines, and such displayed in initiation situations, one is often struck, as I have been when observing Ndembu masks in circumcision and funerary rites, by the way in which certain natural and cultural features are represented as disproportionately large or small. A head, nose, or phallus, a hoe, bow, or meal mortar are represented as huge or tiny by comparison with other features of their context which retain their normal size. (For a good example of this, see "The Man Without Arms" in *Chisungu* [Richards 1956, 211], a figurine of a lazy man with an enormous penis but no arms.) Sometimes things retain their customary shapes but are portrayed in unusual colors. What is the point of this exaggeration amounting sometimes to caricature? It seems to me that to enlarge or diminish or discolor in this way is a primordial mode of abstraction. The outstandingly exaggerated feature is made into an object of reflection. Usually it is not a univocal symbol that is thus represented but a multivocal one, a semantic molecule with many components. One example is the Bemba pottery emblem *Coshi wa ng'oma*, "The Nursing Mother," described by Audrey Richards in *Chisungu*. This is a clay figurine, nine inches high, of an exaggeratedly pregnant mother shown carrying four babies at the same time, one at her breast and three at her back. To this figurine is attached a riddling song:

> My mother deceived me!
> *Coshi wa ng'oma*!
> So you have deceived me;
> I have become pregnant again.

Bemba women interpreted this to Richards as follows:

*Coshi wa ng'oma* was a midwife of legendary fame and is merely addressed in this song. The girl complains because her mother told her to wean her first child too soon so that it died; or alternatively told her that she would take the first child if her daughter had a second one. But she was tricking her and now the girl has two babies to look after. The moral stressed is the duty of refusing intercourse with the husband before the baby is weaned, i.e., at the second or third year. This is a common Bemba practice (1956, 209–210).

In the figurine the exaggerated features are the number of children carried at once by the woman and her enormously distended belly. Coupled with the song, it encourages the novice to ponder upon two relationships vital to her, those with her mother and her husband. Unless the novice observes the Bemba weaning custom, her mother's desire for grandchildren to increase her matrilineage and her husband's desire for renewed sexual intercourse will between them actually destroy and not increase her offspring. Underlying this is the deeper moral that to abide by tribal custom and not to sin against it either by excess or defect is to live satisfactorily. Even to please those one loves may be to invite calamity, if such compliance defies the immemorial wisdom of the elders embodied in the *mbusa*. This wisdom is vouched for by the mythical and archetypal midwife *Coshi wa ng'oma*.

---

### Reading I.5

Initiation does not take place only with reference to the formation of the individual. On the contrary, its greatest significance lies in the purpose it serves for society as a whole. In his discussion of the Gikuyu society, Jomo Kenyatta speaks of initiation under the topic of education and also under the topic of government in traditional life. In the following reading he shows that circumcision was the means by which the whole society progressed: individuals moving through the ranks and through time, and the group not simply maintaining itself but also producing its own history.

---

## Jomo Kenyatta, *Facing Mount Kenya*

In all tribal education the emphasis lies on a particular act of behaviour in a concrete situation. While the emphasis lies in the sphere of behaviour, it is none the less true that the growing child is acquiring a mass of knowledge all the time....

To return to our analysis of the Gikuyu system of government. We have seen that the circumcision ceremony was the only qualification which gave a man the recognition of manhood and the full right of citizenship. It is therefore necessary to take the circumcision ceremony as our starting-point.

Before a boy goes through this ceremony he is considered as a mere child, and as such has no responsibility in the tribal organisation; his parents are responsible for all his actions. If he commits any crime he cannot be prosecuted personally, it is his parents' duty to answer for him. But this liberty ceases immediately he is circumcised, because he is now "full grown," and has assumed the title of *mondomorome* (a he-man), and as such he must share the responsibility with other "he-men" (*arome*). As soon as his circumcision wound heals he joins in the national council of junior warriors, *njama ya anake a mumo*. At this stage his father provides him with necessary weapons, namely, spear, shield, and sword; then a sheep or a male goat is given to the senior warriors of the district, who receive it in the name of the whole national council of senior warriors. The animal is killed for a ceremony of introducing the young warrior into the general activities and the etiquette of the warrior class.

In former days the ceremony was more elaborate. The weapons of the young warrior were sprinkled with the blood of the ceremonial animal, then the leading warrior shouted a war-cry (*rohio*), his companions stood up brandishing their spears and lifting their shields upwards; and in a ritual tone they chanted in unison the following warrior's resolution (*mwehetwa wa anake*): "We brandish our spears, which is the symbol of our courageous and fighting spirit, never to retreat or abandon our hope, or run away from our comrades. If ever we shall make a decision, nothing will change us; and even if the heaven should hold over us a threat to fall and crush us, we shall take our spears and prop it. And if there seems to be a unity between the heaven and the earth to destroy us, we shall sink the bottom part of our spear on the earth, preventing them from uniting; thus keeping the two entities, the earth and the sky, though together, apart. Our faith and our decision never changing shall act as balance." ...

## Eldership

The third stage in manhood is marriage. When a man has married and has established his own homestead, he is required to join the council of elders (*kiama*); he pays one male goat or sheep and then he is initiated into a first grade of eldership (*kiama kia kamatimo*). The word *matimu*, which means spears, signifies the carriers of spears, which denotes the warriors who have joined the *kiama* while still functioning as warriors, and who are carrying spears because they have not yet been given the staff of office. They are not yet elders; they are learners of the *kiama*'s procedures. The *kamatimo* act as messengers to the *kiama*, and help to skin animals, to light fires, to bring firewood, to roast meat for the senior elders, and to carry ceremonial articles to and from the *kiama* assemblies. They must not eat kidneys, spleen, or loin, for these are reserved for the senior elders. Any *kamatimo* who dares eat one of these portions from a ceremonial animal is fined a ram, which is killed to purify the offender and at the same time to initiate him into the secret of the higher grade of eldership.

Next to *kamatimo* comes *kiama kia mataathi*, i.e. the council of peace. This stage is reached when a man has a son or daughter old enough to be circumcised. Before the child enters in the circumcision ceremony, the father is called upon by the *kiama kia mataathi* of his village, and asked to prepare himself for a ceremony called *gotonyio kerera*, that is, to be initiated into the core of the tribal tradition and custom....

### Religious Sacrificial Council (*Kiama Kia Maturanguru*)

The last and most honoured status in the man's life history is the *kiama kia maturanguru* (religious and sacrificial council). This stage is reached when a man has had practically all his children circumcised, and his wife (or wives) has passed the child-bearing age. At this stage the man has passed through all age-grades, has been initiated to them all. Apart from his staff of office, he wears brass rings (*icohe*) in his ears, but he is not yet invested with the power to lead a sacrificial ceremony at the sacred tree (*mogumo mote wa Igongona*). To acquire this privilege he has to pay a ewe. This is taken to the sacred tree where the animal is slaughtered by the elders of the sacrificial council. This ceremony is performed in secrecy and only by the selected few who are fortunate enough to live to that esteemed age. No one outside the members of the sacrificial council is allowed anywhere near the sacred tree when this ceremony is in progress. Half of the animal is eaten by the elders and the other half is burned in the sacrificial fire. The main feature of this ceremony is dedication of the man's life to *Ngai* (God) and to the welfare of the community. What actually happens at the sacred tree with regard to preparation of the ceremony is very hard to say, for the writer has not had the opportunity of attending the ceremony, having not yet reached the required age. But he had the privilege of watching the elders going to and from the sacred tree while herding sheep and goats near the ceremonial grove called *mogumo wa Njathi*.

On coming out from the sacred tree the elders carry bunches of sacred leaves called *maturanguru*. The elders of this grade assume a role of "holy men." They are the high priests. All religious and ethical ceremonies are in their hands.

---

### Reading I.6

In the reading from Jomo Kenyatta, we have seen the central role played by circumcision in Gikuyu society. Suppression of the form practiced by and on women, clitoridectomy, was a major focus of early missionary effort in Kenya. As a consequence, the practice became a central rallying point for the early stages of Gikuyu cultural nationalism—a movement in which Kenyatta's book itself played a part, though at a later date. An issue as complex as that of clitoridectomy demonstrates the difficulty of passing judgment on the practices and norms of other cultures. The status of women in African societies is similarly difficult to judge. How would you assess the status of women as depicted in Audrey Richards' study of the Bemba of Zambia?

---

## Audrey I. Richards, *Chisungu: A Girls' Initiation Ceremony among the Bemba of Zambia*

The ideal of a Bemba in the old days was military success and with it the exaction of tribute and slaves from conquered peoples. This is arrogantly expressed in the phrase "We Bemba cultivate with the spear and not the hoe." Patient industry in agriculture was not as much admired as the power to command service from others. The ability to attract followers by generosity, the elegant exchange of courtesies, and by personal popularity was highly rated. The organizing powers and judgement which are essential to the achievement of either of these aims are admired in themselves.

Thrift and the slow accumulation of property are not admired since they cannot be achieved in terms of Bemba economy. Children are brought up to share everything they have with the group they are with and easy and even reckless giving is praised. Bemba also admire display of all kinds, but here, as may be imagined, the display is not so much of personal possession but of followers and adherents, who walk about with a man of note and praise him.

Bemba admire ceremonious behaviour in personal relations, exact forms of address, the recognition of social precedence and rights to respect, and the avoidance of quarrels, unpleasantness and "scenes" which might disturb the delicate balance of village relations. They praise suavity and self-control in personal relations. They delight in circumlocutions and allusive speech, and seem sophisticated in social contacts, as compared with their neighbours, the Bisa.

Bemba ideal behaviour is that of the *mwina umusumba* or man living at the court, as distinct from the *mwina impanga* or inhabitant of the bush; the country bumpkin.

A commoner is expected to be loyal to the death to his chief, and to accept the fact that his rulers have the right to all his time and all his possessions. He must be silent and respectful. Members of the crocodile clan are expected to be arrogant and even ruthless, but they must be generous in feeding their adherents.

Extreme deference is paid to age. Each child knows his exact position of seniority in a group of village children and is given precedence in games. Each group of men sitting in the village shelter does the same. A younger child is scolded for putting itself forward before its elders.

Bemba women share many of these ideals. They work for their chief in his gardens and make the same abject obeisance to him. They have a lively interest in the ritual centred in the court. They play an important part in attracting followers and kinsmen to a village. A headman's following or "crowd" (bumba) is attracted by means of beer, good entertainment and company, and these depend both on the successful organization of labour, which is largely a man's job, and on the wise and tactful distribution of food, and happy personal relations, which are mainly in the women's sphere.

Women, unlike men, are admired for industry and for resource in finding food in the bush. They are honoured for bearing and rearing many children and for courage in childbirth which is often, under Bemba conditions, a terrible ordeal. They are expected to be loyal to their own sex and to accept the domination of older women.

In the sphere of tribal life women have an important part to play, or rather one that is thought to be important. As we saw, two senior princesses have districts of their own; and junior princesses often act as village "headmen." In all these cases they wield political authority but are regarded as chiefs with feminine attributes, that is to say, with more gentleness and hospitality to the needy. They are not expected to be ruthless in discipline. They have male counsellors to advise and support them. Besides these real political functions the senior women have important ritual duties since, like their "brothers," they are in charge of ancestral shrines. They are also the potential mothers of future chiefs and provide their brothers' heirs. Senior princesses stride in and out of their brothers' royal enclosures, advise them, hector them and borrow their things. The senior wives of chiefs are also honoured highly since they hold in their charge the royal fire and they can, by their conduct, destroy or maintain the supernatural powers of the chief. They are thus able at any time to "spoil the land."

In courts of law women can plead their own cases; this is most unusual in the patrilineal societies to the south. When contracting their first marriage they are under the control of their fathers' and their mothers' brothers, but they are fairly free to contract second marriages at their own wish. They are certainly able to break a marriage contract with much greater ease than women in patrilineal Bantu societies who pass under the control of the husbands' patrilineage on the transfer of cattle at marriage, and divorce is rather frequent in this society. Bemba women have the reputation on the copper belt of Northern Rhodesia for being quite unmanageable by men of other tribes. Such men shrug their shoulders, raise their eyes to heaven and say, "These Bemba women! My word! They are fierceness itself."

Compared to many patrilineal tribes, the Bemba women seem to have a high status. Parents welcome the birth of girls since they bring husbands into their village and build up its strength. Daughters become founders of new lines since the succession passes through them. When they first marry they are under the very definite authority of their relatives, but they are "at home" whereas their husbands are outsiders from other villages. They have the support of their parents and may form part of a solid phalanx of married sisters, and they are therefore in an extremely strong position. As they become mothers and grandmothers their authority increases. Teknonymy is practised and women are called by the names of their sons or daughters with the female prefix "na." On the birth of the first grandchild their name is changed to grandmother of so-and-so—this is a title of respect.[1] The Bemba woman is shy and submissive as a girl, but once a grandmother she often becomes imperious and managing and obviously enjoys her position as she sits on the verandah of a large hut, directing operations and dividing food. This is the position a woman achieves by a stable marriage, and one which she longs to achieve.

Sex relations are openly desired by Bemba and celibacy for men or women is not admired. A girl who rejects men is criticized as having "pride of the womb" (*cilumba ca munda*). Abstinence is only practised for ritual reasons, by a woman nursing a child, for instance. Adultery in women was, however, savagely punished in the old days and is a cause of divorce. It is still thought to cause death in childbirth. Men are not very seriously criticized for adultery although it is thought a terrible crime for them to "kill" their children by not submitting to the purification rites.

The two sexes are divided in everyday life as regards their work and recreations. Men sit in their own shelter at night and eat together there. Women, on the other hand, are grouped round their own house verandahs. Men have their own economic tasks and women theirs. Girls do not enter marriage with any ideal of companionship with their husband. A young couple is not expected to show affection in public and a bridegroom tends to be despised for spending time with his wife. But affection grows over the years in the case of a stable marriage.

There are certain obvious contradictions in the husband's position. Menfolk are dominant in Bemba society. Women used to greet men kneeling, and they still do so on formal occasions today. Men receive the best of the food and take precedence at beer drinks and on other social occasions. They speak first in family matters. Men are expected to take the initiative in sex affairs. Women are married (*ukuupwa*—the passive form) while men marry (*ukuupa*—the active form). Girls are taught to please their husbands and are considered responsible for giving them pleasure in sex relations. Women calmly accept the fact that their husbands will beat them "when they are young and their hearts get hot quickly."

The contradiction between the masterful male and the submissive son-in-law, between the secure young married woman backed by her own relatives and the submissive kneeling wife, is one which first stuck me forcibly in the course of the chisungu ceremony.

---

[1] E.g., *Na-Kampamba* = The mother of Kampamba; *Kakulu-Canda* = The grandmother of Canda.

## Reading I.7

We come back to a point similar to the one from which we departed—the ideas of rhythm, balance, and coordination. This time, however, instead of finding them in music, we find these qualities dispersed throughout the whole environment. If we think of beauty as motion and the aesthetic as the strategic, we begin to understand a sensibility that stresses the artistic dimensions of the body and its labors. In the following passage, Marcel Griaule recounts a conversation with Ogotemmêli, the elder who began Griaule's instruction in the deeper meanings of social life and religious thought. Here we see the ways in which farming, weaving, bodily decoration, and fertility are all connected through the use of a single aesthetic concept—the Word.

## Marcel Griaule, *Conversations with Ogotemmêli: An Introduction to Dogon Religious Ideas*

"The old method of cultivation," he went on, "is like weaving; one begins on the north side, moving from east to west and then back from west to east. On each line eight feet are planted and the square has eight lines recalling the eight ancestors and the eight seeds."

Furthermore, inside the line the cultivator advances first on one foot and then on the other, changing his hoe from one hand to the other at each step. When the right foot is in front, the right hand on the handle is nearest the iron, and *vice versa* when he changes step.

Cultivation being thus a form of weaving, a field is like a blanket made of eight strips, the black and white squares being represented by the alternation of the mounds made at each step and the gaps between them; a mound and its shadow represent a black square....

If a man clears ground and makes a new square plot and builds a dwelling on the plot, his work is like weaving a cloth.

Moreover, weaving is a form of speech, which is imparted to the fabric by the to-and-fro movement of the shuttle on the warp; and in the same way the to-and-fro movement of the peasant on his plot imparts the Word of the ancestors, that is to say, moisture, to the ground on which he works, and thus rids the earth of impurity and extends the area of cultivation round inhabited places.

\*   \*   \*

On the social aspects of clothing Ogotemmêli had much to say.

"The loin-cloth is tight," he said, " to conceal the woman's sex, but it stimulates a desire to see what is underneath. This is because of the Word, which the Nummo put into the fabric. That word is every woman's secret, and is what attracts the man. A woman must have secret parts to inspire desire. If she went about in the market with nothing on, no one would run after her even if she were very beautiful. Undressed and unadorned she is not desirable; but dress and ornament make men desire her, even if she is not beautiful. From a very beautiful woman without adornment men turn away."

He reflected a few moments before adding:

"To be naked is to be speechless."

\* \* \*

In the symbolism of the body already discussed by the old man, the ear was bi-sexual: the external ear was male, and the auditory aperture female. But in fact the Word, according to its nature, can enter by two apertures in a woman—the ear or the sexual organ.

Bad words enter by the ear and pass into the throat, the liver, and finally the womb. The unpleasant smell of the female sexual parts comes from the bad words heard by the ear. The smell, apparently, completing a cycle of words.

On the other hand good words, though taken in by the ear, go directly to the sexual parts where they encircle the womb as the copper spiral encircles the sun. This Word of water provides and maintains the moisture necessary for procreation, and the Nummo, by this means, introduces a germ of water into the womb. He changes the water of the Word into a germ, and gives it the appearance of a human being but the essence of a Nummo. Or rather, the Nummo, present in the moist sexual organ, as in all water, by means of efficacious words which mingle with the woman's seed, moulds a tiny watery creature in his own image.

Thus at the very beginning of human life is to be found a divine germ which lies waiting in the womb of every fertile woman. It is shaped by the Nummo: but the living matter of which it is composed is produced by human action. All good words, whether spoken by the mouths of men or women, enter the bodies of all women, and prepare them for future mating and childbirth.

---

## Reading I.8

In addition to highly abstract conceptualizations like Ogotemmêli's idea of the Word, cultures on the African continent provide vivid aesthetic concepts. Ideas of color and light not only refer to objects in reality but also describe personal qualities of human beings. In the following excerpt from Godfrey Lienhardt's study of the Dinka of the Sudan, we see how the color configurations of cattle relate these animals both to things in nature and to their human owners.

## Godfrey Lienhardt, *Divinity and Experience: The Religion of the Dinka*

There is a vast Dinka vocabulary referring to cattle, and particularly to the varieties of their colouring and shading in their almost innumerable blends and configurations. The interest and, one might almost say, obsession which produces and develops this vocabulary is not primarily practical in nature; for the colour-configuration of a beast is not related to its usefulness as a source of food or other material necessities and, moreover, the rich metaphorical cattle-vocabulary of the Dinka relates primarily to oxen, which are of least utilitarian importance.

Cattle are described by many composite terms, each indicating by a prefix or suffix the sex and stage of maturity of a beast, combined with a term for its particular kind of colour-configuration. Bulls and oxen have the prefix *ma*, and if it is necessary to distinguish between the whole and the castrated beast the former takes as a suffix the term *thon*, meaning "whole male," and the latter the term *bwoc*, castrated. A short-horn bull is further distinguished by the term *acoot*. Heifers have the prefix *nya*, "young female," and cows the prefix *a*. Bull-calves may have the prefix *manh*, from *meth*, child, added to their other names.

There is a general parallelism between the prefix for "bull" and "ox," and for men's personal names, and between that for "cow," and women's personal names, so that on the whole personal names with the prefix *ma*, for "bull," are likely to be the names of men, and those with the prefix *a*, for "cow," are likely to be the names of women.

Almost the whole extensive colour vocabulary of the Dinka is one of cattle-colours. A particular pattern or colour in newly imported cloth or beads is thus necessarily referred to by the name of the configuration of colour in cattle which it is thought most to resemble. A black and white spotted cloth, for example, would be *alath (-nh) ma kuac, ma kuac* being the term for a spotted bull or ox, which is itself connected explicitly with the spots of the leopard, *kuac*. A striped cloth would be *alath (-nh) ma nyang, ma nyang* being the term for a brindled bull, which is connected with the brindling of the crocodile, *nyang*. I think that the only Western Dinka words for colours, other than terms connected also with colour-configurations in cattle, are *toc*, green, which also means rawness and freshness in vegetables, and *thith*, red, which means also the redness of raw meat. These colours are not in any case found in cattle.[1] *Agher*, white, which refers to bright white light, may be connected with the term *yor* or *yar* in the names for white cattle, and *col*, black and also

---

[1] Though *thith* may be added to the term for a brown beast to indicate a strong reddish tone—*malual thith*, "a very red-brown ox."

"soot," though absent from the term for a black bull, *ma car*, is included in the names for black cows and heifers, *a col* and *nyan col*.

The basic vocabulary of names for configurations of colour in cattle is fixed and traditional, consisting of words for colours and combinations of light and shade which a Dinka learns to use from childhood, perhaps without initially having seen what it is, in wild nature, to which they refer. Thus any spotted pattern in which the spots generally resemble in size and distribution those of the leopard will be called *ma kuac*, and in this and many other cases the child may well have seen the *ma kuac* configuration in cattle before he has seen the leopard, *kuac*, to the configuration of which the name refers. A Dinka may thus recognize the configuration in nature by reference to what he first knows of it in the cattle on which his attention, from childhood, is concentrated.

The Dinkas' very perception of colour, light, and shade in the world around them is in these ways inextricably connected with their recognition of colour-configurations in their cattle. If their cattle-colour vocabulary were taken away, they would have scarcely any way of describing visual experience in terms of colour, light, and darkness.

When boys reach manhood they take the colour-names of oxen in addition to the personal names they have been previously known by, and are called by intimate friends and age-mates by the ox-names they have then taken at initiation. A young man then becomes in a manner identified with an ox of some particular colour, which he proudly displays before the girls. He will praise his ox in songs, delighting in inventing new ways of referring to its appearance, and in introducing into song imagery fitting to an ox of that colour. The ability to create new imagery based upon the traditional colour-names of cattle is considered a mark of intelligence in a man; and though some men are acknowledged to be more gifted than others in this respect, every Dinka can attempt a measure of poetic ingenuity and originality.

---

## Reading I.9

The aesthetic sensibility we first touched on in music and have described as it relates to objects, animals, and activities also functions to define appropriate styles of conduct in interpersonal relations. Here, it takes on a political dimension, for *how* a thing is accomplished often determines what its consequences are for shaping ongoing social relations. The two excerpts that follow portray interactions among the Jelgobe, a subgroup of the Fulani. Paul Riesman describes first the aesthetic of interpersonal relations as such and then the respect in which this aesthetic provides the means for people to maintain the quality of life apart from the demands of the money economy.

## Paul Riesman, *Freedom in Fulani Social Life*

### The Father's Respect for His Son

We have dwelt considerably on the relations between parents—especially the father—and little children, first because these relations form psychological attitudes which persist largely unchanged throughout life and, second, because these relations remain the model of what the relation between parent and child should be. But in reality, as we have just indicated, this relation changes when the child grows up. Let us look more closely at what happens. We have noted that it is in having children that a man establishes his own group of dependents, which permits him to free himself from his dependence on his father. And we have just said that the father may tell his child what to do in part because the child is truly incapable of guiding himself. The difficulty here is the following: during the period when the child is really not capable of becoming responsible for himself, he is at the same time too young to be useful to his father, whether in actual work or morally. When the child becomes big enough to be useful to his father for physical labor, if he could not at the same time be responsible for himself, it is easy to see that that usefulness would be greatly limited; should the father treat his child like a slave, the child's support would be inconsequential for the father in his relations with his equals. The child must have weight himself if he is really to second his father, and he must be worthy of him if he is to represent him.

That can only happen if the father respects his child. For, the greater part of the child's education takes place neither within the family nor with his father, but in the company of his age-mates. It is they who are the first judges of the child's *pulaaku*, and that ideal, as we have seen, is essentially one of self-control. If one behaves like a slave, and not like one's father's son, one lacks *pulaaku*, which is a shame for the father himself as well as for the son. If a young man is with his comrades when his father calls him, the son answers with a sort of loud grunt ("Hunh!") which only means that the call has been heard. He does not move, and he continues to chat with his friends. It is only some minutes later that he will get up to join his father. He knows that his father wants to see him, but in refusing to act mechanically the son is demonstrating that he acts as a free man. The father is aware of this and ordinarily he does not repeat his call.

Another factor which prevents the father from giving orders to his son in public is the risk of seeing the latter refuse to carry them out, for everyone would then know that the father's authority is only pretense. That damages the father's reputation, but it is bad for the son as well, not only because he is recognized as disobedient, but also because he is the son of a father who has no authority over his children, which diminishes the father's weight in the society and, as a result, diminishes the respect accorded to his son. For the system to function well, the father's authority over his children must appear real, which comes down to saying that it must be real, since the act of obeying and that of pretending to obey cannot be distinguished from one another. But at the same time it is equally essential that the son be regarded as free, to the very point of being able to refuse or to revolt, for otherwise his obedience would be valueless. In reality we find in Fulani society the entire gamut between blind obedience and complete revolt. In the Fulani mind, both extremes are unwholesome, but the first is worse than the second since only a man who is incomplete in some way blindly obeys another man. In the second case, though the men are both complete, their discord nevertheless diminishes their strength in relation to others; they are just individuals and do not form a common bloc. When relations between father and son deteriorate to this point, they stop living together: the son keeps his herd separate, cultivates his field separately, and pays his own tax. The tax receipt is today a symbol of an individual's independence from his parents.

* * *

## The Rejection of Money as a Means of Influencing People

The contrast between the use of money in Western society and in Fulani society is instructive in this respect. In both cases, money may serve as remuneration for work, but in Jelgoji society this never happens between Fulani, only between members of different social groups (*riimaaybe*, artisans), between members of different ethnic groups (Dogon, Mossi, Songhai), or between strangers. To work for money is to work because one needs that money to live. To work for another Fulani would therefore reveal to him one's state of need and would constitute a lack of *pulaaku*. Moreover, such work cannot, consequently, be seen as assistance given to the person one works for; instead of reinforcing a social bond, this course would tend to weaken it. That is why the Jelgobe will neither work for one of themselves for money nor allow others to work for them under these conditions. To pay someone for work is to insinuate, or to note as a fact, that he did not do it to be useful to you, to help you deal with the difficulties of life, but that he was forced to do it by his own needs. If a man does not work freely, that means that he is not free, and the Fulani find it very painful to see one of their own in such a state, a state below the level of humanity as they conceive it. According to circumstances, this pain is transformed into *yurmeende* or into ridicule, but the latter is often nothing but the public expression of what would be *yurmeende* if other people were not present. Even more important for our purposes, however, is the fact that the Jelgobe try to prevent such situations from arising within their communities. For the most part, those who are richer than others avoid using their money to create a dependency around them, and those who might be tempted to do so would meet only refusal and flight, not cooperation.

*Reading I.10*

Cultural forms shape everyday life by infusing it with networks of interrelated meanings, concepts of beauty, and ideas of morality. These connections also form the basis for a creativity which extends beyond everyday life into the domains of art. In the songs excerpted below, universal human longings become manifest in individual expression. The first two, collected by Paul Riesman, are praise songs sung of women by Fulani men. They draw on the imagery of cattle to evoke women's beauty in movement. The last two songs, collected by Godfrey Lienhardt, are Dinka hymns sung in time of sickness and misfortune. They express wrath and despair precipitated by loss.

## Praise songs from *Freedom in Fulani Social Life*

*Ngaari Baydi boɗewol poyngol*
*Na laamna danewol girrayel Aayi*
*Nari dawla tiinde tilsaay*
*Sabu soodataake*
*Naafiki nangaay ma*
*Rawni mooso*
*Kelloy girrayel Aayi*

The bull of Baïdi, red like the dawn
Makes brighter [by comparison] the whiteness of Ayi, the little
    long-necked one.
No need to bedeck a face already lucky
Because [beauty] cannot be bought.
Backbiting's not for you,
[You are] white like a smile,
Oh the little hand-clappings of Ayi, the little long-necked one.


*Dunna dabbunde mbaadoy na cimta malleeji na njuura*
    *Njimanen Suumayel Umaru*
*A juurnaay na nyannde nyalloyɗen Hammadi Sagidi*
*Kurukutu e nyeeke Nyodel*
    *Njimanen Suumayel Umaru*


Grey sky in the cold season, droplets are drizzling,
    speckle-necked cows come to drink—
    Let us sing for "little black-muzzle," Umaru's cow.
You came with the cows the day we went to Hammadi Sagidi

To make music while Nyodel's face shone with sweat droplets—
  Let us sing for "little black-muzzle," Umaru's cow.

---

## Hymns from *Divinity and Experience: The Religion of The Dinka*

If I am hated, then I hate,
If I am loved, then I love,
If a kite swoops upon what is mine
Then it regrets it, seeing what I am
It trembles inwardly.[1]
If a kite swoops upon what is mine, ee
Its wing breaks.
When it sees, it fears and trembles.


Children of the ants, we have suffered from dryness[2]
Why I am without cattle, why I am without grain—
That is what I ask, ee!
I am a man who boasted of himself
I slaughtered in my greed my *majok* ox[3]
Children of Aghok, my father, the children of the ants are forsaken(?)
[Yet] my father the creator indeed created men
We honour our lord (*banydan yeku rok*) that he may look in upon us
Mayan [a diviner or prophet] honours (*rok*) Divinity
Mayan son of Deng divines
It is GOLONG[4] which devours our cattle.

---

## Reading I.11

Indigenous culture in Africa can also be used as a resource by artists creating in modern genres such as plays, poems, and novels. In the following passage from one of her novels, Nigerian writer Buchi Emecheta uses features of traditional Ibo culture to create many aspects of the story. In her hands, culture functions to illuminate

---

[1] In Dinka, *yic ager*...translates as "to have compassion." I think more widely it means to weaken and shrink inwardly, so that the source of action is paralysed.
[2] "Suffered from dryness" is represented in Dinka by the one word *yal*—a holophrasis compared with the English, which suggests the holistic nature of this Dinka experience.
[3] He connects his past pride and self-complacency with the present decline in his fortunes.
[4] GOLONG is an injurious Power of the same class as the fetish MATHIANG GOK, but less widely known among the Western Dinka. It devours the cattle because many beasts are sacrificed to satisfy its greed. Now Divinity is asked to help.

character, to convey the mood of a relationship, and to further plot development. For us, Emecheta's artistry also serves to give a sense of how traditional beliefs *feel* as part of a life as lived. Here, we see how the passionate ambivalence of two lovers, Agbadi and his mistress Ona, is made elegant and intriguing by cultural restraints and necessities.

## Buchi Emecheta, *The Joys of Motherhood*

Agbadi's senior wife, Agunwa, became ill that very night. Some said later that she sacrificed herself for her husband; but a few had noticed that it was bad for her morale to hear her husband giving pleasure to another woman in the same courtyard where she slept, and to such a woman who openly treated the man they all worshipped so badly. A woman who was troublesome and impetuous, who had the audacity to fight with her man before letting him have her: a bad woman.

Agbadi and Ona were still sleeping the following morning when the alarm was raised by one of the children.

"Wake up, Father, wake up! Our mother is having a seizure."

"What?" Agbadi barked. "What is the matter with her? She was all right last night." Momentarily he forgot himself and made as if to get up; Ona, wide awake now, restrained him. "Damn this shoulder," he grumbled. "But what is the matter with Agunwa?"

"That's what we're trying to find out," said the reassuring voice of Idayi, who had been keeping vigil over his friend.

"Lie still, Agbadi," other voices advised.

He watched helplessly as they took his senior wife away to her hut in her own part of the compound. "Send her my medicine man. What is the matter with the woman?" he fumed.

Soon his friend came from Agunwa's hut and told him, "Your chief wife is very ill. Your *dibia* is doing all he can for her, but I don't think she will survive."

"Why, Idayi, why at this time?"

"Nobody knows when their time will come. Your wife Agunwa is no exception. The strain of your illness...since the day we brought you back from Ude, she has watched over you from that corner of your courtyard. She was even here last night."

"Oh, come, my friend. What are you trying to tell me? She's my chief wife, I took here to Udo the day I became an Obi. She is the mother of my grown sons. You are wrong, Idayi, to suggest she might be sore or bitter just because last night with Ona I amused myself a little. Agunwa is too mature to mind that. Why, if she behaved like that what kind of example would that be to the younger wives?"

"You talk of last night as only a little amusement. But it kept all of us awake. You and your Ona woke the very dead..."

Goats and hens were sacrificed in an attempt to save Agunwa. When, on the eighteenth day, Agbadi was able to get up and move about with the help of one of his male slaves and a stick, the first place he visited was his senior wife's hut. He was shocked to see her. She was too far gone to even know of his presence.

He looked around and saw two of his grown sons watching him. "Your mother is a good woman. So unobtrusive, so quiet. I don't know who else will help me keep an eye on those young wives of mine, and see to the smooth running of my household."

Two days later, Agunwa died and Agbadi sent a big cow to her people to announce her death. Having died a "complete woman," she was to be buried in her husband's compound.

"Make sure that her slave and her cooking things go with her. We must all mourn her."

Ona moved about like a quiet wife. She knew that people blamed her for Agunwa's death though no one had the courage to say so openly. That night, after she had given Agbadi his meal and helped his men rub life into his stiff side and shoulder, she curled up to him and asked: "Would you like me to go now? My father will be worrying, wondering what your people are saying."

"And what are my people saying, woman? That I took my mistress in my own courtyard, and that I take her every night as I see fit? Is that it? Haven't I got enough to worry about without you adding your bit? Go to sleep, Ona, you're tired and you don't look too well to me. Tomorrow is going to be a busy day. The burial of a chief's wife is not a small thing in Ibuza."

The funeral dancing and feasting started very early in the morning and went on throughout the day. Different groups of people came and went and had to be entertained. In the evening it was time to put Agunwa in her grave. All the things that she would need in her after-life were gathered and arranged in her wooden coffin which was made of the best mahogany Agbadi could find. Then her personal slave was ceremoniously called in a loud voice by the medicine man: she must be laid inside the grave first. A good slave was supposed to jump into the grave willingly, happy to accompany her mistress; but this young and beautiful woman did not wish to die yet.

She kept begging for her life, much to the annoyance of many of the men standing around. The women stood far off for this was a custom they found revolting. The poor slave was pushed into the shallow grave, but she struggled out, fighting and pleading, appealing to her owner Agbadi.

Then Agbadi's eldest son cried in anger: "So my mother does not even deserve a decent burial? Now we are not to send her slave down with her, just because the girl is beautiful?" So saying, he gave the woman a sharp blow with the head of the cutlass he was carrying. "Go down like a good slave!" he shouted.

"Stop that at once!" Agbadi roared, limping up to his son. "What do you call this, bravery? You make my stomach turn."

The slave woman turned her eyes, now glazed with approaching death, towards him. "Thank you for this kindness, Nwokocha the son of Agbadi. I shall come back to your household, but as a legitimate daughter. I shall come back..."

Another relative gave her a final blow to the head and at last she fell into the grave, silenced for ever. As her blood spurted, splashing the men standing round, there was a piercing scream from the group of mourning women standing a little way off. But it was not their feelings for the dead woman that caused this reaction, Agbadi saw; they were holding Ona up.

"Now what is happening?" Agbadi said hoarsely. "My friend Idayi, take the burial kolanut and finish the ceremony. I think Umunna's daughter Ona wants to die on me, too. She has been ill all day, I don't know why. I must take her inside." He limped over to her with his stick as fast as he could.

Ona was lain on a goatskin in Agbadi's courtyard while the medicine man went on praying and performing in the centre of the compound. For a while that night Ona went hot and cold, but before dawn it was clear that although the illness was tiring and weakening her she could bear it. Agbadi's early fear had been that it might be *iba*, the malaria which killed anyone in a short time.

Obi Umunna came in the morning and said to Agbadi without preamble: "I think there is something in your family killing everyone. First you barely escaped death, then your Agunwa was taken, now my healthy daughter who came to look after you—"

"My friend, if you were not an Obi like me, and not Ona's father, I would tell you a few home truths. If she is ill because of a curse in my household, would it not be right for you to leave her with me until she gets better? I will look after her myself."

Over the next few days, Agbadi's practised eyes noted the pattern of the sickness, and he said to Ona one morning as she sat beside him, "Ona, the daughter of Umunna, I think I am making you into a mother. You are carrying our love child."

He said it so lightly that she was too surprised to say a word.

"Well, it is true. What are you going to say to your father?"

"Oh, please, Agbadi, don't take my joy away. You know I like staying here with you, but I am my father's daughter. He has no son. Your house is full of children. Please, Nwokocha the son of Agbadi, your bravery is known afar and so is your tenderness. Don't complicate this for me—the greatest joy of my life."

"But what of me? You and your father are using me as a tool to get what you wanted."

"We did not force you, remember," Ona said, anger rising in her. "Is it my fault that you decided to treat me as a wife and not a lover? You knew of my father's determination before you came to me. We did not use you. You used me, yet I don't regret it. If you want to regret it, well, that is up to you."

"So when are you leaving me?" Agbadi asked eventually.

"As soon as I feel stronger. You are getting better every day, ready to go back to your farm."

"Forget about my farm. Hurry up and get well and go back to your shameless father."

"Don't call him names," she cried, and felt very weak.

"You see, you won't even allow yourself to be a woman. You are in the first weeks of motherhood, and all you can do is to think like a man, raising male issue for your father, just because he cannot do it himself."

"I am not going to quarrel with you," Ona declared.

That day, for the first time since the accident, Agbadi went to his farm, much to everybody's surprise. "I want to see how the work is going," he replied to questions people put to him.

Ona felt lonely during his absence. But she sent word to her father to come for her the next day.

On that last night, she tried to reason with Agbadi, but he gave her his stiff back. "All right," she said in compromise, "my father wants a son and you have many sons. But you do not have a girl yet. Since my father will not accept any bride price from you, if I have a son he will belong to my father, but if a girl, she will be yours. That is the best I can do for you both."

They made it up before morning, Agbadi being tender and loving the rest of the night.

The next day, the women from Obi Umunna's compound came with presents for Agbadi's household. They were all very polite to each other, and Ona was relieved to note that her father had not come; she could not stand another argument between the two men, though she supposed she should regard herself as lucky for two men to want to own her.

Nwokocha Agbadi visited her often in her hut, and slept there many an Eke night when he did not have to go to the farm or hunting. People had thought that after a while he would get fed up with her, but that was not so. Each parting was painful, just as if they were young people playing by the moonlight.

Some days when he could not come to her, she knew he was with his other wives. Being Agbadi, however, he never talked about them to her, and she respected him for it. It was on such a night that she came into labour. She cried quietly as she agonised alone through the long hours of darkness. Only when the pain became unbearable did she enlist the help of the women in her father's compound.

Her baby daughter was very merciful to her. "She simply glided into the world," the women around told her.

Ona was dazed with happiness. Agbadi had won, she thought to herself, at the same time feeling pity for her poor father.

Agbadi came the very second day and was visibly overjoyed. "Well, you have done well, Ona. A daughter, eh?"

He bent down and peeped at the day-old child wrapped and kept warm by the fireside and remarked: "This child is priceless, more than twenty bags of cowries. I think that should really be her name, because she is a beauty and she is mine. Yes, 'Nnu Ego,' twenty bags of cowries."

He called in the men who came with him and they brought enough yams and drinks to last Ona a long time, for custom did not allow him to go near her again until after twenty-five days.

Obi Umunna came in and for a while the two men toasted and prayed for the happiness of the new child.

"Did Ona tell you of our compromise? She agreed that if she bore a baby girl she would be mine, if a boy, he would be yours," Agbadi said coolly.

"That may be true, my friend. I am not a man who can take seriously talks lovers have on their love mat. She was your guest, and you were a sick man then."

"What are you trying to say, Umunna? That your daughter should go back on her promise?"

"She is a woman so I don't see why not. However, because she is my daughter, I am not asking her to violate her word. Yes, the baby is yours, but my daughter remains here. I have not accepted any money from you."

"How much do you want for her? What else do you expect? Is it her fault that you have no son?" Agbadi was beginning to roar like the wild animals he was wont to hunt and kill.

"Please, please, aren't you two happy that I have survived the birth? It seems nobody is interested in that part of it. I made a promise to Agbadi, yes; but, dear Agbadi, I am still my father's daughter. Since he has not taken a bride price from you, do you think it would be right for me to stay with you permanently? You know our custom does not permit it. I am still my father's daughter," Ona intoned sadly.

Agbadi drew himself up from the mud pavement where he had been sitting and said, "I have never forced a woman to come to me. Never, and I am not going to start now. The only women I captured were slaves. All my wives are happy to be such. You want to stay with your father? So be it." And he left alone.

For months, Ona did not see Agbadi. She heard from people that he more or less lived in thick, swampy Ude where game was plentiful. Ona missed him, yet she knew that, according to the way things were, she was doing the right thing.

A year after the birth of Nnu Ego, Obi Umunna died, and Ona cried for days for him, especially as he had gone without her producing the wanted son. Agbadi relented when he heard of it, for he knew how close Ona was to her father.

For over two years, he persisted in trying to persuade her to come and live in his compound. "You are no longer bound by your father's hopes. He is dead. But we are still living. Come and stay with me. You are all alone here among your extended relatives. Please, Ona, don't let us waste our lives longing for each other."

"You know my father would not have liked it, so stop talking like that, Agbadi. I refuse to be intimidated by your wealth and your position."

Yet Agbadi went on visiting his Ona.

Nnu Ego was the apple of her parents' eyes. She was a beautiful child, fair-skinned like the women from the Aboh and Itsekiri areas. At her birth it was noticed that there was a lump on her head, which in due course was covered with thick, curly, black hair. But suddenly one evening she started to suffer from a strange headache that held her head and shoulder together. In panic, Ona sent for Agbadi who came tearing down from Ogboli with a *dibia*.

The *dibia* touched the child's head and drew in his breath, feeling how much hotter the lump was than the rest of her body. He quickly set to work, arranging his pieces of kolanut and snail shells and cowries on the mud floor. He soon went into a trance and began to speak in a far-off voice, strange and unnatural: "This child is the slave woman who died with your senior wife Agunwa. She promised to come back as a daughter. Now here she is. That is why this child has the fair skin of the water people, and the painful lump on her head is from the beating your men gave her before she fell into the grave. She will always have trouble with that head. If she has a fortunate life, the head will not play up. But if she is unhappy, it will trouble her both physically and emotionally. My advice is that you go and appease the slave woman."

"Ona, you must leave this place," Agbadi ordered, "you have to leave your father's house, otherwise I am taking my daughter from you. She can't worship her *chi* from a foreign place, she must be where her *chi* is until all the sacrifices have been made."

So Ona finally had to leave her people, not because she allowed her love for Agbadi to rule her actions but because she wanted the safety of her child. As soon as they arrived at Ogboli, Nnu Ego got better. The slave woman was properly buried in a separate grave, and an image of her was made for Nnu Ego to carry with her.

Soon after that, Ona became pregnant again. From the very beginning she was ill, so that it was not a surprise to Agbadi's household when she came into premature labour. After the birth, Ona was weak but her head was clear. She knew she was dying.

"Agbadi," she called hoarsely, "you see that I was not destined to live with you. But you are stubborn, my father was stubborn, and I am stubborn too. Please don't mourn for me long; and see that however much you love our daughter Nnu Ego you allow her to have a life of her own, a husband if she wants one. Allow her to be a woman."

Not long after this, Ona died; and her weak new-born son followed her only a day later. So all Nwokocha Agbadi had to remind him of his great passion for Ona was their daughter, Nnu Ego.

# PART II

# EXAMINING THE TRIPLE HERITAGE

## 1

# ANATOMY OF A CONTINENT

### Merrick Posnansky

It is difficult to understand either the history of Africa or its contemporary situation unless we know something about its physical background. Like the human body, the African continent is made up of many different parts. In this chapter Professor Posnansky explores the general features of Africa that give it its distinctive geographic personality and discusses the ways in which different communities have adapted to their environment. Eds.

The key to the geography of Africa is its shape. It is attached to Asia at its northeast Sinai corner by an isthmus only 70 miles wide, which helps to explain the linguistic, cultural, and religious ties of North Africa and the Horn of Africa to southwest Asia. The continent thrusts south for some 5,000 miles separating the Atlantic from the Indian Ocean. Due west lies South America, and due east lies Australia, each more than 4,000 miles away. The nearest land mass is Europe, separated by the Mediterranean Sea, only nine miles across at the Straits of Gibraltar. Africa's early influences from other continents came from the north and northeast. Southern Africa was not influenced by the outside until much later than North Africa.

Africa is a solid continent, approximately as long as it is broad, some 4,500 by 5,000 miles. (See Map 1.1.) Much of its surface is composed of the world's oldest Precambrian rocks planed down to an upland plateau. Cutting through this plateau from the northeast, linking it geologically with Asia, is the great Rift Valley, running its 3,200-mile course from the Dead Sea in Palestine to Malawi. The last

MAP 1.1    **Physical Features of Africa**

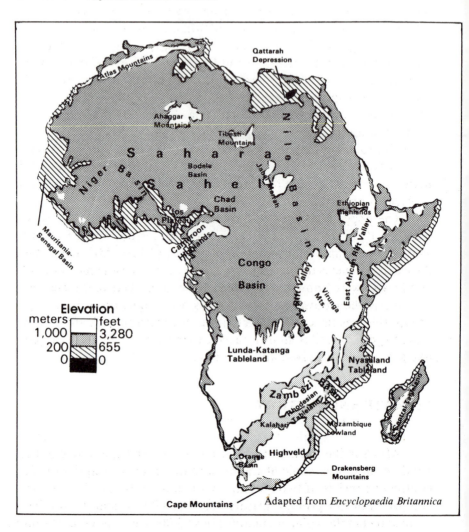

Adapted from *Encyclopaedia Britannica*

stages of the formation of the Rift Valley were contemporaneous with the emergence of humanity three million years ago.

The Rift Valley is the most striking feature of East Africa's landscape, with escarpments over 4,000 feet high in places. The valley provides an area of inland drainage with a series of deep high-level lakes from Lake Turkana in the north to Lake Nyasa (Malawi) in the south. Lake Victoria lies in a basin between the two main arms of the Rift Valley and is much shallower—rarely deeper than 250 feet—than the 4,708 feet maximum of Lake Tanganyika.

The coastline of the continent is remarkably straight, free from the indentations that make for good natural harbors. The rivers plunge off the southern plateaus in a series of falls and rapids, and much of the coast is fringed with coral reefs, sand bars, mangrove swamps, and lagoons, which make access to and from the sea harrowing and make passage by river to the interior difficult. In addition, several rivers, like the Rufiji in Tanzania, have braided mouths or delta swamps, which complicate their use for navigation. The channels of the Rufiji are so difficult to disentangle from the sea that in World War I the Germans were able to hide their cruiser Königsberg there from the British Navy for nearly a year. Because of the difficult coastline, the interior, with better land, climate, and resources, has provided the setting for much of Africa's history.

The upper Nile's insect-infested swamps in the southern Sudan were another barrier to movement, this time from north to south. Though the Sahara blocked passage between North Africa and West Africa, it was nevertheless crossable once the few oases and sources of good water were known to travelers. Even in the days of the medieval caravans, when upwards of 12,000 camels might cross in a single group, this was never an easy crossing. It normally took 100 days or more to go 1,200 miles, limiting access to the most precious of cargoes, like gold, minerals, civet, and kola nuts.

## CLIMATE AND HISTORY

Africa is the most tropical of continents and the only one that straddles both the tropic of Cancer and the tropic of Capricorn. The continent consists of two rectangles: the horizontal one in the north comprised of low ground, mainly below 3,000 feet; and the southern vertical rectangle, a plateau mainly above 3,000 feet. The climate south of the equator mirrors that north of the equator, but the shape of the northern half of Africa reduces any maritime amelioration of the prevailing southwest winds. This shape difference results in a very large desert, the Sahara, in the north and a much smaller one, the Kalahari, in the south. In Southern Africa the existence of the high plateau makes the climate of Zambia much cooler and much more humid than that of Niger, yet both are crossed by the 15 degree parallel. It was the altitude which made the tropical location of East Africa attractive to European settlement in contrast to the less comfortable, more humid lowlands of West Africa.

The climate of Africa has not always remained the same. It was once believed that the Ice Ages in the temperate latitudes corresponded to wet periods or "pluvials" in the tropics. This is now seen as too simplistic a theory. The high mountains certainly had their expanding and contracting ice caps. Evidence exists, however, of significant climatic changes over the last 30,000 years. Around 18,000 B.C., an unusually dry period began which lasted nearly 10,000 years. During this time the Niger River ceased to exist as a continuous river, and Lake Chad completely dried up. The sand dunes of the Sahara advanced at least 300 miles farther south than today, as far as Kano in northern Nigeria. The sands of the Kalahari spread outwards, reaching across Angola towards Kinshasa. This was certainly a period when the food procurement capabilities of Stone Age hunters and gatherers were sorely taxed. It is believed that in the Nile Valley at this time, the first tentative steps may have been taken toward reliance on a few carefully selected varieties of wild grains. Other societies probably became more specialized hunters and fishers.

Around 10,000 B.C., conditions became more humid; and between 7000 and 3000 B.C., there was a period much wetter than today. That period is known to archaeologists as the climatic optimum. At that time the desert was quite small and many areas that are now parts of the Sahara were more like the Sahel, experiencing annual rainfalls of over 10 inches per year. Lake Chad grew to at least eight to ten times its present size. At many archaeological sites, abundant fish remains and bone harpoons indicate that the Stone Age inhabitants practiced an aquatic way of life—fishing, fowling, and hunting around the lakes and waterways. Population was probably somewhat restricted, however, by insect-borne disease. Stone Age populations also left a graphic record of a more humid climate through their pictures of crocodiles, hippopotamuses, giraffes, elephants, large antelopes, buffalo, and other game that can no longer exist in the Sahara. By 5500 B.C. paintings of cattle provide abundant testimony to the beginnings of pastoralism in the Sahara. In the Nile Valley, the more humid conditions allowed the populations to once again hunt, fish, and fowl in the swamps and lakes along the river. Besides the evidence of the rock art of Stone Age sites, satellite images have shown that the enlarged rivers of this period cut through the sand dunes of the previous dry period. By around 3000 B.C., however, conditions more like those of today had begun to develop.

Among the best sources of information about Africa's climate during the last few thousand years are the records of the Nile floods kept in Early Dynastic times (2920–2575 B.C.). The Nilometer provides unique evidence of the rise and fall of river levels, which can be correlated with the known history of Egypt. Even though drastic climatic changes on the order of the previous 15,000 years did not occur, some major fluctuations characterized this historical period. We know, for instance, from historical evidence, from flood levels, and from geomorphological work that the Nile dropped to one of its lowest levels around 2100–1950 B.C., and again around the period 1150–1100 B.C. We know also that it rose during the period 300–800 A.D. The first low levels coincided with the collapse of the Old Kingdom (2575–2134 B.C.) and the chaos of the First Intermediate period (2134–2040 B.C.). The second set of low levels, which persisted for a long time, coincided with the decline of the New Kingdom (1550–1070 B.C.). A fall in the Nile level meant that it was more difficult to raise the water for irrigation. Thus, agricultural productivity dropped as large areas fell out of cultivation. In late New Kingdom times, this fall in agricultural productivity coincided with a decline in gold production, an enlarged bureaucracy, and an unwieldy army and urban slave force that were difficult to feed. There were repeated military reversals. The result was the collapse of Ancient Egypt. During the period 300–800 A.D., when the rise of Nile floods took place, the new technology of the water wheel enabled more water to be drawn from the Nile to higher levels at faster rates. The result was more land under cultivation and a period of prosperity.

Climate was also a factor in West Africa, where it appears that the last quarter of the first millennium A.D. was a somewhat wetter period. At this time Ancient Ghana, West Africa's first major state, emerged on the stage of world history. The second quarter of the second millennium A.D. witnessed a dry period; lake levels dropped and wells dried up. It is quite significant that this latter period was the era when Mali declined and when several major movements of population began to take place elsewhere in Africa, such as those of the Galla in Ethiopia and the Nilotic Lwoo into East Africa from the southern Sudan. A return to somewhat wetter conditions from the 16th to the 18th centuries coincided with further expansion of trade and towns, such as those of the Hausa in Nigeria or along the southern savannah in modern Ghana.

The study of past climate and our speculations (and they can only be speculations) about their implications for African history have never been more relevant. Even the recent much shorter droughts of Africa, felt severely in the Sahel and Ethiopia between 1970 and 1977

and again between 1981 and 1985, displaced large populations as
historical perspective, we should be able to take precautions in the
famished herds and starving, diseased peoples sought dwindling water
supplies and grazing land. By putting these natural disasters into
future to ameliorate their severity. Current research indicates that
there are cycles to weather patterns, though the reason for their existence
is still unknown.

On the edge of the Sahel (the semidesert southern fringe of the
Sahara), rainfall has decreased steadily over the past 40 years. Whether
this is part of a long or a short cycle is still not known. We do know that
human beings throughout history have often exacerbated the impact
of unreliable rains. (For rainfall reliability, see Map 1.2.) At the end of
the climatic optimum, for example, there were trees on many of the
Saharan and North African ranges. There was a naturally renewable
scrub vegetation of bushes and grass in the Sahel. This vegetation
helped to delay the runoff of ground water and reduced surface radiation
and air temperatures. With the introduction of cattle, sheep, and goats,
overgrazing led to erosion, a rapid runoff of surface water, a lowered
water table, and eventually the abandonment of the lands marginal to
the desert. Farther to the south, population increased with the beginnings of agriculture around the fourth millennium B.C. At first the
demands for building timber and firewood had little impact on the
landscape, but with the invention of ironworking, sometime after 1000
B.C., the demands for charcoal severely depleted the supply of trees,
particularly in the Sahel and savannah belts. Candice Goucher (1984)
calculated from her research in Togo and Ghana that a single furnace
site, in a five-year period of average output, can exhaust the suitable
timber supplies within a 1.5-kilometer radius. The loss of tree cover
ultimately leads to higher surface radiation temperatures and lower
humidity levels, since the hot air is less likely to condense into rain.
Considering that a single iron-smelting area, like that of the Bassar in
Togo, might have hundreds of furnace sites operating over several
hundred years, it is easy to appreciate the impact that iron technology
had on the environment. Further, it is clear that the substitution of
alternative fuel supplies for the charcoal that presently supplies so
many African towns, the creation of dams to capture limited rainwater,
the programs of afforestation and sand-dune reclamation, and the
restriction of livestock numbers in marginal lands not only conserve
Africa's limited resources but also help guard against future ravages of
drought. It is hoped that these programs will provide some recompense
for the despoliation of the past and also adjust the demands of modern
communities to their limited natural resources.

**Map 1.2    Rainfall Reliability**

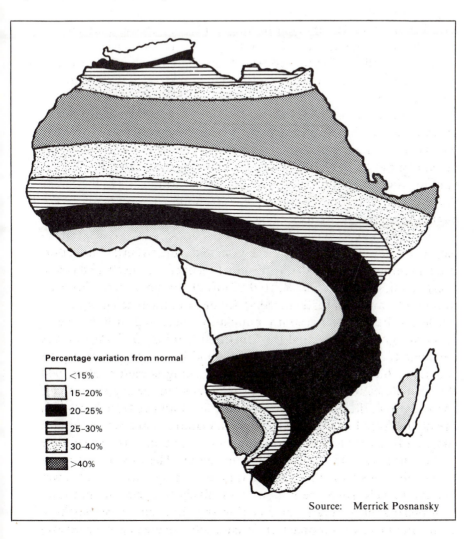

Percentage variation from normal

- [ ] <15%
- 15–20%
- 20–25%
- 25–30%
- 30–40%
- >40%

Source:    Merrick Posnansky

## VEGETATION

Vegetation follows the climatic belts. More than half of Africa's land surface is covered by the Sahel and savannah. (See Map 1.3.) The Sahel consists of scattered shrubs and grass on the edge of the desert. These are areas with highly unreliable rainfalls—five to 15 inches annually. Such vegetation can at best support nomadic pastoralists and in the better watered areas an annual crop of the hardier varieties of millet can be grown. Savannah can include quite tall trees and 12- to

**Map 1.3    Vegetation Zones of Africa**

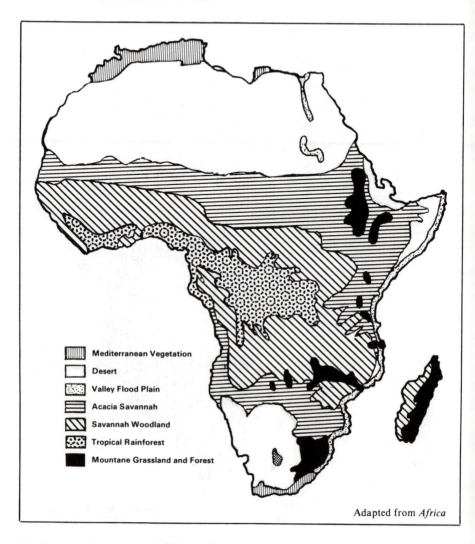

Mediterranean Vegetation

Desert

Valley Flood Plain

Acacia Savannah

Savannah Woodland

Tropical Rainforest

Mountane Grassland and Forest

Adapted from *Africa*

15-foot elephant grass in its wetter range (up to 55 inches per year). Most of the savannah is characterized by relatively open vegetation and scattered woodland, especially along waterways. One feature of the savannah is its prolonged dry season. It is an area that has been especially susceptible to annual fires which are followed by a healthier flush of grass at the beginnings of the rains. To protect themselves, the savannah trees have developed rough, scaly, fire-resistant barks.

Originally, tropical forest covered as much as ten percent of the African continent, which had adequate rainfalls more evenly dispersed throughout the year. Now, less than ten percent of that original forest cover is preserved. Some 25 percent of the continent is desert, a figure that is increasing rapidly. Every year vast stretches of the Sahel lose their ground cover, and sand dunes advance.

The variety of vegetation zones resulted in many different ecological niches. In the forest, settlements tended to be highly nucleated, and communications were slow or tenuous unless there was access to a large river. As a result of their often richer agricultural resources, the populations of the forest were often more concentrated and numerous than those in the Sahel or savannah. It was no coincidence that the largest towns in pre-colonial Africa were located in southern Nigeria. The towns that developed in the Sahel or the drier parts of the savannah were large because they were centers, or desert "ports" for complex trade networks. These towns were often located at the junctions of different ecological zones.

## SOILS

Only about half of Africa contains either easily-worked or productive soils. Soils reflect both climatic zones and patterns of use. The thinner and more easily exhaustible soils are found in some of the highest rainfall areas and in the Sahel, where the nutrients are rapidly lost through exploitation. (See Map 1.4.) The relatively poor soils of the tropics have led to a pattern of shifting cultivation. Under this system a main crop, like yams, is cultivated in a cleared area for about a year, followed by a less important crop, such as cassava or maize. The area is then left fallow and allowed to return to bush or secondary forest. Clearance of new land often involves burning, which adds such nutrients as sulphates to the soil. Sometimes the shifting pattern involves a small area, so the farmer returns to the original area fairly soon. In other cases, shifting involves an actual movement to another location. In order not to exhaust the soil, the land should be left uncultivated for 15 to 20 years. As population pressure on the land has developed, however, farmers have returned at shorter intervals to the same land they cultivated, and the soil has rapidly become exhausted. The areas of richest soils in Africa are those along some of the river valleys. The annually flood-renewed alluvium of the Nile and the inland Niger delta in Mali are outstanding. The volcanic soils of East Africa are also especially fertile.

**Map 1.4    Soils**

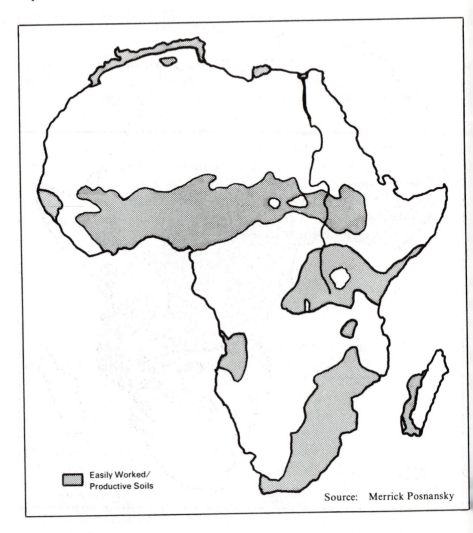

Easily Worked/
Productive Soils

Source:    Merrick Posnansky

## DISEASE PATTERNS

Disease has always been a major factor in African history. There is geological evidence that disease carried by the tsetse fly, which affects both animals and humans, goes back at least 25 million years. Major epidemics of sleeping sickness, now controllable by medicine, have periodically decimated large populations. The high incidence of sickle-cell anemia in many areas, particularly West Africa, is an indica-

**Map 1.5**       **Area of Tsetse Fly Infestation**

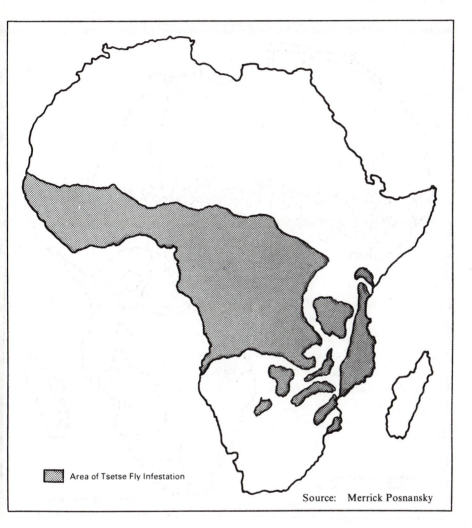

Area of Tsetse Fly Infestation

Source:   Merrick Posnansky

tion of an endemic pattern of resistance that has been established to fight malaria. Little simulium flies and snails carry river blindness (onchocerciasis) and bilharzia and affect the rivers, swamps, and lakes. Numerous intestinal diseases, such as paratyphoid, which result in varying degrees of debilitating diarrhea; parasitic worms; and fly-borne eye infections are common where drinking water is dirty and domestic animals are present. The only areas relatively free of the tsetse fly are the lands above 5,000 feet or those that are too dry to support vegetation.

(Compare Maps 1.1 and 1.5.) Some of the areas surrounding the desert are not immune to insect-borne catastrophe; locusts, for example, swarm into the more fertile areas and destroy both food and grazing. Even the camel falls prey to a form of trypanosomiasis carried by the horsefly. Similarly, the very small quelea bird, which flies south from the desert, has been responsible for significant losses of vegetation, particularly in East Africa. When swarming, the birds can be a major cause of desertification. Even in the desert, the camel caravans played host to fleas and rats, which enabled certain diseases, possibly including bubonic plague, to cross the Sahara. The incidence of disease along the rivers was a deterrent to their use for transport, except for the Nile and, to a more limited extent, the middle Niger, though even along their banks populations still suffer a high incidence of bilharzia. The presence of the tsetse fly forced farmers in tropical Africa to till their soil by hand, using hoes, without the benefit of oxen or horses. (See Map 1.5.)

The high incidence of malaria, yellow fever, and other diseases was certainly an important factor discouraging the colonization of Africa after the voyages of the Portuguese opened up the coastline to European contact. Before the middle of the 19th century, Europeans working for the trading companies regularly lost between a quarter and a half of their manpower on two-year tours of duty. There are well-authenticated cases where over 90 percent of the staff of European trading stations died from disease. It was their relative resistance to disease that made Africans so valuable as slaves in the New World, where European labor was prone to tropical disease and American Indians rapidly succumbed to the most elementary of European diseases, like measles and chicken pox.

## AGRICULTURAL ADAPTATIONS

When one takes into consideration climate, vegetation, soils, and disease, it is possible to see that certain areas were more conducive to population growth than others. Initially, in the Stone Age, the favored areas were the more open grassland and bush, where game was either more abundant or easier to hunt. With the introduction of agriculture, the emphasis shifted to those areas with a more reliable rainfall, better soils, and—for pastoralists—freedom from the tsetse fly. Africa's agricultural systems began in the late Stone Age, sometime after 10,000 B.C. Experimentation with different plants probably led to the selective use of such grains as barley in Upper Egypt, tef and millet in the Ethiopian highlands, and millets and sorghums in the northern savannah and Sahel of West Africa. Agriculture, once believed to have been introduced to Africa from the Near East, is now known to have a respectable antiquity in Africa with the earliest village site at Nabta Playa, in the Aswan area of Egypt, dating around 6250 B.C.

In several studies of farmers in a traditional area of the southern savannah of Ghana it has been estimated that villagers may utilize up to 200 different plants on an annual basis. The plants are used to make food, sauces and relishes, medicines, soaps, building materials, charcoal, and, until recently, bark cloth, adhesives, dyes, and even poisons. In addition, villagers know the names and uses of several hundred more plants. This knowledge was gained over thousands of years by trial and error, and its survival provides evidence of the indigenous beginnings of West African agriculture among the late Stone Age hunters and food gatherers. Though they no longer hunt large game, many farmers retain the hunting ethic. Small animals, such as the ubiquitous grass-cutters and other large rodents, birds, giant forest snails, and oil palm grubs form an essential part of these farmers' limited intake of nonvegetable food. Honey is another important staple. The economic crisis that is now restricting the import or distribution of cane sugar has caused an expansion in rural honey consumption. Other clues to the ancestry of West African crop systems lie in their folklore and religion. New-yam festivals and the linking of oil palms and yams with different deities and folk heroes distinguish these crops from those which we know were later introduced from outside the region.

## RESOURCE LOCATION AND STATE FORMATION

We know that sheep, poultry, and possibly cattle were introduced from outside Africa, spreading slowly from North Africa until cattle and sheep reached the Cape area of South Africa 1,800 to 2,000 years ago. As agriculture spread, including some new crops from Southeast Asia as bananas and taro, the population of Africa grew. The largely transitory existence of the Stone Age was replaced by settled life in village communities.

Agricultural expansion ultimately required a new technology. Iron was needed for hoes to break up the soil, and slashing blades or machetes were needed to clear bush and weeds. With the beginnings of agriculture we start to see the true foundations of traditional African society, and we first recognize the major ethnic groupings that have survived to the present day. This was also the period when major differential growth meant that some societies expanded at the expense of others. The anatomy of the continent became important in determining which areas were to become historically more significant.

The areas which ultimately developed fastest were those with key resources and the appropriate technology to exploit those resources or those areas with access to key resources that enabled them to control the trade to or from areas of supply and demand. In its prime, Ancient Egypt had both these advantages. The Nile Valley provided the most fertile, irrigable alluvial soil in the eastern Mediterranean, and the river itself provided access to excellent sources of gold, building stone, slaves, skins, and other tropical goods in Nubia and areas farther south. There was easy access to copper in the Sinai, timber in Lebanon through trade, and semi-precious stones for bead-making in the nearby Saharan mountains.

Trade allowed agriculture and mineral surpluses to be exchanged for commodities not produced locally. In West Africa, for example, imports included fine textiles to supplement their own cotton cloth, brassware, glass beads, salt from the north, and such forest products as kola nuts, civet for perfumes, skins, and ivory from the south. Camels and horses also were regularly brought in from North Africa. Tentacles of long-distance trade were linking different areas of Africa several centuries before the Arabs invaded North Africa in the seventh century A.D. These networks were enlarged by north Arab traders who crossed the Sahara using camels. Islamized Mande moved south from the middle Niger, relying on donkeys and, when donkeys were lost to the tsetse fly, human carriers.

In Southern Africa the location of copper around the headwaters of the Congo and in the Copper Belt of northern Zambia concentrated population and helped to initiate trade and coastal contact in the late first millennium A.D. Some of the trade probably followed routes already pioneered in local networks for the distribution of salt. Gold was the key resource across the Zambezi in Zimbabwe at a slightly later date. But the supply of highly localized resources would have been unimportant if there had been no demand. The demand came from the coast, where traders had been visiting from the Red Sea and the Persian Gulf since classical times, first in search of frankincense and myrrh, and later for a variety of tropical goods, including spices and sea shells. The tsetse-free highlands of central Africa encouraged movement and the expansion of cattle-keeping, and the builders of the town and monuments of Great Zimbabwe probably owed their wealth partly to their control of the overland trade in precious metals, and also to the success of their cattle ranches.

To the north of Lake Victoria after the 17th century, the small kingdom of Buganda expanded because its home area possessed good soils and reliable year-round rainfall. The Baganda built their wealth on an intensive horticulture based primarily on the banana. Altogether, they grew 50 different varieties of banana, carefully pruning and mulching the plants in order to avoid having to shift the plantations to other areas of the tropics. Agricultural prosperity encouraged population growth. At the same time, the settled, well-fed population and the stable crop enabled their ruling *kabakas* (kings) to raise armies quickly. This was in contrast to their neighbors, who ruled over more dispersed populations of herders, and found it more difficult to abandon their livestock to fight their ruler's battles. Because of their position on the north shore of Lake Victoria and their ability to provide a rich market, the Baganda also were able to develop a highly prosperous canoe trade that ultimately reached the coast. This control of important lines of communication also meant that they could block trade access to rivals who lay further inland.

## THE FRAGILE ENVIRONMENT
## AND RESOURCE EXHAUSTION

Though resources stimulated growth, they were exhaustible. Ancient Ghana may have declined as much because of its overexploitation of the Bambuk gold of Guinea and the rapid growth of both its human and domestic animal populations as because of invaders. Norwegian research on the small kingdom of Mema, the contemporary of Ancient Ghana on its southeastern flank, revealed huge iron slag mounds which stopped being used in the 11th century. The area is now dry Sahel, but the waste from the iron extractive industry that served Ghana in its heyday is mute testimony to the environmental destruction caused by endless cords of timber being consumed for charcoal. Mali, in the 13th century, became the predominant power in the western Sudan, drawing gold supplies from both the upper Niger and the forest. Mali used the Niger as an artery of trade and had thriving towns—some with perhaps over 20,000 people—which served as entrepots for desert caravans. In the 1400s, Mali also declined. Though political disintegration and weak leadership played roles, the Black Death epidemics of the 14th century and the climatic deterioration that caused people of the desert and Sahel to move into better watered lands must also have been important. Medieval Zimbabwe, similarly, may have been abandoned because of environmental stress, perhaps a shortage of grazing lands, a depletion of wood for firewood and charcoal, or an advance of the tsetse belt in the 15th century.

## THE IMPACT OF THE ENVIRONMENT ON THE INDIVIDUAL AND SOCIETY

We have dealt with the way the anatomy of Africa affected historical societies. But what about the impact of the environment on the individual? The story of humanity is basically one of adaptation to environment. The human species is the most successful of all living species, in that it has adapted to every single environment. Other species adapt to a particular ecological niche; away from that environment, they cannot survive.

A particular society has a highly specialized relationship with its environment, depending on the nature of the economy. For the hunter and gatherer as well as the farmer, the relationship with the environment is a very direct one, an almost mystical or religious bond; whereas for the pastoralist, the link is indirect—through the family herds. The intimacy of the environmental link, as possessed by the hunter, the herdsman, or the village farmer, was weakened with the development of the richest parts of Africa as specialists in trade, industry, and government. The echoes of that intimacy, however, were retained in the religion and art of much of Africa. The pantheon of gods of ancient Egypt was surmounted by the cosmic family of Ra, Nut, Osiris, Isis, and Seth, all of whom were linked with the cycle of nature, the sun, the sky, the fertility of the earth, and the flow of the Nile. Similarly, many of the traditional deities of the Yoruba and the Ibo, in Nigeria, and the *balubaale* of the Baganda represented such natural forces as thunder, water, the moon, and fertility. The pattern of disease and the indeterminate way in which people survived was also a matter of some mystery. It is no wonder that in many societies there was a deity of smallpox who needed to be placated. The religious link with the environment was strengthened by the association of specific animals or rivers with specific forces. A healthy respect for nature was thus maintained, along with a respect for what the environment could and could not provide. The relationship with the land was particularly important in matters of death. For many traditional societies the dead represented continuity with the present. They were buried within the village itself, sometimes within the very house in which they had lived, rather than in some special cemetery away from the community of the living. Among the Baganda, continuity was and is symbolized by burial within the *lusuku*, or banana grove, which provides nourishment for the living.

The pattern of the seasons governed the lives of Africans, particularly the coming of the rains and the resulting harvest. Where there was a need to know exactly when events would take place, systems for regulating human activities were sought. It is no coincidence that the most accurate calendrical system before modern times was devised in Ancient Egypt. These people needed to know when the annual floods would occur. Accurate to within a quarter of a day, the Egyptian calendrical system depended on keen observation of the stars. The floods brought fertility to the land; but, if uncontrolled, they also brought destruction to homes and fields. There was a need to control the floods and, ultimately, to harness the waters for irrigation.

Time was important elsewhere in Africa, but not the linear concept of time which has developed in the West. Unlike Western time, in which fixed dates were important, the sense of time in most traditional African societies was cyclical; it was related to other events rather than to a single time scale. The exact time involved was less important than that the relationship was made. When a cycle was employed it consisted of an annual agricultural cycle, an individual or group life growth cycle (such as age-grade systems), or the weekly or monthly cycles of certain West African peoples. Markets were held at regular intervals, according to the weekly cycle used. In an age-grade system, each new age-grade is initiated every seven to 15 years and given a new name, so that every member of the age-grade can be readily identified as belonging to the group which has just been admitted. Age-grades provide social cohesion. Names are repeated after a normal life span, so that reference to a particular age-grade or cycle provides some indication of time. Members of a group will remember distinctive external events that may have taken place at the time they entered the age-grade. A Ghanaian or Togolese child knows the day of the week she or he was born, but not necessarily the year. In most societies, genealogies provide an indication of time since they relate to generational identity, which is important in the social context or in the context of such matters as land inheritance. Thus, time can be seen as belonging to the cycle of nature, the web of family, and kin relationships, as it is part of a society's economic activities rather than a philosophical or physical concept.

## CURRENT PERSPECTIVES

We have looked at aspects of Africa's history and at the beliefs of traditional societies that were derived from the intimate relationship between the societies and their environment. But what about present realities? In some areas, the custom of pouring libations to ancestors still occurs; ancestors still reside within the earth. Children are given day names, and yam or maize festivals still mark the passage of time, calling the attention of city workers, intellectuals, and farmers to a natural cycle based on an ancestral tradition. The close attachment of many urban middle classes to the land can be seen in their preference of purchasing land or homes in the village or town from which they came rather than in the city in which they live. The strength of environmental knowledge can also be seen in the expansion and official recognition in towns of traditional healers, who make use of a wide variety of well-tried herbal remedies. Although a great deal of urbanization (estimated at five percent growth per year) has taken place since the era of independence, tropical Africa is still predominantly a rural continent. Few countries, among them Ghana and Cameroon with 35 percent, and the Ivory Coast and Zambia with 38 percent, have more than 30 percent of their populations in towns of more than 5,000 people (compared to over 70 percent in North America and over 90 percent in most of Europe). With high urban unemployment and underemployment, food shortages significantly affect most African governments, making agricultural policy and food-pricing prime governmental concerns. With food problems affecting the towns and scarce foreign currency reserves being spent on food imports, the environmental relationship affects the town-dweller as much as the traditional farmer. The drought years of the 1970s and 1980s diverted money from the social services and physical infrastructure of the new countries to buy imported food to feed the towns. Political instability was a direct consequence of the drought, including the collapse of the monarchy in Ethiopia.

At the village level, however, various studies have indicated a resilience in the face of adversity. This is well illustrated in my own research at the village of Hani in rural Ghana. Just after independence, in 1957, there was a period of relative prosperity, largely because of the rise in cocoa prices. Towns were the chief recipients of development, and the urban wage grew relative to the income of the traditional farmer. The urban worker could buy more for a day's labor than his rural counterpart. Consequently, there was a movement away from the villages. The economy in Ghana weakened in the 1970s, the cocoa production declined, and so the development of the 1960s began to dwindle. Foreign indebtedness increased and imports declined, bringing hardships to the towns. The villagers were able to feed and shelter themselves; and while foreign food imports decreased, local food supplies increased, bringing higher incomes to individual farmers than had previous cash crops such as tobacco. Increased rural spending power was reflected in greater self-reliance, house-building, and community projects, including an occasional feeder road, health center, and dam. Shelter in the town was a problem for the urban worker; but for the villager, the cost of shelter is mainly the cost of labor and the application of indigenous skills. While imported items, such as aluminum, enamel, and galvanized ware, became scarce, rural industries, such as potting, expanded to meet the demand. In areas where blacksmiths still existed, they began to make hoes again from scrap metal. Many of the herbal remedies fast being forgotten were just as quickly remembered when medicines from hospitals became scarce. Soaps were made from a half dozen different natural substances when packet soap became unobtainable. This suggests that in countries under stress, individual societies have the ability to draw upon their accumulated knowledge of the environment in order to adapt to adverse economic change. But the experience of the two periods of acute drought in Africa has indicated the vulnerability of Africa to different kinds of environmental stress.

This vulnerability is nothing new, nor is it confined to a particular region of Africa. In many areas gross over-exploitation of the environment has occurred. In other areas, agricultural systems that were appropriate for subsistence have broken down as population has expanded. The traditional societies of Africa each developed unique adaptations to environments in which they were located, adaptations which shaped their religious systems, philosophical outlook, and patterns of daily life. The challenge for African societies in the future is to adapt to new technologies and to an environment ravaged by overexploitation, while facing the continent's usual problems: endemic disease, unreliable rains, and inadequately distributed natural resources.

---

## Reading 1.1

In these extracts from a contemporary study of one of the last major groups of foraging people in Africa, the !Kung San of Botswana, we learn both of the importance of water in an area of unreliable rainfall and we learn of the different but highly specialized roles of men and women. The San now number less than 60,000 in Namibia, Botswana, and South Africa. Hunters and gatherers in Africa presently comprise around one fortieth of one percent of Africa's population. Groups similar to the !Kung, known by the rather derogatory term of *Bushmen* in much of Western literature, were responsible for some of the finest rock art in the world, in the Drakensburg mountains of Natal and Lesotho. Living in an environment with more abundant natural resources, these groups had a rich folklore and an almost mystical and symbolic religious life, in which the eland played an important role. They were lost to the rest of humanity by the advance of civilization, the last Drakensburg Bushmen having been hunted or driven out of existence in the early 19th century.

The story of Nisa is told both by the anthropologist Marjorie Shostak and by Nisa herself.

---

## Marjorie Shostak: *Nisa: The Life and Words of a !Kung Woman*

The northern fringe of the Kalahari Desert is a capricious and demanding environment. Total rainfall of the wet season can vary from as much as forty to as little as five inches from one year to the next. Forty inches fills depressions in the land and forms pools that often remain full for weeks or even months. Travel to distant places is easy, and people are able to disperse in small groups over the area in search of game and other food. Lesser-known plants, seen only once in several years, flourish, but some of the more basic foods may drown. Continuous rains may even cause the fruit of the staple food, the protein-rich mongongo nut, to rot; even worse, rare heavy downpours early in the season may damage the mongongo flowers before they bear fruit.

Five inches of rain, in contrast, is a drought condition, and many of the edible plants gathered by !Kung women may not be found. Severe drought occurs in the Dobe area on the average of one year in four. Knowing where permanent water springs are located, being able to see the shriveled vines that signal large water-storing roots hidden several feet under the ground, remembering the partially enclosed recesses of the thick mongongo and morula tree trunks that hide trapped water, can mean survival. All of this is compounded by the geographical variability of rainfall within one season; one area may receive twice as much as another just a few miles away.

An untrained visitor set down in this sand-and-thorn scrub brush on a typical spring day (September to November), would first look for some shade, and would be grateful to find some where the temperature was only 100° F. The visitor might not see water anywhere, and might find little if anything to eat. Even in the middle of the nut groves, with hundreds of thousands of mongongo nuts lying on the ground, the newcomer might go hungry; it would be necessary to find stones strong enough to crack the quarter-inch shell, then to determine how to hold the nut between the stones and, without smashing a finger, to hit it with just enough power in just the right spot to make it crack along the fault line, releasing the filbert-sized nut inside.

Suppose an animal were sighted and suppose further that the visitor had had the foresight to have fashioned arrowheads from bone remnants, shafts for the arrows from a tall, reed-like grass, poison from the larvae of a certain beetle, a bow from a partly dried green branch, and a string from fibrous plant threads rolled into twine. Even for such a well-prepared visitor, it would take the most extraordinary luck to make a hit without years of training and experience in tracking, stalking, and shooting. And even then, how long might it take for the animal to die? Hours? Days? Would the visitor be able to follow its tracks? To find enough plant food to survive in the meantime?

Even the !Kung average only one kill for every four days of hunting. The hunter must know how to read animal tracks—to know when they were made and what species of animal made them, as well as the animal's age, size, and condition of health. The quarry must not only be tracked but stalked, and the hunter must understand the vagaries of the wind in order to get close enough for a clear shot. If the arrow strikes, he must determine how far the poisoned shaft has entered, how long the animal will take to die, and where it is likely to travel as it dies. If the animal is large, the hunger may go back to the village for the night, and return the next day with others to help. They will pick up the tracks again, find the animal, and, if it is not yet dead, kill it with spears. If already dead, the animal may have attracted lions, leopards, hyenas, jackals, wild dogs, or vultures, separately or in combination, and these will have to be chased away, sometimes at great risk. The carcass will then be butchered and the skin carefully removed to be tanned later and made into clothing or blankets. The liver will be roasted and eaten immediately and the rest of the meat prepared for carrying back. Nothing will be left behind or wasted.

\* \* \*

**NISA:**

Once we went to live near a water hole, but there was no water in it. That was another time we were all thirsty. The only water came from kwa, a large water root. My mother scraped the white pulp into mounds, squeezing out the water for me to drink. She'd say, "Nisa's only a little child, yet she's dying of thirst." Because, although the kwa roots were plentiful, they were also bitter. When I'd drink the juice, I'd cry.

We lived there and after some time passed we saw the rain clouds. One came near, but just hung in the sky. It stayed hanging, just like that. Then another day, more rain clouds came over and they, too, just stood. Then the rain started to spill itself and it came pouring down.

The rainy season had finally come. The sun rose and set and the rain spilled itself. It fell and kept falling. It fell tirelessly, without ceasing. Soon the water pans were full. And my heart! My heart within me was happy. We lived and ate meat and mongongo nuts and more meat and it was all delicious.

My heart was so happy I moved about like a little dog, wagging my tail and running around. Really! I was so happy, I shouted out what I saw: "The rainy season has come today! Yea! Yea!"

There were caterpillars to eat, those little things that crawl along going, "Mmmm...mmmm...mmmm..." And people dug roots and collected food and brought home more and more food. There was plenty of meat and people kept bringing more back, hanging on sticks, and they hung it up in the trees where we were camped. My heart was bursting and I ate lots of food and my tail kept wagging, wagging about like a little dog. And I'd laugh with my little tail, laugh a little donkey's laugh, a tiny thing that is. I'd wag my tail one way and the other, shouting, "Today I'm going to eat caterpillars...cat—er—pillars!" Some people gave me meat broth to drink and others prepared the skins of caterpillars and roasted them for me to eat and I ate and ate and ate!

* * *

**SHOSTAK:**

As a subsistence strategy, gathering for a living is quite satisfying. It can be energetically engaged in, no matter what the size of a woman's family. The schedule is flexible, the pace is self-determined, and the work is accomplished in the company of others. Although each woman basically gathers for herself, this does not isolate her from other women. Women present choice findings to each other as offerings of good will and solidarity. The work is challenging: each expedition taps a woman's ability to discern, among the more than two hundred plants known by name and in the general tangle of vegetation, which plants are edible, which are ripe for harvesting, and which are most worthy of her efforts. It is also efficient: a day's work is usually enough to feed a family for a few days. Unlike !Kung hunters, !Kung gatherers have the solid assurance that when their families are hungry they will be able to find food—an assurance that fills them with pride. As one woman explained, "I like to gather. If I just sit, my children have nothing to eat. If I gather, my children are full." Finally, although gathering requires considerable stamina, the four days a week that women are not gathering afford them abundant time for visiting and for leisure.

When a woman returns to the village, she determines how much of her gatherings, if any, will be given away, and to whom. She sets aside piles of food for those she feels inclined to give to, and places the rest in the back of her hut or beside her family's fire. The food she and her family eat that night, the next day, and perhaps even the next, will consist primarily of the things she has brought home. From start to finish, her labor and its product remain under her own control.

Another indication of the high standing of !Kung women is their relationship to the gift-giving network called *hxaro*. All !Kung adults (and some children) are part of this network; each has a discrete number of partners with whom certain goods are exchanged. Women's participation in hxaro is basically the same as that of men, with no significant difference in the number of exchange partners or in the quality or quantity of exchanges.

In addition, core membership in a band, as well as "ownership" of water holes and other resources, is inherited through women as well as men. No male prerogative can be exercised in relation to this important source of influence in !Kung society.

This picture of !Kung women's lives might seem to challenge Margaret Mead's observation about the universality of the male bias. Unfortunately, though, the !Kung are not the exception they at first appear to be. !Kung women do have a formidable degree of autonomy, but !Kung men enjoy certain distinct advantages—in the way the culture values their activities, both economic and spiritual, and in their somewhat greater influence over decisions affecting the life of the group.

Meat, the economic contribution of men, is considered more valuable than gathered foods. Most gathered foods, except the mongongo nut, are described as "things comparable to nothing," while meat is so highly valued that it is often used as a synonym for "food." Squeals of delighted children may greet women as they return from gathering, but when men walk into the village balancing meat on sticks held high on their shoulders, everyone celebrates, young and old alike. It may even precipitate a trance dance. The one thing women can bring in that causes a comparable reaction is honey, but the finding of honey is a much rarer event and one that men are usually enlisted to help with. !Kung women may control the distribution of their gathered products, but the distribution of meat, while more constrained by formal rules, involves men in a wider sphere of influence.

---

## Reading 1.2

In these extracts from the first and best known of the novels by distinguished Nigerian author Chinua Achebe, we are introduced to the world of Okonkwo, the farmer whose whole life is affected by his relationship to the land and particularly to the yam, the chief crop of the Ibo people. Though rainfall in the forest is normally reliable, we find out in the first extract what happens if the rains come at the wrong time or are insufficient, as happened in many West African countries as recently as 1982 and 1983. The second extract indicates the religious nature of the bond between the farmer and the land, and the link between the ancestors and the gods. In many West African societies, libations are poured to the living dead, whose souls stay with the earth they tilled and to whom offerings are normally given at the time of the yam festival or at any other gathering associated with a festival or time of gladness, sadness, or dedication. The yam festival was traditionally a time of renewal, a time when the community could join together to rejoice in the bounty of the earth.

---

## Chinua Achebe, *Things Fall Apart*

The year that Okonkwo took eight hundred seed-yams from Nwakibie was the worst year in living memory. Nothing happened at its proper time; it was either too early or too late. It seemed as if the world had gone mad. The first rains were late, and, when they came, lasted only a brief moment. The blazing sun returned, more fierce than it had ever been known, and scorched all the green that had appeared with the rains. The earth burned like hot coals and roasted all the yams that had been sown. Like all good farmers, Okonkwo had begun to sow with the first rains. He had sown four hundred seeds when the rains dried up and the heat returned. He watched the sky all day for signs of rain-clouds and lay awake all night. In the morning he went back to his farm and saw the withering tendrils. He had tried to protect them from the smouldering earth by making rings of thick sisal leaves around them. But by the end of the day the sisal rings were burnt dry and grey. He changed them every day, and prayed that the rain might fall in the night. But the drought continued for eight market weeks and the yams were killed.

Some farmers had not planted their yams yet. They were the lazy easy-going ones who always put off clearing their farms as long as they could. This year they were the wise ones. They sympathised with their neighbours with much shaking of the head, but inwardly they were happy for what they took to be their own foresight.

Okonkwo planted what was left of his seed-yams when the rains finally returned. He had one consolation. The yams he had sown before the drought were his own, the harvest of the previous year. He still had the eight hundred from Nwakibie and the four hundred from his father's friend. So he would make a fresh start.

But the year had gone mad. Rain fell as it had never fallen before. For days and nights together it poured down in violent torrents, and washed away the yam heaps. Trees were uprooted and deep gorges appeared everywhere. Then the rain became less violent. But it went on from day to day without a pause. The spell of sunshine which always came in the middle of the wet season did not appear. The yams put on luxuriant green leaves, but every farmer knew that without sunshine the tubers would not grow.

That year the harvest was sad, like a funeral, and many farmers wept as they dug up the miserable and rotting yams. One man tied his cloth to a tree branch and hanged himself.

Okonkwo remembered that tragic year with a cold shiver throughout the rest of his life. It always surprised him when he thought of it later that he did not sink under the load of despair. He knew he was a fierce fighter, but that year had been enough to break the heart of a lion.

\* \* \*

Yam, the king of crops, was a very exacting king. For three or four moons it demanded hard work and constant attention from cock-crow till the chickens went back to roost. The young tendrils were protected from earth-heat with rings of sisal leaves. As the rains became heavier the women planted maize, melons and beans between the yam mounds. The yams were then staked, first with little sticks and later with tall and big tree branches. The women weeded the farm three times at definite periods in the life of the yams, neither early nor late.

And now the rains had really come, so heavy and persistent that even the village rain-maker no longer claimed to be able to intervene. He could not stop the rain now, just as he would not attempt to start it in the heart of the dry season, without serious danger to his own health. The personal dynamism required to counter the forces of these extremes of weather would be far too great for the human frame.

And so nature was not interfered with in the middle of the rainy season. Sometimes it poured down in such thick sheets of water that earth and sky seemed merged in one grey wetness. It was then uncertain whether the low rumbling of Amadiora's thunder came from above or below. At such times, in each of the countless thatched huts of Umuofia, children sat around their mother's cooking fire telling stories, or with their father in his *obi* warming themselves from a log fire, roasting and eating maize. It was a brief resting period between the exacting and arduous planting season and the equally exacting but light-hearted month of harvest.

\* \* \*

The Feast of the New Yam was approaching and Umuofia was in a festival mood. It was an occasion for giving thanks to Ani, the earth goddess and the source of all fertility. Ani played a greater part in the life of the people than any other deity. She was the ultimate judge of morality and conduct. And what was more, she was in close communion with the departed fathers of the clan whose bodies had been committed to earth.

The Feast of the New Yam was held every year before the harvest began, to honour the earth goddess and the ancestral spirits of the clan. New yams could not be eaten until some had first been offered to these powers. Men and women, young and old, looked forward to the New Yam Festival because it began the season of plenty—the new year. On the last night before the festival, yams of the old year were all disposed of by those who still had them. The new year must begin with tasty, fresh yams and not the shrivelled and fibrous crop of the previous year. All cooking-pots, calabashes and wooden bowls were thoroughly washed, especially the wooden mortar in which yam was pounded. Yam foo-foo and vegetable soup was the chief food in the celebration. So much of it was cooked that, no matter how heavily the family ate or how many friends and relations they invited from neighbouring villages, there was always a huge quantity of food left over at the end of the day. The story was always told of a wealthy man who set before his guests a mound of foo-foo so high that those who sat on one side could not see what was happening on the other, and it was not until late in the evening that one of them saw for the first time his in-law who had arrived during the course of the meal and had fallen to on the opposite side. It was only then that they exchanged greetings and shook hands over what was left of the food.

The New Yam Festival was thus an occasion for joy throughout Umuofia. And every man whose arm was strong, as the Ibo people say, was expected to invite large numbers of guests from far and wide. Okonkwo always asked his wives' relations, and since he now had three wives his guests would make a fairly big crowd.

---

## Reading 1.3

Francis Deng was one of the first African anthropologists. In his book, he describes the life of his own people, the Dinka, the largest ethnic group in the Republic of the Sudan. He describes not only the difficulties of the environment, but also its beauty, and he demonstrates how their environment and way of life has resulted in a very definite Dinka personality. Pride, ethnocentrism, and individualism are distinguished as particular Dinka qualities. The Dinka area, in common with other areas of the southern Sudan, is presently struggling to retain the measure of local autonomy that was obtained under the Addis Agreement of 1972. Pastoralism is still a major economic activity within the area, though the Jonglei canal and irrigation work in the south will eventually increase agricultural potential and economic prosperity and also streamline river communication.

---

## Francis Mading Deng, *The Dinka of the Sudan*

The land of the Dinka is in the rich savannah, segmented by the waters of the Nile and its tributaries. Large in numbers, widespread in settlement, and divided by many rivers, some are unaware of one another as fellow Dinka. A congeries of about twenty-five mutually independent tribal groups, they are united by their physical characteristics, their ethnocentric pride, and their striking cultural uniformity....

The cultural continuity of the Dinka is often ascribed to their pride and ethnocentrism, which are conspicuous in their own name for themselves. They do not call themselves "Dinka" but *Monyjang*, which means "The Man [or the husband] of Men." This denotes that they see themselves as the standard of what is normal for the dignity of man and asserts their superiority to "the others" or "foreigners" (the *juur*: singular, *jur*).

While viewing themselves as "Lords of Men" the Dinka are loving slaves of cattle and they will gladly admit this. In the spirit of a devout slave, a Dinka will kill and even risk his life for a single cow. They have a myth that explains their involvement with, and suffering for, cattle: The Dinka went hunting and killed the mother of the buffalo and the cow. Both, bereft and provoked, vowed to take vengeance against man. The buffalo chose to remain in the forest and attack man whenever he laid eyes on him. (To this day, the buffalo is one of the few animals that will charge against man without provocation.) The cow on the other hand ingeniously preferred to fight man within man's own system: to be domesticated to make man slave for her; to play man off against man; and to cause him to fight and kill for ownership, possession, or protection of her.

But, if the cow is subtle, the Dinka too has his reasons for being allured into her trap. Cattle provide him with much of his worldly needs. Cows provide dairy products that the Dinka consider not only the best, but also the most noble, food. While they deplore killing the animal out of craving for meat and will do so only in sacrifice to God, spirits, and their ancestors—and sometimes in honor of guests, or for special feasts—almost every animal is eventually destined for the fire or the pot, since every animal is eaten whatever the cause of its death. Through dedication and sacrifice, cattle protect the Dinka against the evil forces of illness and death. Their payment as "bride-wealth" guarantees the continuation of the Dinka race, and the distribution of the bridewealth among a wide circle of relatives cements the network of human ties so highly regarded by the Dinka. Cattle are also paid as blood-wealth in homicide and in compensation for a variety of other wrongs. Their dried dung provides the Dinka with fuel and fertilizer, their urine with disinfectant, their hides with bedding skins, and their horns with snuffboxes, trumpets, and spoons. So important for the welfare of the Dinka and so honored by them are their cattle that the Dinka speak of the cow or the bull as the "creator." With bridewealth sometimes going as high as 200 cows, the Dinka are probably the richest cattle-owners on the continent of Africa and certainly in the Sudan. They also keep sheep and goats. But to these animals they afford only a fraction of their devotion to cattle.

Less known is the fact that the Dinka are cultivators, although their production is generally on the subsistence level and sometimes below it. This is partly because of their lavish hospitality, extravagant festivity, and resentment of saving as miserly. Much, however, has to do with their rudimentary implements and the adverse climate both of which limit the size of the land they can till and the amount they can produce. So irregular are the rains that they may fall and people plant, then stop, and crops die, or soak the fields and drown the crops. While their land is full of all-season rivers, the Dinka do not use irrigation except on their small plots of tobacco which are cultivated during the dry season. Worms, locusts, birds, and a variety of animals are additional threats at all stages of cultivation.

For human beings and animals there is much discomfort in Dinkaland. The blazing sun of the dry season kills the grass and deceives the traveler with moving mirages of rivers and lakes. The soil dries up, forming wide and deep cracks into which humans and animals fall. The ground and trees are covered with sturdy thorns. Swarms of restless flies torment both men and herds. Armies of mosquitoes necessitate exhaustive fanning or escaping into the smoky and stuffy huts. The wet season comes with heavy and stormy rains that may fall for days, leveling the tall grass and impeding even milking and cooking. Thunder and lightning leave behind fallen trees, burning huts, and sometimes dead relatives—tragedies that for the Dinka are divine manifestations calling for dedication and sacrifice. The Nile and its tributaries overflow, leaving floods, swamps, and mud. Lions, leopards, hyenas, wild dogs, rhinos, buffaloes, hippos, crocodiles, snakes, and scorpions are a continuous threat—so much more real than travelers' tales can tell.

Although the Dinka is always in direct contact with a hostile environment, he loves his country. He is self-sufficient in a way not easily explained by the simplicity of his desires. As he sees it, God has been most generous to him. He has cattle, sheep, and goats and he grows a wide variety of crops. His rivers and lagoons teem with fish just as his land is covered with animals. There are also many kinds of wild crops, vegetables, and fruits to satisfy his craving. Honey is in plenty. Depending on the season, his skies and pools are marvelously decorated with birds of every color, shape, and size. His fields and home sway with butterflies. The land is flat, changing from dark clay to white sand; from desertlike openness to junglelike forests. The greenness of infant grass carpeting the land after the early rains, the reflection of the sun through falling rains, and the bright rainbow linking opposite ends of his horizon are only examples of the beauties the rainy season brings. The radiant golden yellow rays of the setting sun spreading over the plains, the cattle returning to graze near the homes and bellowing to their tethered calves, the calves lowing to their mothers—near but unreachable, a boy singing as he starts a fire and tethers the cattle, the smoke from the fire mingling with the rays of the setting sun, and the sweet smell of the dried, smoking cow dung make a dry-season dusk.

Because the country is flat, vision goes far; and in the evenings when fires are lit in distant cattle-camps, one sees a beacon orange, pink, and yellow rising bright into the sky to spotlight the camps for a Dinka traveler. The sounds of distant drums, of bellowing herds, of howling boys, of singing birds all combine to produce the harmonious tunes of the slow rhythm of tribal life. At night, the high-pitched sounds of crickets, the cries of frogs, of a mother singing any song as a lullaby at the peak of her voice while jiggling an accompanying gourd, of a gentleman's singing of his favorite ox, while the ox bellows with gratification are a pleasant break to the stillness of rural nights. Moonlit nights attract children to play for long hours when they would otherwise be asleep and young men to travel long distances to visit their girlfriends and to sit all night in the open air conversing until dawn.

Against the dangers of his hostile environment, the Dinka builds huts for himself and cattle byres for his herds. His walls of wood and mud and his roofs of rafters and grass have won great admiration from many a visitor. The length and firmness of the roof grass and the slimness and the straightness of the tall trees from which he cuts his rafters make his thatch remarkably smooth. Dinka buildings can last for well over ten years, and in a country of rudimentary technology where termites and other pests threaten timber, this is no easy feat.

To a Dinka, his country, with all its deprivations and troubles, is the best in the world. Until very recently, going to a foreign land was not only a rarity but a shame. For a Dinka to threaten his relatives with leaving Dinkaland was seen as little short of suicide. What a lot to give up, and for what!

In character, the Dinka is a socially conscious yet individualistic person, gentle and humorous, but sensitive, temperamental, and prone to violent reaction when his sense of pride and dignity is hurt—and that may not take much. Dinka society is an exceedingly violent society, and from very early age one of the central values in a boy's education is valor and physical strength.

In sharp contrast with the violent disposition of militant youth, who provoke wars that are fought by all, is the emphasis on "ideal" human relations and on the attributes of unity, harmony, and persuasion. The chiefs and elders are largely persuasive, even though they admire the coercive character of their youth. Valor is institutionalized by means of organized warrior age-sets, and every Dinka joins one upon his initiation into adulthood. But this nurtured valor is ideally to be used against the aggressor and not for aggression. In fact, the Dinka never admit to being the aggressors. In their war-songs, they exalt themselves as ferocious resisters of aggression.

Proud and ethnocentric as the Dinka are, they are nevertheless hospitable and friendly to all visitors. Their high moral standards and sense of personal dignity and integrity prevent their taking advantage of foreigners. But once they are given a reason for disrespect by the misconduct of a foreigner, that foreigner barely qualifies as a human being. The Dinka are then prone to use their wits against him without the least feeling of guilt.

While the Dinka now form part of modern Sudan, they remain among the least touched by modernization. Their pride and ethnocentrism has always been given as an important factor in their conservatism and resistance to change.

---
*2*
---

# THE TRIPLE HERITAGE OF LIFESTYLES

————————— Elliott P. Skinner —————————

The previous chapter explored aspects of the environment that deeply affect life in Africa. In this chapter, noted anthropologist Elliott P. Skinner describes the three religious heritages that have coexisted in Africa for centuries, identifying their basic tenets, history, and role in contemporary African life. The coexistence and juxtaposition of these three legacies help to explain the diversity of the continent and the people who are called African. Eds.

Africans are heirs to three heritages: Africanity or the indigenous, the Islamic, and Western Christendom. Each has provided guides for human conduct and solutions to the questions of life and the universe.

## AFRICANITY

Africanity, a term we use to mean the variety of indigenous customs, has provided Africans with answers to the basic questions of their existence, from how they came into being to how they cope with the problems of daily life. The solutions to these problems varied as specific African societies adapted to particular ecologies, but to a remarkable degree all African societies are similar. Common to the now biologically and linguistically differentiated African peoples is the idea that neither religion nor society can be understood in isolation, for they are one. African religions are essentially human-centered. There is relatively little speculation about God and the universe. The object is to deal with mankind. God is almost everywhere, self-created and the Creator; but there is little speculation about his origin, essence, or designs. Nevertheless, almost every single day of their lives Africans invoke God. They do so when they greet each other and when they converse about health, happiness, and the most routine affairs.

God's power, majesty, and interest in human beings is most frequently viewed as mediated through Earth (often viewed as female and intimately linked to the Creator), lesser gods, deified kings and ancestors, spirits of various types, statues or icons, and phylacteries or sacred objects. All are perceived as part of or emanating from the Creator and are often the objects of cults of worship, the source of help, and the agencies by which order in human societies is maintained.

The principal supernatural references for human behavior are the ancestors who founded certain families and nations. Having once lived on earth, the ancestors are acquainted with the problems of human life and are ready to forgive as well as to punish transgressors. They try to protect their descendants as well as to prevent them from doing evil so that they may have health, long life, and children. In this way, the ancestors will be remembered and honored through sacrifices. Ill or troubled persons are notified by ancestors through dreams or consulting priests of the source of ancestral displeasure and make appropriate amends.

Africans are quite realistic about the problem of evil in human societies. They believe that some people, through envy or malice, deliberately harm their fellow human beings. Others who do harm may not even know they harbor such intentions or evil thoughts. Their propensity to do evil may have been inherited from parents or other relatives. Those who have been affected by evil may seek help from persons with supernatural power who can initiate or remove evil. Individuals also attempt to protect property or other persons through the use of holy objects.

While human beings are subject to the overall will of the Creator and the supervision of the ancestors, they are not helpless in the face of adversity. There is general recognition that God gives people specific gifts or weaknesses and that in complex societies statuses in life are ascribed. In the final analysis, however, people are held responsible for their lives. *Olorun* (the Yoruba name for God) is involved in a system of divination called *Ifa*, by which people seek to ascertain their destiny and thus attempt to deal with its problems or shortcomings. Often an *orisha* (ancestor) is beseeched to take a sacrifice and prayer directly to Olorun. While the Yoruba do not believe that Olorun necessarily intervenes, the Ibo of Nigeria are more inclined to believe that a person's *chi* (destiny) can be changed by prayers and sacrifices. An Ibo maxim holds: "If a man says yes, his chi says yes, also." Like destiny or personality, the fate of the spiritual essence which every person possesses is ultimately in the hands of God. Wickedness hastens death.

Elaborate funerals often mark the physical separation of a person from the community, but more important is the ability of a person to join the ranks of ancestors. This is determined by whether a person lived a good life and left descendants who could honor the deceased. The notion of final judgment of the soul is not common. What is expected, however, is that the final essence of the ancestors will continue to be honored along with the collective ancestors of the community.

The animals, plants, and techniques which make life possible are all said to come from God directly or through one of his agents. The name for God among the Ovimbundu of Angola, for example, translates as "He who supplies the needs of His creatures." This view of God has largely conditioned how Africans regard economic affairs. Amma (creator God of the Dogon people in Mali) sent the ancestors down to Earth in a great ark with all the species of animals and plants in the company of Nommo, an Osiris-like being. As the ark descended, Nommo shouted out Amma's creative words, thereby transmitting language to all mankind. Nommo stepped on the soil to demonstrate dominion over the Earth, and he impregnated it with Amma's creative signs. On the other side of the continent in Kenya, Ngai, the supreme being of the Gikuyu people, is believed to have identified specific occupations for each group living in the region. To the Ndorobo people of Kenya he gave a spear, thereby indicating their occupation as hunters; to the Maasai of Kenya he gave all the cattle in the world for their sustenance, and to the Gikuyu of Kenya he gave a hoe, the symbol of their livelihood as cultivators.

Africans seldom perform any economic activity without symbolic references to the supernatural. San hunters of the Kalahari invariably apologize to the spiritual essence of the animals they kill, explaining the need of human beings for food. The BaTwa hunters of Zaire are careful to respect the sanctity of the forests in whose vastness they obtain sustenance. To do evil in the forest is to run the risk of having it refuse to yield animals for food. Dinka and Nuer pastoralists of the Sudan not only treasure cattle, an essential food gift and important social asset, but view them as links to ancestral spirits. We are told that by rubbing ashes along the back of a cow or ox one may communicate with the spirit or ghost associated with it and ask for assistance. The Fulani herders of West Africa perform many rituals to help preserve the life of young calves and to safeguard the supply of cows' milk. In many other African pastoral societies, meat is eaten mainly in association with sacrifices and rituals.

Rituals that show respect for the earth mark the opening of the agricultural season for most African cultivators, especially in those regions where rainfall is precarious. In the forest regions trees and plots believed to be associated with spiritual beings are not defiled, and cultivators perform the necessary rituals invoking the aid of the earth and nature spirits. Rituals welcoming the harvest, such as the yam festivals in West Africa, millet festivals in the Sudan, or the first fruits in Swaziland, are widespread. These involve thanksgiving and sacrifices to God and his referents, including the ancestors.

Africanity also gives a great deal of importance to such significant rites of passage as childbirth, marriage, and death. Among the Akan peoples of West Africa, there are out-dorring, or coming out, ceremonies, in which the new child is introduced into its community. The Gikuyu on the other side of the continent seclude women during childbirth and perform similar rituals welcoming both mother and child back into the community. The names given African babies frequently indicate the day on which they were born, the ancestors they commemorate or whose place they have taken, or the spiritual benefactors who gave them to their parents. Twins often pose a problem since their advent is deemed unnatural. They may be honored, as among the Fanti of Ghana, or despised, as among the Udhuk of Ethiopia. Most children, however, find a niche in their families. They are socialized and educated according to the accepted norms for males or females and the status groups into which they were born.

Specialized training normally takes place at puberty when youth are prepared for adulthood. The Kore ritual among the Bambara of Mali takes several years and involves six distinct stages designed to create men who are morally and intellectually enlightened and metaphysically endowed with immortal souls. In most societies, the youth are removed from their communities, taught how to behave like adults, how to perform specific tasks, and how to respect social and political authority and the history and beliefs of their societies. Judged to be at a dangerous threshold, Bakongo youngsters in Zaire undergo religious rituals symbolizing their death as children and their rebirth as adults. Male circumcision and its female counterpart, clitoridectomy, are often associated with these rituals. In most cases, initiation rituals are viewed as preparatory and often obligatory for marriage. It is reported that the Dogon of Mali believe that an infant must be given its own sexual, social, and spiritual identity by the community into which it is born in order to be considered human. They believe that every child is born with twin—male and female—souls and has an unstable personality until circumcision removes the physical part (the prepuce or the clitoris) that contains the soul of the opposite sex.

Descent, kinship, and other social relationships are central values in Africanity. Also characteristic of Africanity is the transfer of valuables or services from the family of the bridegroom to that of the bride. Known in some regions as *lobolo*, the so-called bride-price, bride-wealth, or child-price legitimizes marriages and the children born to them. Sterility is considered a grave misfortune, and African couples seek advice from both diviners and herbalists on how to become fertile. Grateful parents often name subsequent children after the orisha or divinity that came to their rescue. Lactation sexual taboos often function to space the birth of children and to preserve the health of mothers and their children. Cases of abortion are not unknown, but a basic premise of Africanity is that women should have as many children as God gives them.

Motherhood is such an honored status in African societies that it modifies almost all other statuses held by women, whether servile, commoner, or royal. Men may insist that their daughters' behavior bring credit to the family; that young wives be supervised lest they stray; that they respect fathers' sisters, often considered male mothers; and that they avoid mothers-in-law who may create domestic problems for them. But African men and women alike deeply resent any disparaging remarks about their mothers. What this demonstrates is that the roles and status of African women vary as a function of their stage of life. Young wives who are quite circumspect in their attitudes to husbands become confidantes in later years and assume a great deal of responsibility for the status and welfare of their families.

Social activities, economic activities, and politics almost always involve rhythmic singing and movement. Music and movement are used to invoke the gods as well as to provide accompaniment for most activities. Intricate dances signal that deities are present. Special dances are performed to honor guests and to mark every important rite of passage from birth to death. Verbal skills in the use of proverbs, orations, or praise songs are valued by Africans for their functions as well as for their form. Sometimes, as among the Kalabari in southern Nigeria, masquerades combine art, music, oratory, song, and dance in the interest of aesthetics, economics, social relations, and politics, forming a conscious link between the natural and the supernatural. This connection is one of the most basic characteristics of Africanity.

## ISLAM

Islam emerged in Mecca and Medina on the Arabian Peninsula during the seventh century and was taken to North Africa initially by militant Arabs waging holy wars in the name of God (*Allah*) and His prophet, Mohammed. It was adopted by indigenous Africans and carried into the Sudan by mystics, traders, and conquerors as part of a movement which also took Islam into the Iberian Peninsula. Islam entered the Horn and East Africa with settlers, traders, and slave raiders. Faced with the power of the Muslims, many African tradition-alists and some Christians adopted Islam to avoid retribution and to take advantage of its benefits. Still other Africans rejected Islam, preferring their own indigenous religions. Finally, Islam took advantage of the European conquest of Africa to move into new areas. This process, in which Muslims lived side by side with non-Muslims, was often subtle and unobtrusive but gradually resulted in conversions.

While Islam has a diversity of specific beliefs and practices, it had to adapt to the African milieu, resulting in many regional variations. In all regions *Islam* (literally, *surrender*) has retained basically the same meaning: a sacred way of life, representing God's final revelation to His prophet Mohammed, which was recorded in the Koran.

For *Muslims* (meaning here, *those who surrender themselves*), Islam involves practices and beliefs in which all realms of life are interconnected and are viewed as manifestations of the sacred. Islam is also rigidly monotheistic, a belief made explicit in the *Sharia*, the law or code of righteousness. For Muslims, Islam is "the Way." It provides both theories and practices by which individuals and societies may obtain salvation. African Muslims, like Muslims everywhere, attempt to obey the following specific rules (the pillars) as a function of their faith: bear witness to the belief that there is no God but Allah and Mohammed is His prophet; pray five times a day, the first time just before dawn; observe fasts and other forms of abstinence during the month of Ramadan; give alms; and make the pilgrimage to Mecca. In addition, good Muslims must follow specific calendar (lunar) rites and observances; observe certain taboos and prescriptions; use Islamic elements in such rites of passage as naming; acknowledge the efficacy of Islamic supernatural powers, such as amulets and divinatory lore; believe in the power of saints and holy persons; and use holy war (*jihad*) to spread the faith, if necessary.

Throughout Africa, belief in Allah has coalesced with the creator-God of African cosmologies; but often the African name for God is used interchangeably with *Allah*. The Mossi use *Allah* along with *Winnam,* and the Swahili of East Africa use *Allah* and *Mungu* as synonyms. Subsidiary supernatural powers in indigenous African religions also have tended to be Islamized according to Koranic principles. Good spirits are equated with angels and the evil ones with *jinn* (a group of evil spirits). Muslim clerics, who are persons endowed with mystical power, divine the sources of evil and seek to exorcise it using verses of the Koran.

While African Islam has clerics, it has no established religious hierarchy. The local cleric, or *imam*, whether itinerant or living in rural or urban communities, performs such religious functions as leading the faithful in prayer; teaching the young to recite the sacred texts, especially the Koran; and performing the first sacrifices at great feasts, such as Ramadan. He also officiates at such rites of passage as the naming of the newborn; conducts marriage ceremonies; washes the dead; and leads funeral prayers. Often the only literate person in a rural community, the local imam frequently lives the ordinary life of a cultivator, herder, or tradesman.

Learned and holy men versed in Arabic and the Koran often preside over Koranic schools. They are believed to possess ritual power manifest by such charismatic qualities as the ability to perform miracles. Such men have often founded religious orders or brotherhoods with unique rituals and beliefs that differ from other Muslims. In many parts of Africa, there are cults of saints that honor especially devout Muslim clerics. In certain regions, the tombs of these men are Muslim pilgrimage sites.

African Islam, like its progenitor in Mecca or Medina, has always been associated with urban life and those concomitants of urban life (crafts, industry, and commerce) that are the attributes of a complex civilization. Muslim traders appeared in ancient Ghana long before that empire was conquered by the Almoravids and were, in fact, responsible for peacefully converting many western Sudanese states to Islam. In East Africa, Muslim ivory and slave traders functioned as Islamic missionaries. Because they were specialists in the intricacies of long-distance trade, Muslims were able to introduce into West Africa family-based commercial corporations with local credit and distribution systems. Muslim traders introduced new clothing styles into many parts of Africa, diffused certain notions of personal adornment, fostered novel food habits to replace those despised by Muslims, and encouraged the appreciation of representational art as well as forms of speech and manners from more highly developed regions.

Islamic law has affected the social organization of African peoples. The patrilineal emphasis in Islam has weakened the matrilineality of such people as the Yao in Tanzania. The Sharia also weakened the corporate nature of African lineages. Greater individualism is stressed, as is the right of women to inherit some property. And while Islam has generally regarded women as minors, few African Muslims seclude them entirely, since that would restrict female pastoral and other occupational duties.

African Muslims have largely accepted Islamic marriage practices. The Sharia's conception of marriage as a voluntary contract between individual spouses has been incorporated into the African practice of arranged marriages between two families. And while Islam does not dictate marriage between cousins, marriage between the children of brothers is increasingly viewed as preferred by this religion. Daughters can be given in marriage without a bride-price as a form of alms. The marriage settlement, intended to go to the bride, is often linked to the traditional bride-price, and a dowry often takes the form of the bride contributing utensils and food to the household. Arab cattle nomads in the Nilotic Sudan pay the bride's family and give valuables to the bride's mother to pay for the trousseau and the wedding.

The actual marriage is performed by the male relatives of the bride and groom before a cleric. This ceremony includes the formal acceptance of the bride-price and the recitation of formulas and specific prayers by the cleric. Post-ceremonial practices include ritually transporting the bride to the groom's house, as among the Hausa; taking her to a specially erected nuptial house, as among the Tuareg; or ritual bathing and unveiling of the bride, as among the Nilotes. In contrast to the lengthy marriage procedures, divorce among African Muslims is fairly easy, at least for the husband. Wives are often pressured to maintain even intolerable marriages.

Only wealthy African Muslims can take advantage of the permission to marry four wives. The payment of the marriage settlement gives men full rights to spouses as sexual and domestic partners and to all children born of the union. With this payment, matrilineal Yao men gain substantial control over their wives and their wives' children. This is important since many such men live with their wives' relatives. The marriage settlement gives Somali men rights to the fertility of their wives during the union regardless of the genitor of the offspring. On the other hand, payment does not entitle a man to a female replacement from the wife's family if the wife dies, nor does it allow a kinsperson to automatically inherit a widow.

Birth rituals are significant communal events among African Muslims. The naming ceremony is normally conducted by a cleric eight days after birth. Usually the child receives a Muslim name, is honored with sacrifice, and has its hair shaved. The Songhay believe that, at the naming, the *biya* (personality characteristics) of an ancestor enter and the baby becomes a person. At the end of the naming ceremony, Mossi give all witnesses grains of millet to distribute throughout the community as they announce the child's name. Muslim mothers must participate in a purification ceremony which normally takes place on the 40th day after childbirth. Nilotic Muslim women go to the Nile with female friends to perform this ablution.

Circumcision and clitoridectomy among African Muslims, normally part of the initiation ceremonies, are both linked to cleanliness. Muslims profess disdain for the uncircumcised. The Malinke of Guinea, the Mossi, and even the urban Swahili separate boys from their communities, educate them in the Koran, and have them operated upon by a cleric. The Songhay practice collective circumcision but have eliminated the other rituals. Elaborate ceremonies marked by prayers and sacrifices welcome the initiates back into the community. The Nilotic Jaliyyin practice an individual ceremony resembling a wedding procession in which the boy is decorated, mounted on a horse, and clad in women's robes and ornaments to protect him from the evil eye.

Burial rituals for African Muslims are fairly similar throughout the continent and involve ritual washing, incense, prayers, specific types of grave clothes, the use of stretchers for the dead, mourners' assistance in carrying the body, funeral prayers by clerics, specific orientation of the grave, and casting earth on the grave. After burial, ceremonies include gathering at the home of the deceased to pray and recite the Koran, and making offerings. There are also widows' ritual mourning, washing, seclusion, and purification. Most Muslims hold memorial events on the first, third, seventh, and 40th days after a funeral. The Hausa of Nigeria offer sacrifices to a man's soul and to God for the repose of the soul until the 40th day, but have no further ceremonies. The near relatives of Nilotic Muslims spend several days squatting on mats while they receive visits of condolence. On the final day of mourning the entire Koran is recited, and special prayers are periodically offered, ending with an elaborate ceremony on the last Friday of the month of Ramadan.

## WESTERN CHRISTENDOM

Christianity entered Africa shortly after its origin in Palestine and has persisted in Egypt and Ethiopia, even after having been eliminated in most of North Africa and the eastern Sudan. It gained a new lease on life in Africa when it entered the continent linked to Western imperialism.

Early African Christianity was riven by heretical controversies about the nature of God, Jesus, and the Trinity. Persecutions and attempts to escape the evils of this world resulted in increased numbers of hermits and monasteries, which later became characteristic of Christianity everywhere. The African Christian belief that Christ was a creature of God and therefore subordinated to him was rejected by the rest of Christendom. The African monks rejected the notion that Christ had two natures, human and divine, insisting that he had one (monophysite) nature that was divine. This belief laid the basis for Coptic Christianity in Egypt and Ethiopia. Christians in Roman North Africa suffered for their faith and coined the saying that "the blood of martyrs is the seeds of the church." They produced such eminent theologians as Cyprian, Bishop of Carthage, and St. Augustine, Bishop of Hippo, and they were the first to use the word *trinity*. These early Christians spread their religion among the Berbers and the Nubians, only to have it extinguished with the coming of Islam.

The Christianity that arrived with Western Europeans during the 15th century was quite different from its progenitor. It had been sectarianized by the Protestant Reformation, influenced by capitalism, and conditioned by European culture and nationalism. Spurred on by an evangelistic spirit and eager for personal gain and glory for their sovereigns, European adventurers and missionaries moved into Africa. Soldiers conquered new territories in the name of their king and God; the missionaries spoke in the name of God and their king. But slowly and sometimes painfully Africans realized that Western Christendom was made up of many competing and often conflicting institutions. Within Christianity itself, the various mission groups not only had different rituals and theology and exacted different codes of conduct, but they belonged to different nation states as well. Despite their commitment to religion, many missionaries fervently believed in the superiority of whites and European culture. The Christian missionaries and lay persons who went to Africa sought to impress upon the Africans that Christ died for their sins, and only in Christ would they be made alive. Moreover, they believed that by nature Africans were lowly and depraved savages in need of individual salvation and European civilization. Therefore the self-assigned task of the missionaries was to make a clean sweep of all that was African and to implant a new religion and way of life.

Christianity, as it is increasingly practiced by most Africans, has diverged from its Western European antecedents. Coptic Christianity still survives, however, and although it is embattled with Islam in Egypt, it still functions as the state religion in Ethiopia. European-type churches still persist but are increasingly controlled by black African clergy. In most African countries, early black Roman Catholic cardinals and bishops often were more orthodox than their European colleagues and were not in sympathy with the attempts of their pope to Africanize continental churches. This placed them in opposition to the younger clergy. Similarly, most of the important Protestant churches now have African clergy but still adhere to European theology and liturgy. The exception to even this limited accommodation to the indigenous culture is the Dutch Reformed Church of the Republic of South Africa, which adheres to strict Calvinist doctrine about the nature of God's elect and supports the government's policy of *apartheid*, maintaining separate churches for coloreds and blacks.

The so-called separatist or independent African churches are among the more dynamic Christian churches in the world. Ethiopian-type churches largely accept the Western Christian tradition but prefer African clergy and lifestyles, while the so-called Zionist churches have attempted to adapt Christianity to African culture. Some of the churches contain both tendencies, striving to remain true to both Western Christianity and their African background. Many Africans found the combination they desired in the African Methodist Episcopal Church, which was founded by black Americans.

Theologically, many separatist churches hold the Old Testament in high regard because the patriarchs were so like Africans. They emphasize the role of the Holy Spirit and often equate their leaders or founders with the Jesus Christ of the New Testament. Thus, for the South African Zulu Nazareth Baptist Church, Jehovah alone is "*Inkosi* (king) with power." Its founder, Shembe, is viewed as Jesus Christ; and the Holy Spirit is said to have come to Earth to serve the Zulus.

Similarly, Simon Kimbangu, founder of the Church of Jesus Christ on Earth through the Prophet Simon Kimbangu, is hailed among the Bakongo of Zaire as a messianic martyr chosen by God to sacrifice himself for the gospel and his people.

Christian beliefs have undergone slight changes in regular Western churches in Africa and significant ones in the independent churches. God is more unique in the Christian churches than the Creator-God of Africanity. His uniqueness has also been noted among non-Christian Africans in contact with Christians. God is directly invoked in prayers, and even Roman Catholics say special prayers to him for rain and for other benefits. Female prayer groups, called *manyanos* among South African Christians, believe in the efficacy of prayers to God to mitigate all troubles and difficulties in life. Zulu Christians, both in Western and independent churches, prefer to regard Jesus Christ as the Son of Man rather than the Son of God, and find it illogical that anyone would consider a son as having the same status as his father.

Independent churches also have a high regard for the Holy Spirit, which is thought to possess believers. Under its influence, they dance, sing, and speak in tongues. Invoking the Holy Spirit through the laying on of hands is a quite common event in independent churches. The power of the Holy Spirit is believed to suffuse amulets worn by the faithful; and its essence is said to be in the holy water sprinkled by Roman Catholics as well as independents on homes, fields, farms, and objects to be blessed. Diviners within the independent churches also believe that the Holy Spirit helps them uncover and treat evil. Specific to these churches are special vestments bearing religious talismans, including the cross, the crescent, and other symbols. Dancing groups within the church, whether age-graded or not, are said to have their basis in the Holy Bible.

Western Christendom, which saw no contradiction between its universality (the church, composed of all the followers of Jesus of Nazareth) and individuality (personal salvation to become a member of the body of Christ), posed social dilemmas for Africans. Whereas indigenous Africans accepted differences in personalities within groups, Western Christendom emphasized individuality that went against the group.

The adoption of European notions of monogamy and the family structure has been judged essential to those Africans who opted for Western Christendom. Colonial governments encouraged Western-educated persons, whether Christian or not, to take only one lawful wife by ordinance. Such persons were able to take additional wives by customary marriage, but these marriages were not accepted by church or state. In contrast, some independent African churches argue that monogamy is more European than Christian and that polygyny should be fully accepted by Christianity in Africa. Similarly, many Christianized Africans eschewed the bride-price or, as among urban South Africans, used it to pay for the bride's trousseau or to give her a start in business. Often, when faced with the inability of male converts to obtain wives without the traditional bride-price, mission churches found wives for them among families of converts.

Most Christianized and educated Africans consider the nuclear family to be the ideal domestic unit, although men and women work, socialize, and worship separately. While missionaries have been known to frown upon such African practices as new mothers leaving their husbands to temporarily return to their parents, and the observation of sexual taboos while rearing babies, Christianized Africans only abandon these traditional practices when conditions permit. The traditional tendency of African married couples to become closer to parents later on in life in order to serve the needs of the family is also found among Christians. Similarly, Christian couples contemplating divorce readily mobilize extended kin, fellow workers, and even the clergy to save the marriage, in a manner reminiscent of traditional Africanity where concern over the bride-price is invoked.

Western Christendom has affected traditional African rites of passage but has not succeeded in surpassing them. Infant baptism, quite similar to traditional out-dooring ceremonies in such African societies as the Akan and Malinke of West Africa, is readily accepted by Christians. For many African Christians, especially of the independent churches, adult baptism by immersion in lakes and rivers is most important, being ritually akin to Christ's baptism by John the Baptist.

Some of the early African Christians among the Tswana and BaSotho of South Africa complied with missionary opposition to puberty initiation rituals, but Xhosa and Kikuyu Christians insisted upon retaining them. Boys from Christian homes regularly joined their non-Christian age-mates in initiation camps and took part in ceremonies which, while traditional, were increasingly modernized. Members of the Kikuyu Orthodox independent church defended both male circumcision and female clitoridectomy as necessary for Christian morality and rebelled against missionary opposition to it. Xhosa subtracted certain features of female initiation dealing with sexual education from initiation rituals and made these part of the advice mothers gave daughters on the eve of marriage. Mossi Catholics simply add pictures of the Virgin Mary to the circumcision lodge, asking her blessing on boys in transition from manhood to parenthood. Today, many African Christians, including conservative Kikuyu parents, oppose circumcision and clitoridectomy on grounds of health. When circumcision is practiced, the reason given is also on grounds of health.

Western Christendom has had to compromise with African beliefs and practices concerning death and burial. Western Christians usually defer to traditional customs related to death and the dead, especially in rituals at home and those involving members of the family who may not be Christian. It is, therefore, not unusual for staunchly Christian families among the Ngoni or Xhosa of South Africa or Yoruba and Akan of West Africa to conduct fairly traditional rites at home, follow the offices of the dead in church and cemetery, add customary elements after the cleric leaves the graveside, and continue such rituals on returning home. Christian burials in Mossi homesteads may involve the use of Western-type coffins placed at the bottom of the traditional round hole, which may then be sealed with pots. All this may take place while indigenous dances are performed and a Christian minister simultaneously calls for silence so that he may read verses and psalms from the Bible. Funerals, in contrast to burials, may involve the erection of a tombstone unveiled at a service conducted by a clergyman and attended by Christian and non-Christian relatives and friends of the dead, followed by a Western-style dinner for which a beast has been slaughtered as a means of pacifying or pleasing the dead. Neglecting such rituals is commonly regarded as potential reason for ancestors to send misfortune.

Westerners have left a sometimes bitter legacy in Africa as a result of their disdain for African aesthetics. To Europeans, African art was ugly or primitive; and to Christians, the works were thought of as by or in the image of the devil. This has left a sometimes bitter legacy in Africa. Widespread beliefs that Jesus Christ, the angels, and the saints (if not God and the Holy Spirit) were white did result in many African Christians holding themselves and their physical features in disdain. The Christians of independent churches sought to overcome this by insisting that Christ was black and in their image and likeness. Much to the consternation of many missionaries and administrators, African Christians used drums, rattles, and traditional tunes and adopted

Negro spirituals as models for their music. Often it took the adoption of African art forms by Westerners to convince Africans that their traditional music, dances, and sculpture had a richness and value. Therefore, in a paradoxical way, notions of *Négritude* and the cult of the African personality are, in effect, legacies of Western Christendom. Nigerian author Wole Soyinka suggests "a tiger does not have to proclaim its tigritude—it pounces." This is only one of the many ways in which Africans with a legacy of Western Christendom are attempting to recapture that Africanity which was the earliest African heritage.

---

### Reading 2.1

Kenyatta's description of courtship and marriage among the Gikuyu must be viewed as an attempt of Africans to defend their customs against the criticisms of Europeans, especially of administrators and missionaries. In all likelihood he overstates the case as any protagonist is prone to do. Nevertheless, Kenyatta's description is quite similar to marriage customs common to Africanity. Whether the brideprice, or bride-wealth, was considered payment of the cost to a family for rearing a daughter, in compensation to a family for the children that a daughter would provide to another family, or an indication that the family into which a daughter was being married was able to care for her, the passage of goods and services from one family to another at marriage is more universal than is commonly recognized or admitted. Kenyatta's insistence that Gikuyu husbands knew how to share their love equally among many wives only points to a problem that other African societies have admitted, namely that co-wives were often competitors for special favors for themselves and for their children. It is probably true that while among the Gikuyu, as among many other African groups, men considered polygyny as ideal, many African women would have been quite happy with monogamy.

---

### Jomo Kenyatta, "Marriage System Among the Gikuyu," from *Facing Mount Kenya*

One of the outstanding features in the Gikuyu system of marriage is the desire of every member of the tribe to build up his own family group, and by this means to extend and prolong his father's *mbari* (clan)....

We may mention here that the Gikuyu system of courtship is based on mutual love and gratification of sexual instinct between two individuals. And, therefore, a family is constituted by a permanent union between one man and one woman or several women....

On signing the matrimonial contract the marriage ceases to be merely a personal matter, it becomes a duty to produce children.... The Gikuyu tribal custom requires that a married couple should have at least four children, two male and two female. The first male is regarded as perpetuating the existence of the man's father, the second as perpetuating that of the woman's father. The first and second female children fulfill the same ritual duty to the souls of their grandmothers on both sides. The children are given names of the persons whose souls they represent. A childless marriage in a Gikuyu community is practically a failure, for children bring joy not only to their parents, but to the *mbari* (clan) as a whole. The social position of a married man and woman who have children is of greater importance and dignity than that of a bachelor or spinster. After the birth of the first child the married pair become the object of higher regard on the part of their fellows than they were before.

The most interesting feature in the Gikuyu marriage system is the way in which marriages are solemnized. . . . There has been some confusion in the minds of many writers who have tried to explain the system of marriage and the position of women in the African community. Some, especially missionaries, have gone so far as to say that African women are regarded as mere chattels of the men. Well-informed anthropologists agree that this is erroneous and a misconception of the African's social custom. . . .

A Gikuyu wedding is a thing that baffles many outsiders and terrifies many Europeans who may have an opportunity of witnessing the events. This wedding drama misleads foreign onlookers, who do not understand the Gikuyu custom, into thinking that the girls are forced to marry, and even that they are treated as chattels.... On the wedding day the boy's female relatives set out to watch the girl's movements. She might be in a garden, weeding, or in a forest collecting firewood, etc. When they have obtained the necessary information as to where she is working they search for her. On finding her they return with her, carrying her shoulder high. This is a moment of real theatrical acting. The girl struggles and refuses to go with them, protesting loudly and even seeming to shed tears, while the women giggle joyously and cheer her with songs and dances. The cries and cheers can be heard for miles around, and the Gikuyu people will know that the son of So-and-so has taken the daughter of So-and-so in marriage—while foreigners may imagine that the girl has been forcibly seized. It is probable that any person who is not well acquainted with the Gikuyu customs may easily mistake the drama for reality.... This provides great entertainment for the women and is followed by a liberal feast at the bridegroom's homestead. The girl's cries, which are uttered theatrically in a singing manner, include such phrases as "I do not want to get married! I will kill myself if you take me away from my parents! Oh! How foolish I was to leave my home alone and put myself into the hands of merciless people! Where are my relatives? Cannot they come and release me and prevent my being taken to a man whom I do not love?" and so on. This goes on until the girl reaches the boy's homestead, where she is led into her new hut, while children greet her, singing praises for their new bride. On her way home the bride is cheered by passers-by, who utter blessings for the bride and bridegroom and for their future homestead.

After the bride is comfortably settled in her new hut, the whole party of women from both clans, who a short while ago were engaged in a mock fight, join together and start dancing, singing, and cheering hilariously. In the evening the bride is visited by her age-group of both sexes, who bring presents in way of food and ornaments. The bride entertains them with songs called *kerero*, i.e., weeping, in which girls only take part while the boys listen. The *kerero* songs are mostly connected with the collective activities of the girl's age-group, and the part played by the girl. It is considered as the age-group mourning for the loss of the services and companionship of one of their number who, by marriage, has passed to another age-group.

The mourning songs are continued for eight days, during which time the bride is frequently visited by her friends and age-group of both sexes.

During this period the bride may not go out publicly or do any work. She has a special back path which she may use when she leaves the house during the day to sit under a tree for fresh air. Her girl friends keep her company, together with the children of the family. The *kerero* goes on the whole day and a part of the evening, except for a few intervals between the arrival and departure of the visitors. About ten o'clock in the evening the bride and bridegroom are left to themselves until the neighborhood of nine o'clock next morning, when the visitors begin to pour in.

The question of physical virginity is very important, and parents expect their daughters to go to their husbands as physical virgins. This must be reported to the parents of both sides. The boy has to show by certain signs that the girl was a virgin; the girl, too, has to do the same to show that the boy is physically fit to be a husband. In case of impotency on either side, the matter is put before the families and the marriage is annulled at once.

On the eighth day, when the *kerero* ceases, a sheep is killed, the fat of which is fried, and the oil is used to anoint the bride in a ceremony of adoption into the new clan. After she has been admitted as a full member of the husband's family, she is free to mingle with its members and take an active part in the general work of the homestead. When the adoption ceremony is concluded, a day is fixed immediately for her to pay a visit to her own parents. Care is taken in appointing the day, for she must not travel or cook during her menstrual period. On this particular visit she carries a small calabash with beer in it for the use of her parents in blessing her. On her way she is led by a small girl, who goes before her holding one end of a stick, the other end of which is held by the bride, who follows as though she were blind. She is supposed to be unable to see, and may not speak with any stranger she may meet during her journey. She goes all the way with bent head, hiding her face shyly, especially when somebody passes by her. She returns back in the evening (if the parents are in the neighborhood) with presents from her parents. Sometimes when parents are rich she is given two or three sheep or goats. Her father-in-law also gives her presents; these vary in some cases from five sheep and goats to ten or a cow and a piece of fertile land. These presents are regarded as an act of "warming" the bride's hut, and they end the marriage ceremonial.

---

## Reading 2.2

Born in Tangier, North Africa, on February 24, 1304, and named Mohammed, son of Abdallah, the man known to us as Ibn Battuta, an upper class Berber, set off for Mecca at the age of 21 to make the pilgrimage required of all devout Muslims. He traveled by caravan to Egypt and to Syria before arriving in Mecca, and from there set out for India by way of Jedda. His wanderings and adventures took him to Calicut (Calcutta), the Maldive Islands, Malabar, Ceylon, China, Sumatra, back to Morocco, and the western Sudan, a voyage of some 75,000 miles. He therefore had the opportunity to see Islam in many areas. It was against this background that he was able to comment about Islam in the Mali empire, which he visited in 1352. Ibn Battuta was not uncritical of the Malians, especially their political organization, attitudes toward women, and use of animals not killed according to ritual or forbidden by orthodox Islam. However, he does give us some of the earliest information that we have of ancient Mali and the behavior of the Muslims who lived there. One aspect of Africanity most puzzling and disturbing to Muslims was the relative freedom of women in the western Sudan. The ability of these women to control a great part of their lives no doubt stemmed from matrilineal descent which, while only occasionally resulting in a line of female rulers such as Queen Amina of Hausaland, was linked to their power of passing on descent to men, including royalty. Ibn Battuta's reference to the beauty of the Malian women is also revealing in light of his wide acquaintance with standards of beauty in much of Africa and Asia. But while it is not clear whether it was attitudes such as those of Ibn Battuta towards women that finally persuaded some West African Muslims to introduce the purdah (seclusion of women), it is quite likely that African Islam experienced a great deal of pressure to curb their autonomy.

---

### *Ibn Battuta: Travels in Asia and Africa, 1325–1354* (H.A.R. Gibb, tr.)

I was at Málli during the two festivals of the sacrifice and the fast-breaking. On these days the sultan takes his seat on the *pempi* after the midafternoon prayer. The armour-bearers bring in magnificent arms—quivers of gold and silver, swords ornamented with gold and with golden scabbards, gold and silver lances, and crystal maces. At his head stand four amírs driving off the flies, having in their hands silver ornaments resembling saddle-stirrups. The commanders, qádí, and preacher sit in their usual places. The interpreter Dúghá comes with his four wives and his slave-girls, who are about a hundred in number. They are wearing beautiful robes, and on their heads they have gold and silver fillets, with gold and silver balls attached. A chair is placed for Dúghá to sit on. He plays on an instrument made of reeds, with some small calabashes at its lower end, and chants a poem in praise of the sultan, recalling his battles and deeds of valour. The women and girls sing along with him and play with bows. Accompanying them are about thirty youths, wearing red woollen tunics and white skull-caps; each of them has his drum slung from his shoulder and beats it. Afterwards come his boy pupils who play and turn wheels in the air, like the natives of Sind. They show a marvelous nimbleness and agility in these exercises and play most cleverly with swords. Dúghá also makes a fine play with the sword. Thereupon the sultan orders a gift to be presented to Dúghá and he is given a purse containing two hundred *mithqáls* of gold dust, and is informed of the contents of the purse before all the people. The commanders rise and twang their bows in thanks to the sultan. The next day each one of them gives Dúghá a gift, every man according to his rank. Every Friday after the *'asr* prayer, Dúghá carries out a similar ceremony to this that we have described.

On feast-days, after Dúghá has finished his display, the poets come in. Each of them is inside a figure resembling a thrush, made of feathers, and provided with a wooden head with a red beak, to look like a thrush's head. They stand in front of the sultan in this ridiculous make-up and recite their poems. I was told that their poetry is a king of sermonizing in which they say to the sultan: "This *pempi* which you occupy was that whereon sat this king and that king, and such and such were this one's noble actions and such and such the other's. So do you too do good deeds whose memory will outlive you." After that, the chief of the poets mounts the steps of the *pempi* and lays his head on the sultan's lap, then climbs to the top of the *pempi* and lays his head first on the sultan's right shoulder and then on his left, speaking all the while in their tongue, and finally he comes down again....

The negroes possess some admirable qualities. They are seldom unjust, and have a greater abhorrence of injustice than any other people. Their sultan shows no mercy to anyone who is guilty of the least act of it. There is complete security in their country. Neither traveller nor inhabitant in it has anything to fear from robbers or men of violence. They do not confiscate the property of any white man who dies in their country, even if it be uncounted wealth. On the contrary, they give it into the charge of some trustworthy person among the whites, until the rightful heir takes possession of it. They are careful to observe the hours of prayer, and assiduous in attending them in congregations, and in bringing up their children to them. On Fridays, if a man does not go early to the mosque, he cannot find a corner to pray in, on account of the crowd. It is a custom of theirs to send each man his boy [to the mosque] with his prayer-mat; the boy spreads it out for his master in a place befitting him [and remains on it] until he comes to the mosque. Their prayer-mats are made of the leaves of a tree resembling a date-palm, but without fruit.

Another of their good qualities is their habit of wearing clean white garments on Fridays. Even if a man has nothing but an old worn shirt, he washes it and cleans it, and wears it to the Friday service. Yet another is their zeal for learning the Koran by heart. They put their children in chains if they show any backwardness in memorizing it, and they are not set free until they have it by heart. I visited the qádí in his house on the day of the festival. His children were chained up, so I said to him "Will you not let them loose?" He replied "I shall not do so until they learn the Koran by heart." Among their bad qualities are the following. The women servants, slave-girls, and young girls go about in front of everyone naked, without a stitch of clothing on them. Women go into the sultan's presence naked and without coverings, and his daughters also go about naked. Then there is their custom of putting dust and ashes on their heads, as a mark of respect, and the grotesque ceremonies we have described when the poets recite their verses.

---

## Reading 2.3

Western Christendom was comprised of religious, social, economic, and aesthetic factors that served the populations of Western Europe, and as such had difficulty dealing with the socio-cultural realities of Africa. There was almost inevitable conflict, but Christianity was too valuable to be neglected by the Africans. Instead they systematically examined Christianity to identify those elements that they found adaptable to their reality, rejecting those which in their view were detrimental to their ways of life. The result has been a more dynamic African Christianity, one which in many ways is more ecumenical than its Western predecessor and is making greater inroads in Africa than in other parts of the world.

## Erasto Muga, *African Response to Western Christian Religion*

It is important to note here that African reaction to Christianity in East Africa as I have shown in this book is not a total rejection of Christianity by the African independent church and political leaders. The rejection of some over-Westernised aspects of Christianity and the subsequent formation of African independent church and political movements are due to Western Christian missionary approach, their proselytization and education of the Africans, their attitude toward African way of life, and their actual encounter and relationship with the African people.

I, therefore, wish to propose that the effects of missionary work in East Africa would have been different, in that the African separatist church and political movements would not have emerged had Western Christian missionary approach in their proselytization and their dealings with the African people been different in some ways.

The important point to remember is that in their approach the Western Christian missionaries had the attitude that Western European culture was superior to the African culture. This attitude was concomitant with the denigration of African culture by the Western Christian missionaries. Hence the refusal of the Western Christian missionaries to accept polygyny, female circumcision and other African rites of passage, and the use of any African musical instruments as accompaniments in the singing of songs and hymns in churches, to mention only a few practices among those that were not acceptable to the missionaries.

The above observation is important when it is recognised that out of... fifteen African independent church movements... two became independent because of the question of female circumcision, five were motivated by the desire to be free to practise polygyny, another five were motivated by the desire to be free from European leadership and control, one decided to be free to practise all necessary aspects of African culture, and one decided to abolish the multiplicity of Christian denominations by establishing only one church and one faith for all (although by establishing it the members also helped increase the number of existing religious denominations at that time).

In the light of the above observation it could be inferred that if the Western Christian missionaries accepted African culture as it was, provided some aspects of it were not condemned by the Christian Bible, it is doubtful if African independent church and political movements would have been established because the reasons for establishing them would have been lacking.

In the same way, it could be inferred from the foregoing statements that African independent church and political movements which came into being because of African desire to be free from European leadership and control in churches could not have arisen had the European missionaries shared that leadership and control fairly on equal footing with the qualified Africans.

The many Christian denominations in East Africa teaching many different religious beliefs or dogmas is a phenomenon that has baffled many African Christians. It has been pointed out by Western Christian missionaries working in East Africa today, that much could be done to eliminate African suspicion of Western Christian missionaries as being mere organisers of different Christian denominations for their own interests by seriously discussing and introducing ecumenism of all the different Western Christian denominations working in East Africa. In fact ecumenism today is being organised in East Africa, and it is possible that in the future this will be a great factor in re-establishing the foundation of Christianity which has been shaken and weakened by African independency.

If Western Christian missionaries introduced only one Christian faith in East Africa this would have done much to discourage African independent church movements in East Africa. The central points for discussion in the ecumenical movement in East Africa today entail important sociological problems which must be looked into if ecumenism is to succeed. For example ecumenical leaders in East Africa today discuss African values and customs vis a vis Western values and customs, and particularly how these affect the relationship that has existed and still exists between the Western Christian missionaries and the African Christians and African people as a whole. The discussions now centre around the nature of the relationship that must now exist between Western Christian missionaries and the African Christians and peoples.

Concerning African values and customs ecumenism now discusses among other things polygyny versus monogamy, dowry versus non-dowry, and the introduction of certain appropriate African musical instruments to be used in church during worship and in the singing of songs of praise to God. As a result of this discussion, some Christian churches in East Africa now accept polygynists and their wives, and the dowry system is not being discouraged and preached against by Western Christian missionaries. This attempt at reconciliation of differences between Western Christian leaders and the African Christian leaders is a clue as to the kind of approach that the Western Christian leaders could have used in the beginning in introducing Christianity to the Africans—that is, the acceptance of certain fundamental African customs and way of life, provided there is no basis in the Christian Bible for their rejection. Their rejection laid a foundation for religious movements as a protest against the possibility of loss of important African aspects of culture and values.

## 3

# NEW GODS

### Lamin Sanneh

Long before either Western or Arab religions were introduced into African life, a rich legacy of African religious practices existed. In this chapter, Professor Sanneh discusses how the "new gods"—Islam and Christianity—were assimilated into the fabric of indigenous African religious life and how all three religious legacies now coexist and are interwoven. Eds.

Both Christianity and Islam are a thousand years old in some places in Africa, and where they are of less antiquity they are no less distinguished by the depth and range of their appeal. The depth of their penetration over a long period of time has combined with the assimilation of new religious practices into indigenous beliefs and rituals to establish the two religions as permanent features of the African religious landscape.

It is customary to deal with the issue of Christian and Muslim expansion in Africa in terms of how successful *they* were in winning converts, a view of religious change which belittles the immense contribution of Africa to the process. Instead we should approach the matter by asking how successful *Africa* was in assimilating the two religions, understanding "Africa" to mean its diverse religious traditions and practices. This second way of looking at the subject assumes the enduring vitality of the indigenous African religions under the Christian or Islamic garb. It is essential, therefore, to sketch in aspects of the African background on the basis of which the "new gods" of the two religions were successfully domesticated.

It would be misleading to pretend that Africa is a unity of form and spirit. On the contrary, nowhere is its diversity and complexity more evident than in the religious sphere. Yet a basic persistent trait of African societies is the importance of religion. It falls like a shaft of light across the entire spectrum of life, fused and undifferentiated at one end, and refracted and highly refined at the other. From casual, daily, and spontaneous incidents to somber, highly structured public occasions, it is the focus of elaborate and detailed interest. In art and ritual; in speech, work, and leisure; in the fields, at home, and in travel; on land or on water; in health and in sickness; in need and in contentment, religion occurs with authoritative force. African communities have consequently lived, moved, and had their being in religion.

Even the Greeks of classical antiquity noted this fact. Diodorus of Sicily, an historian of the first century B.C., comments that the blacks were the first to honor the gods with sacrifices, and that the sacrifices of the Ethiopians "are the most pleasing to heaven." The power of religion, he claims, protected them from foreign invaders. (Snowden, 1970:146–147)

## THE CHRISTIAN DIMENSION

Christianity reached Alexandria and Cyrene from Palestine during the first decades of the religion. By the middle of the second century, it had spread along the North African coast from Rome. There is evidence that sections of the indigenous African population were converted at this time and that some of them joined the ranks of the early martyrs. Several African converts appear on a list of people martyred in 180 A.D. The Berber element was important in the church: St. Augustine (d. 430), for example, was almost certainly of Berber stock. His birthplace, Thagaste, was a center of Berber culture; and his son's name, Adeodatus, meaning "God-given," is emphatically un-Roman. One writer, Julian of Eclanum, dubbed Augustine "the African sophist," so deeply African were his thoughts and feelings. (Ferguson, 1969:184)

At this time the religion of the local population consisted largely of the worship of Saturn, also called Ba'al, whose symbols appeared in churches. Formulae associated with its worship were adopted by bishops. Even the term *senex*, a local African religious title, was adopted by the church. Some of the ideas of Saturn-worship infiltrated Augustine's thinking, especially the notion that Saturn was capable of dark human passions and vengeance. Augustine wrote: "God orders man to love him, and threatens deep miseries if he does not do so," indicating the vengeful attribute of Saturn. (Ferguson, 1969:189) It has been suggested that even the passionate attachment to martyrdom was more likely a hangover of the deep-rooted African tradition of human sacrifice. For example, Tertullian, a second century African church

Father, asserted that God does desire human blood. Some Christians provoked their enemies in order to make a sacrifice of themselves.

The new god of Christianity clearly arrived in Africa by the routes long frequented by the old gods, and proceeded at a pace they had made familiar. Often the two sets of gods surfaced in a frank acknowledgment of parallelism. A member of Augustine's congregation, for example, told him how his worship of the old gods of indigenous Africa could be maintained without conflicting with his Christian profession. "Oh, yes," he confessed to Augustine, who was himself the supreme master of the art, "I go to idols. I consult seers and magicians, but I do not abandon God's church. I am a Catholic." (Ferguson, 1969:189)

Modern archaeological excavations have established the existence of some 200 churches and chapels in Berber villages, suggesting the depth of Christian penetration beyond the Roman quarters of Carthage. (Frend, 1952:53) The proximity, then, to sources of indigenous assimilation could not have been greater. As one writer aptly put it, Christianity "did not burst [upon Africa] like a clap of thunder, but stole into ears already prepared. Neither on her popular nor on her philosophic side was [Christianity] a creed apart." (Forster, 1961:75)

In Ethiopia a similar development appears to have taken place. The institutionalized indigenous religion of Ethiopia resulted from the presence of Sabean immigrants who crossed the Red Sea about 1000 B.C., and, later, from an amalgamation of Greco-Roman religious materials. The religion was based on the trinity of the moon god, the sun goddess, and the morning star, a pattern clearly evocative of Egypt's Isis, Osiris, and Horus. Though the names varied, especially after Greek gods were introduced, the main temples practiced a cult of three divinities. King Ezana (reigned 320–360 A.D.), for example, before his conversion, presided over the cult of Astar, Beher, and Meder. An important feature of the ancient religion was the integration of state and society with religion at the core. Consequently, the king, assuming a divine status, was high priest as well as ruler and military commander. In inscriptions made by him, Ezana styles himself at one point as "King of kings, the son of the invincible god Ares." (Tafla, 1967:29) Thus, as Diodorus observed, religion played a critical role in assuring the cohesion of society and the stability of the states.

By the time Christianity was officially established in the fifth century, Ethiopia, or areas in active contact with it, had known the religion from the first decades of its existence. Much later, monophysite refugees, fleeing the persecution unleashed by the Council of Chalcedon of 451, sought sanctuary in Ethiopia, itself in the monophysite camp, and thus added to the number of active Christians who helped to spread the religion.

It is clear in Ethiopia, too, that the new religion gravitated towards the most active centers of indigenous worship, and made use of the old gods to articulate the creed and to confirm an identical interest in healing and miracles. The old gods were, therefore, baptized, given Christian names, and invested with scriptural sanction. The tension that might occur from Christian expansion was averted by submitting Christian materials to the force of local paradigms. But, far from parodying the old religions, Christianity initiated a strong renewal of Ethiopian culture, resulting in the efflorescence of Ethiopian literature. Translation of religious works fueled the spread of learning and language study and the founding of schools.

Having succeeded in penetrating Ethiopian culture, the new religion was challenged to determine its final attitude to the old gods. This issue was never settled once and for all, so that in the modern period of Ethiopian history it was to surface as an unresolved phenomenon. In times of crisis—such as the abortive Italian invasion of 1896, and the later attack of 1935 by the Fascist regime of Mussolini—the spirit of the nation, knit of both old and new, reasserted itself to avert permanent ignominy. The religious authorities of the Ethiopian Orthodox Church were mobilized to drive out the invaders—who indeed departed in 1941. Diodorus might after all have a clue to the secret force of religion in Africa.

Despite the doctrinal struggles of intervening centuries and the attempt to reform Ethiopian Christianity, the indigenous religious paradigms survived, not so much in opposition to Christianity as in subtle alliance with them. The rise of Islam in the seventh century served to isolate Christian Ethiopia from its successfully Islamized neighbors, and the old gods rose to add their share to a sense of Ethiopian identity. The isolation from the outside world was deepened within Ethiopia itself by the absence of a central ecclesiastical structure, and that left the new gods at the mercy of indigenous infiltration. In the survival of the nation both forces had a stake and a contribution.

## CHRISTIANITY AND COLONIALISM

The close interplay between Christianity and indigenous culture should be borne in mind when we reflect on the historical coincidence between the 19th-century missionary movement and colonialism. Mission assumed an identity of interest with colonialism, and this led to a complicated relationship in which missionaries felt entitled to colonial support and backing, and, on the other hand, colonial administrators felt justified in incorporating missionary spheres into the empire. Missionary objections, for example, to such local customs as dancing, nakedness, or polygamy, and to such religious practices as sacrifice, mortuary rites, or drumming, might be translated into administrative ordinances with legal force. Furthermore, the operation of missionary schools might be given government sanction, thus adding political authority to the use of schools as proselytizing agencies or as instruments of social control.

Yet missions were not always viewed with favor by colonial administrations, in Africa or elsewhere. Political alliances shifted radically, for instance, after World War I. When German interests in Africa were sequestered, German missionary fortunes correspondingly declined, often with no adequate replacement by other countries. In other places colonial administrations adopted a pro-Islamic policy which placed missions under severe restrictions. Furthermore, in areas where Christian schools operated, their success as instruments of conversion was very limited, though they might open the way for other unforeseen changes. Vernacular translations of Christian writings led to literacy and national awakening; thus we have a curious irony in the fact that most of the nationalist leaders, including Muslims, were educated in Christian schools. Under the seemingly suffocating heat of cultural imperialism, the spirits of the old gods, in consort with the new gods, discovered the conditions congenial to incubate a full-blown pride that some have characterized as *Négritude*. (Wilson, 1969:266)

## AFRICAN CHRISTIAN INDEPENDENCY

One spectacular result of the translations of the Scriptures into local languages was the emergence of prophet movements and African independent churches. With the ability to read the Scriptures in their mother-tongue, Africans developed a powerful sense of their own indispensability for the enterprise from which the missions had excluded them. The point of historical friction was the Niger Mission (1841–1891), led by Bishop Samuel Ajayi Crowther (ca. 1807–1891). In untidy maneuvers to unseat Bishop Crowther, the (Anglican) Church Missionary Society dismantled the Niger Mission, removing 12 of the 15 African agents between 1880 and 1890. Crowther himself was replaced by European leadership. That added fat to the fire, and the African response flared up in calls for separation from the mission. Before long the revolt spread to other missions, with the Baptists and Methodists joining the Anglicans in demanding separation. The experience was repeated all over Christian Africa, and today we have more than 8,000 such movements. Independency is the term employed to describe the phenomenon. (Barrett, 1968)

Independency represents Africa's unique contribution to the story of Christianity. It is the dramatic adaptation of new teachings to the African environment. The carriage of Christianity, bearing down on a straight line from the Western world, has been remodeled to fit it out for the different terrain of Africa. It now rocks to the tune of colorful processions and shouts of praise and song.

We may summarize the characteristics of independency as follows. The important religious agents remain the prophets, preachers, and healers; and they mediate between the pull of the old and the push of the new. In their hands the vocabulary of salvation is made to conform to the grammar of kin obligation. Prayer, dreams, and healing occupied a prominent place in the origin and development of independency. The goals might be described as power, community, and wholeness. Religion was more than a solitary affair for the African, and independency has demonstrated that social character to the fullest possible extent. It has also in this regard encouraged a rich and diverse manifestation in established standards of regalia, music, and dance. As a consequence, Christianity is encountered in its vividness, its sounds, and in movement, rather than as a processed, cognitive system. Thus Christianity came to impinge on the entire spectrum of life in the manner of the old religions. In the successful assimilation of the "new gods," therefore, we catch a luminous reflection of the old spirits, arrayed in creative alliance with the new rather than in inhibiting parody.

## ISLAM AND THE AFRICAN EXPERIENCE

Like Christianity before it, Islam made its appearance in Africa from the beginning of its history. The accounts describe how the Prophet Mohammed dispatched a body of his followers to seek sanctuary in Christian Ethiopia following fierce persecution in Mecca. (Ibn Ishaq, 1967:146–153) Subsequently, the Prophet and his companions emigrated as a body to Medina in 622, a move that is called the *hijrah*. The next time Muslims appeared in Africa it was as a conquering army in 647. The Prophet had passed away in 632. Further military incursions followed, with one in 711 opening the way for the permanent establishment of the faith in North Africa.

North Africa came to nurture its own brand of Islam with the extremist Kharijites and later with the Fatimids, whose rule spread from Egypt to Morocco. As Ibn Khaldun (d. 1406) was to demonstrate, Islam provided a successful framework for political integration and social cohesion of North Africa. (Khaldun, 1982) Two reform movements sprang up there in an effort to overturn isolationist pressures and rechannel local forces into the orthodox mainstream. One was the Almoravid movement led by Ibn Yasin (d. 1059), a devout, ascetic character resolved to remedy what he considered the scandalous ignorance of the Berbers of the most basic tenets of the religion they professed to follow. He swept over the area, sword in one hand and the Koran in the other, waging a struggle of radical Islamization. He achieved astonishing success. But power spoilt the Almoravids, and their vision of a true Islam dimmed from the conflicting attractions of civilized splendor.

Then arose the Almohads—literally, *monotheists*—under the charismatic Ibn Tumart (d. 1130). In 1127, they launched a campaign to institute Sunni Islamic orthodoxy, denouncing the Almoravids as corrupters of the faith and the scholars as their unholy allies. Stern and energetic, Ibn Tumart was a deeply learned man. He carried out his campaigns with utter ruthlessness, convinced he was the inaugurator of a fresh religious dispensation for his people.

Ibn Tumart outreached himself, however, and his successors were consumed by the demands of the far-flung Almohad empire, from the southern Sahara to the high ranges of Andalusian Spain. From the inevitable decline that came with political decay, Islam descended to the levels of the pre-reform era in which the synthesis of law and ascetic practice predominated over undiluted formalism.

Yet the legacy of the reformers did not die completely, and in many parts of West Africa enough was transmitted to prime the local Muslim temper with an ideological commitment to orthodox rectitude. Thanks to the infusion of reform ideas from beyond the Sahara, African Islam embodied an internal dynamism: on the one hand, a steady assimilation into the local setting, and on the other, a corresponding impulse to check uncritical syncretism. More than in African Christianity, in African Islam we come upon dramatic examples of a religious polarity between rampant syncretism and radical iconoclasm.

The *jihad* wars, which carried to spectacular lengths the radical iconoclastic tendencies of Islam, achieved their greatest victories in Hausaland in the 19th century, with similar happenings in Masina, Adamawa, and Senegambia. But the dramatic nature of jihad should not mislead us about its enduring significance. The struggle to establish a reform ethos in Islam through more peaceful means was more representative of the history of the religion in Africa, and here the dialogue with the indigenous religions was one of mutual influence. Jihad had undeniable importance for the subsequent direction of the local practice of Islam. (Hiskett, 1984:303) But it was no substitute for peaceful reform and expansion which, through the channels of education and pilgrimage, outdistanced and outlived the reign of the sword. (Wilks, 1968:162–195)

The peaceful promotion of Islam encouraged greater collaboration with African religious agents. Muslim religious officials evoked their counterparts in the indigenous culture. The channels of this peaceful transmission of Islam included traders, trade routes, commercial centers, and organized states and the institutions that served them. Settled Muslim communities intermarried with local populations, and family bonds became bearers of Islamic influence.

In order to show how Islam first arrived at a convergence with the old Africa before it struck on an independent course, I would like to consider a number of examples concerning the underlying indigenous perception with which the new religion had to align itself. It is necessary for this purpose to focus on religious agents, especially in their role as transition agents.

Local cults and shrines have often been the center of activity for the blending of the old and new, and religious agents in these settings may be lapsed Muslims or emancipated shrine priests, fostering a rich sort of eclecticism. An example given by Nehemia Levtzion (Levtzion, 1968:66) tells how one shrine priest in Ghana offers two prayers morning and evening and fasts three days in the month of Ramadan. He carries a rosary, a copy of the Koran, and a bundle of Arabic manuscripts, although he himself cannot read Arabic at all. Although the shrine priest came from a once-Muslim family, he now offers a mix of Islam and traditional religion, the kind of bridge that eases the path of transition. This helps maintain a certain rudimentary familiarity with Islam without implying a dramatic lurch towards formal conversion. Islam at this stage exists in the feelings of non-Muslims as a reinforcement rather than as a principle of critical differentiation.

Another example concerns an intinerant Muslim cleric. He, too, blends his practice of Islam with a heavy dose of local religious materials. He is given the title *alfa*. On one occasion in June 1945, the cleric appeared before an audience headed by the paramount chief of a Mende chiefdom in Sierra Leone. He spoke of a once-powerful chief who was seized on a walk and transported to heaven where he fell victim to searing hunger and "wept bitterly," realizing what hunger was like. Then the cleric spoke about the value of obedience to constituted political authority as a mirror of obedience to God. He went on to paint a particularly idyllic picture of heaven where, in some contradiction to his earlier assertion, there was no hunger or death or drowsiness. There was no darkness, only pure light. But it was also a place where sensuous desires were fulfilled, with the means available in inexhaustible abundance. Finally, the cleric asked the chief to make a sacrifice to ease his path to heaven. The sacrifice consisted of a large quantity of seed-rice, cooked sweet potatoes, an old coat, a pair of sandals to protect the feet from thorn-pricks, two cocks, an old mortar and pestle, two pails, and a quantity of kerosene. These were to be contributed by the rich. The poor were to give a bundle of wood and seven bamboo slats; and the alfa himself, not to be outdone, would donate seven kola-nuts, one old pot, and three splinters of wood.

Clearly this sacrifice belongs to the local religious tradition, where the name for it is *kpakpa*, and that was the inspiration and the paradigm for the alfa's action. Islam, at least initially, did not deny this tradition or even compete with it; it took advantage of it, with a gentle hint that it could add the element of hope in a future life. In the meantime, those who converted to Islam would continue to benefit by the providence of the old gods. (Little, 1946:111–113) The widespread use of amulets, charms, and other forms of instrumental religion in Muslim Africa indicates a deep level of indigenization, with Islam being transposed into local terms as a religion of power, whatever the scruples of the orthodox party.

In another example, Islam came upon a secret society—the Poro, which is widespread in West Africa—in Sierra Leone. Here again the society Islam encountered was better organized, more ably maintained, and more articulate in economic and political terms than were the invading Muslims. The consequence was that Islam was reduced to a subordinate position without, of course, losing its separate identity. The society and Islam came together when the local population decided on a campaign of economic boycott. Traditionally the people initiated this campaign by placing an interdiction on the harvesting of oil-palm, represented by a Poro medicine being left in the field. In this particular case Islam was incorporated into the arsenal of Poro by the inclusion of two wooden slates containing Arabic material in magic squares, a combination that was believed to add greater potency. At this level, too, Islam was conceived to be in continuity with the old gods, following the direction in which they always pointed. (Alldridge, 1901:133–134)

The reference to chiefs and authority brings us to an important theme in the domestication of Islam in Africa. Islam has always been attracted to organized societies, finding in local hierarchies a natural affinity for the institutions of its religious life. This identity of interest would first occur at the level of indigenous customs. Among the Dagomba of Ghana, for example, there is a *Damba* festival that commemorates the birthday (*mawlid*) of the Prophet. Yet the chiefs who observe this ceremony are far removed from Islam, and the Damba has lost any connection with the mawlid of Islam. The festival is really "an occasion for sub-chiefs to pay homage to their senior chief. The Damba, more than any of the other Muslim feasts in Dagomba, is a chiefly affair." (Levtzion, 1968:98) Islam is thus adopted, if at all, to bolster traditional political authority and to add color to a local ceremony. Thus domesticated, the foreign religion exhibits the marks of local familiarity, even though at an advanced stage of participation the earlier loyalties might be weakened. That advanced stage, however, may remain in an indefinite future for a considerable number of people.

In *The Jakhanke: The History of an Islamic Clerical People of the Senegambia (1979)*, I have indicated the richness of the pacific tradition in African Islam, using an example where clerical mediation has offset any sharp break with the religion and spirituality of the old Africa. (Sanneh, 1979) All the material in that study confirms the African destiny of the religion in its new environment. Without a central religious structure to direct practice and enforce a common code of faith and conduct, the incidence of local variation would remain very high indeed.

One further example throws an important light on the persistence of older religious attitudes even in exemplary Muslim communities. In March 1824, Hugh Clapperton, a Scottish Calvinist, arrived in Sokoto, the heart of the puritan revolution initiated by the Shehu Usuman dan Fodio (d. 1817) in northern Nigeria. Clapperton was quite disconcerted to find that the iconoclasm of the reformers had failed to change the outlook that provoked reform in the first place. Describing a meeting with Mohammed Bello, the son and heir to the Shehu, Clapperton recounts with surprise the informed interest of the Sultan in matters arcane. "I first exhibited a planisphere of the heavenly bodies," he wrote. "The sultan knew all the signs of the Zodiac, some of the constellations, and many of the stars, by their Arabic names." (Bovill, 1966:679) On a visit in the same city to the vizier of the Sultan, Clapperton appears to be pursued by a similar difficulty.

> This morning (April 9, 1824) I paid the *gadado* a visit, and found him alone, reading an Arabic book, one of a small collection he possessed. "Abdallah," he said, "I had a dream last night, and am perusing this book to find out what it meant. Do you believe in such things?" "No, my lord *gadado*; I consider books of dreams to be full of idle conceits. God gives a man wisdom to guide his conduct, while dreams are occasioned by the accidental circumstances of sleeping with the head low, excess of food, or uneasiness of mind." "Abdallah," he replied, smiling, "this book tells me differently." (Bovill, 1966:695)

In one incident Clapperton himself became the subject of religious curiosity. "I was," he says, "unluckily taken for a *fighi*, or teacher, and was pestered, at all hours of the day, to write out prayers by the people.... Today my washerwoman positively insisted on being paid with a charm, in writing, that would entice people to buy earthen-ware of her; and no persuasions of mine could either induce her to accept money for her service, or make her believe the request was beyond human power." (Bovill, 1966:669–670) Thus even at the height of the reform movement in the Sokoto Caliphate, there was a strong tendency to recast the leading protagonists as medicine men in conformity with the older paradigm.

## SUFISM AND ISLAMIZATION

The Sufi orders have been major factors of Islamization in Africa, and in the successful adaptation of Islam to the African environment. The term *Sufi* is used to describe the mystical and spiritual tradition in Islam, in distinction from the orthodox legalism of the scholars (*ulama*). One of the earliest Sufi orders in black Africa was the Qadiriyah, founded after Abd al-Qadir al-Jilani (d. 1166) of Baghdad. The order spread to West Africa from Saharan centers during the 15th and 16th centuries. Qadiri Sufis were known for their attachment to education, their moderation in religious matters, their encouragement of popular religious devotion, and their relative abstention from political affairs. Of them it could be said with some truth that the best of the worldly rulers are those who consort with religious scholars and the worst of the religious scholars are those who fraternize with worldly rulers.

We have evidence that in the 15th and 16th centuries Qadiri-inspired religious centers in black Africa maintained the character of a republic, with the king banned from setting foot in the center except once a year at the annual religious festival of fasting.

Some other Sufi orders were also active in black Africa, although many of them departed quite radically from the quietist tradition of the Qadiriyah. One such order, which also split off from the Qadiriyah, was the Shadhiliyah. It arrived in West Africa in the 18th century and played an active political role in hinterland Guinea. There it was the dominant religious force, except for a brief spell when it was eclipsed in the mid-19th century by a rival order. The French eventually proscribed it in 1912.

The order that challenged the political dominance of the Shadhiliyah was the Tijaniyah, founded by Shaykh Ahmad al-Tijani (d. 1815). The man responsible for introducing the order to West Africa was al-Hajj Umar Tal al-Futi (1794–1864). Under his leadership it spread widely in the region. During his extended return from Mecca where he had been on pilgrimage (*hajj*), al-Hajj Umar brought the order to such places as Bornu east of Lake Chad, Bauchi, Kano, Zaria, and Katsina—all in Nigeria and all previously attached in a loose way to the Qadiriyah. The order was also taken to Masina (modern Mali) where a son of al-Hajj Umar became the caliph.

However, the continuity of organized Tijani affiliation in Nigeria was only established in this century when Abbas, the *emir* (ruler) of Kano from 1903 to 1909, adopted the Way (Islam). Several important Tijani dignitaries from North Africa and elsewhere visited the community in Kano, encouraging new initiatives in organization, discipline, and doctrine.

One of the most eventful visits to Kano in this connection was that by the Tijani leader Shaykh Ibrahim Niass (d. 1975) of Koalack, Senegal. He visited Kano in 1937 and was able to confirm several important Kano Tijanis in the order. One such Kano leader was the emir Abdullahi Bayero, and another was the charismatic scholar Wali Sulayman (d. 1939). Thus the influence of Shaykh Niass on Tijani organizational life was profound. Subsequently the order campaigned vigorously for mass recruitment, and its leaders—known as the Reformed Tijaniyah, to distinguish them from older individual followers of al-Hajj Umar—went on to play an important role in the social and political life of northern Nigeria.

Several new initiatives have emerged as a result of the influence of the Sufi brotherhoods. In the 1960s a new organization of Sufi scholars was set up in Kaduna, and under its aegis the leaders were able to collaborate on a number of issues of public importance. More recently Muslim religious scholars have been active in discussions on the issue of the Islamic religious code, the Sharia, and its possible adoption as part of the constitution of Nigeria. Even under military rule the religious scholars have remained active in the public arena.

In Senegal itself the Sufi brotherhoods, including the Tijaniyah, have been active in recruiting disciples in town and country districts. The Tijaniyah is represented there by the older community of al-Hajj Umar, led by Sayyid Nur Tal and based in the Senegal River Valley; the family of Malik Sy, based in Tivaouane in the district of Thies; and the house of Niass at Kaolack, which has been the most successful in developing links and contacts outside Senegal.

However, within Senegal itself one of the most active Sufi orders is the Mouride Brotherhood, founded by Ahmad Bamba (d. 1927), and since his death vigorously propagated by his successors, called *khalifas* (caliphs), who have succeeded in winning the rural masses. The Mourides have instituted a rigorous program of agricultural labor, with the majority of disciples being farm laborers put to cash-crop farming on peanut plantations, the staple cash crop of Senegal. Once every year throngs of disciples make for the village of Touba in Senegal for the annual pilgrimage, and in 1975 it was estimated that about half a million people participated.

The Mourides are significant in embracing many aspects of African culture. For example, they have adopted the strict code of etiquette which governs relations between slaves and their masters and used that to regulate the behavior of the disciple towards his religious master. They have also taken the traditional farming calendar and made it the basis for organizing the life of Mouride followers. The pervasive African custom of mortuary ceremonies, to take another example, has been preserved in the Brotherhood's annual pilgrimage to Touba, called the Grand Magal, created to commemorate the death of the founder. As Léopold Sédar Senghor, former President of Senegal, said, the Mourides are an example of the successful adaptation of

Islam to African conditions, with the leaders able to assimilate the new religion with the old in imaginative and productive ways.

## THE TRANSLATION OF RELIGIONS

In Islam, the Koran is regarded as untranslatable, and there is a corresponding negative attitude toward indigenous languages as *ajami* (foreign). However, the foregoing examples and others suggest that Islam itself is engaged in a subtle process of translation, whereby it is made accessible to the indigenous population. Islamic gains in Africa are thus freighted with many indigenous values and attitudes, confirming the success of Africa in harnessing the power of the new gods to serve its purposes.

Unquestionably, both Islam and Christianity have had a stimulating effect on indigenous African culture. The impact of Christian translations of scripture strengthened the vernacular and led to a sense of national identity. Muslim religious itinerancy engaged in a profound dialogue with African customs and strengthened cross-cultural relations within Africa itself. Together both religions have contributed in their own ways to the multifaceted heritage of Africa. For contemporary Africa, the challenge is to preserve its pluralist heritage against the pressures of doctrinaire statism and religious fundamentalism.

**REFERENCES**

Alldridge, T.J. 1901. *The Sherbro and Its Hinterland*. London and New York: Macmillan.
Barrett, David B. 1968. *Schism and Renewal in Africa: An Analysis of Six Thousand Contemporary Religious Movements*. Nairobi: Oxford University Press.
Bovill, E.W., ed. 1966. *Missions to the Niger*, vol. iv: *The Bornu Mission 1822–25*. London: The Hakluyt Society.
Ferguson, John. 1969. "Aspects of Early Christianity in North Africa." In *Africa in Classical Antiquity*, ed. L. Thompson and J. Ferguson, 182–191. Ibadan: Ibadan University Press.
Forster, E.M. 1961. *Alexandria: A History and a Guide*. New York: Anchor.
Frend, W.H.C. 1952. *The Donatist Church*. London: Oxford University Press.
Hiskett, Mervyn. 1984. *The Development of Islam in West Africa*. London: Longman.
Ishaq, Ibn. 1967. *The Life of Muhammad [Sirat Raul-u-llah]*, edited and translated by Alfred Guillaume. Karachi: Oxford University Press.
Khaldun, Ibn. 1982. *Histoire des Berberes et des Dynasties Musulmanes de l'Afrique Septentrionale*. Paris: Librairie Orientaliste, Paul Geuthner, S.A.
Levtzion, Nehemia. 1968. *Muslims and Chiefs in West Africa: A Study of Islam in the Middle Volta in the Pre-Colonial Period*. Oxford: Oxford University Press.
Little, Kenneth. 1946. "A Muslim Missionary in Mendeland." *Man*, Journal of the Royal Anthropological Institute, Sept.–Oct.:111–113.

Sanneh, Lamin. 1979. *The Jakhanke: The History of an Islamic Clerical People of Senegambia*. London: The International African Institute.

Snowden, Frank M., Jr. 1970. *Blacks in Antiquity*. Cambridge, MA: Belknap Press.

Tafla, Bairuh. 1967. "The Establishment of the Ethiopian Church." *Tarikh*, Historical Society of Nigeria, *2*(1):28–42.

Wilks, Ivor. 1968. "The Transmission of Islamic Learning in the Western Sudan." In *Literacy in Traditional Societies*, ed. Jack Goody, 162–195. London: Cambridge University Press.

Wilson, Monica. 1969. "Co-operation and Conflict: The Eastern Cape Frontier." In *The Oxford History of South Africa*, vol. i, *South Africa to 1870*, ed. M. Wilson and L. Thompson, 233–271. London: Oxford University Press.

## *Reading 3.1*

The Nuer are a Nilotic, cattle-herding people who live in the southern Sudan. They cultivate grain and live in intense intimacy with their cattle. They are not hunters and, in fact, seem to abhor the practice. Although they have no priesthood, the Nuer have highly developed religious rites at the center of which is a clear and consistent notion of God. In the passage below, the reader is introduced to this central subject of Nuer religious life. The people have a strong sense of trust in *kwoth*, Spirit, who is described in a number of ways. There are broad questions concerning the nature of kwoth and more detailed ones pertaining to characteristics and manifestations. For the Nuer, kwoth has his dwelling place in the sky, although, like the wind, he is everywhere at the same time. The Nuer conceive of a difference, though not necessarily a conflict, between kwoth and human beings, who belong to the created order. Kwoth is the living breath of life, the source of personal life. Kwoth is also spoken of as ancestor to stress the genealogical basis of Nuer self-representation. Kwoth is thus related to human beings in both a general and a specific sense, and is invoked to express objective facts of kin relation and subjective notions of personal understanding. Kwoth is creator of the phenomenal world and progenitor of the race; he is also friend, comforter, and arbiter. Before kwoth we are nothing and can give nothing. Yet as source and provider of all, kwoth owns everything and may thus properly claim everything. Good and evil are controlled by him, although human conduct is subject to righteousness. Just as the sky and the earth are represented as articulate parts of a coherent moral universe ("it is thine earth, it is thy universe"), so human conduct is integrated in a world whose true source has no limits. The confidence of the Nuer in appealing to God is not weakened by a corresponding awareness of the gulf that cannot be removed.

# From: *The Prayers of African Religion,* John S. Mbiti

In the beginning was God,
Today is God,
Tomorrow will be God.
Who can make an image of God?
He has no body.
He is a word which comes out of your mouth.
That word! It is no more,
It is past, and still it lives!
So is God.

# Edward Evans Evans-Pritchard, "God," from *Nuer Religion*

The Nuer word we translate 'God' is *kwoth*,[1] Spirit. Nuer also speak of him more definitely as *kwoth nhial* or *kwoth a nhial*, Spirit of the sky or Spirit who is in the sky. There are other and lesser spirits which they class as *kuth nhial*, spirits of the sky or of the above, and *kuth piny*, spirits of the earth or of the below. I discuss the conception of God first because the other spiritual conceptions are dependent on it and can only be understood in relation to it.

The Nuer *kwoth*, like the Latin *spiritus*, the Greek *pneuma*, and the English derivatives of both words, suggests both the intangible quality of air and the breathing or blowing out of air... In its verbal form it is used to describe such actions as blowing on the embers of a fire; blowing on food to cool it; blowing into the uterus of a cow, while a tulchan is propped up before it, to make it give milk; snorting; the blowing out of air by the puff fish; and the hooting by steam pressure of a river steamer. The word is also found, and has the same general sense, in some of the other Nilotic languages.

As a noun, however, *kwoth* means only Spirit, and in the particular sense we are now discussing it means *kwoth nhial* or *kwoth a nhial*, Spirit of the heavens or Spirit who is in the heavens, the copula *a* in the second designation being one of the verbs we translate 'to be'. *Nhial* is the sky, and combined with verbs the word may also refer to certain natural processes associated with the sky, as raining and thundering; but it may also have merely the sense of 'on high' or 'above'. We may certainly say that the Nuer do not regard the sky or any celestial phenomenon as God, and this is clearly shown in the distinction made between God and the sky in the expressions 'Spirit of the sky' and 'Spirit who is in the sky'. Moreover, it would even be a mistake to interpret 'of the sky' and 'in the sky' too literally.

---

[1] The word has been variously spelt by European writers. I shall throughout use *kwoth* (pl. *kuth*), neglecting the genitive and locative forms.

It would equally be a mistake to regard the association of God with the sky as pure metaphor, for though the sky is not God, and though God is everywhere, he is thought of as being particularly in the sky, and Nuer generally think of him in a spatial sense as being on high. Hence anything connected with the firmament has associations with him.... I have never heard a spontaneous reference to the sun as a divine manifestation, but if one asks Nuer about it they say that it too belongs to God, and the moon and the stars also. They say that if a man sees the sun at night this is a divine manifestation, and one which is most dangerous for him; but I think that the light they say is occasionally seen is not regarded as an appearance of the physical sun but as some peculiar luminous vision. When Nuer see the new moon they rub ashes on their foreheads and they throw ashes, and perhaps also a grain of millet, towards it, saying some short prayer, as 'grandfather, let us be at peace' or 'ah moon, *nyadeang* (daughter of the air-spirit *deng*) we invoke (God) that thou shouldst appear with goodness. May the people see thee every day. Let us be (*akolapko*)'....

Thus anything associated with the sky has virtue which is lacking in earthly things. Nuer pathetically compare man to heavenly things. He is *ran piny*, an earthly person and, according to the general Nuer view, his ghost is also earth-bound. Between God and man, between heaven and earth, there is a great gulf, and we shall find that an appreciation of the symbolism of the polarity of heaven and earth helps us to understand Nuer religious thought and feeling and also sheds light on certain social features of their religion, for example the greater prestige of prophets than of priests....

Before discussing further the separation of God from man I will mention some of the chief attributes of God. He is in the sky, but his being in the sky does not mean that he is not at the same time elsewhere, and on earth. Indeed, as will be seen, Nuer religious thought cannot be understood unless God's closeness to man is taken together with his separation from man, for its meaning lies precisely in this paradox....

God, Spirit in the heavens who is like wind and air, is the creator and mover of all things. Since he made the world he is addressed in prayers as *kwoth ghaua*, Spirit of the universe, with the sense of creator of the universe. The word *cak*, used as a noun, can mean the creation, that is, all created things, and hence the nature or character proper to a person or thing; it can be used in a very special sense to refer to an abnormality, *cak kwoth*, a freak; and, though I think rarely, it is used as a title of God, the creator, as in the expression *cak nath*, creator of men. As a verb 'to create' it signifies creation *ex nihilo*, and when speaking of things can therefore only be used of God. However, the word can be used of men for imaginative constructions, such as the thinking of a name to give a child, inventing a tale, or composing a poem, in the same figurative sense as when we say that an actor creates a part. The word therefore means not only creation from nothing but also creation by thought or imagination, so that 'God created the universe' has the sense of 'God thought of the universe' or 'God imagined the universe'.

The complementary distinction made in Genesis between 'the heaven and the earth' is made, by implication at least, in a slightly different way by the Nuer. A parallelism often heard in their prayers is '*e pinydu, e ghaudu*', 'it is thine earth, it is thy universe'. *Piny* is the down-below, the earth in the sense of the terrestrial world as the Nuer know it. *Ghau* has many meanings—world, sky, earth, atmosphere, time, and weather—which taken together, as they should be in a context of prayer, mean the universe. Another common, and related, strophe in prayers is '*e ghaudu, e rwacdu*', 'it is thy universe, it is thy word'. *Rwac* in ordinary contexts means speech, talk, or word, but when used in prayers and invocations in the phrase '*e rwacdu*', 'it is thy word', it means the will of God; and when used in reference to creation it has almost the meaning of the creative word: 'he created the world, it is his word'.... Everything in nature, in culture, in society, and in men is as it is because God made or willed it so. Above all else God is thought of as the giver and sustainer of life. He also brings death. It is true that Nuer seldom attribute death—in such cases as death by lightning or following the breach of a divinely sanctioned interdiction—to the direct intervention of God, but rather to natural circumstances or to the action of a lesser spirit, but they nevertheless regard the natural circumstances or the spirits as instruments or agents of God, and the final appeal in sickness is made to him. Nuer have often told me that it is God who takes the life, whether a man dies from spear, wild beast, or sickness, for these are all *nyin kwoth*, instruments of God.

In the Nuer conception of God he is thus creative Spirit. He is also a *ran*, a living person, whose *yiegh*, breath or life, sustains man. I have never heard Nuer suggest that he has human form, but though he is himself ubiquitous and invisible, he sees and hears all that happens and he can be angry and can love (the Nuer word is *nhok*, and if we here translate it 'to love' it must be understood in the preferential sense of *agapō* or *diligo*: when Nuer say that God loves something they mean that he is partial to it). However, the anthropomorphic features of the Nuer conception of God are very weak and, as will be seen, they do not act towards him as though he were a man. Indeed, such human features as are given him barely suffice to satisfy the requirements of thought and speech....

A very common mode of address to the Deity is '*gwandong*', a word which means 'grandfather' or 'ancestor', and literally 'old father', but in a religious context 'father' or 'our father' would convey the Nuer sense better; and '*gwara*' and '*gwandan*', 'our father', and the respectful form of address '*gwadin*', 'father', are also often used in speaking to or about God. God is the father of men in two respects. He is their creator and he is their protector.

He is addressed in prayers as '*kwoth me cak gwadong*', 'God who created my ancestor'. Figuratively, and in conformity with Nuer lineage idiom, he is sometimes given a genealogical position in relation to man. A man in the Jinaca clan, for example, after tracing his pedigree back to Denac, the founder of his clan, may go on to say that Denac was a son of Gee, who was a son of *Ran*, man, who was a son of *Ghau*, the universe, who was a son of *Kwoth*, God. When Nuer thus speak of God as their remote ancestor and address him as 'father' or 'grandfather', and likewise when in praying to him they speak of themselves, as they commonly do, as *'gaatku'*, 'thy children', their manner of speech is no more to be taken literally than are those frequent passages in the Old Testament in which Israel is spoken of as the spouse or son of Jehovah.

God is also the father of men in that he is their protector and friend. He is *'kwoth me jale ka ji'*, 'God who walks with you', that is, who is present with you. He is the friend of men who helps them in their troubles, and Nuer sometimes address him as *'madh'*, 'friend', a word which has for them the sense of intimate friendship. The frequent use in prayers of the word *rom* in reference to the lives, or souls, of men indicates the same feeling about God, for it has the sense of the care and protection parents give to a child and especially the carrying of a helpless infant. So does another word often used in prayers, *luek*, to comfort, God is asked to *'luek nei'* to 'comfort the people'. The Nuer habit of making short supplications to God outside formal and ritual occasions also suggests an awareness of a protective presence, as does the affirmation one hears every day among the Nuer, *'kwoth a thin'*, 'God is present'. Nuer say this, doubtless often as a merely verbal response, when they are faced with some difficulty to be overcome or some problem to be solved. The phrase does not mean 'there is a God'. That would be for Nuer a pointless remark. God's existence is taken for granted by everybody. Consequently when we say, as we can do, that all Nuer have faith in God, the word 'faith' must be understood in the Old Testament sense of 'trust' (The Nuer *ngath*) and not in that modern sense of 'belief' which the concept came to have under Greek and Latin influences. There is in any case, I think, no word in the Nuer language which could stand for 'I believe'. *Kwoth a thin* means that God is present in the sense of being in a place or enterprise, the *a* being here again a verb 'to be'. When Nuer use the phrase they are saying that they do not know what to do but God is here with them and will help them. He is with them because he is Spirit and being like wind or air is everywhere, and, being everywhere, is here now.

---

## Reading 3.2

For the Nuer and the Dinka, all the complex and diverse ways in which human beings respond to God converge and have their most dramatic representation in sacrifice, which may be said to form the cornerstone of the ritual life. Sacrifice is essentially exchange, and in the Low Church tradition of African religions it is the offering of a life to the Supreme Being in exchange for blessings. Thus blood sacrifice comes to constitute the most concentrated and intense aspect of personal religion. In some other parts of Africa sacrifice is elaborated into a complex series of symbols which come to a focus in the drama of priestly intervention. In that High Church tradition, a sacred aura might come to be attached to the priestly lineage, which in turn might be centered on an earth or territorial cult. The examples given here belong, broadly speaking, to the Low Church end of the spectrum.

## Edward Evans Evans-Pritchard, "Sacrifice," from *Nuer Religion*

Nuer sacrifices fall into two broad classes. Most sacrifices are made to prevent some danger hanging over people, for example on account of some sin, to appease an angry spirit, or at the birth of twins; or to curtail or to get rid of a misfortune which has already fallen, as in times of plague or in acute sickness. On all such occasions Spirit intervenes, or may intervene, for better or more often for worse, in the affairs of men, and its intervention is always dangerous. Any misfortune or grave danger is a sign of spiritual activity. Such sacrifices are made for a person or persons and not for social groups and they involve ideas of propitiation, expiation, and related intentions. As they are the most common and the most specifically religious sacrifices I shall devote chief attention to them. There are other sacrifices which accompany various social activities, mostly of the *rites de passage* kind, such as initiation, marriage, and death. We cannot make an absolute distinction between the two sorts of sacrifice. A sacrifice of the *rites de passage* kind may contain elements of meaning characteristic of the other type. Sacrifices in marriage ceremonies—at betrothal, at the wedding, and at the consummation—are the best examples of the second type. A sacrifice to ward off the consequences of serious incest is a good example of the first type. A sacrifice to end mourning is an example of the blending of the two. It is a routine sacrifice in a *rites de passage* context, but it is also intended to get rid of the contamination of death and any evil there may be in men's hearts. For the purpose of discussing the meaning or meanings of sacrifice it is necessary to make the distinction, even if there is some overlapping. I shall speak of the one type as personal sacrifice and of the other as collective sacrifice. . . .

This chapter is mostly devoted to a discussion of personal sacrifices but I say something of the collective ones before giving exclusive attention to them. The primary purpose of collective sacrifices, and also their main function, is to confirm, to establish, or to add strength to, a change in social status—boy to man, maiden to wife, living man to ghost—or a new relationship between social groups—the coming into being of a new age-set, the uniting of kin groups by ties of affinity, the ending of a blood-feud—by making God and the ghosts, who are directly concerned with the change taking place, witnesses of it. The ceremonies are incomplete and ineffective without sacrifice, but sacrifice may be only one incident in a complex of ceremonies, dances, and rites of various kinds, which have no religious significance in themselves. Its importance lies in the fact that it sacralizes the social event and the new relationships brought about by it. It solemnizes the change of status or relationship, giving it religious validation. On such occasions sacrifice has generally a conspicuously festal and eucharistic character.

Collective sacrifices thus have a marked structural character. Sacrifices may be made on behalf of whole communities, as in times of epidemic, but they are then made for a great number of individuals. Here, however, we are dealing with something rather different, with sacrifices made on behalf of social segments, lineages, and age-sets, which are concerned as whole groups, sometimes in relation to groups of like order. This is why they have to be performed by specially appointed representatives of the groups concerned or by public functionaries, as is explained later.

It is indicative of Nuer religious thought that these sacrifices performed as part of social activities are concerned with relations within the social order and not with relations between men and their natural environment. We are often told in accounts of African peoples that their sacrifices are concerned with weather, rain, fertility of the soil, seed-time, fructification, harvest, and fishing and hunting. Generally no rite of any kind is performed by Nuer in connexion with these processes, certainly no regular and obligatory rite; and if in certain circumstances one is performed, as before large-scale fishing, it is rarely a sacrifice, and if it is a sacrifice it is not regarded as either necessary or important. All this may be due to some extent to lack of interest in agriculture and hunting, but it is also because Nuer take nature for granted and are passive and resigned towards it. They do not think that they can influence it to their own advantage, being merely ignorant folk. What happens there is the will of God, and that has to be accepted. Hence Nuer are little interested in ritual for bringing rain and even consider it presumptuous to think of asking God for rain before sowing. This mentality is illustrated in one of their stories which relates how death came to a girl who asked that the setting of the sun might be delayed till she had finished her work. Nuer rather turn their eyes inwards, to the little closed social world in which they live, they and their cattle. Their sacrifices are concerned with moral and spiritual, not natural, crises.

\* \* \*

We have now first to ask to whom sacrifices are made. This brings us again up against the problem of the one and the many. When a sin is expiated or pollution is wiped out by sacrifice it is made to God alone. Likewise in major calamities, such as plagues and murrains. Also when a person is struck by lightning, in connexion with death, and in cases of sickness not attributed to a specific cause. We are here dealing with circumstances common to all men and with universals—with the moral law which is the same for all men, with effects of common interest and concern, and with dangers and misfortunes which fall on each and all alike. Sacrifices may, however, be made on some occasions to one or other spirit, for example, to a spirit of the air before battle or when it is thought to have brought about sickness in a man or if it is feared that it may do so; or to a totemic or other spirit of the below in circumstances already mentioned in earlier chapters. We are here dealing with something more particular and specific, the relation of certain persons to Spirit figured to them, and not to others, in one or other special form as a spirit. Nevertheless, as I have earlier explained, these spirits may be regarded as hypostases, representations, or refractions of God, and in the already defined sense in which this is so we can say that a sacrifice to any one of them is a sacrifice also to God. The cause of sickness, or of any misfortune, is always thought to be, either immediately or in the last resort, Spirit, which in some circumstances may be more specifically defined as a certain spirit. Furthermore, when sickness is attributed to an air-spirit, for example *deng*, whether the patient recovers or not is thought to rest with God, that is, with Spirit in the comprehensive sense which includes *deng* as one manifestation of it. The two representations may thus be separated in the mind in relation to cause and cure, but they are fused in the sacrificial act. If, therefore, it can be said that, in this sense, God is sacrificed to in all sacrifices, it must be added that in particular circumstances connected with particular persons or social groups Spirit conceived of in some lower form may be dominant. This inevitably affects to some extent the character of the rite.

Spirit conceived of as God does not seize people and make them sick as some air-spirits and earth-spirits may. They exact a special tribute which God does not demand, a payment for special protection and favour, and this can hardly fail to affect the meaning of the sacrificial act. We have to take this fact into consideration, and it complicates our problem. To avoid ambiguities and obscurities at this stage I shall take sacrifice to God as my model and describe that, and then state later what modifications and qualifications are required when sacrifice is made to a spirit.

In the case of collective sacrifices, which...may be to Spirit in some totemic or other refraction, the changes in social status and relations they serve to bring about involve the ghosts, who are usually little or not at all concerned in personal sacrifices. At collective sacrifices they may therefore be invoked together with God in some such formula as 'God, thou and the ghosts'. Since the matter has been discussed earlier I need only say here that the sacrifices are made to God, even on those occasions which most directly concern the dead. The ghosts must be summoned as witnesses and the matter must be explained to them because it concerns them, but they are only witnesses as the living are, and what is explained to them is explained to the living also. Even when sacrifice is made at a mortuary ceremony or when a man commemorates his dead father it cannot be said that the victim is sacrificed to the ghost....

Even when a ghost is troublesome and sacrifice has to be made to pacify it the victim is consecrated to God and not to the ghost. It is to God that expiation for the wrong done to the ghost must be made. What is made to the ghost is reparation, where this is possible. It follows from all that has been said about the Nuer notion of faults, and it will be seen that it also follows from the whole character of the sacrificial act, that it is only to Spirit that sacrifice can be made.

Our second question is, What is sacrificed? The sacrificial animal *par excellence* is an ox, and in important social ceremonies, such as weddings and those held for settlement of feuds, the victim must be an ox. Oxen are also sacrificed in times of general calamity, sometimes when people are dangerously ill, and occasionally to spirits. A barren cow may take the place of an ox. Bulls are only sacrificed in one of the rites closing a blood-feud, and occasionally, though only old beasts, in honour of a dead father. Except in these instances a male victim must be a neuter. If it is not, it is castrated before the rites begin. Fertile cows are only sacrificed at mortuary ceremonies, and then only for senior persons, as a tribute to their position in the community. It does not matter what is the colour of the victim, though in certain sacrifices there is a preference for beasts with certain markings....

The animal, whatever it may be—cow or ox or bull, ewe or wether, nanny-goat or castrated billy-goat—is spoken of in invocations and in any sacrificial context as '*yang*', 'cow'. This word, like our 'cow', denotes in ordinary usage any bovine animal of any age and of either sex or, when used more exclusively, a female and, still more exclusively, an adult female. When translating what Nuer have said in sacrifices or about them I have preserved their sacrificial idiom. It must be understood, therefore, that in this context the word 'cow' seldom refers to a cow but almost always, when the victim is an animal, to an ox, a wether, or a castrated he-goat. In a sacrificial context Nuer also always speak of a cucumber-victim as '*yang*', '*cow*'.

Should for some reason no beast be available Nuer may instead, or as a temporary expedient, sacrifice a small trailing knobbly cucumber.... If necessary, animal sacrifice is made later, when a victim can be acquired. Nuer also sacrifice this cucumber in minor anxieties, as when they have bad dreams or have committed petty incest. It is treated as though it were an animal victim. It is presented and consecrated, an invocation is said over it, and it is slain by the spear, being cut in half along its edge. The left, or bad, half is then thrown away and the right, or good, half is squeezed and its juice and seeds rubbed on the chest and forehead of the officiant and maybe on others present. This half is afterwards put in the thatch over the entrance to the byre, or sometimes to the dwelling-hut. In cases of petty incest a fruit of the sausage tree (*Kigelia aethiopica*) may be cut in half, though I am uncertain whether this constitutes a sacrifice *in sensu stricto*.

We have discussed to whom sacrifice is made and what is sacrificed. We have now to ask by whom it is made, and when and where.... Several people may take part in the consecration and several men may deliver invocations. One man may present the victim, another consecrate and make the invocation over it, and yet another slay it. Nevertheless, there are always one or more prime actors, those who make the consecrations and invocations, which, rather than the actual killing, constitute for Nuer the main acts in the series of rites making up a sacrifice; and we may therefore speak of anyone who, after consecrating the victim, makes an invocation over it as the officiant. There may be several of them. In certain sacrifices, particularly those of the collective kind, whoever else may invoke God, one or other particular functionary either must do so or it is thought highly desirable that he should do so.... Normally any senior man, usually the head of the family of the sacrificer, can officiate at personal sacrifices. He would generally be one of the sacrificer's paternal kinsmen but it would not matter if he were not. The sacrifice is to God and not to ghosts, and it therefore does not matter who officiates. A youth would not officiate if there were an older man present, but this is a matter of social convention only: there is no ritual bar to his acting. Women do not sacrifice. They may assist in the act of consecration with ashes and they may pray, but they do not make invocations or slay victims. Neither the sacrificer nor the officiant has to be in a state of ceremonial purity. This is an idea entirely unknown to Nuer....

If there is no urgency a sacrifice may be put off till a time convenient for the sacrificer. The collective sacrifices and sacrifices in honour of spirits of one kind or another are normally held in the villages during the rains, and even in cases of sickness, if it is not acute, in dry-season camps Nuer prefer to put off animal sacrifice till they return to their villages. They may consider that though a sickness is due to neglect of some spirit there is no pressing need for immediate sacrifice. To keep the spirit content in the meantime they may sacrifice a cucumber, if they have one, or offer it some tobacco or a libation; or they may make an animal sacrifice in intention by devoting to the spirit then and there an animal by rubbing ashes on its back and then wait till they are back in their permanent homes to sacrifice it. Consequently one rarely sees animal sacrifices in dry-season camps.

A sacrifice is also a feast, and a feast is more suitably held in the surrounding of huts and byres. Nuer, especially the older people, think of the *cieng*, the homestead and village, rather than of the *wec*, the cattle camp, as their home. This is all the more weighty a reason in the case of collective sacrifices, because the kin who should attend them and have rights in the sacrificial flesh may be scattered in the drought. There is also plenty of beer and porridge in the rains to add to the meat of the sacrifices for feasting, and little or none in the dry-season camps, for even if their millet is not exhausted people are often too far from their granaries to transport it. Moreover, the social activities which are the occasion of collective sacrifices take place, largely because there is plenty of food, in the rains. I think also it is possible that there is more, and more serious, sickness in the rains and hence the greater need for sacrifices then.

It does not seem usually to matter at what time of day a sacrifice takes place, though the early morning is preferred on big occasions when oxen are sacrificed; but I have witnessed sacrifices when the sun was high and also in the evening. Early morning and evening are the most convenient times because then the men are at leisure and it is cool, but the early morning has the additional advantage that it gives time for what are sometimes lengthy cere-monies to be performed with slow dignity. I suppose that if there were need Nuer would sacrifice at night, but I have never known this to happen, and it would cause certain inconveniences....

Before giving an account of the succession of acts which constitute a sacrifice it is advisable to say further that though the acts are almost always the same and performed in the same order they are much more elaborate on some occasions than on others. A mortuary ceremony must begin between dawn and sunrise and is carried out by long, slow, solemn stages. The rites of sacrifice at marriage ceremonies are, on the contrary, often carried out in a perfunctory manner, giving the impression that they are regarded as little more than a formality. Likewise there is much variation in the attention paid to the rites by those present but not taking an active part in them. In some sacrifices they pay little attention to them, or even ignore them altogether, continuing their dancing or talking among themselves about their own affairs. Thus, in my experience, at sacrifices in marriage ceremonies only close kin of the persons immediately concerned take much, or even any, interest in the ritual. Even sacrifices in honour of a spirit may be performed in a perfunctory manner, it being thought that all that is required is that a beast be offered so that the spirit may know that it has not been forgotten. But on occasions of serious sickness, of grave danger, and of death the spectators sit quietly in a line or semicircle and give silent attention to what is being said and done. The amount of attention paid and its intensity depend on the nature of the occasion and the degree to which spectators are personally involved.

Therefore the many attempts that have been made to explain primitive religions in terms of supposed psychological states—awe, religious thrill, and so forth—are, as far as the Nuer are concerned, inept because the feelings of officiants and spectators are, in so far as they are discernible, clearly different on different occasions and in different parts of the same ceremony. This is obvious to anyone who sees a few Nuer sacrifices. Some people are paying attention and others not. Some are solemn, others gay. Wedding and funeral sacrifices do not evoke the same response, nor do initiation and incest sacrifices, nor even the opening and closing sacrifices of a mortuary ceremony. The feelings of close kin are not the same as those of distant kin. There is no need to labour the point. What is important in sacrifice is not how people feel, or even how they behave—a serious mien when the occasion is a solemn one is a matter of sentiment and good manners, not of religion. What is important is that the essential acts of sacrifice be carried out and, especially in personal sacrifices, with a right intention, which is a matter of disposition, not of emotion.

# EXPLOITATION

## Robert I. Rotberg

In this chapter Professor Rotberg discusses various forms of exploitation that took place in Africa before and during the colonial period from the late 19th through the mid-20th century. The readings he has selected provide an intimate view of these different kinds of exploitations, written by individuals who either experienced them or observed them. **Eds**.

## TWO DISTINCT AFRICAS

Between the 17th and 19th centuries, there were two Africas. The first consisted of the bulk of the interior of the continent. This Africa was only indirectly influenced by the economic, social, and political trends of Europe. The second was coastal Africa, where Africans first interacted with both Europeans and Arabs and where the impact of new ideas, new theologies, and new organizational methods was initially felt. It was coastal Africa also where Africans initially and for many years to come confronted the realities of exploitation. The second Africa ultimately encompassed the first, and Western and Middle Eastern ideas were introduced to the interior of the continent.

Africa has never been static. For at least several centuries before 1600, peoples in coastal Africa encouraged conflict between ethnic groups, the migration of whole peoples, and the transformation of regions of Africa from one to another religious and political persuasion as they pursued goals of economic self-sufficiency and political growth. A good example of the process of generation and regeneration which can be called quintessentially African occurred in the Central African lake region (the area of Lakes Victoria, Tanganyika, and Albert) during the period 1600–1800, well before the arrival of outsiders. Without any apparent non-African outside influence, the peoples of what would become Uganda, Kenya, Tanzania, Rwanda, and Burundi established a succession of durable kingdoms which engaged in long-distance trade, boasted sophisticated forms of government, and were as achievement-oriented as many European polities of the time. These centralized, highly stratified kingdoms replaced the egalitarian, clan-based societies of an earlier era. A similar growth in centralization occurred in the grasslands of the Cameroons and in and around the Gold Coast (Ghana). During the 18th century, in the basin of the Congo and on the high plateau along its rim, many agricultural peoples were absorbed into larger groups ruled by innovative migrants.

In other areas, too, these two centuries constituted a time of elaboration and differentiation. Economically, it was a period of expanding horizons, of new exploitations, of the intensification of long-distance trade involving astonishing journeys from the center of the continent to either coast, and of the development of markets, especially in the west and the north. In parts of Africa that had not yet fully entered the iron age, people embraced metal and its uses, enhancing their abilities to cultivate and hunt and their propensity for wars. The stakes of competitive exploitation and of war had grown higher, too, making conflict everywhere more frequent and more costly.

## FROM SUGAR TO SLAVES

The first Africa merged into the second Africa in and because of the clash of armies. From the 17th century onward, coastal Africa was thoroughly involved with the wider world, especially with the Arabs in the east and Europe in the south after the settlement of the Dutch at the Cape of Good Hope in mid-century. Its predominant involvement was the enslavement and sale of men and women. The combat of armies supplied captives; and, as the needs of the Americas increased, the frontier of European and Arab influence expanded. If we seek an underlying villain for this process, it was sugar. Only in the 17th century did sugar begin to be cultivated successfully and extensively in the West Indies. Sugar demands backbreaking labor, especially during the cane-cutting season. Without ready supplies of African labor, it would have proved costly—perhaps impossible—to grow cane successfully in the West Indies and Brazil.

Fueled by this foreign demand, the slave trade enveloped Africa throughout the 17th and 18th centuries and for a large part of the 19th century. (See Maps 4.1 and 4.2.) The apparatus necessary for obtaining

**MAP 4.1    Eighteenth-Century Slave Trade**

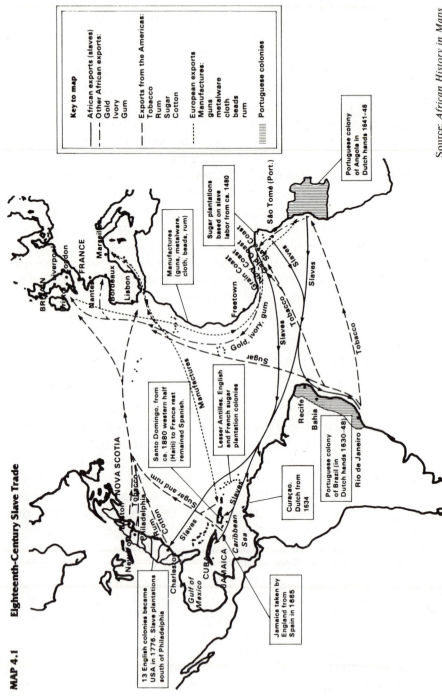

Key to map

African exports (slaves):
Other African exports:
Gold
Ivory
Gum

Exports from the Americas:
Tobacco
Rum
Sugar
Cotton

European exports
Manufactures:
guns
metalware
cloth
beads
rum

Portuguese colonies

Source: *African History in Maps*

13 English colonies became USA in 1776. Slave plantations south of Philadelphia

Santo Domingo, from ca. 1880 western half (Haiti) to France rest remained Spanish.

Lesser Antilles, English and French sugar plantation colonies

Curaçao, Dutch from 1634

Portuguese colony of Brazil (in Dutch hands 1630–48)

Jamaica taken by England from Spain in 1665

Sugar plantations based on slave labor from ca. 1480

Manufactures (guns, metalware, cloth, beads, rum)

Portuguese colony of Angola in Dutch hands 1641–48

BRITAIN
Liverpool
London
FRANCE
Marseille
Nantes
Bordeaux
Lisbon

New orleans
NOVA SCOTIA
Philadelphia
Charleston
Gulf of Mexico
CUBA
JAMAICA
Caribbean Sea

Tobacco
Rum
Cotton
Sugar and rum
Slaves
Manufactures

São Tomé (Port.)
Slave Coast
Gold Coast
Grain Coast
Freetown
Gold, ivory, gum
Slaves
Tobacco
Sugar
Slaves

Recife
Bahia
Rio de Janeiro
Tobacco

**MAP 4.2**     **Nineteenth-Century Slave Trade**

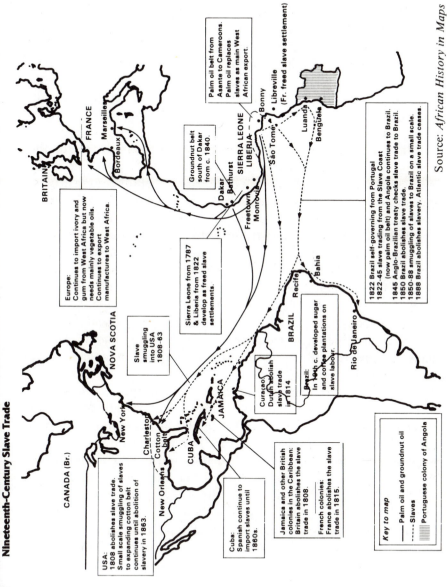

Source: *African History in Maps*

**Europe:**
Continues to import ivory and gum from West Africa but now needs mainly vegetable oils. Continues to export manufactures to West Africa.

Palm oil belt from Asante to Cameroons. Palm oil replaces slaves as main West African export.

Groundnut belt south of Dakar from c. 1840.

Sierra Leone from 1787 & Liberia from 1822 develop as freed slave settlements.

Slave smuggling into USA 1808-63

**USA:**
1808 abolishes slave trade. Small scale smuggling of slaves to expanding cotton belt continues until abolition of slavery in 1863.

Curaçao Dutch abolish slave trade in 1814.

**Brazil:**
In 19th c. developed sugar and coffee plantations on slave labour.

Cuba:
Spanish continue to import slaves until 1860s.

Jamaica and other British colonies in the Caribbean: Britain abolishes the slave trade in 1808.

French colonies: France abolishes the slave trade in 1815.

1822 Brazil self-governing from Portugal
1822-45 slave trading from the Slave Coast (now palm oil belt) and Angola continues to Brazil.
1845 Anglo-Brazilian treaty checks slave trade to Brazil.
1850 Brazil abolishes slave trade.
1850-88 smuggling of slaves to Brazil on a small scale.
1888 Brazil abolishes slavery. Atlantic slave trade ceases.

*Key to map*
—— Palm oil and groundnut oil
----- Slaves
▨ Portuguese colony of Angola

CANADA (Br.)
NOVA SCOTIA
New York
Charleston
Cotton belt
New Orleans
CUBA
JAMAICA
Recife
Bahia
BRAZIL
Rio de Janeiro

BRITAIN
FRANCE
Marseilles
Bordeaux

Dakar
Bathurst
SIERRA LEONE
Freetown
Monrovia
LIBERIA
São Tomé
Bonny
Libreville (Fr. freed slave settlement)
Luanda
Benguela

111

slaves; walking them to the marshalling yards of the coast; fattening and feeding them there; and selling them, individual by individual, to ship captains for transport overseas, demanded entrepreneurial initiative and managerial competence of a high and complex order. It presumably also required a strong stomach and a hard heart on the part of Europeans and Africans alike. Certainly the treatment of slaves in the African ports was degrading. Even more inhumane were the shackling and the cramming of cramped ships with anxious, potentially rebellious slaves, and their transport across often stormy seas to an auction yard in the Americas. If enslavement were an abomination—even by the standards of the day—the sea voyage, the so-called Middle Passage of six to ten weeks, was totally destructive.

In round numbers, about ten million Africans were forcibly removed from Africa. Many must have lost their lives during the Middle Passage, others as a result of abortive rebellions or the original opposition to capture. As cruel as being enslaved was for individuals, however, the societies of Africa may themselves have suffered far less than has often been supposed. For individuals fortunate enough to have remained behind, the trade in slaves brought new sources of capital for development, markets for commodities other than slaves, the transfer of technology from the West to Africa, and an outlet—however perverse—for the talents of certain groups within the coastal and forest states. The rise of Ashanti, Dahomey, Oyo, and many less well-known peoples in the Congo basin and the hinterlands of Angola, stems directly from the important role they played in the new, slave-centered terms of trade.

When pressure from humanitarians in Europe was brought to bear on the iniquities of the slave trade in the late 18th century, the merchants of Africa were among the loudest in defending their livelihood. After Britain abolished slavery in the early 19th century and persuaded France, Portugal, and Spain—and later Zanzibar in the east—to follow suit, Africans complained even more bitterly and sought to frustrate the activities of Britain's antislave patrol in the Atlantic. Yet, as they gnashed their teeth, many of these Africans found that their commercial talents could be put to good use supplying industrializing Europe with palm oil (for soap and industrial lubricants) and other items.

The effects of the slave trade and its abolition were felt increasingly in the upcouuntry regions as well as in areas nearer the coast. The quest for slaves naturally involved peoples farther and farther afield. In the mid-19th century, for example, Arabo-Swahili caravan leaders from Zanzibar scoured the lands within the distant Congo Basin for humans to supply the developing markets of Arabia and the Indian Ocean islands (where sugar was being grown) as well as the clove plantations of Zanzibar itself. Earlier, the hinterlands of Malawi and Zambia had been crisscrossed innumerable times for slaves and ivory, and virtually no part of Africa was unacquainted with the horrors of enforced enslavement. Accordingly, some peoples erected effective barriers against the traders. Those who were warlike and aggressive, like the Masai and their herding cousins, the Turkana and the Karamojong (of East Africa), were never molested. Likewise, where there were centralized kingdoms like Rwanda and Buganda on the great lakes, Africans moved freely and little feared the slave trade.

When Arabs and Europeans arrived in East Africa in the 19th century, they found strong states which proved a magnet for foreigners. Buganda, the nucleus of modern Uganda, was an outstanding example. There a king (or *kabaka*) ruled autocratically with the assistance of a complex bureaucracy. Throughout the middle 19th century, successive rulers of Buganda increased their personal power by curbing the religious authority of the indigenous priests, phasing out the autonomy of clans and their leaders by installing regional subordinates in their place and enlisting an army. As a result of breaking the old societal bonds, the kabakas of Buganda thus created a society that was remarkably fluid and achievement-oriented. Commoners could obtain advancement and prestige more easily than they could elsewhere in Africa. As a result, the people of Buganda were receptive to Islam and Christianity when each arrived toward the end of the century. They were also open to modernization when it eventually arrived from Europe in the shape of conquest. A similar situation prevailed with the Ibo society of eastern Nigeria.

## AFRICAN RIVALRY AND NEW NATION-STATES

The rise of Buganda was paralleled in time by the rise of other aggressive new states. Each was stimulated by a set of local circumstances—by a shift in ecological fortunes or the nature of trade, or by the rise of a great man. Each, too, in one way or another was the result of a chain of reactions set off by the increasing activity and encroachment of Europeans. Among the more dramatic and far-reaching of these developments was the forcible integration of a number of Nguni-speaking clan units of southeastern Africa (what is now Natal) into the great Zulu nation.

The leader of this nation was the charismatic Shaka, who modernized methods of warfare, introduced new, superior weapons, and greatly influenced the history of Africa. Under his leadership, Zulus were able to present a solid front to the British and Afrikaners (the descendants of the Dutch and Protestant French who settled the Cape of Good Hope during the 17th and 18th centuries). Shaka was a tyrant who came to power behind an *assegai* (a powerful stabbing spear) and left a legacy of autocratic centralization.

Yet Shaka could not gain the obedience of all Zulu. After their defeat by his armies, several of the clans created a far-ranging diaspora which, before mid-century, engulfed virtually the whole of southern and central Africa. Three Zulu segments conquered their way northward, creating havoc and ending the independence of numerous peoples across whose territories they marched. In nearby Rhodesia, the Ndebele offshoot established a major state which ruled south of the Zambezi River until the coming of the Europeans. The Kololo offshoot gained control of the kingdom of the Lozi on the upper reaches of the Zambezi River. A larger detachment of Nguni smashed its way northward through Mozambique, eastern Zimbabwe, and modern Zambia, until, in about 1839, it, too, suffered from internal rivalry. Fission resulted, one Nguni group carving out a niche for itself in western Tanzania, another in southwestern Tanzania, a third in eastern Zambia, a fourth in northern Malawi, and two others in southern Malawi. In addition, a separate segment gained control of southern Mozambique. Taken as a whole, the Nguni diaspora profoundly altered the nature of government and society in most of central and southern Africa. By laying waste to the territories through which they passed and thoroughly cowing the agricultural peoples over whom their juggernaut rolled, the Nguni made conditions easier for slavers and, ultimately, for the conquest of the area by Europeans.

This cataclysm in the east had its counterpart in the west. However, while the Nguni were thoroughly traditional in their culture and religion, in their delight in cattle, and in their willingness to absorb the conquered into their new states, in the west there was a different approach. The significant upheavals there (as in the north later) were based on the promise of religious purification. Without the support of the doctrines of fundamentalist Islam, the leaders of that religious revival might not have been able to stimulate a war between believers and traditionalists throughout the breadth of Hausaland—now northern Nigeria. Most of the believers were also immigrants, largely Fulani from the west who, like so many minorities, felt themselves disadvantaged under the various rulers of the separate Hausa city-states. Usuman dan Fodio, a Fulani cleric who had studied with Muslim theologians, was in the forefront of this movement of reform.

Usuman sought to reintroduce a spirit of religious orthodoxy into Hausaland that was in keeping with the literal teachings of the Koran and which he supposed would help foster the ideal society of an imagined earlier golden age. In the opening years of the 19th century, Usuman therefore went from leading a crusade on behalf of purified Islam into open rebellion against the city-states of what later became Niger and northern Nigeria. He and his followers attacked Gobir. Then, gathering adherents among the Fulani and Hausa alike, the new soldiers of Islamic orthodoxy swiftly carried their revolution into the other states of Hausaland. Young leaders advanced on distant Bornu. Within a few years they overran Kano, Katsina, and Zaria, the other major cities of Hausaland. By 1810, the victory had been won. Usuman ruled 180,000 square miles and 15 city-states. A heavy-handed rule was imposed on peasants, and Usuman himself retired into a life of religious contemplation. His successors appropriated traditional and political institutions for their own purposes, the revolution replacing one ruling class with another. This was neither the first nor the last example of Africans preying on other Africans as Europeans had long conquered other Europeans and Asians exploited fellow Asians.

Two other Islamic revolutions transformed sub-Saharan Africa on the eve of colonial rule. In 1818 Ahmadu bin Hammadi Boubou, a Fulani cleric who had studied under Usuman, led Muslims in the Macina region of the upper Niger River to wage war against their Bambara overlords. By 1827, his state reached the northern extremities of the Volta River in the south and Timbuktu in the north. Ahmadu ruled as the head of an intolerant theocracy over its five emirates. Beer, tobacco, and dancing were banned. Even foreigners were compelled to order their daily lives according to the dictates of the new government.

Naturally there was a reaction. In the 1850s al-hajj Umar, another clerical reformer who had studied with the descendants of Usuman, led a further revival along the upper reaches of the Niger River. His armies were victorious against the Bambara and against peoples to the west, in what is now Senegal. They even battled the French, who were approaching from the west. Toward the east, al-hajj Umar conquered Ahmadu's empire, proclaiming a holy war against it, although it had earlier been created by the same process. But these victories were short lived. Umar died soon after, and the French destroyed his state a decade later.

Usuman's revolution prevented the carving up of northern Nigeria. It also accustomed Africans to autocratic, large-scale rule and contributed to the economic growth of the region. When the German explorer Heinrich Barth traversed the area in mid-century, he marveled at the commercial activity, at the manufacturing, and at the general prosperity of the region.

## SEARCHING THE INTERIOR

The conquest of Africa began with the slave trade and the subsequent establishment of commodity exchange centers along the coasts. But for a long time these were no more than trading toeholds. Africans were reluctant to permit foreigners to venture inland for fear that they would steal commercial secrets. For many years, therefore, Europeans lacked reliable information about the African interior, and only a few intrepid merchants and soldiers ever ventured upcountry before the end of the 18th century. Then, as a byproduct of enlightenment in Europe and successful explorations in Asia and America, intellectuals and adventurers in Britain and on the Continent sought to cover their maps of Africa with actual rivers, towns, and peoples. Private individuals and geographical societies more than governments propelled this quest for the unknown. Without meaning to, however, they and the explorers who went out to Africa also paved the way for Africa's conquest.

The dramatic, epochal explorations of the continent gained public significance with the career of David Livingstone, a Scottish medical missionary, who wrote gracefully of his triumphs over misfortune in inner Africa and used his fame to demand the end of the Arabo-Swahili slave trade. In 1849, Livingstone guided a successful trek across the Kalahari desert from the south to Lake Ngami in modern Botswana. In 1851 he saw the mighty Zambezi River for the first time. He hoped that it might provide an easily accessible avenue into the unevangelized center of the continent. Obsessed for the rest of his life with the need to open up the continent to Western and Christian influence, he undertook three major journeys. Between 1853 and 1856, he accompanied a small group of Africans from the Zambezi to the Atlantic Coast of Angola, and then went back into the interior to walk to the Indian ocean coast of Mozambique. This was the first known foreign crossing of Africa's middle. Along the way, Livingstone found the magnificent falls that he named Victoria. On the second journey he reached Lake Malawi from the south and east and encouraged missionaries to follow. His third journey, from 1866 to 1873, propelled him from Zanzibar to Lake Tanganyika, then westward to the upper reaches of the Congo River, to Lake Mweru, and finally to Lake Bangweulu (modern Zambia), near which he died in 1873.

Livingstone's last search was for the sources of the Nile. Already, however, the British explorers Sir Richard Burton and John Hanning Speke had followed the tracks of African traders to Lake Tanganyika. Speke was told that Lake Victoria was the main source of the Nile. In 1862, after spending months in the capital of Buganda, Speke stood above a point where Lake Victoria cascaded down the White Nile on its long way to Cairo and Alexandria. Samuel White Baker, a Briton, and his Hungarian wife, added to Speke's knowledge in 1864 when they reached Lake Albert, thus confirming another link in the chain of Nile evidence. Some years before, two German missionaries stationed on the coast of East Africa had—to the astonishment of armchair geographers in Europe—reported that there were two snowcapped mountains, Kilimanjaro and Kenya, near the equator. They supposed, and Speke and Baker confirmed this, that waters from their upper reaches contributed to the torrent of the Nile.

## CARVING UP THE CONTINENT

The great explorations provided a prelude to the partitioning and exploitation of Africa. So did the activities of Roman Catholic and Protestant missionaries who intrepidly entered the interior in the wake of the explorers, reduced languages to writing, and then explained why and how Western influence would benefit Africa. The commerical interests were equally important, especially in western Africa in the 19th century where the early toeholds turned into enclaves ruled by Europeans with the cooperation of collaborating Africans. Minor wars led to the gradual, unanticipated growth of these outposts. In South Africa, too, animosity between English- and Afrikaans-speaking whites led to wars with Africans, the expansion of the frontier there, and the occupation by Europe of all of southern and central Africa. Everywhere the actions of a few commercial promoters were important. The most important was Cecil Rhodes, a young British entrepreneur, who gained control of the diamond mines of South Africa in the late

1880s, and used that wealth to occupy Zimbabwe, Zambia, and Malawi and to give Britain control over Botswana.

But above all it was the political rivalries of the new Europe which accelerated the decisive division of the continent. Throughout the late 19th century, France, Germany, and Britain each attempted to gain a competitive edge over the others by controlling sources of raw materials overseas (in East and South Asia, in the Pacific Islands, and so on). An unthinkable alternative, then, was a war in Europe to end competition. For 13 weeks in 1884–1885, the representatives of 14 European nations and the United States therefore considered the establishment of freedom of commerce in the basin and mouth of the Congo River, freedom of navigation on both the Congo and Niger rivers, and a definition of what constituted effective occupation of African territory.

Instead of curtailing occupation, the West African Conference in Berlin (more commonly called the Berlin Conference) created formal rules for a scramble for territory in tropical Africa that in time divided tribes indiscriminately, disrupted traditional patterns of migration, and resulted in the partition of tropical Africa into arbitrary, untidy colonial aggregates of heterogenous territories. Between 1880 and 1914, Europe systematically occupied Africa. (See Map 4.3.) Persuading Africans to sign treaties requesting protection, or using machine guns to silence opposition when treaties were disdained, Europeans systematically annexed one region after another and cynically determined among themselves where respective borders would lie. In some cases there were races between European emissaries or small armies to reach and gain control of a strategic place, such as a junction point on the Nile River or an area (like Katanga) that was rich in copper.

Because the Europeans had superior weapons and access to ammunition and other supplies, there was surprisingly little resistance. Most of all, Africans were rarely united, and many welcomed whites for the protection they would bring against more powerful Africans (like the Nguni of the diaspora). Nevertheless, there were bitter battles in opposition. The Ashanti resisted British conquest from the 1820s to 1902. The French had to overcome the armies of Ahmadu and Umar as well as those of a late-19th-century mercenary state created by Samori of Guinea. Along the coast opposite Zanzibar, Arabo-Swahili warriors kept the Germans away for two years in the late 1880s. Upcountry, Hehe warriors were subdued only after long, costly battles. In South Africa the Zulu defeated the British and the Afrikaners twice before being humbled by bigger and better guns. In Zimbabwe the Ndebele fought against the end of their power. There were innumerable rearguard

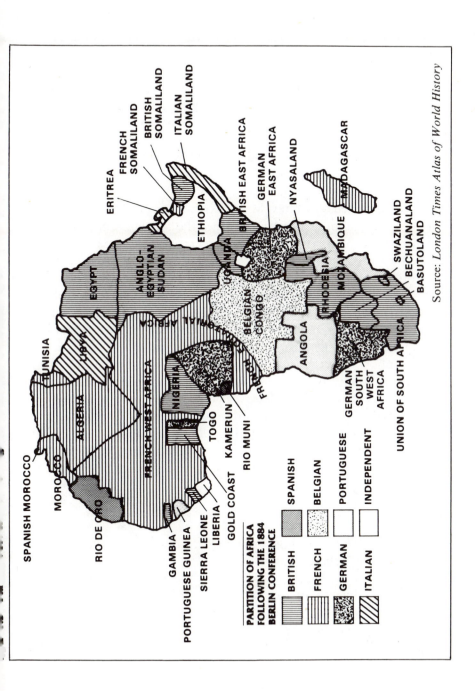

PARTITION OF AFRICA
FOLLOWING THE 1884
BERLIN CONFERENCE

BRITISH
FRENCH
GERMAN
ITALIAN
SPANISH
BELGIAN
PORTUGUESE
INDEPENDENT

SPANISH MOROCCO
MOROCCO
RIO DE ORO
GAMBIA
PORTUGUESE GUINEA
SIERRA LEONE
LIBERIA
GOLD COAST
TOGO
KAMERUN
RIO MUNI
NIGERIA
FRENCH WEST AFRICA
TUNISIA
LIBYA
ALGERIA
EGYPT
ANGLO-EGYPTIAN SUDAN
ERITREA
FRENCH SOMALILAND
BRITISH SOMALILAND
ITALIAN SOMALILAND
ETHIOPIA
UGANDA
BRITISH EAST AFRICA
GERMAN EAST AFRICA
NYASALAND
MADAGASCAR
BELGIAN CONGO
ANGOLA
RHODESIA
MOZAMBIQUE
SWAZILAND
BECHUANALAND
BASUTOLAND
GERMAN SOUTH WEST AFRICA
UNION OF SOUTH AFRICA

Source: *London Times Atlas of World History*

119

actions, too, where isolated clans burned European camps and attacked their soldiers for years before finally being worn down. In Ethiopia, however, King Menelik was able in 1896, at Adwa near the capital of much earlier Aksum, to oust a large army of invading Italians. In his case he had sufficient guns of European manufacture and a large, well-trained army. His intelligence was better informed, too. As a result Ethiopia remained undominated by outsiders until 1936, when the Italians revenged their previous defeat and governed the empire until 1941.

By 1900 in many places, and certainly by 1914, it was clear to the peoples of Africa that their white rulers had come to stay. A new generation grew up that had never known any life other than that ultimately directed by whites. Many Africans, in fact, adapted easily: Africans in the administrative age learned the languages, customs, and organizational requirements of their rulers. They studied in schools staffed by white missionaries, worked for white administrators, farmers, and traders, and attended to the household needs of white families. They were bound to rely for advancement upon the patronage of the colonists rather than traditional societies. For the most part whites encouraged these responses; but they generally discouraged assimilation and, instead, concentrated upon the administration rather than the tutelage of the Western colonies. They also tried to develop their colonies economically, at least by furthering the extraction of minerals and tropical crops. Nevertheless, the colonial approach remained for much of its duration essentially static and divorced from the social and economic changes taking place in the respective mother countries. It defined the context within which Africans lived and labored. Nevertheless, it molded decisively their aspirations for change and modernization.

---

## Reading 4.1

Alexander Falconbridge was a physician, serving in the late 18th century on British slave ships plying the West African coast and taking their captives to the West Indies. He later became an opponent of the slave trade, and wrote an account of its horrors.

---

## Alexander Falconbridge, *Account of the Slave Trade on the Coast of Africa*

After permission has been obtained for *breaking trade*, as it is termed, the captains go ashore, from time to time, to examine the negroes that are exposed to sale and to make their purchases. The slaves are bought by the black traders at fairs, which are held for that purpose, at the distance of upwards of two hundred miles from the sea coast; and these fairs are said to be supplied from an interior part of the country. Many negroes, upon being questioned relative to the places of their nativity, have asserted that they have travelled during the revolution of several moons (their usual method of calculating time) before they have reached the places where they were purchased by the black traders. At these fairs, which are held at uncertain periods, but generally every six weeks, several thousands are frequently exposed to sale who had been collected from all parts of the country for a very considerable distance round. During one of my voyages, the black traders brought down, in different canoes, from twelve to fifteen hundred negroes which had been purchased at one fair. They consisted chiefly of men and boys, the women seldom exceeding a third of the whole number. From forty to two hundred negroes are generally purchased at a time by the black traders, according to the opulence of the buyer, and consist of all ages, from a month to sixty years and upwards. Scarcely any age or situation is deemed an exception, the price being proportionable. Women sometimes form a part of them, who happen to be so far advanced in their pregnancy as to be delivered during their journey from the fairs to the coast; and I have frequently seen instances of deliveries on board ship....

As soon as the wretched negroes fall into the hands of the black traders, they experience an earnest of the sufferings which they are doomed in future to undergo. And there is not the least doubt that even before they can reach the fairs, great numbers perish from cruel usage. They are brought from the places where they are purchased, to Bonny, &c., in canoes, at the bottom of which they lie, having their hands tied with a kind of willow twigs and a strict watch is kept over them. Their usage in other respects, during the time of the passage, which generally lasts several days, is equally cruel. Their allowance of food is so scanty that it is barely sufficient to support nature and they are also much exposed to the violent rains which frequently fall, being covered only with mats that afford but a slight defence; and as there is usually water in the bottom of the canoes they are scarcely ever dry....

And after they become the property of Europeans their treatment is no less severe. The men, on being brought aboard ship, are immediately fastened together, two and two, by handcuffs on their wrists and by irons rivetted on their legs. They are then sent down between the decks and placed in a space partitioned off for that purpose. The women also are placed in a separate space between decks, but without being ironed. An adjoining room, on the same deck, is set apart for the boys.

At the same time, however, they are frequently stowed so close as to admit of no other position than lying on their sides. Nor will the height between decks, unless directly under the grating, allow them to stand; especially where there are platforms on either side, which is generally the case.

*   *   *

The diet of the negroes while on board, consists chiefly of horse-beans boiled to the consistence of a pulp; of boiled yams and rice and sometimes of a small quantity of beef or pork. The latter are frequently taken from the provisions laid in for the sailors. They sometimes make use of a sauce composed of palm-oil mixed with flour, water and pepper, which the sailors call *slabber-sauce*. Yams are the favorite food of the Eboe or Bight negroes, and rice or corn of those from the Gold and Windward Coasts; each preferring the produce of their native soil.

In their own country the negroes in general live on animal food and fish, with roots, yams and Indian corn. The horse-beans and rice, with which they are fed aboard ship, are chiefly brought from Europe.

\* \* \*

Upon the negroes refusing to take food, I have seen coals of fire, glowing hot, put on a shovel and placed so near their lips as to scorch and burn them. And this has been accompanied with threats of forcing them to swallow the coals if they persisted in refusing to eat. This generally had the desired effect. I have also been credibly informed that a certain captain in the slave-trade, poured melted lead on such of his negroes as obstinately refused their food.

Exercise being considered necessary for the preservation of their health they are sometimes obliged to dance when the weather will permit their coming on deck. If they go about it reluctantly or do not move with agility, they are flogged; a person standing by them all the time with a cat-o'-nine-tails in his hand for that purpose. Their music, upon these occasions, consists of a drum, sometimes with only one head; and when that is worn out they make use of the bottom of one of the tubs before described. The poor wretches are frequently compelled to sing also; but when they do so, their songs are generally, as may naturally be expected, melancholy lamentations of their exile from their native country.

\* \* \*

A certain Liverpool ship once took on board at Bonny, at least seven hundred negroes. By shipping so large a number, the slaves were so crowded that they were obliged to lie one upon another. This occasioned such a mortality among them that without meeting with unusual bad weather or having a longer voyage than common, nearly one half of them died before the ship arrived in the West Indies.

That it may be possible to form some idea of the almost incredible small space into which so large a number of negroes were crammed, the following particulars of this ship are given. According to Liverpool custom she measured 235 tons. Her width across the beam was 25 feet. Length between the decks, 92 feet, which was divided into four rooms, thus:

| | |
|---|---|
| Store room, in which no negroes were placed | 15 feet |
| | |
| Negroe's rooms—men's rooms—about | 45 feet |
| women's ditto—about | 10 feet |
| boy's ditto—about | 22 feet |
| | |
| Total room for negroes | 77 feet |

---

## Reading 4.2

Heinrich Barth, a perceptive, learned German geographer, visited the lands of the Sahel in the middle years of the 19th century. This portion of the report of his explorations discusses the agricultural and economic promise of northern Nigeria, particularly Kano.

---

## Heinrich Barth, *Travels and Discoveries in North and Central Africa...1849–1855*

The great advantage of Kanó is, that commerce and manufactures go hand in hand, and that almost every family has its share in them. There is really something grand in this kind of industry, which spreads to the north as far as Múrzuk, Ghát, and even Tripoli; to the west, not only to Timbúktu, but in some degree even as far as the shores of the Atlantic, the very inhabitants of Arguin dressing in the cloth woven and dyed in Kanó; to the east, all over Bórnu, although there it comes in contact with the native industry of the country; and to the south it maintains a rivalry with the native industry of the I'gbira and I'gbo, while toward the southeast it invades the whole of 'Adamáwa, and is only limited by the nakedness of the pagan *sans-culottes,* who do not wear clothing.

\*   \*   \*

The chief articles of native industry, besides cloth, which have a wide market, are principally sandals. The sandals are made with great neatness, and, like the cloth, are exported to an immense distance; but, being a cheap article (the very best, which are called "táka-sárakí," fetching only 200 kurdí), they bear, of course, no comparison in importance with the former. I estimate this branch at ten millions. It is very curious that the shoes made here by Arab shoemakers, of Sudán leather, and called "bélgh'a," are exported in great quantities to North Africa. The "nesísa," or twisted leather strap, is a celebrated article of Kanó manufacture, and "jebíras," richly ornamented ... are made by Arab workmen.

* * *

Besides these manufactures, the chief article of African produce in the Kanó market is the "gúro," or kola-nut; but while, on the one hand, it forms an important article of transit, and brings considerable profit, on the other, large sums are expended by the natives upon this luxury, which has become to them as necessary as coffee or tea to us.... The import of this nut into Kanó, comprising certainly more than five hundred ass-loads every year, the load of each, if safely brought to the market—for it is a very delicate article, and very liable to spoil—being sold for about 200,000 kurdí, will amount to an average of from eighty to one hundred millions. Of this sum, I think we shall be correct in asserting about half to be paid for by the natives of the province, while the other half will be profit.

* * *

A very important branch of the native commerce in Kanó is certainly the slave-trade; but it is extremely difficult to say how many of these unfortunate creatures are exported, as a greater number are carried away by small caravans to Bórnu and Núpe than on the direct road to Ghát and Fezzán. Altogether, I do not think that the number of slaves annually exported from Kanó exceeds* 5000; but, of course, a considerable number are sold into domestic slavery, either to the inhabitants of the province itself or to those of the adjoining districts. The value of this trade, of which only a small percentage falls to the profit of the Kanáwa, besides the tax which is levied in the market, may altogether amount to from a hundred and fifty to two hundred millions of kurdí per annum.

Another important branch of the commerce of Kanó is the transit of natron from Bórnu to Núpe or Nýffi, which here always passes into other hands, and in so doing leaves a considerable profit in the place. The merchandise is very cheap, but the quantity is great, and it employs a great many persons, as I shall have ample occasion to illustrate in the course of my proceedings. Twenty thousand loads, at the very least, between pack-oxen, sumpter-horses, and asses, of natron must annually pass through the market of Kanó, which, at 500 kurdí per load, merely for passage-money, would give 10,000,000 kurdí.

I here also mention the salt-trade, which is entirely an import one, the salt being almost all consumed in the province. Of the three thousand camel-loads of salt, which I have above computed as comprising the aïri with which I

---

*This trade will now be greatly affected by the abolition of the slave-trade in Tripoli.

reached Kátsena, we may suppose one third to be sold in the province of Kanó, and therefore that hereby a value of from fifty to eighty millions annually is drained from the country. But we must not forget that the money which is paid for this requisite (and not only for that consumed in Kanó, but also in other provinces) is entirely laid out by the sellers in buying the produce of Kanó, viz., cloth and corn. Here, therefore, is an absolute balance—a real exchange of necessaries and wants.

\* \* \*

The principal European goods brought to the market of Kanó are bleached and unbleached calicoes, and cotton prints from Manchester; French silks and sugar; red cloth from Saxony and other parts of Europe; beads from Venice and Trieste; a very coarse kind of silk from Trieste; common paper with the sign of three moons, looking-glasses, needles, and small ware, from Nuremberg; sword-blades from Solingen; razors from Styria. It is very remarkable that so little English merchandise is seen in this great emporium of Negroland, which lies so near to the two branches of "the Great River" of Western Africa, calico and muslins (or tanjips, as they are called by the merchants) being almost the only English articles. Calico certainly is not the thing most wanted in a country where home-made cloth is produced at so cheap a rate, and of so excellent a quality; indeed, the unbleached calico has a very poor chance in Kanó, while the bleached calico and the cambric attract the wealthier people on account of their nobler appearance. In Timbúktu, on the contrary, where the native cloth is dearer, unbleached calico is in request; and it would be so in an extraordinary degree if it were dyed dark blue. It is very interesting to observe that a small proportion of the calico imported into Kanó is again exported, after having been dyed, returning even the long way to Ghadámes. I estimate the whole amount of Manchester goods imported into Kanó at about forty millions, but it may be somewhat more.

\* \* \*

Of sugar, I think about one hundred camel-loads are imported every year, each containing eighty small loaves of two and a half pounds each, which are sold in general at 1500 kurdí, so that the import of this article would amount to about twelve millions. It is very remarkable that in all Central Negroland the large English sugarloaf is scarcely ever seen, while it is the only one seen in Timbúktu. However, I was greatly surprised when, on my return from that place in 1854, 'Aliyu, the Emír el Mumenín of Sókoto, presented to me an English loaf of sugar; and I heard that he had received several of them as presents from a merchant of Tawát. The small loaf has certainly a great advantage in such a country, where money is scarce; and I found in 1854 that its weight had even been reduced to two pounds.

*Reading 4.3*

George Simeon Mwase was an African clerk, storekeeper, and indigenous politician in Nyasaland (Malawi) during the early colonial period. In his own idiom he wrote a controversial but authentic account of Chilembwe's rebellion. To it he added reflections on white rule, including this brief discussion of white attitudes. Mwase called his manuscript "A Dialogue of Nyasaland Record of Past Events, Environments and the Present Outlook within the Protectorate." He completed the manuscript about 1932.

## George S. Mwase, *Strike a Blow and Die: A Narrative of Race Relations in Colonial Africa* (Robert I. Rotberg, ed.)

In those days, if a native had complaint against a whiteman, the whiteman was not to be called up to answer the charge, or the suit against him in Court, but only a letter was written to him, and whatever he will reply, that was to be relied upon, and the native was to be judged upon that reply. Often times natives complained of being beaten by whiteman to the Boma (i.e., *complained to the Boma*) but all without satisfactory results. The only conclusion received was that whiteman cannot beat you without offending him (without your having offended him). I know you have offended him; "Choka" (scram!). In those days a whiteman could administer whipping and flogging at his house, or Estate, [and] the Government never interfered or warn him of his actions. I cannot say whether this was out of their view or hearing. For this reason a native feared the whiteman as he fears the polegoblins (?) of heaven. Surely he did not believe there will be a sign of [better] relationship in the future. Often times, [Africans] feared when their master a whiteman has given them a letter to the Boma, if that letter, after addressing it, it had a straight line like this——— at the bottom of the envelope. If they were two they talked to each other, "see, the whiteman has put 'Chikoti' (a whip) on this letter, so we are going to be flogged." Some other times, they did not deliver such letters, they were to throw or torn [it] even to burn it on a fire. That was through fear of being beaten at the Boma or by any whiteman where that letter was to go. Why they did this? Because they saw a lot of their men being beaten just after the letter was delivered to the Boma or to the whiteman concerned.

Native, sometimes, was to work about two to three months without paying him (being paid). When complaining why they should not be paid, the whiteman said "Choka, ngati ufuna ku Boma pita" (bearing the interpretation as go away, if you want to go to the Boma go); and if the native will insist on that, he is to be beaten severely, and afterwards send him to Boma with a letter, in which he (the planter) has had to write that this boy gave me insolence, and such like. There also he would write anything which has made that whiteman not to pay the native, which the whiteman had thought to be important, and for which the Boma would think serious against the native. As the system was to rely on a letter, the native then had to lose his two or three months' pay.

[There were] Many other things, which looked favourable to a whiteman and contrary to the native. This was Law market, as that slave market. The think (I thank) the Blue skies, that such Law market is dispensed. I hope will not be seen again.

I have again asked, if the country has won something extraordinary since then? Yes, the country is far enjoying its quarter betterments tho' not half yet [has been achieved.] Of course, the child born you cannot expect it to walk and run by the very [first] week or month. It grows gradually, until it will reach its height. The country has indeed won the best Government, best measures of ruling and even won the Government of no respect of colour. No letter is now used as evidence against a native, does not matter what value is the person who has written if anyone is to lose the case through lack of evidence. "Chapeau bas" system is entirely diminished and vanished. No native fear the town when he has his hat on, [although] this was a very big offence in the days of Chilembwe. Native were often and often beaten for this respect, their complaints were not listened to. This grew worse indeed. The native knew not what to do, in a way of defending his head from the heat of the sun, when passing the whiteman's town.

---

## Reading 4.4

André Gide, the French novelist and critic, visited French Equatorial Africa in the 1920s. By car, by rail, and on foot, Gide explored the French Congo, Gabon, Cameroon, Chad, and what is now the Central African Republic. In the upcountry areas of the Congo he discovered that French rubber concessionaires had instituted a system of forced labor that was akin to slavery. Gide's book and the publicity that followed helped bring this particular form of exploitation to an end. The excerpts are from the English translation by Dorothy Bussy.

---

## André Gide, *Travels in the Congo*

We went to bed early and were both fast asleep under our mosquito-nets in the post hut when, at about two o'clock in the morning, a noise of steps and voices woke us up. Someone wanted to come in. We called out in Sango: "*Zo niè?* (Who is there?)" It was a native chief of some importance, who had called before that same evening while we were at dinner, but, being afraid of disturbing us, he had put off the interview he wished to have until the next morning; in the mean time a messenger, sent after him by Pacha, the administrator of Boda, had just arrived with orders that he should return at once to his village. He was obliged to obey. But in despair at seeing his last chance of speaking to us vanish, he had made so bold as to wake us up at this impossible hour. He talked with extreme volubility in a language of which we understood not a single word. We begged him to let us sleep. He could come back later when we should have an interpreter. We promised to take the responsibility of the delay on ourselves and to shield him from the terrible Pacha. Why should this latter be so anxious to prevent the chief Samba N'Goto from giving us his message? We easily understood the reason when next morning, with Mobaye acting as interpreter, we learnt the following circumstances from Samba N'Goto.

On October 21 last (six days ago, that is) Sergeant Yemba was sent by the administrator of Boda to Bodembéré in order to execute reprisals on the inhabitants of this village (between Boda and N'Goto), who had refused to obey the order to move their settlement on to the Carnot road. They pleaded that they were anxious not to abandon their plantations and urged besides that the people established on the Carnot road are Bayas, while they are Bofis.

Sergeant Yemba therefore left Boda with three guards (whose names we carefully noted). This small detachment was accompanied by the capita Baoué, and two men under his command. On the road, Sergeant Yemba requisitioned two or three men from each of the villages they passed through, and after having put them in chains, took them along with the party. When they arrived at Bodempéré, the reprisals began; twelve men were seized and tied up to trees, while the chief of the village, a man called Cobelé, took flight. Sergeant Yemba and the guard Bonjo then shot and killed the twelve men who had been tied up. Then followed a great massacre of women, whom Yemba struck down with a matchet; after which he seized five young children, shut them up in a hut, and set fire to it. In all, said Samba N'Goto, there were thirty-two victims.

We must add to this number the capita of M'Biri, who had fled from his village (Boubakara, near N'Goto) and whom Yemba came upon at Bossué, the first village north of N'Goto.

We also learnt that Samba N'Goto was returning to Boda, where he lives, and had nearly reached it when on the road he met Governor Lamblin's car, which was taking us to N'Goto. At this he turned back, thinking that it contained the governor himself and anxious to appeal to him in person. He must have walked very quickly, as he arrived at N'Goto a very short time after us....

\* \* \*

We were so much upset by Samba N'Goto's deposition and by Garron's tales that when, in the forest, we came across a group of women who were mending the road, we had no heart even to smile at them. These poor creatures, more like cattle than human beings, were in the streaming rain, a number of them with babies at the breast. Every twenty yards or so there were huge pits by the side of the road, generally about ten feet deep; it was out of these that the poor wretches had dug the sandy earth with which to bank the road, and this *without proper tools*. It has happened more than once that the loose earth has given way and buried the women and children who were working at the bottom of the pit....

As they usually work too far from their village to return at night, the poor women have built themselves temporary huts in the forest, wretched shelters of branches and reeds, useless against the rain. We heard that the native soldier who is their overseer had made them work all night in order to repair the damage done by a recent storm and to enable us to pass.

* * *

*29 October*

This morning I went to see one of the native chiefs who came to meet us yesterday. This evening he returned my visit. We had a long conversation. Adoum, sitting on the ground between the chief and me, acted as interpreter.

The information of the Bambio chief confirms everything that I heard from Samba N'Goto. In particular, he gave me an account of "the ball" last market day at Boda. I here transcribe the story as I copied it from Garron's private diary.

"At Bambio, on September 8, ten rubber-gatherers... belonging to the Goundi gang, who work for the Compagnie Forestière—because they had not brought in any rubber the month before (but this month they brought in double, from 40 to 50 kilogrammes)—were condemned to go round and round the factory under a fierce sun, carrying very heavy wooden beams. If they fell down, they were forced up by guards flogging them with whips.

"The 'ball' began at eight o'clock and lasted the whole day, with Messrs. Pacha and Maudurier, the company's agent, looking on. At about eleven o'clock a man from Bagouma, called Malongué, fell to get up no more. When M. Pacha was informed of this, he merely replied: *'Je m'en f—'* and ordered the 'ball' to go on. All this took place in the presence of the assembled inhabitants of Bambio and of all the chiefs who had come from the neighbouring villages to attend the market."

The chief spoke to us also of the conditions reigning in the Boda prison; of the wretched plight of the natives and of how they are fleeing to some less accursed country. My indignation against Pacha is naturally great, but the Compagnie Forestière plays a part in all this, which seems to be very much graver, though more secret. For, after all, it—its representatives, I mean—knew everything that was going on. It (or its agents) profited by this state of things. Its agents approved Pacha, encouraged him, were his partners. It was at their request that Pacha arbitrarily threw into prison the natives who did nqt furnish enough stuff; etc....

As I am anxious to make a good job of my letter to the governor, I have decided to put off leaving here till the day after tomorrow. The short time I have passed in French Equatorial Africa has already put me on my guard against "authentic accounts," exaggerations and deformations of the smallest facts. I am terribly afraid, however, that this scene of the "ball" was nothing exceptional, if the stories of several eyewitnesses, whom I questioned one after the other, are to be believed. The terror Pacha inspires makes them implore me not to name them. No doubt they will withdraw everything later on and deny that they ever saw anything. When a Governor goes on tour, his subordinates usually present reports containing the facts they think most likely to please him. Those that I have to place before him are of a kind, I fear, that may never come to his notice, and the voices that might inform him of them will be carefully stifled. A simple tourist like myself may, I feel sure, often hear and see things which never reach a person in his high position.

When I accepted this mission, I failed to grasp at first what it was I was undertaking, what part I could play, how I could be useful. I understand it now and I am beginning to think that my coming will not have been in vain.

During my stay in the colony I have come to realize how terribly the problems which I have to solve are interwoven one with the other. Far be it from me to raise my voice on points which are not within my competence and which necessitate a prolonged study. But this is a matter of certain definite facts, completely independent of questions of a general order. Perhaps the *chef de circonscription* has been already informed of them. From what the natives tell me, he seems to be ignorant of them. The circumscription is too vast; a single man who is without the means of rapid transport is unable to keep his eye on the whole of it. One is here, as everywhere else in French Equatorial Africa, brought up against those two terrible impediments: want of sufficient staff; want of sufficient money.

\*    \*    \*

*30 October*

Impossible to sleep. The Bambio "ball" haunted my night. I cannot content myself with saying, as so many do, that the natives were still more wretched before the French occupation. We have shouldered responsibilities regarding them which we have no right to evade. The immense pity of what I have seen has taken possession of me; I know things to which I cannot reconcile myself. What demon drove me to Africa? What did I come out to find in this country? I was at peace. I know now. I must speak.

But how can I get people to listen? Hitherto I have always spoken without the least care whether I was heard or not; always written for tomorrow, with the single desire of lasting. Now I envy the journalist, whose voice carries at once, even if it perishes immediately after. Have I been walking hitherto between high walls of falsehood? I must get behind them, out on to the other side, and learn what it is they are put to hide, even if the truth is horrible. The horrible truth that I suspect is what I must see.

\* \* \*

Some chiefs came out to meet us with two tamtams, carried by children. There are two considerable "Bakongo" villages here. ("Bakongo" is the name given indiscriminately to all natives who work for the Forestière.) And near by is a tiny little village called N'Délé, which is at present inhabited by only five sound men (and they are away collecting rubber in the forest), and five invalids, who look after the plantations. Needless to say, these men in the forest, who are under no supervision, work as little as possible at a task that is so little paid. Hence the punishments with which the representatives of the Forestière try to recall them to a sense of their *duty*.

Long conversation with the two chiefs of the Bakongo village. But the one who was at first talking to us alone, stopped as soon as the other came up. He would not say another word; and nothing could be more harrowing than his silence and his fear of compromising himself when we questioned him about the Boda prison, where he has himself been confined. When he was again alone with us later on, he told us that he had seen ten men die in it in a single day, as a result of ill treatment. He himself bears the marks of flogging and showed us his scars....

He spoke of the fines that the Compagnie Forestière are in the habit of inflicting on the natives who fail to bring in sufficient quantities of rubber—fines of forty francs—that is to say, the whole of one month's pay. He added that when the wretched man has not enough to pay the fine, he can only escape being thrown into prison by borrowing from someone better off than himself, if he can find such a person—and then he is sometimes thrown into prison "into the bargain." Terror reigns and the surrounding villages are deserted. We talked to other chiefs. When they are asked: "How many men in your village?" they count them by putting down a finger for each one. There are rarely more than ten. Adoum acts as interpreter.

---

## Reading 4.5

Jomo Kenyatta became Kenya's first president in 1963. In the early 1950s after the outbreak of the Mau Mau uprising against British rule, Kenyatta was detained. He spent the years until 1961 under arrest in a remote part of the country. Many years before, in 1938, after studying anthropology at the London School of Economics, he wrote *Facing Mount Kenya.* The following critique of colonial rule is taken from his conclusion.

## Jomo Kenyatta, *Facing Mount Kenya*

There certainly are some progressive ideas among the Europeans. They include the ideas of material prosperity, of medicine, and hygiene, and literacy which enables people to take part in world culture. But so far the Europeans who visit Africa have not been conspicuously zealous in imparting these parts of their inheritance to the Africans, and seem to think that the only way to do it is by police discipline and armed force. They speak as if it was somehow beneficial to an African to work for them instead of for himself, and to make sure that he will receive this benefit they do their best to take away his land and leave him with no alternative. Along with his land they rob him of his government, condemn his religious ideas, and ignore his fundamental conceptions of justice and morals, all in the name of civilisation and progress.

If Africans were left in peace on their own lands, Europeans would have to offer them the benefits of white civilisation in real earnest before they could obtain the African labour which they want so much. They would have to offer the African a way of life which was really superior to the one his fathers lived before him, and a share in the prosperity given them by their command of science. They would have to let the African choose what parts of European culture could be beneficially transplanted, and how they could be adapted. He would probably not choose the gas bomb or the armed police force, but he might ask for some other things of which he does not get so much to-day. As it is, by driving him off his ancestral lands, the Europeans have robbed him of the material foundations of his culture, and reduced him to a state of serfdom incompatible with human happiness. The African is conditioned, by the cultural and social institutions of centuries, to a freedom of which Europe has little conception, and it is not in his nature to accept serfdom for ever. He realises that he must fight unceasingly for his own complete emancipation; for without this he is doomed to remain the prey of rival imperialisms, which in every successive year will drive their fangs more deeply into his vitality and strength.

## 5

# NEW CONFLICTS

Pearl T. Robinson

During the colonial period in Africa, Western and traditional African political systems were juxtaposed. In this chapter, Professor Robinson describes some of the key concepts in traditional African political systems and discusses how they converged or came into conflict both with colonial and post-colonial forms of governance. Particular attention is given in this chapter to the role of women in African political systems. **Eds.**

Islam, Christianity, and colonial rule brought new conflicts to African societies. Although earlier times were far from idyllic, in the past Africans traditionally had had numerous means of dealing with sociopolitical conflict. Because the changing realities of power have blurred the lines of authority, today we find that struggles over who is in charge and what ought to be done can erupt in communal violence or provoke a national crisis. Religious divisions, especially those based on Islam and Christianity, are increasingly a focus of social tensions and a vulnerability for those in power. Most present-day conflicts, however, stem from the difficulty of state building, a process which is complicated by the competing claims of authority and new forms of stratification introduced under European hegemony.

Although pre-colonial political patterns continue to influence behavior, current developments result from the convergence of Islamic and Western institutions with the indigenous African heritage. The continent's political traditions run the gamut from government without states to states without fixed territorial boundaries. Within those broad parameters there were many different kinds of authoritative rule. Since Africa has only recently adopted the Western state model, indigenous authority structures remain the focus of important political loyalties. These institutions, which formerly compelled people to obey the same rules and accept a common authority, are among the building blocks of politics today. For this reason it is necessary to look at the foundations of indigenous systems as we examine the structures of political conflict in Africa and their transformation over time. African polities were typically organized on the basis of lineage, or individuals who claim descent from a common ancestor; age-groups, or persons born within specified time intervals; separate spheres of authority for men and women; and kingship.

## LINEAGE

Lineage functions as a basic element of social organization throughout Africa. Lineage is defined as a group of persons who, depending on their cultural background, trace a common ancestry through either male or female descent and can actually establish their kinship. It is possible for strangers who meet special criteria to be absorbed into a lineage and given a fictitious relationship to the group. What is important is the notion of kinship. Lineages have corporate responsibilities, duties, and rights. They oversee marriages, regulate the use of property and access to land, share certain liabilities incurred individually, and may assume collective injury if one of their members is harmed. By the same token, the lineage can make certain claims on the material possessions of its members, even if such assets have been acquired without its evident support.

Responsibility falls to the lineage heads to maintain order among their kin. Traditionally what this involved varied widely depending on the complexity of social organization. In relatively egalitarian situations, lineage heads occasionally took on representative roles in councils of their peers to coordinate the activities of related lineages or lineage segments. Such councils might also be mobilized in the event of conflict with outsiders, especially when no overarching state authority systems existed. In hierarchical societies the rulers belonged to separate noble lineages, and stratification was maintained with administrative, caste-like, and servile corporate groups.

Because the lineage is internally divided into smaller kinship segments and creates a bond of solidarity among people who may be widely dispersed, it is an institution that has proved well-suited for a variety of political purposes. For those who wish to consolidate power, lineage facilitates both the proliferation of coalitions based on kinship and recourse to long-distance networks of patronage and support. In the case of personal rivalries or intragroup competition, lineage segments may break apart and form the structure for organizing factions or cliques. Even with the eclipse of autonomous traditional polities, the authoritative control of lineage continues to influence African political life.

## AGE COHORTS

A very different outcome reflects the political influence of social groupings based on age. Institutionalized generational stratification is widespread in Africa and has been associated with most models of indigenous political systems. These age-grades or age-classes are established through initiation rituals associated with puberty. Boys and girls who are roughly contemporary submit to rites of passage in separate ceremonies which transmit their society's cultural history along with the duties and responsibilities of adulthood. The initiates are consolidated into age-grades, which exist throughout the members' lives. The effect of these procedures is to stratify the adult population into an age hierarchy with corresponding social responsibilities and duties.

In indigenous African polities which developed into centralized states, age-grades provided a framework for social solidarity distinct from the lineage or extended family. Mutual aid, communal labor, and cooperative agricultural activities could all be accomplished through this system. Age-grades also were important mechanisms for the maintenance of social order. For other societies which traditionally functioned without chiefs or a supreme ruler, the system of age classes sometimes served as the basic structure of government. In these cases, such categories as young singles, recently married, warriors, and elders took on special political significance. The elders, for example, usually managed public affairs, kept the peace, served as judges, and looked after community welfare. The warriors had specific responsibilities related to raiding expeditions and the execution of war. Different strata within the warrior and elder classes might be given the right to proclaim and enforce rules. Whatever the particular variations from one culture to the next, a basic premise of age-grade systems was the duty to respect one's elders. Age led, while youth followed. A person's respect and authority increased as a function of age.

Esteem for the elders remains a prominent feature of African social life, even though its political importance waned with the arrival of the Europeans. Youth educated in colonial schools acquired skills unknown to their ancestors. Those who were employed in the administrative or commercial sector earned a cash income that elevated their status in the money economy. In the new urban centers, with modern pressures and demands, the prestige of age could not speak with an authoritative political voice. This trend has been accelerated in today's urban-based states.

## WOMEN IN AUTHORITY

A third system of organization common to many African societies defines separate spheres of authority based on sexual identity. Under the sexist bias of the Western world, men predominate in all key political roles. In a number of African systems, however, each sex managed its own affairs, ensuring that women and their interests were represented at all levels.

Though not ubiquitous, these dual-sex political systems have functioned both in segmentary and in highly centralized African polities. Under the rules of these systems, each sex has its own kinship institutions, age-grades, and titles. Men and women are members of councils which may enact laws and settle disputes in their respective jurisdictions. For example, in a society where marketing is the woman's affair, the women's council would oversee marketing. In the case of a dual-sex monarchy, two rulers are enthroned, and they live in separate palaces. The male may be acknowledged as the head of the community as a whole and the female charged with special concern for women's affairs, but the entire population pays homage to both monarchs.

Dual-sex systems institutionalized the parallel exercise of power by women and men. By mandating social structures with certain high-status positions slated for females, these systems assured that African women were included among the ranks of monarchs, councilors, title holders, religious dignitaries, political advisors, and lineage heads. Women leaders participated in the running of public affairs, acted as political pressure groups, interceded with the supernatural on the community's behalf, and shouldered significant responsibility for the general welfare.

The diminished status of women in Africa today is attributable to many factors, but a good deal of the blame lies with the anti-feminist bias of Western institutions. During the colonial period, traditional chiefs who were incorporated into local administrative structures reaped material rewards in the form of salaries, a percentage of tax receipts, and substantial revenues from cash crops. Because official recognition was only accorded to male chiefs, many of the female authority figures fell behind in the new money economy. This preference for transferring resources to men also meant that women were rarely provided the means to grow cash crops or to benefit from agricultural extension services. With independence, Western aid donors have continued to slight women by directing the most lucrative development assistance primarily toward men. Thus it should come as no surprise that the realm of women's authority is less strategic at present than in the past.

## KINGSHIP

To say that Africa's male traditional rulers fared better than their female counterparts does not mean that kings have retained their former glory. Indeed, colonial conquest suppressed indigenous sovereigns, and they will not be restored by the new national states. In the exceptional case of Ethiopia, which never experienced full-fledged colonial rule, the emperor assured his own demise. Nevertheless, kingship remains a powerful legacy even today.

Pre-colonial African states had no fixed territorial borders. Heading such systems were hereditary kings or chiefs imbued with both secular and sacred authority who functioned as supreme rulers. These sovereigns claimed superiority because of conquest, a special relationship with the supernatural, or descent from the original occupants of the land. They could levy taxes, wage war, try cases, punish disobedience, regulate trade, and issue public commands. Their directives were carried out with the aid of administrative officials and supportive networks of district rulers and village headmen. In the more bureaucratic states, certain powers were delegated, but the main activity remained with the king at his court.

Although kingship signified centralized political authority, constitutional checks and dual-sex authority arrangements guarded against unlimited power. Governance usually involved a council of notables, and in the case of a dual-sex monarchy, authority was divided into male and female domains. Possible contenders to the throne often sought to expose abuses of power if for no other reason than to advance their own political fortunes. Even the circumscribed authority of title holders and age-grade associations was used to restrain autocratic tendencies. And most states had procedures for removing unsuitable rulers.

With the arrival of Western colonialism, these African systems of kingship collapsed. The incorporation of traditional rulers and institutions into colonial administrations strengthened those individuals who were able to use the new situation to their advantage. But the old kingdoms no longer exist. Their most important legacy today is political. What remains is the seductive precedent of a system of governance which enabled the person at the top to implement directives and influence decisions down to the grass roots level. Many of the politicians and soldiers who present rule Africa consider the practice of statecraft to be a modern form of kingship. As Ali Mazrui has noted, the monarchical tendency is a distinctive feature of African political culture. (Mazrui, 1966:14–16)

## COMMUNAL CONFLICT

Years before the dawn of independence, Westernization, urbanization, and imperialism expanded the scope of African politics. With the spread of capitalism and its attendant social changes, subsistence farmers, nomadic herders, market women, and religious clerics developed economic interests linked to the colonial state. Today, everything from language policy to adherence to the Sharia can be mandated by the new national state. Politics determines who will get loans to buy tractors or plows, what criteria will affect career mobility in the bureaucracy, and how funds will be allocated for building schools, wells, and roads. The conflicts engendered in the wake of these developments have fostered competitive structures organized around communal loyalties.

Communalism refers to identity based on race, ethnicity, religion, language, or geographical homeland. It connotes certain shared cultural norms and values, but loyalties and obligations toward members of the group are diffuse. Some communal identities are situational and may change according to the setting. Political entrepreneurs may have considerable latitude to expand or even redefine their constituencies. The conflict in Chad illustrates this point.

Chad is divided into two distinct population zones: agriculturalists in the south and nomadic pastoralists in the north. Both regions are ethnically heterogeneous, but the north-south religious division is frequently given as a reason for Chad's two decades of war and civil strife. Indeed, the conflict officially began in 1966 when Chad's first president, François Tombalbaye, a southerner and a Christian, was challenged by the formation of the Front de Liberation National du Tchad (FROLINAT). The movement was launched in the Sudan by Muslims from northern Chad who pledged to fight a revolutionary, anti-imperialist war for national liberation. In addition to advocating a socialist path to development, FROLINAT called for the official use of Arabic alongside French as a Chadian national language. It is important to note that FROLINAT was not pushing secession but was struggling for control of the country as a whole. The fluidity of communal group identities is key to understanding the dynamics of this conflict.

Although no reliable census exists, northern Chad is thought to be around 95 percent Muslim, with estimates for the country as a whole ranging from 41 percent to 55 percent. The south is about 30 percent Christian, with the remainder of its people following indigenous African religions or, to a lesser extent, Islam. Christians are clearly a minority group in Chad. So are Arabs, who comprise approximately nine percent of the population. But many non-Arabs who live in northern Chad are bilingual, and people educated in Islamic schools speak Arabic. The fact that French was retained as the sole official language when Chad became independent in 1960 put northerners at a disadvantage with respect to mobility in the civil service and competition for jobs in the modern economy. Christians, who are almost always educated in French, also have benefited disproportionately as an outcome of the language policy. In terms of the politics of communalism, FROLINAT's appeal to people in the north was to groups who had certain linguistic and religious identities in common. These groups were encouraged to express their dissatisfaction over patronage and recruitment issues by vying for control of the state.

Chad is also a good case for noting that communal appeals need not be confined within state borders. Libyan leader Muammar Qaddafi has repeatedly manipulated alliances with Chadian political factions based on militant Islam and extensions of Arab ethnicity. Proclaiming that Arab culture is the prevailing culture in Chad, he attempted to merge the country with Libya in 1981. Qaddafi has alternatively provided military aid to various Muslim faction leaders in Chad's civil conflict and dispatched troops to fight against government forces on Chadian soil. Although this particular example is extreme, it reminds us that the politicization of communal loyalties has an entrepreneurial aspect, and that the boundaries of communal group identities are quite fluid.

## PATRON-CLIENT RELATIONSHIPS

Along the broad spectrum of group loyalties, patron-client ties are a frequent locus of political competition in Africa. Such relationships are based on the exchange of noncomparable goods and services between people unequal in status, wealth, and influence. The aim of such alliances is to maximize individual interests through personalized contacts. In exchange for loyal service and obedience to the patron, the client receives protection, economic security, or material rewards.

Numerous African societies have indigenous forms of social clientage. In the initial years of colonial rule, these patron-client ties remained largely outside the realm of the new sovereign authority. But after World War II, Western-inspired representative institutions created unprecedented opportunities for political clientelism. Funds available for investment in development activities gradually increased, and progress toward independence meant that Africans were beginning to influence the distribution of these resources. In the wake of such changes, patron-client relationships found a new field of operation in the government sphere.

With the rise of the nationalistic movements and the formation of political parties, many of the new politicians used clientelist structures as a means of garnering votes. Clients were thus socialized into a new pattern of expectations and obligations which centered around government resources and electoral support. Since independence, the politicization of patron-client bonds has carried over and become a pattern of political mobilization throughout Africa. For example, it was a feature of Nigerian multi-party democracy in the first and second republics, has anchored both the single-party state and military rule in Niger, and functions as the centerpiece of Kenya's one-party dominant political oligarchy.

Clientelism defines the boundaries of the political society in functional terms, emphasizing mutual interests. According to anthropologist Michael G. Smith, functional flexibility accounts for the versatility of these networks. (Smith, 1960:260) Patron-client bonds can consolidate linkages across divisions of ethnicity, occupational status, lineage, and urban-rural distinctions. The major disadvantage of clientelistic politics, however, is factionalism, which is endemic to the system. To the extent that clientage ties are mobilized in the quest for jobs, licenses, government contracts, loans, and development funds of all sorts, conflict over access to these valued goods can become highly destabilizing.

## CLASS AFFILIATIONS

The final category examined here is class affiliations. Class refers to people who share common economic interests based on their similar positions in the processes of production. Education, income, and occupation are the standard indicators of class status. Because economic class position determines a person's life chances, class creates a mutuality of interests among people who may never see one another and who may have no emotional ties.

One basic idea of Marxist analysis is that the ruling capitalist class promotes and protects its interests through control of the state. In Africa, where indigenous capitalism is in its early stages, international capital controls the means of industrial production, while the national bureaucratic bourgeoisie controls the means of state coercion. The Republic of South Africa, with its racially stratified advanced industrial economy, has a history of pronounced class conflict. But in most African countries, the rural economy dwarfs the industrial sector, and class consolidation is far from complete. Kenya is a good example of how state intervention can accelerate this process.

When Kenya became independent in 1963, President Jomo Kenyatta's new government was zealously committed to closing the racial gap between the white settler and African populations. On the critical issue of land tenure, blacks were to regain control of the rich and fertile highlands, which the British colonial government had turned over to white settler estate agriculture. Because the independence agreement stipulated that this land be purchased at market value, Britain and the World Bank financed loans to African farmers through the Kenyan government. By 1976, two-thirds of the farms in this region were in African hands, but holdings were generally so small that most peasant owners could not earn enough to pay back their loans. The Kenyan government renegotiated the payment schedules and began evicting those farmers who failed to meet their obligations. Soon, credit-worthy Africans were purchasing large estates or reconsolidating the small plots. Over time, a class of landed African gentry appeared alongside the rural, landless poor.

Class formation in Kenya's urban areas also has been advanced by the policy of Africanization. Regarding the sensitive issue of employment equity, the government moved as rapidly as possible to replace the expatriates in the civil service with Kenyan nationals. In the private sector, the state encouraged foreign-owned subsidiaries to hire African executives for their firms. Such initiatives created a new class of well-paid Africans but did nothing to alleviate poverty among the urban poor. Nor have government efforts to promote job creation in the industrial sector done much to cut the rates of unemployment and underemployment.

Clearly, those who control the state in Africa may use its prerogatives for their own personal advantage and to consolidate their economic class interests. But they also seek to promote the welfare of politically relevant elements within their respective constituencies. Because these constituencies are typically based on such communal affiliations as ethnicity, region, or religion; on clientelistic relations which bridge class boundaries; or on such kinship ties as lineage, class affiliations are obscured. As a result, the structural patterns of African politics often mask the existence of class conflict and distort the perception of internal class struggles.

## AGENTS OF CHANGE

What emerges from this overview of the African political landscape is a picture of social diversity and organizational complexity. The heterogeneous institutional framework provides many channels of competition and support. But the political plane is restricted to narrowly based power held tightly by a small inner core. Within these parameters, the undervalued political potential of women and youth looms on the horizon.

Nigerian sociologist Kamene Okonjo, in reference to politics in her own country, observed that the present diminished political role of women is largely due to the introduction of a Western political model that superseded traditional dual-sex systems. She also finds fault with the anti-feminist bias of Christianity and Islam. (Okonjo, 1983:211–222) The current male-dominated national politics is virtually institutionalized in military regimes. In competitive electoral systems as well as in one-party states, female candidates are usually avoided by the established political machinery and are rarely elected to representative office. Even though virtually every African political party has a women's wing and most governments appoint at least a few females to high political posts, women are rarely integrated into politics at the national level in their own right. At sub-national levels, however, there is currently a resurgence of traditional dual-sex political institutions along with the emergence of new types of women's organizations. These developments suggest that far from being resigned to the prevailing pattern of marginalization, women are becoming more assertive in addressing the problems of narrowly shared power and unequal access.

We are now seeing a different kind of reversal regarding the role of youth. Renouncing the traditional norm of rule by elders, groups of young people today—students in particular—have become the opposition. Whether in a military regime, a bureaucratic empire, a one-party state, or a racialist state, students form the one group most likely to articulate dissatisfaction and publicly air social grievances. Open confrontation with the autocratic rule of Ethiopia's Haile Selassie, for example, came from the university. And since the 1976 Soweto rebellion, the steady upsurge of internal resistance and violent protest to South Africa's apartheid regime has been routinely spurred by children. The old age-grade structures seem to be assuming new roles. Less concerned with the traditional emphasis on social control, these modern equivalents of the youth cohorts are now advocates for change. They have taken up the gauntlet of denouncing economic injustices, political corruption, autocratic rule, and barriers to social mobility.

## REFERENCES

Mazrui, Ali A. 1966. "Nkrumah: The Leninist Czar." *Transition*, Kampala, 26.

Okonjo, Kamene. 1983. "Sex Roles in Nigerian Politics." In *Female and Male in West Africa*, ed. Christine Oppong. London: George Allen and Unwin.

Smith, Michael G. 1960. *Government in Zazzau*. London: Oxford University Press.

---

## *Reading 5.1*

Tibiri is the capital-in-exile of the former Hausa state of Gobir. Its emir, whose title is Sarkin Gobir, is one of Niger's five paramount chiefs. When the French colonial reforms of 1946 introduced represen-

tative institutions based on a limited African franchise, the Parti
Progressiste Nigerien (PPN) emerged as Niger's first political party. It
was soon challenged by the Union Nigerienne des Sympathisants et
Indépendants (UNIS), the political organ of the chiefs. By 1958 five
parties had been organized in Tibiri—each led by a prince with a weak
claim to the Gobir throne. In 1960 Niger gained independence with
President Diori Hamani of the PPN at the helm. Despite his consolidation of a one-party state, PPN control from the national capital in
Niamey had only limited impact in Tibiri. The following profile of
Moussa Marafa, one of Gobir's "politician-princes," shows the convergence of indigenous and modern political conflict structures in this
rural Hausa community.

## Pearl T. Robinson, "Traditional Clientage and Political Change in a Hausa Community," from *Transformation and Resiliency in Africa*

Moussa Marafa was the first president of the party's local committee
and a prominent member of Tibiri's small Christian community. A man who
combined strong leadership qualities with a sharp mind, Moussa was another
Gobir aristocrat who found his ambitions stifled by his status as a second-
generation prince.

Back in 1927, when Protestant missionaries arrived in a Tibiri that was
nominally Muslim but predominantly traditionalist in its religious practices,
Moussa Marafa was their first convert. Moussa's stature as a proponent of the
new Western faith grew as his evangelistic work carried him throughout
Hausaland even into northern Nigeria. Christianity seemed initially to offer a
unique leadership opportunity until [Pastor Osborne of the Sudan Interior
Mission] announced that Moussa would not be allowed to become a deacon in
the church that was to be built in Tibiri. Revealing his own concern with
maintaining control, [Osborne] reasoned that Moussa's personal following
had become so strong that the Gobir prince-turned-evangelist would ultimately
emerge as the dominant power on the church's governing board. Though he
remained a member of the congregation, Moussa was obliged to look elsewhere
to satisfy his desire for stewardship. Years later, party politics and the PPN
provided an opportunity.

Combining the support of his personal clients, the Christian community
and local PPN sympathizers, Moussa attempted to build a political base as an
advocate for the commoners against Sarkin [Gobir] Labo and his retinue of
traditional officeholders. During the years that Moussa headed Tibiri's PPN
party (1959–1962), the population became polarized into two mutually exclu-

sive competitive groups. As one resident of Tibiri explained, "If you went to Moussa Marafa's compound, you did not go to the Sarki's palace."

Moussa's overt opposition to the Sarki was a source of embarrassment to the national PPN leaders because they had only managed to come to power through an alliance forged with the chiefs via the UNIS party. Although Niamey did not move immediately to oust Moussa, under his tenure as president the local party committee had to operate without the benefit of patronage from the postindependence single-party state. In 1962 Sarkin Labo finally prevailed upon the PPN's National Political Bureau to put an end to this contentious situation. Moussa was removed from office and replaced by one of the Sarki's personal retainers. With help from Niamey, the hierarchical authority structure of Tibiri's traditional political system was thus reaffirmed.

Of all Tibiri's "politician-princes," Moussa Marafa was the only one who consistently followed a course intended to create a sphere of authority outside the Sarki's control. He was much more interested in becoming a leader in his own right than in improving his advantage in the quest for traditional offices. The decision to embrace Christianity led to new opportunities for status mobility, but it also precluded the possibility of being eligible to fulfill the religious duties of a Sarki. That is why being denied membership on the church's deacon board was more a political than a religious setback for Moussa.

Perhaps because he was the most skilled of the local politicians in his use of client networks to build a broad base of support, Moussa chose to defy the principle of hierarchical authority by functioning as an antitraditionalist crusader for the rights of commoners. Such a political strategy could be successful in Tibiri only if it were backed up by an incentive system strong enough to match the Sarki's. The Niamey government might have provided the material basis for Moussa to build a patronage machine, but such was not to be.

President Diori's own weak position made him unwilling to side with a mercurial political upstart against a traditional leader of proven power and influence. The fact that Moussa Marafa headed a local branch of the ruling PPN party was not enough to keep Sarkin Labo from striking back. Antitraditionalism as a political strategy therefore failed in this particular instance because it was articulated uniquely through traditional structures of social clientage and was not supplemented by modern sector resources or political patronage.

---

## Reading 5.2

Secessionist tendencies based on geo-ethnicity have plagued the Sudan since the British negotiated independence in 1956. Although the country's cultural heritage includes numerous ethnic groups, distinctive regional identities have developed among the northern and southern Sudanese. Rebelling against emergent internal colonialism, the Nilotic and Sudanic peoples of the south have refused to accept the political hegemony of the Arabized and Islamized north. Sudanese political scientist Dunstan Wai, himself a southerner, explains the historical background and characterizes the contemporary struggle as a conflict between Arab and African nationalism.

---

## Dunstan Wai, *The Afro-Arab Conflict in the Sudan*

The prevalence of communal conflicts in Africa, and indeed, in the world at large, is not a revelation. What is lacking is a clear differentiation between such conflicts, and a critical examination of some of those cases which defy comparison.

The African-Arab confrontation along the Nile Valley is a case in point. In essence, it is a conflict of nationalism: One rooted in Africanism and the other in Arabism. It is not a mere case of ethnicity. The Northern Sudanese view themselves as Arabs and whether their Arabness is more by acquisition than heredity is of less importance. Whereas the Southern Sudanese feel themselves to be authentically Negroid Africans in every way. We see here two identities with differing perspectives on the universe.

Imperial Britain recognized the differences between the two collectivities within the area it named the Anglo-Egyptian Sudan: Arab and Muslim in the North, and African and "pagan" in the South. Colonial common sense dictated that two separate administrations must be set up for two regions, which were two distinct worlds culturally, racially, as well as geographically. Such differences were reinforced by historical hostilities and mutual distrust.

The imperial regime decided to keep the South as a human zoo and to concentrate economic and educational development in the North. Subsequently, British interests dictated on the eve of imperial withdrawal that the two regions should be united administratively and that political power should be handed to the Arabs. The Southern Sudanese were deliberately excluded from the constitutional negotiations preceding independence, while the Northern Sudanese were effectively represented. The North pleaded for its right to self-determination and was fully involved in determining the nature of the political arrangement that would sanctify its sovereign rights in the international community of mankind; the South was not considered fit to participate in discussions which were meant to shape its destiny as well.

It was, therefore, not surprising that the South resorted to violence to protest the change of colonial rulers, from the British to the Arabs, which took place without their consent. It took to arms in the transitional period with the hope that imperial Britain would review the situation and allow it to exercise its right to self-determination. The British were not about to retreat from their agreement with the Northern Sudanese and the Egyptians, who were a junior colonial partner in the Sudan. Indeed, they intervened militarily to help the North subdue the South and establish its hegemony over the region.

For the Southern Sudanese, the end of British colonialism in their land meant the beginning of Arab domination and colonialism. That was unacceptable and needed to be challenged in order to preserve Southern Sudanese identity and to gain their self-determination. For the Northern Sudanese, the British withdrawal meant assumption of political power and it also meant gaining of sovereign status by the Sudan which, in their view, included the South as well. Any challenge to the political and constitutional arrangements worked out with the departing imperial power by any group, such as the Southern Sudanese, was viewed by the North as treason.

The Southern Sudanese were willing to compromise in settling for autonomous status within the framework of one Sudan. But the Northern Sudanese political elites of the time were not prepared for such an arrangement, infringing on their ability to dominate the South. Hence, armed conflict continued for seventeen years until the point of a military stalemate was reached, at which time both parties agreed to negotiate. The talks resulted in the granting of self-rule to the South within a united Sudan.

The Sudanese war helps us to make a distinction between political conflicts inherent in the coexistence of diverse racial, ethnic, and cultural groups within a single state in which all of them participated in forming on the eve of the colonial withdrawal, and those conflicts in which one of the parties contests the legitimacy of the sovereignty that it is supposed to enjoy. In both situations the aggrieved group may evoke the right to self-determination, and indeed, the distinction between the two types of conflict may be blurred by the tragedy of violence committed along the structural lines of pluralism and by the cultural biases of propaganda. Nevertheless, in making this distinction here, it is asserted that the sources of motivation for the emergence of cultural loyalty as a medium for political secession can be differentiated along a broad continuum. [The conflict in the Sudan] was not simply a war arising out of hostilities which are generated through the evocation and manipulation of ethnic sentiments by elites competing for power at the national level. It was deeper than that in that it essentially arose from the dynamics of direct interaction between peoples of different cultures and races as experienced through the perceptual prism of their respective heritages and value systems, coupled with the history of antagonism and distrust....

The Southern Sudanese did not feel that any Khartoum government in the North had a legitimate right to rule them. They resented the manner and the fact of being handed over by the British to their traditional enemies. Moreover, the monopoly of political power by the North confirmed to them the beginning of a second colonial era. On the other hand, the North felt that it had the legitimate right to formulate and carry out policies which would affect the entire country. The failure of the Northern Sudanese politicians to share political power with political elites from the South continually reinforced a feeling of alienation by the South and the belief that the North was, in essence, a colonial successor to Britain. Also, attempts to coerce the South into the Northern fold worsened rather than benefited the perception of Khartoum governments as illegitimate, ultimately leading to armed rebellion.

The resort to extraconstitutional means by the Southern region to challenge the perceived illegitimate rule by what it considered to be a racially and culturally alien group was facilitated by the ineptitude and lack of responsiveness of Khartoum governments. Absence of channels for the legitimate expression of discontent and for the peaceful mediation and settlement of Southern grievances, coupled with application of coercion by successive governments on the disenchanted Southern political elites, led to violent confrontation along the Nile Valley. The frustrated, disaffected, and injured Negroid Africans challenged the Arab hegemony over them.

---

## Reading 5.3

In 1980, shortly after his installation as Kenya's second president, Daniel arap Moi pushed a resolution through his ruling KANU party (Kenya African National Union) banning all ethnic welfare associations. Groups such as the Gikuyu, Embu and Meru Association; the Luo Union; and the New Akamba Union had politicized ethnicity and institutionalized communal competition. In the view of Kenyan writer Ngugi wa Thiong'o, such cultural organizations merely mask intra-class conflict over property, wealth, and power among ethnic factions within the national elite. His novel *Petals of Blood* expands on this theme. In the following selection the story's protagonist, Godfrey Munira, receives an invitation to a tea hosted by a new ethnic association. The oath of African unity taken by Mau Mau warriors during their armed struggle against British colonialism is the historical foil for scenes in which oath-taking foments factionalism and communal conflict.

---

## Ngugi wa Thiong'o, *Petals of Blood*

Munira took the envelope and opened it. He could not believe it. He read it over and over again. Kamwene Cultural Organisation (Ilmorog Branch) invited the Headmaster of Ilmorog School and all his staff to join Nderi wa Riera in a delegation that would go to tea at Gatundu... He was trembling...

Munira's heart was glowing with pride. And so he was making something of himself after all. A headmaster. And now an invitation to tea. To tea at Gatundu! Admittedly, the note was handwritten, and came from the district office and it asked him to organise all his teachers and their wives. He had never heard of KCO (Ilmorog Branch). But it was something to remember. A headmaster. An invitation to tea. Tea at Gatundu... But now he had to hurry home to tell his wife of the news. A headmaster! Invitation to tea! Ilmorog had given him greatness. Hoyee!...

As Munira approached his home, a headmastership and an Invitation to Tea all in one pocket, he felt happy. His first big initiative, occasioned by the general idealism that had gripped the country just before and for a little while after independence, had produced a fruit however small. Invitation and a promotion. He could now even stand up to the profile of his father looming large in Munira's imagination as he rode through the brisk air toward his home.

It turned out that most teachers and their wives had been invited to tea at Gatundu. They had also been asked to take twelve shillings and fifty cents for a self-help project. Munira's wife, despite attempts to cover it with a Christian grace, was also excited. For Munira the Saturday would remain tattooed in his mind so that he would pass it alive to his children: he, Munira, was going to tea with a living legend which had dominated the consciousness of a country for almost a century. What wouldn't one give for the honour! Once again Munira felt a little bit above the average.

The bus that took them came around six to the Ruwa-ini post office, and everybody was worried: someone even suggested that they should cancel the trip, but he was hushed by the others. It was better late than never: tea in such a place would mean a night's feast. The solemn-looking government official assured them that all was well.... They were taken past Gatundu, through some banana plantations where they found yet another crowd of people solemnly waiting for something. A funeral tea? Munira wondered, numbed to silence by the eerie sombreness of everything. He looked around: the government official had vanished. They were now ordered into lines—one for men, the other for women. A teacher asked loudly: is this the tea we came to have? He was hit with the flat of a panga by a man who emerged from nowhere and as suddenly disappeared into nowhere. How did Mzigo and the government official come into all this? It was dark: a small light came from a hut into which people disappeared in groups of ten or so. What is it all about? thudded Munira's heart. And then it was his turn!

On the way back, around midnight, Munira knew that [his wife] Julia was silently weeping. He felt her withdrawal, the accusation of betrayal: but how could he answer her now, how could he tell her that he truly did not know? He was hungry and thirsty and all throughout the bus was this hush of a people conscious of having been taken in: of having participated in a rite that jarred with time and place and persons and people's post-Uhuru expectations! How could they as teachers face their children and tell them that Kenya was one?

Later Munira was to learn that a very important person in authority, with the tacit understanding and approval from other very important persons in authority like Nderi, some even from other national communities, was the brain behind this business. But the knowledge did not reconcile him to the act.

For the first time in his life Munira felt that he must have a man-to-man talk with his father.... His father listened rapt in thought and this encouraged Munira.

'What I could not understand...what I shall never forget was this man...he was so poorly dressed...rags...no shoes even...and he stood there, when all of us were trembling, and he said: "I am a squatter—a working-man in a tea plantation owned by Milk Stream Tea Estates. I used to work there before 1952. During the movement I was in charge of spying and receiving guns and taking them to our fighters. I was later detained. Now I am working on the same estate owned by the same company. Only now some of our people have joined them. It is good that some of our people are eating. But I will not take another oath until the promises of the first one have been fulfilled." They beat him in front of us. They stepped on his neck and pressed it with their boots against the floor, and only when he made animal noises did they stop. He took the oath all right. But not with his heart. I shall never forget his screaming.'... His father suddenly stood up, took his coat and beckoned Munira to follow him.

They walked to the top of the ridge looking down upon the vast estate. Waweru was always proud of this estate because it was the one he had acquired when he was beginning to accumulate, before the Second World War.

'Do you see all this?'

'Yes.'

'Flower. Fruit trees. Tea...cows...everything.'

'Yes.'

'It has not come into being just because of the strength of my limbs alone. It is the Lord's doing. It is true that this land of the Agikuyu is blessed by the Lord. The prosperity has multiplied several times since independence.... Now all that prosperity, all that hard-won freedom is threatened by Satan working through other tribes, arousing their envy and jealousy. That is why this oath is necessary. It is for peace and unity and it is in harmony with God's eternal design. Now you listen to me. I have been there. I used the Bible. I want your mother to go. She is refusing. But Christ will soon show her the light. Even highly educated people are going there, of their own accord. My son, the fear of the Lord is the beginning of wisdom. This KCO is not a bad thing...We shall even have a Church Branch. It's a cultural organisation to bring unity and harmony between all of us, the rich and the poor, and to end envy and greed.'

Munira was not sure if he had heard his father correctly.

'You mean that you...'

'Yes, yes,' he said quickly, almost impatiently. Munira for the first time tried to argue back with his father.

'But before God there are no tribes. We are all equal before the Lord.'

'My son,' he said, after considering his words for a few minutes. 'Go back and teach. And stop drinking. If you are tired of teaching, come back here. I have work for you. My estates are many. And I am aging. Or join KCO. Get a bank loan. Start business.'

---

## Reading 5.4

Emperor Haile Selassie of Ethiopia reigned for 44 years and was considered one of Africa's most venerable traditional rulers until his overthrow by the army in 1974. Then the praise singers heaped scorn on this monarch who had lived in extravagant luxury and shown little concern while millions of his subjects starved through five years of drought. But university students attacked the regime much earlier, spearheading anti-palace conflict that presaged Selassie's downfall. Polish journalist Ryszard Kapuscinski traveled to Ethiopia shortly after the military takeover and talked with some of the Emperor's former associates and courtiers. The following interview segment with the servant Z. S.-K. is a somber recollection of a father's sense of impending doom as he watched his son's growing involvement with challenges to imperial authority.

---

## Ryszard Kapuscinski, *The Emperor: Downfall of an Autocrat*

A year after the Cojam uprising—which by showing the furious and unrelenting face of the people stirred the Palace and threw a fright into the dignitaries (and not only them: we servants also started getting the creeps)—a singular misfortune happened to me: my son Hailu, a university student in those depressing years, began to think. That's right, he began to think, and I must explain to you, my friend, that in those days thinking was a painful inconvenience and a troubling deformity. His Unexcelled Majesty, in his incessant care for the good and comfort of his subjects, never spared any efforts to protect them from this inconvenience and deformity. Why should they waste the time that ought to be devoted to the cause of development, why should they disturb their internal peace and stuff their heads with all sorts of disloyal ideas? Nothing decent or comforting could result if someone decided to think restlessly and provocatively or mingle with those who were thinking. And yet my harebrained son committed exactly that indiscretion. My wife was the first to notice it. Her maternal instinct told her that dark clouds were gathering over our home, and she said to me one day, "Hailu must have started to think. You can see that he's sad." That's how it was then. Those who surveyed the Empire and pondered their surroundings walked sadly and lost in thought, their eyes full of troubled pensiveness, as if they had a presentiment of something vague and unspeakable. Most often one saw such faces among students, who, let me add, were causing His Majesty a lot of grief. It truly amazes me that the police never caught the scent, the connection between thinking and mood. Had they made that discovery in time they could easily have neutralized these thinkers, who by their snorting and malicious reluctance to show satisfaction brought so many troubles and afflictions on His Venerable Majesty's head.

The Emperor, however, showing more perspicacity than his police, understood that sadness can drive one to thinking, disappointment, waffling, and shuffling, and so he ordered distractions, merriment, festivities, and masquerades for the whole Empire. His Noble Majesty himself had the Palace illuminated, threw banquets for the poor, and incited people to gaiety. When they had guzzled and gamboled, they gave praise to their King. This went on for years, and the distractions so filled people's heads, so corked them up, that they could talk of nothing but having fun. Our feet are bare, but we're debonair, hey ho! Only the thinkers, who saw everything getting gray, shrunken, mud-splashed, and moldy, skipped the jokes and the merriment. They became a nuisance. The unthinking ones were wiser; they didn't let themselves get taken in, and when the students started holding rallies and talking, the nonthinkers stuffed their ears and made themselves scarce. What's the use of knowing, when it's better not to know? Why do it the hard way, when it can be easy? Why talk, if you're better off keeping your mouth shut? Why get mixed up in the affairs of the Empire, when there's so much to do closer to home, when there's shopping to be done?

Well, my friend, seeing what a dangerous course my son was sailing, I tried to dissuade him, to encourage him to participate in amusements, to send him on excursions. I would even have preferred that he devote himself to nightlife rather than to those damned demonstrations and conspiracies. Just imagine my pain, my distress: the father in the Palace, the son in the anti-Palace. In the streets I'm protected by the police from my own son, who demonstrates and throws rocks. I told him over and over again, "Why don't you give up thinking? It doesn't get you anywhere. Forget it. Fool around instead. Look at other people, those who listen to the wise—how cheerfully they walk around, laugh. No clouds on their foreheads. They devote themselves to the good life, and if they worry about anything it's about how to fill their pockets, and to such concerns and solicitations His Majesty is always kindly inclined, always thinking of how to make things smooth and cozy." "And how," asks Hailu, "can there be a contradiction between a person who thinks and a wise person? If a person doesn't think, he's a fool." "Not at all," I say. "Wise he still is—it's just that he has directed his thoughts to a safe, sheltered place, and not between rumbling, crushing millstones." But it was too late. Hailu was already living in a different world; by then the university, located not far from the Palace, had turned itself into a real anti-Palace where only the brave set foot, and the space between the court and the university increasingly resembled a battlefield on which the fate of the Empire was being decided.

---

## Reading 5.5

Protest became rebellion in Soweto on June 16, 1976, when police fired on a group of black students demonstrating against the use of the Afrikaans language in their schools. Two months later the unrest spread to Cape Town's three black townships of Langa, Nyanga, and Guguletu. Maria Tholo, a resident of Guguletu, kept track of these events in her diary. As the proprietor of a day care center and the wife of a retail chain supervisor, Tholo is part of South Africa's small urban black middle class. Her prescient commentary on funerals as a surrogate political arena evokes the mood of defiance. In the scenes that follow, children become heroes. Their deeds rival Christianity as a force for black redemption. Reversing traditional African roles, the youth step ahead of their elders and take responsibility for the fate of the community.

---

## Carol Hermer, *The Diary of Maria Tholo*

*Sunday, August 22*

Yesterday was a day of funerals. The first one was that of the Mosi boy. Now because he was the first student to be killed in the riots, the police were worried that there would be trouble at the funeral, so they told Mrs. Mosi that only very close relatives could attend, not more than 20 people. I hear that they threatened her that if she allowed a crowd she would be endorsed out of Cape Town because she is here illegally....

Now with Africans twenty people is impossible. Who can decide who is a close relative? Why, when I got married to Gus he had to adopt my whole family. If you keep counting his people and her people and her sister's people and their people's people you'll never stop counting. Everybody who belongs to that clan or that totem belongs to the family.

The students insisted that they were going to be at the funeral even though the teachers had told them that the police had forbidden this. We heard this from Arthur....

Police were watching the stations and the bus terminals to see that the children didn't gather together. Because they wear their uniforms they are easy to spot.

But the children were too clever for the riot squad. The girls put their mothers' overalls over their uniforms and the boys took off their ties and blazers and only when they were safely in Langa, away from the eyes of the police, did they strip and get into uniform. I don't know where they did it but as we turned the car into the road that runs straight to the graveyard, we saw a whole crowd of children dressed in the uniforms of all four township high schools, and some of the higher primary ones as well.

We parked and followed the students through the knots of curious people flanking the side of the road till we came in sight of the actual grave. You could see from this distance that there were very few people there, a handful. There was nobody at the gate, no sign of riot cars or police.

Out of nowhere they appeared. All you could see were camouflage uniforms charging for the gate. One policeman, dressed in proper light blue, appeared in front shouting, 'Stop, or we shoot.' I thought wow, they really are all armed. They had those big guns on slings and revolvers. We quickly slunk into one of the gates but stayed in the yard, watching.

The children didn't stop. One of the boys called out, 'They say they don't shoot school children. Let them prove it today.' The policemen crowded together to stop them entering the gate.

And then as if a switch had been pulled the girls started wailing. You know how Africans can scream. 'Wah, wah, wah. It's not a dog that's being buried. We want to see our comrade. We want to see our fellow-student.' The people around took up the chorus and the next moment it was just pandemonium with everybody screaming 'Yes! Yes! Yes!' and then the teargas shot out. One minute Gus was screaming 'You can't shoot children. Let them go!' and the next he was diving away. I saw him dodging the canisters, off down the road.

Everyone was watching the canisters go up, watching to see where they fell and quick as anything the women around were organised. Some tore off their doeks, others had buckets of water. As the canisters fell they were doused with water. They pulled nappies, clothes off the lines, dipping them in water and throwing them to the children to cover their noses.

The boys had thrown a cordon around the girls, cautioning them to stand firm and sit out the gas fumes. I looked around just in time to see Gus driving off around the corner. He had dodged, dodged, disappeared and left me to myself. That's a fine husband for you, leaving me there in the lurch with all the teargas.

The children were carrying a big wreath to put on the grave but there was no way to get through, so eventually they moved off slowly towards Langa High. I ran to where I'd seen the car disappearing. It was a couple of streets away. Gus says he left to protect the children. I know better.

Either way he was not having any more of Langa. He wouldn't even go to church. We drove straight out and back to Guguletu. There was still another funeral to go to. This one was of the boy who had gone to Nomsa's school. We didn't expect trouble because they had a permit to be in Cape Town and there were no restrictions on the number of people attending. I don't know why there was a difference, possibly because he was only a primary school boy.

There were no incidents. The police kept far away, just watched from a distance. The only funny thing was watching the change in the attitude of the adults to the children. There were well over eighty children present though the teachers had tried to restrict it to just the standard fives. Even the high-school children turned up in numbers. They hitchhiked from Langa and collected together.

There was a tremendous moment of tension as we saw the horde of children approaching. By now they were the fear of the township. You could see everyone's eyes turn but they just came in quietly and the bigger men gave way for them.

Now at most African funerals everyone who wants to make a speech does so but the M.C. asked that because this was not an ordinary funeral he'd appreciate it if they would stick to the programme and just hear the appointed speakers.

He couldn't stop one old man from jumping up. 'I'm not in the programme, ' he said, 'but I just want to say that I have learned something in my old age when my hair is turning grey. We have always said that Christianity is what is asked of us in the Bible. I have learned the truth from these children. I'm sure all the parents here will tell you that they can get nothing out of their children. They will not tell what the others have been saying. They are as one. They speak as one and they act together. Christians are supposed to be people who are united, who are brother and sister to each other. Whereas we turn around and gossip about each other, these children cry together, laugh together.

'We must learn a lesson from them. According to African custom this is not a boy lying here. This is a man because we say that a man shows that he is one by his deeds. Here lies a hero. He has died for you and me.' Before he could go on the M.C. jumped up. 'Please friends, can we just stick to the verse that is in front of you and not flounder.'

But the man had said his piece. At least one person stood up for the truth. When we went back to the house for refreshments it was the children who were given first preference. I never thought I'd see that.

---
*6*
---

# IN SEARCH OF STABILITY: INDEPENDENCE AND EXPERIMENTATION

Fred M. Hayward

The decolonization of Africa and the resulting independence of numerous states created a need for Africans to establish new systems of governance. Several models emerged during the 1960s, some of which have proved successful, others of which seem, on reflection, to pose difficulties for long-term stability. In this chapter, Professor Hayward identifies several systems of governance that emerged during the independence period and discusses their strengths and weaknesses. Eds.

The period of the late 1950s and early 1960s witnessed the independence from colonial rule of more than 30 African states. This was an era of great excitement, optimism, and romanticism. The people of Africa were about to move into the modern era from a period of suspended animation under colonial occupation; and there was every expectation that this could be done relatively quickly and easily by building on the knowledge, experience, and technology of the last century. It was expected that the few remaining colonies in Africa would soon be independent, that a solution was forthcoming to end minority rule in South Africa and southern Rhodesia, and that the Portuguese colonies soon would join the rest of Africa as free and independent states.

The optimism about political developments in Africa was shared by scholars and observers from much of the rest of the world. Many foreign countries and international organizations such as the United Nations were eager to assist with the changes and growth which were underway. Further, there was great faith that the skills and knowledge of the industrialized nations could easily be transferred to Africa to bring about rapid and dramatic change. Africa was about to be transformed by great achievements in development, exciting innovations in the political systems, and a resurgence of those African cultural contributions to social and political life which had been stunted by colonialism.

While the initial hope for rapid political and economic development had to be tempered for some African states and some of the expectations about the benefits of external assistance proved unrealistic, there were notable achievements. These included the economic miracles of the Ivory Coast and Kenya and the political experimentation in Ghana and Tanzania. There were also successes with multi-party parliamentary democracy in Sierra Leone, Nigeria, and Botswana, as well as the promise of creative new institutional arrangements in many other African states.

## SEARCH FOR A NEW ORDER

The independence of most African states in the late 1950s and early 1960s came about largely by peaceful means. There were such exceptions as Algeria, Kenya, Guinea-Bissau, Angola, and Mozambique; but the continent as a whole witnessed a period in which the vast majority of African states moved to independence with the cooperation and often the blessing of the former colonial powers, who recognized that continued occupation was no longer possible. The tone of this period is represented in comments made by Kwame Nkrumah in Parliament at the time of the introduction of the government's White Paper on independence for the Gold Coast (which became Ghana). He noted on July 10, 1953:

> Mr. Speaker, we have traveled a long distance from the days when our fathers came under alien subjugation to the present time. We stand now at the threshold of self-government and do not waver. The paths have been tortuous, and fraught with peril, but the positive and tactical action we have adopted is leading us to the New Jerusalem, the golden city of our hearts' desire! I am confident, therefore, that I express the wishes and feelings of the chiefs and people of this country in hoping that the final transfer of power to your Representative Ministers may be done in a spirit of amity and friendship, so that, having peacefully achieved our freedom, the peoples of both countries—Britain and the Gold Coast—may form a new relationship based on mutual respect, trust and friendship. (Nkrumah, 1973:106–107)

This hope was shared by British officials, who for the most part had pride in their achievements in the Gold Coast, by outside observers, and by the populace as a whole. The Convention People's Party (CPP) seemed to be successful in mobilizing the nation, creating a sense of intimacy and solidarity that encouraged its leaders, and developing a program designed to move Ghana forward. All this was done under the charismatic leadership of Kwame Nkrumah who had, in effect, turned politics into religion. (Apter, 1963:304) This positive perception of Ghana's achievements was almost universally shared by observers and participants both inside and outside Ghana.

This was a period of experimentation and innovation all over the continent. Among the cases of particular interest were African socialism in Senegal and Tanzania; party competition and parliamentary democracy in Nigeria, Sierra Leone, and Botswana; traditional rule in Ethiopia; the one-party state in the Ivory Coast, Ghana, and Tanzania; revolutionary regimes in Algeria; and very soon the involvement of African armies in the governance of a number of African states. While not all of these political systems were as successful as some had hoped, they created an aura of movement and action which raised expectations about what was to follow.

## AFRICAN SOCIALISM

One of the experiments which received a great deal of attention during this period was that of Tanzania, one of the poorest countries in Africa. Tanzania was working to devise a formula that would promote development without making the country dependent on massive amounts of external aid which might compromise its newly gained independence. The president of Tanzania, Julius Nyerere, contributed substantially to the credibility of this experiment with his quiet, persuasive leadership, his sincerity, and his determination. He talked of self-reliance and hard work, of democracy and mass participation, and of education and rural development. He tried to inspire the political leadership to be dedicated to service rather than personal gain. Many of the basic principles of this experiment were laid out in the Arusha Declaration of January 29, 1967, which became the party program for moving the nation forward. This was a war against poverty and oppression in which Tanzania was going to try to substitute human energy for money rather than borrowing from abroad. It would emphasize self-reliance instead of foreign aid and would insure that the advantages of development reached the rural masses rather than only urban residents. All this was to be done within the context of socialism which Nyerere saw as having its roots in traditional African values. He viewed socialism as a philosophy based on simple principles which were fundamental to most African societies and suggested that "...socialism is an attitude of mind. The basis of socialism is a belief in the oneness of man and the common historical destiny of mankind. Its basis, in other words, is human equality." (Nyerere, 1968:257)

Not everyone greeted Tanzanian socialism with enthusiasm. Some critics were people in Tanzania or abroad who were affected by the nationalization of businesses (for which compensation was paid), and others were individuals who felt that Tanzanian socialism was a poor policy that would require the transformation of fundamental political and economic values as well as expectations of its citizenry. Nonetheless, major political changes were carried out including the establishment of a one-party state, which confounded the skeptics by organizing truly competitive parliamentary elections in which many senior party officials were defeated.

An important part of the Tanzanian effort was the establishment of *ujamaa* (socialist) villages, designed to bring together the country's scattered rural population. Originally planned as a voluntary effort, the idea was based on the assumption that it was economically and organizationally impossible to provide a widely dispersed rural population with the educational, social, health, water, and sanitation services they needed. The initial results seemed very positive, but the overall impact was hard to determine because the actual number of villages developed under this voluntary scheme was small. It was sometimes hard to get people to move voluntarily from their homes and ancestral lands to new settlements. Thus, the voluntary nature of the villagization program was altered in 1974 to one in which large numbers of people— about one third of the country's population, or about five million people—would be required to move by 1976.

## CONTROLLED POLITICAL DEVELOPMENT AND AN OPEN ECONOMY

Other countries were involved in experiments of particular interest during this period. The Ivory Coast chose to continue in the pattern set out by France during the colonial period. Free enterprise was encouraged, and citizens were urged to build on the parliamentary system they had inherited. While political activity was highly controlled within the confines of the one-party state, there was little repression, and economic development seemed to move ahead at an impressive pace. In fact, people began to talk about an economic miracle in the Ivory Coast, due to an increase in the GNP (Gross National Product) of 125 percent from 1958 to 1965, an annual increase of almost 15 percent. It was estimated that real output grew by 11 or 12 percent from 1960 to 1965, export earning increased by 11 percent annually from 1958 to 1967, and the volume of turnover in manufacturing grew by about 40 percent a year. (Foster and Zolberg, 1971:215–230) All this was accompanied by political stability, high levels of employment, and a general sense of well-being throughout the country.

There were some who argued that the economic gains were illusory and represented large-scale external investments which would soon have to be offset to accommodate the extensive outflow of profits. (Arrighi and Saul, 1968:141–169) Nonetheless, the Ivory Coast was generally seen as an example of both political and economic success, and any visitor to the country would have found it hard to argue otherwise.

## THE LEADER AS GUIDE

Ghana's post-independence political development was another case which attracted a great deal of attention. Ghana was the first sub-Saharan African state to gain its independence, and it did so with much fanfare, goodwill, and the advantage of a budget surplus of $400 million from the cocoa stabilization fund. This fund was set up by the British to guarantee African farmers a relatively stable price for their cocoa in the context of an international market in which the prices fluctuated greatly, sometimes by more than 50 percent. When the price was low, a supplement was added from the fund—money having been put away during periods when prices were high. Ghana also had the advantage of dynamic leadership under Kwame Nkrumah, who had devoted considerable skill to political organization and a great deal of thought to African independence, freedom, and development. Nkrumah's ability to captivate the masses was a formidable advantage that helped him mobilize people. Ayi Kwei Armah captures these qualities:

> The new man must have begun to speak only moments before we arrived at Asamansudo, because his voice was still low. He was not

making any attempt to shout, and the quietness of his sound compelled us all to listen more attentively.

"...Can we ourselves think of nothing that needs to be done? Why idle then...?" Words about eyes needing to be opened and the world to be looked at. "Then we can think....Then we will act."

There was power in the voice that time, a power quickly retracted, and replaced by the low, calm voice....I stood there staring like a believer at the man, and when he stopped I was ashamed and looking around to see if anybody had been watching me. They were all listening. The one up there was rather helpless-looking, with a slight, famished body. So from where had he got this strength that enabled him to speak with such confidence to us, and we waiting patiently for more to come? Here was something more potent than mere words. These dipped inside the listener, making him go with the one who spoke.

"...in the end, we are our own enslavers first. Only we can free ourselves. Today, when we say it, it is a promise, not yet a fact....Freedom!..." The whole crowd shouted. I shouted, and this time I was not ashamed. (Armah, 1968:100–101)

Ghana, like the Ivory Coast, came to independence with a strong economy, an extensive and impressive educational system, and a good start on the basic infrastructure needed for further development. The CPP was well organized with branches and dedicated supporters throughout the country. Nkrumah charted what he saw as a socialist path for Ghana, although it was a very different one from what we have seen in Tanzania. The early years of independence for Ghana were crowned with successes, including the development of an industrial base in Tema built around the Valco aluminum processing plant and access to cheap electricity produced at the Volta dam. Other projects which brought Ghana international attention included Ghana Airways, the Black Star shipping line, several international conferences such as the All-African People's Conference in 1958, and the new Accra-Tema divided highway.

Despite the early rosy prospects for Ghana, the situation soon turned sour. By 1963 the budget surplus was largely gone, the economy was under severe strain, and the political leadership was resorting to increasingly autocratic and repressive measures. The market women, who had formerly been strong supporters, felt that Nkrumah's wage cuts had hurt their ability to make a living. The masses, once mobilized by CPP, now seemed cut adrift. Much of the party leadership appeared to be more concerned with personal gain than with national development. Widespread discontent grew in the country, and on February 24, 1966, the military overthrew the regime of Kwame Nkrumah and set Ghana on a very different path.

## PARLIAMENTARY DEMOCRACY

Other political experiments were under way elsewhere in Africa at this time, including some interesting examples of multi-party parliamentary democracy in Nigeria, Ghana, Botswana, the Gambia, and Sierra Leone. In Sierra Leone, the 1967 national elections witnessed one of the first victories of an opposition party in Africa with the All People's Congress (APC) defeating the Sierra Leone People's Party (SLPP), which had been the dominant political force in the country since 1951. Part of the undoing of the SLPP was their effort to introduce a one-party state. This idea had generated a great deal of hostility among the electorate, including many of the strongest supporters of the SLPP, and was generally perceived as an attempt by its least successful members to keep themselves in power. Although the SLPP eventually withdrew the bill from Parliament to create a one-party state, much damage had already been done to their image. This proposal awakened a widespread concern about the need to insure political competition to guarantee the possibility of real political change. Further, some of the SLPP leadership had shown themselves to be more interested in personal wealth than in the well-being of the populace, and there had been a growing tendency of the government to try to stifle criticism of its policies. During the 1967 elections, Siaka Stevens, leader of the opposition APC, campaigned throughout the country with eloquence and clarity. He urged voters to express their own views, explained why they should not let chiefs tell them how to vote, and discussed differences between the power of chiefs and those of the central government in ways they could understand, while urging their support for the APC.

The electoral victory of the APC was greeted with widespread enthusiasm throughout most of the country. The APC never had a chance to prove its ability, however, for shortly after Siaka Stevens was sworn in as Prime Minister, the military and police staged a coup overthrowing the APC government. Although the military ruled for only a year, the nature of politics seemed fundamentally altered following military rule.

Elsewhere in Africa the experience with multi-party parliamentary democracy was mixed. The democratic process worked well in Nigeria at the outset, but in time, as in Ghana and Sierra Leone, these institutions were beset with serious difficulties and in 1966 succumbed to military intervention. Several other competitive party systems continued to operate effectively in other parts of Africa, including those in Botswana and the Gambia.

## THE LION OF JUDAH: A SYMBOL OF INDEPENDENCE

There were also states, like Ethiopia, which were built on more traditional forms. In Ethiopia, Haile Selassie I, officially titled the Conquering Lion of Judah, Elect of God and King of Kings of Ethiopia, reasserted his claim to the throne of the ancient Ethiopian Empire. With British help, in 1941 he returned from an exile caused by the Italian occupation of his country. He worked to consolidate his power and enhance the position of the monarchy. While the monarchy itself had maintained its legitimacy during the war, some Ethiopians (often referred to as the patriots) who had continued the war of attrition against the Italians felt the emperor should have remained in Ethiopia regardless of the result. It seems clear that had he done so Ethiopia would not have regained its independence immediately after its liberation from fascist control, would probably have been put under trusteeship, and might well have been carved up into a number of smaller states. Unlike the emperor, the feudal court had lost much of its legitimacy, having failed in its military obligations to protect the peasants and other clients. Haile Selassie's first task was to reassert central authority. He re-established the court, appointed ministers loyal to him, and named governors in the regions, trying to balance practical necessity against his concern about those he feared might not be loyal to him.

During the occupation of Ethiopia, Haile Selassie had become an important symbol of African independence and strength both inside and outside Ethiopia. His impassioned pleas against the Italian invasion and the strong defense of his army (which had defeated the Italians in their first attempt at conquest) had pricked the conscience of the international community. His dignity throughout this period plus his personal presence added greatly to the respect and stature he was accorded. Given Haile Selassie's unique position in Africa, he became an important actor in early efforts to establish cooperation among

African states and eventually provided the site and much of the diplomatic inspiration for the formation and operation of the Organization of African Unity, which established its headquarters in Addis Ababa, Ethiopia. The emperor also seemed to be trying to combine the monarchy with aspects of the modern state, expressing his interest in education, modern technology, and economic development. He was seen as a strong ally of the West and an effective spokesman for the independence and autonomy of Africa.

## FACTIONALISM, CHAOS, AND RESOLUTION IN THE CONGO

Another case which was frequently cited as an example of post-independence problems (a few critics tried to paint it as typical) was that of the Congo—later to be called Zaire. The Congo became the focus of public attention as it suddenly raced toward independence due to Belgium's unexpected decision in January 1960 to pull out in five months. At that point the Congo had never had a national election. There were few Africans in the senior civil service, none in the army, and only a handful with college educations.

As the Congo moved to its first national elections, there were as yet no national political organizations. There were few, if any, political leaders with a following outside their own region; and no effective plans had been made by the colonial officials for the orderly transfer of power. Unfortunately, these deficiencies were not rectified during the remaining few months prior to independence, and few additional plans were made to facilitate the transition. That failure, plus external influence and Belgian public and private vacillation, contributed to the collapse of law and order in many parts of the country soon after the announcement that independence was imminent.

On June 30, 1960, the Congo became independent. A few days before there had been talk of secession in the province of Katanga. By July 5, part of the national Congolese army had mutinied. Efforts to bring them under control proved difficult but not impossible under the courageous guidance of Prime Minister Patrice Lumumba who, with others, restored some measure of calm within two days. On July 11 the President of the Provincial Government of Katanga announced that the province was seceding from the Congo and declared its independence. On the same day Belgian naval forces, without the consent of the government of the now independent Congo, bombarded the port city of Matadi without provocation and landed troops. From this point on the situation deteriorated rapidly. The United Nations tried to be of assistance but was badly hampered in its efforts by both the cold war and its inexperience in peace-keeping efforts.

By early 1961, Lumumba had been murdered in Elisabethville. Four major factions were competing for power or asserting the independence of territory under their control: Joseph Kasavubu in Leopoldville with from 7,000 to 15,000 troops, Antoine Gizenga in Stanleyville with 5,500 soldiers, Moise Tshombe in Elisabethville with from 5,000 to 12,000 troops, and Albert Kalonji in South Kasai with an estimated 3,000 soldiers. A period of strife, civil war, anarchy, and other tragic events followed during the next months. For many people, the Congo became synonymous with chaos. Much of the fault should be laid squarely on the shoulders of the Belgians who failed to lay the groundwork for transition and saddled the newly independent country with a billion dollars in external debts. They were ably assisted by other external actors, both independent nations and private entrepreneurs.

After years of thwarted efforts to bring the Congo under central administrative control (frequently with the help of the United Nations and a number of African, Asian, and European nations) and in the wake of yet another failure to do so, Joseph Mobutu, head of the Congolese armed forces, led a successful military coup on November 24, 1965. For the first time in years a semblance of peace and unity was restored, and Mobutu's assumption of power was greeted with both enthusiasm and relief.

## THE MILITARY IN POLITICS

As we have seen, a new type of political phenomenon began to rear its head in the 1960s in many African states—the involvement of the military (and sometimes police) in the political process. In most cases this involvement began with a coup, or military takeover of the government, which was usually accompanied by a great deal of violence but consolidated quickly. The phenomenon of military intervention became an increasingly familiar feature of African political life over the next few years. Such intervention involves the transformation of the military establishment (at the top levels at least) into a political organization whose major function is running the nation, with direct operation of the military becoming a secondary interest at least as far as the new military/political elite is concerned. In most instances military rule also involved suspension of the constitution; elimination of political parties and other political organizations; and restrictions on speech, the press, public participation in government, and public meetings.

Many of the early coups were looked on with favor both at home and abroad. The military was seen as intervening on behalf of the people to protect the nation from a tyrannical ruler, the collapse of political institutions, instability, corruption and greed, incipient or actual rebellion, ethnic conflicts, or all of the above. These interventions were often popularly received by the public, as was the case in Ghana where there was general public rejoicing about the overthrow of Kwame Nkrumah. The later period of his rule was seen as authoritarian, repressive, rife with corruption (though little was attributed to him personally), fraught with economic difficulties, and divisive of the unity that had been forged in earlier years. Colonel A.A. Afrifa, one of the architects of the coup and later the popular and flamboyant head of state, justified military intervention in *The Ghana Coup: 24th February 1966*:

> A *coup d'etat* is the last resort in the range of means whereby an unpopular government may be overthrown. But in our case where there were no constitutional means of offering political opposition to the one-party government, the Armed Forces were automatically made to become the official opposition of the government. (Afrifa, 1966:31)

Others saw the military as providing the heroic, strong leadership necessary to create the conditions for development. The military was depicted as having the ability to impose order and discipline on an elite (and in many cases a populace) that had run amuck because of greed, ineptitude, unrealistic expectations, false ideologies, and other failings. (Pye, 1962; Shils, 1962) Some saw the military as part of a new class which would serve as a positive force in development—a group of new technocrats with modern skills and ideas who could step in and save a bad situation. (Halpern, 1963) Others focused on its highly organized structure; its embodiment of virtues like bravery, order, obedience, and patriotism; its near monopoly over weaponry; and, frequently, its popularity as a basis for success. (Finer, 1962:9–10) The Ghanaian case seemed to bear this out. The military government rebuilt the economy, worked to eliminate corruption, and set up a program of civic education as a prelude to a return to civilian rule. Then, as they had promised, free elections were held and the military retired from the political scene. The government was left in the hands of popularly elected civilian authorities.

The Nigerian example was generally viewed in much the same way with General Yakubu Gowon and other military authorities described as having saved Nigeria from chaos at the hands of political elites and political parties more concerned with personal gain and factional power than with national unity and development. The Egyptian case also was frequently cited as an ideal example of the positive contribution military intervention could make. In this situation the leaders of the coup overthrew the corrupt and venal regime of King Farouk replacing it with a nationalist government under Gamal Abdel Nasser. Nasser's government was dedicated to political and economic development, and he seemed selfless in his personal dedication to making that happen.

The military was not always viewed in such a glowing light. In his classic early study *The Man on Horseback: The Role of the Military in Politics* (1962), S.E. Finer warns that the military has many weaknesses affecting its ability to rule. These include: its limited administrative skills, its lack of legitimacy, and its difficulties in overcoming citizen preferences for civilian rule. Experience in Africa has identified other problems. For example, the hierarchical structure of the military tends to block normal channels for citizen input into the political process. Similarly, early successes at solving short-term problems do not seem to carry over to more basic problems. There is a tendency for the military to see issues in far too simplistic terms. Thus the military regime in Ghana under Jerry Rawlings blamed Ghana's economic difficulties on the market women. The military's solution was to blow up the market. Another military regime had tried to make the civil service more efficient by subjecting those seen to be derelict in their duties to the humiliation of such exercises as marching in proper file or doing calisthenics in the heat of the day.

Military governments also seemed to be no less immune to corruption than civilian regimes and in some respects even less likely to feel any limits on their right to divert public funds. The corruption of the Acheampong military regime in Ghana set the stage for economic collapse from which the country is still trying to extricate itself ten years later. Military governments also have fewer restraints on their spending decisions than do most civilian regimes, and many have spent an increasingly large percentage of the national budget on military hardware, salaries, and other benefits. Most serious of all, however, is the fact that once involved in politics the military comes to see itself as guardian of the state even after the return to civilian rule and is prepared to regularly intervene "on behalf of the people." Thus we see a kind of cyclical re-emergence of military rule as exemplified particularly by the cases of Ghana and Nigeria. No civilian government can rule while constantly worrying about what the military is doing and thinking.

## THE REVOLUTIONARY REGIME

One final political system deserves mention at this point: the revolutionary regime. While there was much talk of revolution in Africa, the peaceful transition to independence in most states and the existence of basic institutional structures in others made radical change unlikely. There were, however, several exceptions of which two warrant mention here: the cases of Algeria and Guinea-Bissau. The Algerian revolution began on November 1, 1954, as an attempt to free Algeria from French colonial rule and lasted almost eight years until March 1962. It was a particularly bloody and brutal struggle in which there were almost one million casualties. Approximately one third of the Algerian population was moved to controlled areas or fortified camps, and nearly half a million children became orphans.

The revolution was designed not only to achieve independence but to create a radical new political order which would make the resources of the nation available to all of its people, create a more egalitarian society, and provide health, education, and social services to all citizens. Despite the solidarity created by eight years of struggle, the post-independence political situation was one of internal strife and conflict, and the efforts of the government to develop a new political and economic system did not live up to expectations. There was a mass exodus of men migrating to France in search of work leaving women and children to live as best they could on remittances. In the end, this regime too was brought to an end by a military coup.

The revolution in Guinea-Bissau was the first real success against the Portuguese. The liberation movement was organized by the African Party for the Independence of Guinea and Cape Verde (PAIGC), a political party working in secret from the late 1950s under the leadership of Amilcar Cabral. It began the armed struggle in 1963 when all other efforts to gain independence failed. By this time much of the rest of Africa was already independent. Portugal, however, was in no mood to consider independence and moved ahead to suppress opposition at any cost. Despite these efforts by the Portuguese, the PAIGC gained extensive support and by the late 1960s controlled almost the entire country. The party worked hard to build a new political and economic structure. It mobilized women to play an active role in the struggle and in this way provided new political roles and expectations for both women and men. In the context of extreme difficulties created by the war, the PAIGC was very well organized, worked to instill its values widely, and tried to build a revolution that would depend on the values and desires of the people for its success, rather than on a handful of leaders. (Cabral, 1969) The PAIGC was socialist in orientation, pragmatic in action, and seemed not to be tied to a particular international camp. To those who watched from a distance, the goals seemed to succeed to a remarkable degree.

Although Portugal had lost the war in Guinea-Bissau by 1967, it would not admit defeat—fearing, one suspects, a kind of domino effect in its other African territories, Angola and Mozambique. Nonetheless, the military and political successes in Guinea-Bissau gave hope and encouragement to the liberation movements in those two states. The Portuguese, for the most part, stayed in the fortified towns and left the countryside to the PAIGC. It was not until 1974 that the Portuguese finally conceded defeat, and Guinea-Bissau officially became a sovereign state.

## THE SEARCH FOR A NEW ORDER: SUCCESS AND FAILURES

In many respects the years immediately after independence were surprisingly successful for many African states. Overall, the transition from colonialism to independence had been remarkably smooth. Cases like the Congo merely serve to emphasize the difficulties which all the newly independent states confronted, the fragility of much of the existing institutional structure, and the potentially very high cost of failure. During the late 1950s and early 1960s there were impressive strides in building the educational facilities necessary for major progress, in mobilizing large numbers of people for development efforts, and in building an economic infrastructure of roads, ports, communications networks, utilities, banking systems, and agricultural extension. Such countries as Kenya, Nigeria, and the Ivory Coast seemed to be making impressive economic gains. The experiments in Tanzania and Senegal were promising; and even where the efforts at political and economic development faltered (as in Ghana), the renewal proposed by the military and the civilian regimes which followed looked good indeed. The visions for the future of Africa expressed by leaders like Kwame Nkrumah, Léopold Sédar Senghor of Senegal, and Amilcar Cabral; the idealism and commitment embodied in the efforts of those like Julius Nyerere and Nelson Mandela in South Africa; and the glorification and defense of African values by political leaders like Senghor, Eduardo Mondlane, and Jomo Kenyatta helped stimulate generations of young people and created values and goals to which many will return again and again.

However, a number of African states did not share in the opportunities of independence. The situation in South Africa continued to deteriorate. Racism and the laws defining it grew worse rather than better. Nationalist leaders like Nelson Mandela were imprisoned for their efforts to create an egalitarian society, and even his trial demonstrated the consequences of a system of justice which fails to recognize the rights and equality of all its people. Even today, some 25 years later, despite some well-publicized changes, there has been little progress for the African and nonwhite populations of South Africa. In many respects the situation is worse now than it was on the eve of independence for most of the rest of Africa. Conditions in the Portuguese colonies also proved to be more difficult to change than expected. A protracted and bloody struggle was fought in these states, depriving the people of many of their young who were killed in battle, died in prison, or were debilitated as a result of the struggle.

By the end of the 1960s, it had become clear that many of the dreams for Africa were not being realized. Some of the political experiments were notably successful, yet too many others appeared to be failing. People wanted economic development, political stability, education, health care, improved agricultural techniques, and the advantages of industrialization. These proved to be more difficult to achieve than most people had expected. Political instability, corruption, repression, military coups, and political disintegration began to thwart plans and frustrate expectations in a number of states. Economic growth proved illusive in many others. While there were successes, the typical rate of growth left an ever increasing gap between the more industrialized nations of the world and most of the newly independent states in Africa.

While some of the expectations and dreams of the independence era were being realized, there was a growing suspicion that the dreams of many African states were not likely to be fulfilled. Furthermore, the difficulties encountered by some of the most promising political and economic experiments were troubling. Part of the reason for the unforeseen difficulties was that nationalist leaders, scholars, advisors, and international organizations had been far too optimistic. Economic development was hindered by the lack of an adequate infrastructure in many states. The economic controls of the former colonial powers and their allies were difficult to eliminate, and it proved harder than expected for African states to alter the existing international economic order and established patterns of trade. Wide price fluctuations, deteriorating terms of trade, tariff barriers in the industrialized states, the increased cost of oil, and the international recession all played a role in hampering development.

As Africa moved into the 1970s, however, there was still a great deal of hope despite the difficulties. The experimentation that had already occurred and that which was currently under way reflected the faith that people could live better and improve their well-being. While there were many different conceptions of what constituted a better life, people were trying new ideas, methods, and strategies to achieve it. A review of the immediate post-independence period suggests that while the prospects were not as bright as they appeared to be in the late 1950s and early 1960s, they still seemed good. There was a sense that a new realism was needed, and with it would come a renewed energy and purpose that would pave the way for political and economic progress for most (if not all) the people of Africa.

## REFERENCES

Afrifa, A.A. 1966. *The Ghana Coup: 24th February 1966.* London: Frank Cass and Co.

Apter, David. 1963. *Ghana in Transition.* New York: Atheneum Press.

Armah, Ayi Kwei. 1968. *The Beautyful Ones Are Not Yet Born.* Boston: Houghton Mifflin.

Arrighi, Giovanni, and John S. Saul. 1968. "Socialism and Economic Development in Tropical Africa." *Journal of Modern African Studies,* 6 (2):141–169.

Cabral, Amilcar. 1969. *Revolution in Guinea.* New York: Monthly Review Press.

Finer, S.E. 1962. *The Man on Horseback: The Role of the Military in Politics.* Middlesex: Penguin Books.

Foster, Philip, and Aristide Zolberg. 1971. *Ghana and the Ivory Coast: Perspectives on Modernization.* Chicago: University of Chicago Press. See especially "Structural Transformation versus Gradualism: Recent Economic Development in Ghana and the Ivory Coast" by Elliot Berg, pp. 187–230.

Halpern, Manfred. 1963. *The Politics of Social Change in the Middle East and North Africa.* Princeton: Princeton University Press.

Nkrumah, Kwame. 1973. *Revolutionary Path.* New York: International Publishers.

Nyerere, Julius K. 1968. *Freedom and Socialism: A Selection From Writings and Speeches 1965–1967*. Oxford: Oxford University Press. See particularly chapters 26 and 30.

Pye, Lucian W. 1962. "Armies in the Process of Modernization." In *The Role of the Military in Underdeveloped Countries*, ed. John J. Johnson. Princeton: Princeton University Press, 69–90.

Shils, Edward. 1962. "The Military in the Political Development of New States." In *The Role of the Military in Underdeveloped Countries*, ed. John J. Johnson. Princeton: Princeton University Press, 7–68.

---

## *Reading 6.1*

In 1955 plans were being made for the forthcoming independence of the Gold Coast (later Ghana), the first of what was to be a number of such colonies in Black Africa to gain independence. (Ethiopia had gained its independence from a brief period of colonial rule under the Italians after liberation from fascist rule in 1941. Liberia had been independent, though under periodic American protection, since 1847.) Ghana became the focus of international attention because of the dynamism of its Prime Minister, Kwame Nkrumah, and its status as one of the most prosperous and successful British colonies. The interest and enthusiasm with which the press followed this case is typical of the hopes and expectations of this period.

---

## The New York Times, "Gold Coast Seeks Lead in Industry," May 1, 1955

### GOLD COAST SEEKS LEAD IN INDUSTRY

### Ambitious Project Foresees Country's Becoming Chief West African Center

ACCRA, Gold Coast, May 1—The Gold Coast Government, eager to establish the country as the leading industrial center of West Africa, has embarked upon an ambitious development program. It includes some of the biggest harbor installation, agricultural research and power projects on the Continent.

The program, if fulfilled, would give the country within ten years the three most modern ports on Africa's west coast, a great power and river development project, the world's leading cocoa research institute and a highly efficient system of interior communications.

At the moment this self-governing African state, once one of Britain's richest colonial possessions, is trying to balance an economy that is largely, and, according to local economists, dangerously dependent upon the cocoa market boom.

Faced by the prospect of full political independence within eighteen months the all-Negro Government of Prime Minister Kwame Nkrumah is intent upon providing assurance that the Gold Coast, when on its own, will be economically stable and will offer reasonable investment opportunities to the international market.

While overseas observers here have felt that some of the plans are overly ambitious, especially in view of the leisurely pace common to African labor, which often drains financial resources through time lag, they also have been anxious to see general encouragement of the development program. The British Colonial Office, through its $360,000,000 Colonial Development and Welfare project, has channeled large sums into the Gold Coast.

Equipped with rich natural resources, a strategic coastline, an ancient international trading tradition and an aggressively commercial-minded people, the Gold Coast is thus making a strong bid to match its acknowledged political leadership in West Africa with a similar lead in industry and commerce.

The major plans in its development program involve overseas interests, either the British Colonial Office or free enterprise, or both. The biggest one of these is the $432,000,000 Volta River plan whereby the waters of that stream, which runs almost diagonally across the country, would be harnessed and used principally for the production of aluminum from the country's bauxite resources at an ultimate rate of 210,000 tons a year.

The capital outlay is to be shared between the British and Gold Coast Governments and Aluminium Limited of Canada and Aluminium Company of England. A preparatory commission of British, Canadian and Gold Coast officials has been studying all aspects of the plan and will submit a report this year. If accepted by all parties, construction may get under way by 1957. The plan, which will provide the West with a valuable new reserve of aluminum, will take about seven years to complete.

Linked directly to the Volta project are several major undertakings that are now under way. The principal of these is construction of a new deep-water harbor at Tema, near the mouth of the Volta.

## Port to Be Finished by 1958

The Tema port will be finished by 1958. A thirty-six-mile railway linking Tema with Achimota, near Accra, was opened last year. Work also has started on a main trunk road that, when completed, will give a first-class route from Tema to Bawku, in the northeast corner of the country.

Roads and railways throughout the country are being improved and extended. The ports at Takoradi and Accra are being improved. Prime

Minister Nkrumah, in a recent review delivered to the Legislative Assembly, said development expenditure is now four times as much as it was in 1950–51. The entire cocoa industry is being reconstructed, he said. Emphasis is on research, eradication of disease, cultivation of improved strains and protection of the watershed.

During the past four years, he added, electricity has been increased 60 per cent. Telephone capacity has been increased threefold; hundreds of miles of new roads and railroads have been built; and cash crops such as coffee and the oil palm are being encouraged.

---

### Reading 6.2

The promise of self-determination and independence for most of Africa was not reflected in the realities of political life in South Africa, Angola, Mozambique, Namibia (South-West Africa), and southern Rhodesia. Racial discrimination, repression, and restrictions on speech, movement, and the press were rampant. The appearance of new legislation further limiting the political, economic, and social rights of those of African descent was a regular fact of the political situation. While development and freedom were in the air for most of Africa, a very different reality confronted the people of Southern Africa on a daily basis. In this part of Africa, Nelson Mandela epitomizes the consequences of a commitment to equality, justice, and full participation in the political life of one's country. Born in 1918, the eldest son of a Tembu chief, he was brought up as a nationalist and an opponent of discrimination and repression. He became active in the African National Congress (ANC) youth league and was soon one of its most articulate and effective spokesmen. He studied law and worked to eliminate the discrimination and racism of apartheid. The South African government regarded his activities with alarm, and he was charged with treason, tried, and imprisoned for his activities. In 1961 he was found guilty and sent to Robben Island. Below are major portions of the testimony he presented in his own defense at the trial.

---

## Nelson Mandela, "Black Man in a White Court," from *No Easy Walk to Freedom*

Your worship, I have elected to conduct my own defence. Some time during the progress of these proceedings, I hope to be able to indicate that this case is a trial of the aspirations of the African people, and because of that I thought it proper to conduct my own defence....

I want to apply for Your Worship's recusal from this case. I challenge the right of this Court to hear my case on two grounds.

Firstly, I challenge it because I fear that I will not be given a fair and proper trial. Secondly, I consider myself neither legally nor morally bound to obey laws made by a Parliament in which I have no representation.

In a political trial such as this one, which involves a clash of the aspirations of the African people and those of Whites, the country's courts, as presently constituted, cannot be impartial and fair.

In such cases, Whites are interested parties. To have a White judicial officer presiding, however high his esteem, and however strong his sense of fairness and justice, is to make Whites judges in their own case.

It is improper and against the elementary principles of justice to entrust Whites with cases involving the denial by them of basic human rights to the African people.

What sort of justice is this that enables the aggrieved to sit in judgement over those against whom they have laid a charge?

A judiciary controlled entirely by Whites and enforcing laws enacted by a White Parliament in which Africans have no representation—laws which in most cases are passed in the face of unanimous opposition from Africans—

### Here the Magistrate interrupted

... It is true that an African who is charged in a court of law enjoys, on the surface, the same rights and privileges as an accused who is White in so far as the conduct of this trial is concerned. He is governed by the same rules of procedure and evidence as apply to a White accused. But it would be grossly inaccurate to conclude from this fact that an African consequently enjoys equality before the law.

In its proper meaning equality before the law means the right to participate in the making of the laws by which one is governed, a constitution which guarantees democratic rights to all sections of the population, the right to approach the court for protection or relief in the case of the violation of rights guaranteed in the constitution, and the right to take part in the administration of justice as judges, magistrates, attorneys-general, law advisers, and similar positions.

In the absence of these safeguards the phrase 'equality before the law', in so far as it is intended to apply to us, is meaningless and misleading. All the rights and privileges to which I have referred are monopolized by Whites, and we enjoy none of them.

The White man makes all the laws, he drags us before his courts and accuses us, and he sits in judgement over us.

It is fit and proper to raise the question sharply, what is this rigid colour-bar in the administration of justice? Why is it that in this courtroom I face a White magistrate, confronted by a White prosecutor, and escorted into the dock by a White orderly? Can anyone honestly and seriously suggest that in this type of atmosphere the scales of justice are evenly balanced?

Why is it that no African in the history of this country has ever had the honour of being tried by his own kith and kin, by his own flesh and blood?

I will tell Your Worship why: the real purpose of this rigid colour-bar is to ensure that the justice dispensed by the courts should conform to the policy of the country, however much that policy might be in conflict with the norms of justice accepted in judiciaries throughout the civilized world.

I feel oppressed by the atmosphere of White domination that lurks all around in this courtroom. Somehow this atmosphere calls to mind the inhuman injustices caused to my people outside this courtroom by this same White domination.

It reminds me that I am voteless because there is a Parliament in this country that is White-controlled. I am without land because the White minority has taken a lion's share of my country and forced me to occupy poverty-stricken Reserves, over-populated and over-stocked. We are ravaged by starvation and disease....

## Interruption by the Magistrate

...It is understandable why citizens, who have the vote as well as the right of direct representation in the country's governing bodies, should be morally and legally bound by the laws governing the country.

It would be equally understandable why we, as Africans, should adopt the attitude that we are neither morally nor legally bound to obey laws which we have not made, nor can we be expected to have confidence in courts which enforce such laws.

I am aware that in many cases of this nature in the past, South African courts have upheld the right of the African people to work for democratic changes. Some of our judicial officers have even openly criticized the policy which refuses to acknowledge that all men are born free and equal, and fearlessly condemned the denial of opportunities to our people.

But such exceptions exist in spite of, not because of, the grotesque system of justice that has been built up in this country. These exceptions furnish yet another proof that even among the country's Whites there are honest men whose sense of fairness and justice revolts against the cruelty perpetrated by their own White brothers to our people.

The existence of genuine democratic values among some of the country's Whites in the judiciary, however slender they may be, is welcomed by me. But I have no illusions about the significance of this fact, healthy a sign as it might be. Such honest and upright Whites are few and they have certainly not succeeded in convincing the vast majority of the rest of the White population that White supremacy leads to dangers and disaster.

However, it would be a hopeless commandant who relied for his victories on the few soldiers in the enemy camp who sympathize with his cause. A competent general pins his faith on the superior striking power he commands and on the justness of his cause which he must pursue uncompromisingly to the bitter end.

I hate race discrimination most intensely and in all its manifestations. I have fought it all during my life; I fight it now, and will do so until the end of my days. Even although I now happen to be tried by one whose opinion I hold in high esteem, I detest most violently the set-up that surrounds me here. It makes me feel that I am a Black man in a White man's court. This should not be. I should feel perfectly at ease and at home with the assurance that I am being tried by a fellow South African who does not regard me as an inferior, entitled to a special type of justice.

In their relationship with us, South African Whites regard it as fair and just to pursue policies which have outraged the conscience of mankind and of honest and upright men throughout the civilized world. They suppress our aspirations, bar our way to freedom, and deny us opportunities to promote our moral and material progress, to secure ourselves from fear and want. All the good things of life are reserved for the White folk and we Blacks are expected to be content to nourish our bodies with such pieces of food as drop from the tables of men with White skins. This is the White man's standard of justice and fairness. Herein lies his conception of ethics. Whatever he himself may say in his defence, the White man's moral standards in this country must be judged by the extent to which he has condemned the vast majority of its inhabitants to serfdom and inferiority.

We, on the other hand, regard the struggle against colour discrimination and for the pursuit of freedom and happiness as the highest aspiration of all men. Through bitter experience, we have learnt to regard the White man as a harsh and merciless type of human being whose contempt for our rights, and whose utter indifference to the promotion of our welfare, makes his assurances to us absolutely meaningless and hypocritical.

I have the hope and confidence that Your Worship will not hear this objection lightly nor regard it as frivolous. I have decided to speak frankly and honestly because the injustice I have referred to contains the seeds of an extremely dangerous situation for our country and people. I make no threat when I say that unless these wrongs are remedied without delay, we might well find that even plain talk before the country's courts is too timid a method to draw the attention of the country to our political demands.

*The application for the recusal of the Magistrate was refused.*

## Reading 6.3

One of the developmental efforts in Africa which sparked the greatest enthusiasm in the post-independence period was that of Tanzania. Of particular interest were the policies laid out in the Arusha Declaration of January 1967 which specified and discussed the basic principles and policies which the country was to follow. Drafted by the President of Tanzania, Julius Nyerere, it was modified by TANU (the Tanganyika—later Tanzania—African National Union), the only political party in Tanzania after a merger with a small opposition party. Among the most significant parts of the Arusha Declaration is the section on self-reliance in which it is suggested that a poor nation like Tanzania must substitute its labor and energy for foreign assistance, loans, and investment if it is to develop as a free and independent state.

## Julius Nyerere, "The Policy of Self-Reliance," from *Freedom and Socialism: A Selection from Writings and Speeches 1965–1967*

### We are at War.

TANU is involved in a war against poverty and oppression in our country; this struggle is aimed at moving the people of Tanzania (and the people of Africa as a whole) from a state of poverty to a state of prosperity.

We have been oppressed a great deal, we have been exploited a great deal and we have been disregarded a great deal. It is our weakness that has led to our being oppressed, exploited and disregarded. Now we want a revolution—a revolution which brings to an end our weakness, so that we are never again exploited, oppressed, or humiliated.

### A Poor Man does not use Money as a Weapon.

But it is obvious that in the past we have chosen the wrong weapon for our struggle, because we chose money as our weapon. We are trying to overcome our economic weakness by using the weapons of the economically strong—weapons which in fact we do not possess. By our thoughts, words and actions it appears as if we have come to the conclusion that without money we cannot bring about the revolution we are aiming at. It is as if we have said, 'Money is the basis of development. Without money there can be no development.'... It is as if we said, 'In the next five years we want to have more food, more education, and better health, and in order to achieve these things we shall spend £250,000,000.' We think and speak as if the most important thing to depend upon is MONEY and anything else we intend to use in our struggle is of minor importance.

When a Member of Parliament says that there is a shortage of water in his constituency and he asks the Government how it intends to deal with the problem, he expects the Government to reply that it is planning to remove the shortage of water in his constituency—WITH MONEY....

When an official of the co-operative movement mentions any problem facing the farmer, he expects to hear that the Government will solve the farmer's problems—WITH MONEY. In short, for every problem facing our nation, the solution that is in everybody's mind is MONEY.

Each year, each Ministry of Government makes its estimates of expenditure, i.e. the amount of money it will require in the coming year to meet recurrent and development expenses. Only one Minister and his Ministry make estimates of revenue. This is the Minister for Finance. Every Ministry puts forward very good development plans. When the Ministry presents its estimates, it believes that the money is there for the asking but that the Minister for Finance and his Ministry are being obstructive. And regularly each year the Minister for Finance has to tell his fellow Ministers that there is no money. And each year the Ministries complain about the Ministry of Finance when it trims down their estimates.

Similarly, when Members of Parliament and other leaders demand that the Government should carry out a certain development, they believe that there is a lot of money to spend on such projects, but that the Government is the stumbling block. Yet such belief on the part of Ministries, Members of Parliament and other leaders does not alter the stark truth, which is that Government has no money.

When it is said that Government has no money, what does this mean? It means that the people of Tanzania have insufficient money. The people pay taxes out of the very little wealth they have; it is from these taxes that the Government meets its recurrent and development expenditure. When we call on the Government to spend more money on development projects, we are asking the Government to use more money. And if the Government does not have any more, the only way it can do this is to increase its revenue through extra taxation.

If one calls on the Government to spend more, one is in effect calling on the Government to increase taxes. Calling on the Government to spend more without raising taxes is like demanding that the Government should perform miracles; it is equivalent to asking for more milk from a cow while insisting that the cow should not be milked again. But our refusal to admit that calling on the Government to spend more is the same as calling on the Government to raise taxes shows that we fully realize the difficulties of increasing taxes. We realize that the cow has no more milk—that is, that the people find it difficult to pay more taxes....

### What of External Aid?

One method we use to try and avoid a recognition of the need to increase taxes if we want to have more money for development, is to think in terms of getting the extra money from outside Tanzania. Such external finance falls into three main categories.

(a) *Gifts:* This means that another government gives our Government a sum of money as a free gift for a particular development scheme. Sometimes it may be that an institution in another country gives our Government, or an institution in our country, financial help for development programmes.

(b) *Loans:* The greater portion of financial help we expect to get from outside is not in the form of gifts or charity, but in the form of loans. A foreign government or a foreign institution, such as a bank, lends our Government money for the purposes of development. Such a loan has repayment conditions attached to it, covering such factors as the time period for which it is available and the rate of interest.

(c) *Private Investment:* The third category of financial help is also greater than the first. This takes the form of investment in our country by individuals or companies from outside. The important condition which such private investors have in mind is that the enterprise into which they put their money should bring them profit and that our Government should permit them to repatriate these profits. They also prefer to invest in a country whose policies they agree with and which will safeguard their economic interests.

These three are the main categories of external finance. And there is in Tanzania a fantastic amount of talk about getting money from outside. Our Government and different groups of our leaders never stop thinking about methods of getting finance from abroad. And if we get some money, or even if we just get a promise of it, our newspapers, our radio, and our leaders, all advertise the fact in order that every person shall know that salvation is coming, or is on the way....

## DO NOT LET US DEPEND UPON MONEY FOR DEVELOPMENT

It is stupid to rely on money as the major instrument of development when we know only too well that our country is poor. It is equally stupid, indeed it is even more stupid, for us to imagine that we shall rid ourselves of our poverty through foreign financial assistance rather than our own financial resources. It is stupid for two reasons.

Firstly, we shall not get the money. It is true that there are countries which can, and which would like, to help us. But there is no country in the world which is prepared to give us gifts or loans, or establish industries, to the extent that we would be able to achieve all our development targets. There are many needy countries in the world. And even if all the prosperous nations were willing to help the needy countries, the assistance would still not suffice. But in any case the prosperous nations have not accepted a responsibility to fight world poverty. Even within their own borders poverty still exists, and the rich individuals do not willingly give money to the government to help their poor fellow citizens.

It is only through taxation, which people have to pay whether they want to or not, that money can be extracted from the rich in order to help the masses. Even then there would not be enough money. However heavily we taxed the citizens of Tanzania and the aliens living here, the resulting revenue would not be enough to meet the costs of the development we want. And there is no World Government which can tax the prosperous nations in order to help the poor nations; nor if one did exist could it raise enough revenue to do all that is needed in the world. But in fact, such a World Government does not exist. Such money as the rich nations offer to the poor nations is given voluntarily, either through their own goodness, or for their own benefit. All this means that it is impossible for Tanzania to obtain from overseas enough money to develop our economy.

## GIFTS AND LOANS WILL ENDANGER OUR INDEPENDENCE

Secondly, even if it were possible for us to get enough money for our needs from external sources, is this what we really want? Independence means self-reliance. Independence cannot be real if a nation depends upon gifts and loans from another for its development. Even if there was a nation, or nations, prepared to give us all the money we need for our development, it would be improper for us to accept such assistance without asking ourselves how this would affect our independence and our very survival as a nation. Gifts which increase, or act as a catalyst, to our own efforts are valuable. But gifts which could have the effect of weakening or distorting our own efforts should not be accepted until we have asked ourselves a number of questions.

The same applies to loans. It is true that loans are better than 'free' gifts. A loan is intended to increase our efforts or make those efforts more fruitful. One condition of a loan is that you show how you are going to repay it. This means you have to show that you intend to use the loan profitably and will therefore be able to repay it.

But even loans have their limitations. You have to give consideration to the ability to repay. When we borrow money from other countries it is the Tanzanian who pays it back. And as we have already stated, Tanzanians are poor people. To burden the people with big loans, the repayment of which will be beyond their means, is not to help them but to make them suffer. It is even worse when the loans they are asked to repay have not benefited the majority of the people but have only benefited a small minority.

How about the enterprises of foreign investors? It is true we need these enterprises. We have even passed an Act of Parliament protecting foreign investments in this country. Our aim is to make foreign investors feel that Tanzania is a good place in which to invest because investments would be safe and profitable, and the profits can be taken out of the country without difficulty. We expect to get money through this method. But we cannot get enough. And even if we were able to convince foreign investors and foreign firms to undertake all the projects and programmes of economic development that we need, is that what we actually want to happen?...

How can we depend upon gifts, loans and investments from foreign countries and foreign companies without endangering our independence? The English people have a proverb which says: 'He who pays the piper calls the tune'. How can we depend upon foreign governments and companies for the major part of our development without giving to those governments and countries a great part of our freedom to act as we please? The truth is that we cannot.

## WE HAVE PUT TOO MUCH EMPHASIS ON INDUSTRIES

Because of our emphasis on money, we have made another big mistake. We have put too much emphasis on industries. Just as we have said, 'Without money there can be no development', we also seem to say, 'Industries are the basis of development, without industries there is no development'. This is true. The day when we have lots of money we shall be able to say we are a developed country. We shall be able to say, 'When we began our Development Plans we did not have enough money and this situation made it difficult for us to develop as fast as we wanted. Today we are developed and we have enough money'. That is to say, our money has been brought by development. Similarly, the day we become industrialized, we shall be able to say we are developed. Development would have enabled us to have industries. The mistake we are making is to think that development begins with industries. It is a mistake because we do not have the means to establish many modern industries in our country. We do not have either the necessary finances or the technical know-how. It is not enough to say that we shall borrow the finances and the technicians from other countries to come and start the industries. The answer to this is the same one we gave earlier, that we cannot get enough money and borrow enough technicians to start all the industries we need. And even if we could get the necessary assistance, dependence on it could interfere with our policy on socialism. The policy of inviting a chain of capitalists to come and establish industries in our country might succeed in giving us all the industries we need, but it would also succeed in preventing the establishment of socialism unless we believe that without first building capitalism, we cannot build socialism.

## LET US PAY HEED TO THE PEASANT

Our emphasis on money and industries has made us concentrate on urban development. We recognize that we do not have enough money to bring the kind of development to each village which would benefit everybody. We also know that we cannot establish an industry in each village and through this means effect a rise in the real incomes of the people. For these reasons we spend most of our money in the urban areas and our industries are established in the towns.

Yet the greater part of this money that we spend in the towns comes from loans. Whether it is used to build schools, hospitals, houses or factories, etc., it still has to be repaid. But it is obvious that it cannot be repaid just out of money obtained from urban and industrial development. To repay the loans we have to use foreign currency which is obtained from the sale of our exports. But we do not now sell our industrial products in foreign markets, and indeed it is likely to be a long time before our industries produce for export. The main aim of our new industries is 'import substitution'—that is, to produce things which up to now we have had to import from foreign countries.

It is therefore obvious that the foreign currency we shall use to pay back the loans used in the development of the urban areas will not come from the towns or the industries. Where, then, shall we get it from? We shall get it from the villages and from agriculture. What does this mean? It means that the people who benefit directly from development which is brought about by borrowed money are not the ones who will repay the loans. The largest proportion of the loans will be spent in, or for, the urban areas, but the largest proportion of the repayment will be made through the efforts of the farmers....

## THE PEOPLE AND AGRICULTURE

The development of a country is brought about by people, not by money. Money, and the wealth it represents, is the result and not the basis of development. The four prerequisites of development are different; they are (i) People; (ii) Land; (iii) Good Policies; (iv) Good Leadership. Our country has more than ten million people* and its area is more than 362,000 square miles.

---

*1967 census showed 12.3 million people.

## AGRICULTURE IS THE BASIS OF DEVELOPMENT

A great part of Tanzania's land is fertile and gets sufficient rain. Our country can produce various crops for home consumption and for export.

We can produce food crops (which can be exported if we produce in large quantities) such as maize, rice, wheat, beans, groundnuts, etc. And we can produce such cash crops as sisal, cotton, coffee, tobacco, pyrethrum, tea, etc. Our land is also good for grazing cattle, goats, sheep, and for raising chickens, etc.; we can get plenty of fish from our rivers, lakes, and from the sea. All of our farmers are in areas which can produce two or three or even more of the food and cash crops enumerated above, and each farmer could increase his production so as to get more food or more money. And because the main aim of development is to get more food, and more money for our other needs, our purpose must be to increase production of these agricultural crops. This is in fact the only road through which we can develop our country—in other words, only by increasing our production of these things can we get more food and more money for every Tanzanian.

## THE CONDITIONS OF DEVELOPMENT

### (a) Hard Work

Everybody wants development; but not everybody understands and accepts the basic requirements for development. The biggest requirement is hard work. Let us go to the villages and talk to our people and see whether or not it is possible for them to work harder....

### (b) Intelligence

The second condition of development is the use of intelligence. Unintelligent hard work would not bring the same good results as the two combined. Using a big hoe instead of a small one; using a plough pulled by oxen instead of an ordinary hoe; the use of fertilizers; the use of insecticides; knowing the right crop for a particular season or soil; choosing good seeds for planting; knowing the right time for planting, weeding, etc.; all these things show the use of knowledge and intelligence. And all of them combine with hard work to produce more and better results.

None of this means that from now on we will not need money or that we will not start industries or embark upon development projects which require money. Furthermore, we are not saying that we will not accept, or even that we shall not look for, money from other countries for our development. This is NOT what we are saying. We will continue to use money; and each year we will use more money for the various development projects than we used the previous year because this will be one of the signs of our development.

What we are saying, however, is that from now on we shall know what is the foundation and what is the fruit of development. Between MONEY and PEOPLE it is obvious that the people and their HARD WORK are the foundation of development, and money is one of the fruits of that hard work.

From now on we shall stand upright and walk forward on our feet rather than look at this problem upside down. Industries will come and money will come but their foundation is THE PEOPLE and their HARD WORK, especially in AGRICULTURE. This is the meaning of self-reliance.

---

## Reading 6.4

Kwame Nkrumah, President of Ghana, in laying out his country's development plan in a radio address to the nation five years after independence, suggests that the country is facing some serious problems in its development effort. In contrast to the Arusha Declaration, the overview of the program is much more an exhortation to support and mobilization than a plan of action. We see in Nkrumah's comments an indication of the fact that the government felt it necessary to coerce and detain those who were deemed to be in opposition to the efforts of President Nkrumah and the Convention People's Party (CPP). At the same time, it is clear in this address that Nkrumah feels confident enough of support to release many of those who were detained at an earlier time.

---

## Kwame Nkrumah, *Revolutionary Path*

Organization presupposes planning, and planning demands a programme for its basis. The Government proposes to launch a Seven-Year Development Plan in January, 1963. The Party, therefore, has a pressing obligation to provide a programme upon which this plan could be formulated.

We must develop Ghana economically, socially, culturally, spiritually, educationally, technologically and otherwise, and produce it as a finished product of a fully integrated life, both exemplary and inspiring.

This programme, which we call a programme for 'Work and Happiness', has been drawn up in regard to all our circumstances and conditions, our hopes and aspirations, our advantages and disadvantages and our opportunities or lack of them. Indeed, the programme is drawn up with an eye on reality and provides the building ground for our immediate scientific, technical and industrial progress.

We have embarked upon an intensive socialist reconstruction of our country. Ghana inherited a colonial economy and similar disabilities in most other directions. We cannot rest content until we have demolished this miserable structure and raised in its place an edifice of economic stability, thus creating for ourselves a veritable paradise of abundance and satisfaction. Despite the ideological bankruptcy and moral collapse of a civilization in despair, we must go forward with our preparations for planned economic growth to supplant the poverty, ignorance, disease, illiteracy and degradation left in their wake by discredited colonialism and decaying imperialism.

In the programme which I am today introducing to the country through this broadcast, the Party has put forward many proposals. I want all of you to get copies of this programme, to read and discuss it and to send us any observations or suggestions you may have about it.

Tomorrow, the National Executive Committee of the Party will meet to discuss the Party programme and officially present it to the nation. I feel sure that it will decide in favour of an immediate release of this programme to the people. The Party, however, will take no action on the programme until the masses of the people have had the fullest opportunity of reviewing it.

This programme for 'Work and Happiness' is an expression of the evidence of the nation's creative ability, the certainty of the correctness of our Party line and action and the greatest single piece of testimony of our national confidence in the future.

Ghana is our country which we must all help to build. This programme gives us the opportunity to make our contribution towards the fulfillment of our national purposes.

As I look at the content of the programme and the matters it covers, such as Tax Reform, Animal Husbandry and Poultry Production, Forest Husbandry, Industrialization, Handicrafts, Banking and Insurance, Foreign Enterprise, Culture and Leisure, I am convinced beyond all doubt that Ghana and Ghanaians will travel full steam ahead, conscious of their great responsibilities and fully aware that the materialization of this bright picture of the future is entirely dependent on their active and energetic industry. Remember that it is at the moment merely a draft programme and only your approval will finalize it.

At this present moment, all over Africa, dark clouds of neocolonialism are fast gathering. African States are becoming debtor-nations, and client States day in and day out, owing to their adoption of unreal attitudes to world problems, saying 'no' when they should have said 'yes', and 'yes' when they should have said 'no'. They are seeking economic shelter under colonalist wings, instead of accepting the truth—that their survival lies in the political unification of Africa.

Countrymen, we must draw up a programme of action and later plan details of this programme for the benefit of the whole people. Such a programme is the one that the Party now brings to you, the people of Ghana, in the hope that you will approve it critically and help to make it a success.

We have a rich heritage. Our natural resources are abundant and varied. We have mineral and agricultural wealth and, above all, we have the will to find the means whereby these possessions can be put to the greatest use and advantage. The Party's programme for work and happiness is a pointer to the way ahead, the way leading to a healthier, happier and more prosperous life for us all. When you have examined and accepted this programme, the Government and the people will base on it and initiate our Seven-Year Development Plan, which will guide our action to prosperity.

This programme constitutes for us a vigorous reminder that we must eschew complacency and push forward more determined than ever before to achieve our goal and, through work and enterprise, to create progress, prosperity and happiness for our people.

And now, Countrymen, I have been speaking to you about our Party programme. From this I turn to a subject of almost equal moment, because it affects what is to me of the greatest importance, namely, the maintenance of the Republic as by law established and the achievement of those aims which under our Constitution I have pledged myself as President to strive for.

An emergent country which attempts to follow a policy of socialism at home and a policy abroad of positive non-alignment, is challenging many vested interests. It would have been the most criminal folly for us not to take note of the lessons of contemporary history.

When you chose me as your President, I took an oath in which I swore that I would preserve and defend the Constitution and that I would do right to all manner of people according to law, without fear or favour, affection or ill will.

I should have been false to my oath had I allowed the Constitution to be overthrown by force, but I consider that the obligations which the Constitution imposes upon me not only call upon me to do justice, but also, wherever possible, to temper justice with mercy.

We have by no means passed through all our difficulties. The need for a Preventive Detention Act still remains, but I believe that the time has come when the security situation has improved sufficiently to allow a number of detainees to be released.

I have therefore ordered the immediate release of many of those at present under detention.

The Government had originally considered that anyone who had been previously detained and released, and who then again engages in subversive activities, should be liable to a maximum imprisonment of twenty years. On this matter, too, I consider that a gesture of reconciliation can be made. The maximum period of five years detention as provided in the existing law will be retained, but the Preventive Detention Act will be so amended as to provide that anyone released from detention who again indulges in subversion, shall be detained again up to the present maximum of five years, and may, in addition, lose all rights as a citizen.

There remains also the question of those few citizens who have fled abroad. In one or two cases detention orders have been made against subversive individuals who have since fled the country, and in the event of such people returning to Ghana, these orders would be reviewed. But in most cases, those who have fled from Ghana have done so because they had a bad conscience or else were frightened by some unscrupulous rumour-monger.

A general amnesty will be extended to all such persons. I call upon them to return and to put their energies into useful purposes for the good of the country. I give them the assurance that they will not be victimized in any way or subjected to any disability for any past act; so long as they remain loyal and law-abiding they will not only have nothing to fear, but will also be assured of the protection which the machinery of the law provides and to which everyone in this country is entitled.

Countrymen, now is the time for reconstruction. We have a gigantic task before us. In solving our problems even those who in the past believed that they could gain their ends by subversion can now, if only they give up illegal methods, find their way back into useful and fruitful work.

# A GARDEN OF EDEN IN DECAY?

—— Victor Olorunsola, with assistance from Dan Muhwezi ——

The previous chapter considered a variety of political systems that evolved in the years immediately following the independence of many African nations. In this chapter, Professor Olorunsola discusses the economic changes that have taken place in Africa during the last 25 years and raises some critical questions about Africa's future. The comparison of post-independent Africa to the Garden of Eden is examined primarily with reference to sub-Saharan Africa. **Eds.**

The title of this chapter is subject to various interpretations. To some it may suggest a former perfect condition and a state of innocence. Those who subscribe to this interpretation may consider pre-colonial Africa to have been such an era. Others may, out of frustration with the present, consider the colonial time as such a period. Still another interpretation considers the Garden of Eden not as a historical fact, but as an ideal construct.

Whatever interpretation one holds, there is a considerable disenchantment with the present economic condition of African states. If there was ever innocence it has vanished, and the great hopes and optimistic expectations of the early independence era are seemingly on the retreat. It is true that there are lost hopes and visible signs of frustrations in the drought-stricken, poverty-ridden, and politically unstable states. But it is also true that there remain great expectations, given the fact that independent African states are still in their infancy.

This chapter attempts to describe the economic state in African countries, to identify decay-producing forces and assess their impact on individuals and societies, and to identify attempts to reverse the current trend. We shall also discuss the notion of appropriate and inappropriate technology in relation to the development of African states.

## PRESENT AND PAST ECONOMIC STATES

The hopes and high expectations which accompanied the dawn of independence in most African states in the 1960s are slowly giving way to despair and nostalgia. African countries seem to be caught in an economic and political morass which may have dire consequences for their existence as viable states and even dash the aspirations of their people.

The main economic features of sub-Saharan Africa can be summed up very briefly. The region is the poorest in the world. (See Table 7.1.) Sixty percent of its population live below poverty level. It has the highest birth rates, the highest—though declining—death rates, and the lowest life expectancy at birth. It has a small modern sector, and the bulk of the population is engaged in agriculture. The economies are small, porous, and dependent on a few primary exports. There are chronic shortages of skilled manpower and inadequate infrastructures.

If the periods before and soon after independence were disappointing for sub-Saharan Africa, the 1970s were catastrophic for most of the continent. For instance, the growth of per capita GDP (Gross Domestic Product) averaged 1.3 percent per year from 1960 to 1970 but fell to 0.7 percent per year between 1970 and 1980 and was estimated at −3.8 percent for 1983. (World Bank, 1984:10) With an annual per capita income of about $411, sub-Saharan Africa is the poorest region of the world. According to the United Nations Conference on Trade and Development (UNCTAD), 20 of the 36 poorest countries of the world and two-thirds of the low-income countries are in Africa. In the last decade, 15 African countries recorded a negative rate of growth of per capita income. (World Bank, 1981:2) There are, of course, considerable variations in the growth and development performance of individual countries. There are oil exporters such as Nigeria and Gabon. Other countries have achieved comparatively greater growth in their per capita incomes, such as Ivory Coast, Kenya, Malawi, and Botswana. In most of the remaining states, however, the situation has been bleak.

Modern economic development in Africa began with the production of cash crops and the extraction of minerals for foreign markets. In most countries, these constitute the predominant sources of foreign exchange. Consequently, the pace of a country's economic growth depends largely on the foreign market for its primary exports. The agricultural export crops include coffee, tea, cocoa, sugar, and oil seeds. This agricultural sector accounts for over 40 percent of the

**TABLE 7.1.  Sub-Saharan Africa and the World: Basic Data**

| Countries | Population (millions) mid-1979 | GNP per capita average annual growth rate (percent) | | Per capita growth 1970-79 (percent) | | Adult literacy rate (percent) 1976 | Life expectancy at birth (years) 1979 | Death rate of children aged 1-4 (per thousand) 1979 |
|---|---|---|---|---|---|---|---|---|
| | | 1960-70 | 1970-79 | Agriculture | Volume of exports | | | |
| Sub-Saharan Africa | 343.9 | 1.3 | 0.8 | -0.9 | -3.5 | 28 | 47 | 25 |
| Low-income | 187.1 | 1.6 | -0.3 | -1.1 | -4.5 | 26 | 46 | 27 |
| Nigeria | 82.6 | 0.1 | 4.2 | -2.8 | -2.8 | .. | 49 | 22 |
| Other middle-income | 74.2 | 1.9 | -0.5 | -0.4 | -3.5 | 34 | 50 | 22 |
| South Asia[a] | 890.5 | 1.5 | 1.5 | 0.0 | 0.6 | 36 | 52 | 15 |
| All developing | 3,245.2 | 3.5 | 2.7[b] | 0.1 | -1.5 | 57 | 58 | 11 |
| Low-income | 2,260.2 | 1.8 | 1.6[b] | 0.1 | -3.1 | 50 | 57 | 11 |
| Middle-income | 985.0 | 3.9 | 2.8[b] | 0.6 | 1.9 | 72 | 61 | 10 |
| All industrialized | 671.2 | 4.1 | 2.5[b] | 0.2 | 5.2 | 99 | 74 | 1 |

.. not available

[a]Bhutan, Bangladesh, Nepal, Burma, India, Sri Lanka, and Pakistan

[b]1970-80

*Source:* World Bank data files

GDP. Over 70 percent of the population is employed in or lives on agriculture. Undoubtedly, the last decade was particularly difficult for agriculture worldwide. The annual growth rate of world agricultural output declined from 2.6 percent between 1960 and 1970 to 2.2 percent from 1970 to 1978, and the corresponding per capita annual growth rate declined from 0.7 to 0.4 percent. In sub-Saharan Africa the deterioration was more notable. The annual growth rate of agricultural output declined from 2.3 percent between 1960 and 1970 to 1.3 percent from 1970 to 1980. Per capita annual growth took a dive from 0.2 percent to −1.4 percent. (Wangwe, 1984:1038; World Bank, 1981:45)

In the 1960s agricultural exports increased by 1.9 percent annually; in the 1970s they fell by the same proportion. In the 1960s Africa grew 70 percent of the world's ground nuts, but today it grows less than 18 percent. To make matters worse, the primary products on which Africa relies for export earnings experienced a sluggish demand. Consequently, Africa's share of the world's trade for most of its agricultural products declined markedly. Given the fact that a large proportion of the population derives its livelihood from agriculture, the fall in production and exports represents a serious loss of income for many African states and dashed hopes—and in some cases untimely death—for some of their people. Moreover, the fact that agricultural growth (1.3 percent) fell behind GDP growth (1.6 percent) suggests widening income disparities between agricultural sector income recipients and others in the rest of the economy. Therefore we can expect worsening conditions in rural areas where the bulk of those who depend on agriculture live. Nor is the problem restricted to cash crop production.

Sub-Saharan Africa is the only region in the world where food production per capita declined over the last two decades. It is estimated that about 20 percent of the population eat less than the minimum needed to sustain good health. In 1978, for instance, per capita food production in Angola, Benin, Ethiopia, Ghana, Nigeria, Senegal, Sierra Leone, Uganda, and Burkina Faso was less than 90 percent of the 1961 to 1965 average. (USDA, 1981:1) Recently the food situation in Ethiopia and Mozambique has been catastrophic. More than three million people in Mozambique and about eight million in Ethiopia have been on the edge of starvation. Accordingly, the grain imports to sub-Saharan Africa tripled between 1960 and 1978.

One is hard pressed to be optimistic on this score. Current estimates indicate that in 1990 Africa may be forced to import about 17 million tons of grain simply to maintain the 1975 level of consumption. (Lofchie and Commins, 1982:2) If correct, these estimates are troublesome, particularly because many African nations that exported food and were relatively self-sufficient in the 1960s are now the net food importers. The magnitude of the current problem is better grasped if we realize that Africa now imports about 9.25 million tons of food. This is equivalent to the food needs of the entire urban population of Africa. (World Bank, 1984)

In addition to agriculture, Africa also depends on mineral exports. For instance, of the total export earnings in 1978, the revenue from minerals accounted for 87 percent in Mauritania, 71 percent in Zaire, 98 percent in Guinea, and 94 percent in Zambia. With the exception of oil-producing countries, Nigeria, Angola, and Gabon, the mining sector made a minimal contribution to the economies of most other African states after mineral prices fell. Heavy reliance on income from exports has made most of these countries prone to earnings fluctuations due to price instability. For instance, the fall in copper prices in the 1970s grossly affected the economies of Zambia and Zaire. These instabilities in income make the planning functions of most states difficult.

The external debt and its service cost or interest are an increasing burden on this region. The former, which stood under $6 billion in the 1960s, rocketed to $32.1 billion in 1979 and $48.1 billion in 1982. At the same time the debt service increased from $0.4 billion in 1970 to $5.5 billion in 1982. Consider the case of Nigeria where the foreign exchange earnings used for debt servicing increased from 10 percent in 1982 to 12 percent in 1983, to 35 percent in 1984, and to about 44 percent in 1985. (*Nigerian Daily Sketch*: 1985) In the Sudan, the external debt was about $7 billion (more than seven times its export earnings) in 1983, while the debt service was estimated at about $1.1 billion (or slightly more than it can generate from its annual exports). Furthermore, the foreign exchange in most African countries has declined sharply to less than two months of import coverage. This encourages borrowing to defray recurrent expenditures, fuels inflation, perpetuates dependency, and ultimately undermines the stability of African states.

High fertility (3.1 percent annual growth rate) and low life expectancy at birth have combined to produce an African population of which 44 percent is below the age of 15. This constitutes a considerable burden on the productive segment of the population and reduces their propensity to save.

Sub-Saharan Africa lacks adequate manpower resources, and 70 percent of the adult population is illiterate. Of the primary-school–age population, 55 percent of the males and 43 percent of the females are enrolled in school. At the secondary level, 39 percent of the males and

24 percent of the females are enrolled. These percentages, although still inadequate, may constitute a ray of hope. More students now go to primary, secondary, and university institutions than before.

Let us turn to the examination of the functions and roles of various economic institutions, particularly development, commercial and cooperative banks, and other financial institutions. Following independence, these institutions were established to provide easy access to capital and to facilitate local trade. Unfortunately, however, banks remain concentrated in urban areas and are reluctant to invest in agriculture because of its initial low investment returns. Most farmers, therefore, do not have easy access to credit while others cannot dispose of their surplus easily. Thus, the existing institutions have failed to uplift the agrarian sector. Consequently, agriculture has remained stagnant. Most farmers feel neglected, disenchanted, frustrated, or apathetic; youth are flocking to towns in search of jobs and better lifestyles. This urban-rural drift has deprived rural areas of potential labor and created a mixed pool of uneducated and educated unemployed.

Trade at the interstate level is relatively negligible. It is true that there are more transport and communication links between African countries today than there were in 1960; but since African economies are more oriented to foreign markets, economic forces continue to ensure that the important routes are those that lead overseas. The trade between individual states is at best intermittent and is often characterized by smuggling of various products across state borders.

The tragic legacy of colonialism in many countries is that the administrative apparatus is unsuited to sustaining growth and development. Indeed, many have argued that the procedures and structures of colonial bureaucracies produced civil servants trained primarily for custodial and punitive tasks. These skills have proved unsuitable for developmental demands placed upon the bureaucracy during the post-independence era. In many African countries, the same administrators who were trained to maintain the colonial system still run the highest offices in the bureaucracy. They are few, but well placed, and thus affect important decisions. Equally perverse is the structure of rewards. The emphasis on seniority rather than competence reinforces a system in which the incompetent may thrive while the more properly trained may be frustrated and confined to the lower echelons of power.

The role of primary and extended families with regard to resource allocation and distribution also has changed significantly. With increasing scarcity of resources, family ties and obligations are being redefined, and extended family relationships are under considerable stress. The successful members of the extended family are often unable to meet their traditional family obligations. Some see this as a partial explanation for corruption and nepotism. For example, agriculture, which previously depended on family labor, is stunted due to lack of labor or appropriate technology. Yet traditional expectations linger on. The father, mother, brother, or sister must provide for the immediate family and is expected to be his or her cousin's keeper beyond the time of working together.

## THE CAUSES OF THE CURRENT ECONOMIC STATE

The failure of most African states to achieve the optimistic goals set at independence or even to keep pace with the levels of the 1960s is a cause of concern and a subject of wide-ranging debate. Could it be that colonial economies were so structured that they could not sufficiently sustain a dynamic state? Could it be that the process of transformation (or the scale and speed of political change) has been so sudden that it destroyed the very foundations of African economies? Could it be that what Africa produces and relies on cannot survive in the present competitive international economic system? Have lack of skills, population pressure, and an increasingly hostile environment contributed to human misery in this region? We believe that all these factors are responsible for the current economic state.

## THE NATURE AND IMPACT OF THE
## COLONIAL ECONOMY

At the turn of the 19th century, European powers partitioned, occupied, and opened up the African continent, establishing systems that were either dependent on or subservient to the colonizing states' own interests. For example, the colonial economy was heavily dependent on the prosperity of its own industries. (Brett, 1973) The industries that processed agricultural and mining products, however, were located in the colonizing state. As a result, transportation and communication networks ran from the coast to mining and agricultural export areas. Each colony was required to produce those primary products for which it had a comparative advantage. Consequently, most of the labor, capital, research, and other inputs were reserved for cash crop or mining activities. This arrangement fitted the interests of the colony, but it has had significant implications for the present states. Although some states have attempted to diversify and reduce their reliance on one or two crops, their economies have remained colonial in outlook. For instance, most of Zaire's minerals are still refined in Belgium. Most states still rely on coffee, cotton, tea, oil seeds, cocoa, palm oil, and timber. Since these products were established primarily to benefit the economies of the colonizing countries, it is difficult for some to perceive how maintenance or expansion of exports of these products can primarily benefit the newly independent states. (McBride, 1978) The emphasis on cash crops has had other negative effects on the society. Food crops, in particular, have either been taken for granted or are regarded as a residual to development. Food production has remained at the subsistence level with women and children providing most of the required labor. Since these workers have not been effectively integrated into the money economy in most African states, the food sector has remained undeveloped.

Education is another area where the colonial legacy was a mixed blessing. Although the importance of education cannot be questioned, colonial education was largely inappropriate and inadequate. In some African countries there were no sufficiently trained personnel to take over the jobs previously held by the expatriates at the time of independence. Perhaps it served the interests of the colonial administration to keep Africans insufficiently trained. But it is difficult to perceive how the new officials could now operate effectively when they were inadequately trained to assume challenging and nonroutine duties. The process of Africanization of the civil service was accomplished in less than a decade in some countries. Some think this time span was inadequate. In any case, there is a fundamental difference between operating a colonial bureaucracy, which emphasizes the maintenance of law and order, and the operation of a bureaucracy of a sovereign state, which must focus on development.

## POPULATION GROWTH

The precise effect of population growth on the present crisis in Africa is controversial. Some argue that population density in Africa is still too low for population to be a critical factor in the explanation of underdevelopment. Others argue that the effect of population growth has been sizeable. (World Bank, 1984; Bothomani, 1984) The estimated population growth rate of 3.1 percent is the fastest growing in the world today. This rate and the structural transformation that accompanies it have several important and complex ramifications for the food situation, basic health and education services, and general economic development. In agriculture, for example, the futile struggle by fast-expanding populations to extract an adequate livelihood from the available resources without the aid of appropriate technology has been wreaking havoc with resources. (FAO, 1982) Additional output traditionally has been obtained by extending cultivation to virgin lands. With an increase in population, however, there is substantial overcropping and overgrazing and a considerable reduction in bush fallow periods. Consequently, cultivation is extended to marginal land. In short, production is increasingly being outpaced by population growth.

One major effect of this trend is an increase in rural-urban migration. This rapid urban growth has put severe pressure on the employment sector, meaning that substantial numbers of people are now dependent on the markets for their daily food, which is now supplied by an agricultural system that is substantially subsistence-oriented. This, together with nontraditional food consumption habits acquired by the emerging urban population, partially explains the growing dependence of African states on food imports.

Most governments have continued to invest heavily in the young. The immediate impact of such investment is a drain on the nations' purses, and this may have caused some countries to forego other productive investments. Further, the long-term economic benefit of such investments is uncertain. The subject of brain drain is a case in point. An increasing number of well trained African scholars, technicians, doctors, and other professionals have taken jobs with foreign countries. Thus, the long-term economic development payoff for investing in a large pool of young people could even turn out to be detrimental. It is paradoxical and costly for Africa to continue hiring expatriate personnel when it cannot retain the very people in which it puts so many scarce resources.

## INVESTMENT LEVELS

One determinant of GDP is investment. In recent years there has been an association between the growth in domestic investment and growth in GDP. In countries where rates of investment were low (Ethiopia, Mozambique, Zaire, Uganda, Ghana, and Zambia) the annual rates of GDP were either low or negative. Conversely, countries which experienced high annual growth rates of investment (Nigeria, Ivory Coast, Cameroon, and Gambia) recorded substantial GDP rates. Overall, gross domestic investment in sub-Saharan Africa increased faster than GDP. (Wangwe, 1984; World Bank, 1984) Although the annual growth rate in investments from 1970 to 1979 was higher, GDP growth rate in this period experienced a deceleration. The question that has to be posed is: What caused the poor performance?

According to the World Bank (1981:31), sub-Saharan Africa lacks the capacity to generate projects which can pay off readily, appraise investment proposals and screen out the good from the not so good, and formulate and implement viable economic policies. It could be deduced from the above that the lack of a domestic pool of skilled personnel in responsible positions and adequate local-specific data generated over longer time periods makes government departments unable to choose wisely with respect to strategic technical assistance, funding, and project selection. Again, let us look at agriculture. As indicated before, agriculture is the traditional cornerstone of African economies. Yet the policies and the institutional framework within which it functions are generally not considered conducive to increasing agricultural output. Price policies are a case in point. In most instances, the official price policies are too low to encourage investment. In other cases, due to existing price distortions generated by overvalued official exchange rates, imported food items are cheaper than locally produced foods. (Watts, 1983:488) At the institutional level, marketing systems are uncertain and inefficient. Public marketing agencies are increasingly high-cost operations due to overstaffing, politicization, poor financial control, lack of accountability, and inexperienced management. (Bothomani, 1984:153; Olorunsola, et al., 1982) Consequently, the incentives to produce have been shattered and urban preferences for imported goods have thrived. The would-be farmers have been pushed out of rural areas and, as if to complete the cycle, more imports have been brought in to fill in the food scarcity gap.

The level of investment usually depends on the volume of savings, which is minimal in the case of the majority of the population. What is astonishing, however, is that those who could invest have either spent their income or invested or banked with foreign banks. This has reduced the size of political investments, affected the confidence and legitimacy of those in power positions, and, in the eyes of international financiers, made most states unworthy of foreign credit.

## POLITICAL INSTABILITY

In addition to the problems discussed so far, sub-Saharan Africa has been gripped by a wave of political instability which has severe implications for the general development process. Coups, countercoups, and civil strife have occurred in one form or another in most countries, with devastating results. For instance, the number of refugees, about 400,000 in the 1960s, is now estimated at about 2.5 million. (World Bank, 1984) It is disturbing to note that sub-Saharan Africa, which has less than a tenth of the world population, has about a quarter of the world's ten million refugees. This represents a major loss to the African continent. The people who are confined in refugee camps and forced to subsist on charity are displaced labor that could have made significant contributions to their own countries.

Furthermore, political instability has deprived many African nations of a favorable climate for investment. While Africa desperately needs the capital and technical know-how to finance and run certain projects, it is difficult to perceive how investors—foreign or local—could be attracted to such highly unstable, uncertain, and sometimes volatile environments. This instability also has encouraged politicians and other government officials in high positions to siphon millions of dollars to foreign banks. Political offices are seen by various competing groups as the only channel for survival.

## THE EFFECTS OF THE INTERNATIONAL ECONOMIC SYSTEM AND PHYSICAL ENVIRONMENT

Africa may not be excused from its own contribution to its underdevelopment, but it is not wholly to blame. External factors beyond the control of sub-Saharan Africa and sheer bad luck are partly responsible. In fact, neither the international economic environment nor nature can plead innocent. According to the secretariats of the Organization of African Unity, Economic Commission for Africa, and African Development Bank, the external factors include stagflation in the industrialized countries, higher energy prices, relatively slow trade growth in primary products, and adverse terms of trade, especially for copper and iron ore. (OAU, ECA, ADB, 1982:7) In the 1970s the prices of cocoa, coffee, ground nuts, sugar, sisal, phosphates, and uranium rose sharply and fell again. (World Bank, 1984) The rise in prices of these primary products was welcome, but the fall sent significant shockwaves through the optimistic development plans, budgets, and revenues of African countries. While the boom improved the creditworthiness of some countries in the eyes of international financiers, the fall made it impossible for them to sustain that position. It also worsened their indebtedness. The benefits from this rise were wiped out by the oil and grain price hikes of the 1970s.

The World Bank has observed that the international economic environment has been difficult for developing countries. In the last four years, trade has stagnated, prices declined, and many developed countries have increased protectionist barriers for goods from developing countries, particularly those goods for which Africa has an edge. (World Bank, 1984:11) This situation is troublesome, not only for the present, but for future hopes for survival.

The physical environment has contributed its own share to the problems of this region. Drought, in particular, has severely curtailed agricultural production in the Sahelian states, Ethiopia, and, until recently, in East Africa. There are fears that the River Niger could dry up completely in the near future. It has also been reported that the surface area of Lake Chad has dropped from its normal 25,000 square kilometers to 3,500 square kilometers. (*Nigerian Daily Times*: 1985) Thousands died in the Sahelian drought of the early 1970s, and others are dying in Ethiopia and Mozambique where the problem is compounded by political turbulence. It could be argued that African methods of production have destroyed the natural habitat and significantly increased the pace of desertification. This is partly true, but the scale of the present drought perhaps defies such a simple explanation.

## TECHNOLOGY AND DEVELOPMENT

Modern technology is one of the major factors which account for differences in levels of development among states. Technology constitutes the knowledge and techniques which pertain to production of goods. (Zadrozny, 1959) It is commonly argued that traditional African technology is archaic and perhaps anachronistic, given the nature of the existing development problems; but imported technologies have not always been appropriate. Often they are either exotic or too sophisticated for the local population.

The Food and Agriculture Organization (FAO) of the United Nations observed several shortcomings and weaknesses of African agriculture including outmoded husbandry practices, the crudest type of production tools, and inadequate and poor storage facilities which result in losses of about 20 to 30 percent of harvested food crops. (FAO, 1982:13) Clearly, then, there is considerable potential for increasing Africa's agricultural output if the farmers use improved technology for proper storage, more disease-resilient seed varieties, and more effective conservation and preservation methods.

A technology is appropriate if it helps in the attainment of societal development goals, maximizes the local resources available, does little or no damage to the environment, and sustains the fundamental and widely treasured values of the society. The matter of appropriate technology is complicated. There may be a need and demand for increased production. A policy of privatization and large-scale farming which will use labor-saving efficient technology may at first seem most appropriate. Nevertheless, in a society characterized by semiskilled and unskilled labor and very high unemployment rates, such a technology may be less appropriate than a more labor-intensive one. Consider the case of Nigeria where the maximization of output was made a priority. Some large mechanized farms were established, private investors with profit-oriented motives were encouraged to farm, and food importation was embraced. Nevertheless, high food prices and insufficient food supply continued to be problems for most of the unskilled and unemployed as well as the ungainfully employed. Former president Julius Nyerere of Tanzania observed:

> I have been telling my people, we have got to change, and must mechanize, we must have better tools. But what better tools? Not combine harvesters. If I were given enough combine harvesters for every family in Tanzania, what would I do with them? No mechanics, no spare parts... I shudder at the thought... we are using hoes. If two million farms could jump from the hoe to the oxen plough, it would be a revolution. It would double our standard of living, triple our produce. (Freeman, 1982:3)

Mechanized agriculture in more developed countries released labor from agriculture to other sectors of the economy. In Africa, however, where population is increasing tremendously and other sections of the economy have a low capacity to absorb labor, the use of technologies that have a potential for releasing more labor may be disastrous. The point is that more productive technologies need to be found, but those must be of an intermediate nature which can easily be maintained by local skills.

Unfortunately, independent African states are generally financially handicapped and, consequently, heavily dependent on foreign aid packages with heavy procurement clause burdens. There is little latitude for decision-making in regard to technology on the part of recipient countries. In a given state, we may find equipment from several countries, a situation that discourages the accumulation and dissemination of knowledge about specific equipment repairs. It also prevents the local accumulation of spare parts, reduces dealer leverage, and breeds equipment incompatibility. For instance, in 1981, the Canadian International Development Agency (CIDA) had to fly three tires from Canada into Tanzania so that the Canadian-made machinery could be available for harvest. (Freeman, 1982:498) Further, much of the equipment is not made or designed for tropical use, and imported technologies are often out of date in more developed countries, making spare parts availability problematic. Appropriate technology will continue to elude us until donor efforts are coordinated with recipient needs, existing aid policies are reformed, and relevant scientific and technological research is given priority by African countries.

## IMPLICATIONS

To some political leaders, public office provides an opportunity to accumulate personal and ill-obtained wealth. Apologists see this enormous desire to accumulate wealth as arising out of a necessity to attain power in a political environment fraught with gross uncertainties and instability. One may argue, however, that it is the reaction to the voracious accumulation of wealth at the expense of citizens which breeds political instability. This is a more credible explanation, given the grossly uneven distribution of wealth, the conspicuous consumption pattern of the wealthy few, and the frustration level of those outside the power circle. Other apologists argue that Africa is experiencing value anomie or dualism which requires that political leaders maintain a patron-client relationship with their supporters and ethnic compatriots even when these individuals do not have the specific objective requirements that are imperative for the operation of the modern economy.

Politicians and bureaucrats excuse themselves and soothe their consciences by pointing to the pressures under which they must operate.

They are expected either to continue to offer financial support to members of extended families who are less fortunate or to practice nepotism. It is common for bureaucrats to ask for a 10 percent commission when dealing with foreign contractors, a practice that has further drained scarce resources. Some argue that corruption at the local level gives the rich but politically excluded elites the access to influence decisions or to cut through bureaucratic red tape. Even if this is granted, there is the danger that corruption can destroy the legitimacy of the government and enfeeble the state because of its potential for sabotaging public policy. Whether one conceives of gross and perpetual instability as the father of a poor economy or vice versa, the fact is that neither has been very productive for Africa. The confidence of political leaders and citizens is shaken when, consistently, resources cannot be found to put carefully conceived development plans into operation. It is shaken when a government cannot provide for its people's basic needs.

Consider the impact of perennial food shortages. In addition to the cost of food imports, which is a drain on scarce foreign exchange resources, there is likely to be a weak and poorly motivated labor force. States are reduced to the status of beggars. Indeed, some observers wonder whether states which seem to chronically fail to meet the elementary needs of their people have legitimacy. Without doubt, there are instances where this has led to a loss of trust in the leaders, the weakening of citizens' support, and increased cynicism about the state, leading to the withdrawal and disengagement of some individuals from the state. Other citizens may feel compelled to use extralegal means to cope with reality or change government or governors. One only needs to do a content analysis of speeches given to justify African military takeovers to realize the potency of inadequate food supply.

## ATTEMPTS TO REVERSE THE DECAY

African states, collectively and individually, have tried to respond to the current problems through various methods. Perhaps the most intriguing is the establishment of ethical codes to ensure certain ethical standards. The leadership code in Tanzania, for example, requires leaders to adhere to a set of prohibitions and to demonstrate sound public morality. This may not only limit the intensity of corruption, but may generate a positive feeling among the citizens about their government and political leaders.

Food has become a focus of attention of many states. Various strategies and policy options are under active consideration, experimentation, or implementation. In May 1981, the Tanzanian government launched the National Economic Survival Program to increase and diversify the production of food crops. In 1980, Zambia launched a ten-year Operation Food Production with the overall objective of increasing production of strategic food and export crops, and Nigeria began a Green Revolution program. The implementation of many such programs is being re-examined.

At the regional level, perhaps the Lagos Plan of Action (LPA) is the most important. This plan emerged at a time of discouraging economic trends: 20 years of stagnation in outputs; deteriorating terms of trade; increased payments for the import of high level skills, capital goods, and spare parts; and increased unemployment and poverty. (OAU, ECA, ADB, 1982:3) It assumes that past and current policies were not adequate to successfully address the present economic problems. Thus the LPA was designed to restructure the economy of Africa, based on the twin principles of national and collective self-reliant and self-sustaining development. (OAU, ECA, ADB, 1982:3) As a corrective measure, the LPA proposed that individual governments involve youth in agricultural development in order to arrest the rural-urban drift, create effective incentives in the agricultural sector, and establish joint efforts to deal with such regional agricultural problems as pest control and seed selection.

Africa operates in an international community of organizations. Accordingly, its road to recovery is, in part, dependent on the supplementary efforts of others. It is therefore encouraging that the 1980 development strategy takes the LPA recommendations into account unlike the past two UN development decades where Africa was unable to make concrete proposals that reflected its needs and aspirations. This is significant because future aid and technical assistance may, to a large extent, reflect priorities and strategies of African countries. (Adedeji, 1982:7)

We seriously doubt that economically Africa was ever the Garden of Eden. It would be a mistake to argue that the colonial period represented such a state. Without question, however, the harsh economic conditions in Africa have not improved; and, in some cases, considerable deterioration has taken place since independence. African states have a long way to go before they can reach the promised land of economic development.

# REFERENCES

Adedeji, Adebayo. 1982. *After Lagos What?* Tripoli: African Center for Applied Research and Training in Social Development.

Brett, A.E. 1973. *Colonialism and Underdevelopment in East Africa.* New York: Nork Publishers.

Bothomani, B.I. Winter 1984–1985. "Food Crisis in East and Central Africa with Special References to Kenya, Malawi, Tanzania, and Zambia." *Journal of African Studies* 11(4):148–155.

Crocker, C. January 1985. "U.S. Assistance and Africa's Economic Crisis." Washington, D.C.: U.S. Department of State.

Food and Agriculture Organization. 1982. *Famine in Africa.* Rome: FAO.

Freeman, L. 1982. "CIDA, Wheat and Rural Development in Tanzania," *Canadian Journal of African Studies* 16(3):479–504.

Lofchie, F.M., and K.S. Commins, 1982. "Food Deficits and Agriculture Policies in Sub-Saharan Africa." In The Hunger Project [San Francisco] Papers. Cambridge: Cambridge University Press.

McBride, H.R. 1978. "How Can Africa Survive?" *Issue,* Los Angeles, 8(4):30–34.

*Nigerian Daily Sketch* (Ibadan), "Exchange Earnings Share Intact," March 16, 1985, p. 1.

*Nigerian Daily Times* (Lagos), "River Niger Drying?" March 16, 1985, p. 1.

OAU, ECA, ADB. 1982. *Accelerated Development in Sub-Saharan Africa: An Assessment.* Addis Ababa: ADB edited version.

Olorunsola, V., H. Marienau, and D. Muhwezi, 1983. "African Government Response to Increasing Food Scarcities." Mimeograph, Political Science Dept., Iowa State University.

USDA. 1981. *Food Problems and Prospects in Sub-Saharan Africa: The Decade of the 1980s.* Washington, D.C.: Foreign Agriculture Research.

Wangwe, S.M. October 1984. "Sub-Saharan Africa: Which Economic Strategy?" *Third World Quarterly* 6(4):1033–1059.

Watts, M. 1983. *Silent Violence: Food Famine and Peasantry in Northern Nigeria.* Los Angeles: University of California Press.

World Bank. 1981. *Accelerated Development in Sub-Saharan Africa: An Agenda for Action.* Washington, D.C.: World Bank.

World Bank. 1984. *Toward Sustained Development in Sub-Saharan Africa: A Joint Program of Action.* Washington, D.C.: World Bank.

Zadrozny, J.T. 1959. *Dictionary of Social Sciences.* Washington, D.C.: Public Affairs Press.

---

## Reading 7.1

This piece examines the transfer of technology and identifies two reasons why much of the technology transferred after World War II has not been beneficial to the recipient countries. In addition, the extract examines the United Nations Conference on Trade and Development's (UNCTAD) proposals for an international code of conduct on the transfer of technology and asks African governments to support and help implement such a code. It advocates the doubling of efforts to enhance African governments' ability to choose appropriate technology which will result in increased productivity.

---

## United Nations Economic Commission for Africa, "Development and Economic Cooperation: Proposals for Consideration by African Governments," from *Economic Bulletin for Africa*

In view of the low level of technological capability in most developing countries, there has been little alternative in the past but to import technology while domestic capability is being developed. Indeed, in those areas where domestic capability is least developed, demand for technology has been greatest, particularly in the following fields: surveys and development of natural resources, modern processes of production, transport and infrastructural facilities. In line with these demands, much technology has been transferred to developing countries in the post World War II period, but there are at least two reasons why receiving countries have not fully benefited from this transfer.

First, the technology which has been transferred has not always been suitable to the factor proportions found in developing countries. In fact, there has been a definite bias in favour of capital, reflecting the relative labour scarcity in developed countries where the technology was developed. In some areas, especially agriculture, this capital bias has been positively harmful. Because of the inflexibility in adapting foreign agricultural technology to rural conditions in developing countries, agricultural development, which directly affects the majority of the African population, has been relatively neglected. In other areas, it must be admitted, the harmful effects have not been so great. Even with the best efforts, it is doubtful that labour-intensive technology could be developed to prospect for oil or minerals and to exploit them on a commercial basis. The elimination of the technological bias favouring capital calls for the formulation and pursuit of effective technological policies and the urgent development of domestic technological capabilities by African Governments. In addition, aid and trade policies pursued by developed countries should be re-examined with the object of promoting the import of labour-intensive products from the developing countries.

Secondly, the market for technology is dominated by transnational corporations controlled by interests in the developed countries. Contractual agreements between developing countries and transnational corporations have often resulted in developing countries' paying too high a price for technology. There are few hard and fast rules in this area, but generally speaking the market for technology is an imperfect market with transnational corporations exercising a monopoly rent over highly specialized technology.

The maximum price for technology is generally determined by the social opportunity cost of land and labour to the host country; no host Government should rationally accept a return to land and labour utilized by the transnational corporation less than the return in their next best uses. The minimum price is determined by the private opportunity cost of capital to the transnational corporation; there is a minimum return on its capital which it will accept in order to invest in the host country. Between these two extremes, the resultant price attached to the technology will depend on the relative strengths of each side and the amount of information available to each side, especially with regard to the other's position. Suffice to say that the price is usually nearer the maximum than the minimum; developing countries are usually in a very weak bargaining position both because of their small size and because of the lack of relevant information available to them. To illustrate the contrast in size, in 1971 the sales of each of the top seven transnational corporations exceeded the GDP of any individual African country.

The Programme of Action on the Establishment of a New International Economic Order called for the formulation of an international code of conduct for the transfer of technology. After exhaustive discussions at the international level, UNCTAD has since proposed such a code with the following main principles:* that suppliers should treat all receivers of technology equally; that problems with respect to factor intensity should be corrected by guaranteeing to receivers the suitability of the technology transferred, a continued supply of information on improvements in the technology concerned during the period of the agreement, and provision of assistance in developing local technological capacity; that monopoly rights granted to a patent holder to restrict the export of goods to other markets where the patent holder has similar operations should be waived; and that adequate training should be provided with a view to taking over management at the end of the agreement period. African Governments should support the activities of UNCTAD in conjunction with other international agencies to implement a code of conduct along these lines.

In the long term, African countries must increase their capacity to absorb and make meaningful use of science and technology. In this area, there is no question that progress will be slow. The dilemma is that demand for technological processes will be great, but the selective and productive utilization of the supply that will be called forth is bound to be limited for a while by inadequate local capability (qualified technologists) to scrutinize the suitability of plant design. The vetting capacity is essential for guaranteeing against over-ready acceptance of the recommendations of the [purveyors] of technology. The purely technological choice has also to be treated in the context of wage, tariff and other fiscal measures which should not unduly cause enterprises to choose capital-intensive rather than labour-intensive techniques. The sudden

---

*United Nations Conference on Trade and Development, Committee on Transfer of Technology, An International Code of Conduct on Transfer of Technology, TD/B/C.6/AC.1/2, Supp. 1, 25 March 1975.

large increase in energy costs calls for even closer examination of technological choices by the African countries, with a view to limiting the process of costly mechanization which they are in no position to afford.

The International Development Strategy contained a programme for the expansion of the scientific and technological capacity of the developing countries and the creation of indigenous technology. It outlined four main components: strengthening scientific and technological manpower development and infrastructure, putting more effort into research and development that are of special interest to developing countries, easier and cheaper access to technological information and the development of new technologies more suitable for adoption by developing countries.

The Committee on Science and Technology has taken up these guidelines and elaborated World and Regional Plans for achieving the objectives of the new international economic order in the field of science and technology. The Africa Regional Plan, while conceived in terms of solving the continent's unique problems, directs special attention to those areas neglected in the past: tropical agricultural research in the field of genetics as a means of spreading the "Green Revolution," research in health, diet and housing improvements, reduction of population pressure and acquisition of literacy.

While there are few short cuts to developing personnel and infrastructure in individual African countries, some economies may be effected through co-operation, especially among smaller countries. Such co-operation should cover higher education and research facilities which can be initiated with outside aid in the form of technical assistance.

---

## Reading 7.2

Adebayo Adedeji addresses some of the necessities for the implementation of the Lagos Plan of Action. In the extract, the author is concerned that the terms *self-reliant* and *self-sustaining* might imply a lack of need for international assistance. Therefore, he specifically outlines ways in which the international environment and assistance can help. He also examines the type of international political and economic environment which would be conducive to the implementation of the plan.

---

## Adebayo Adedeji, "Implementation of the Strategies and the Plan of Action at the International Global Level," from *After Lagos What?*

The Monrovia Strategy for the Economic Development of Africa and the Lagos Plan of Action for its implementation are based on the principles of self-reliance and self-sustainment, which demand that action for the solution of African social, economic, cultural and technical problems should first of all be concentrated on domestic sources. However, such principles do not preach autarchy. Indeed, as some highly-placed African leaders are now wont to tell us, Africa is part of the world and it cannot develop in isolation. Therefore, as declarations on the international development strategy, the Monrovia Strategy and the Lagos Plan have stressed, external resources will be needed to implement these Strategies and Plan. But such resources will only be supplements and should be asked for only after all the available domestic resources have been thoroughly explored.

In the context of the foregoing, the Strategies and the Plan will be implemented at the international global level *inter alia* by:

(i) the provision of grants and loans at concessional terms both bilaterally and multilaterally, and untying of such grants and loans;

(ii) the provision of technical assistance geared to gradual build-up of national capacities and institutions as basis of self-reliance and self-sustainment;

(iii) improved trade terms to enable member States to earn foreign exchange for the purchase of needed and identified factor inputs that are not available at home;

(iv) provision of scholarships for training in appropriate institutions abroad;

(v) provision of facilities in overseas institutions for formal or on-the-job training which may be financed by member States themselves or by aid provided by host governments or third parties; and

(vi) review and appraisal of the progress being made in the implementation of the Strategies and the Plan.

In view of their special status and position as instruments for disbursing aid and technical assistance on a multinational basis and their possession of concentrated and diversified technical expertise, the role of international development organisations deserves further treatment.

These organisations are unique in at least three senses: their expertise is built up on experience from all over the world—West, East and South; their financial resources are mainly made up of the so-called hard or convertible currencies; and they are less susceptible to national policies, politics and politicking. As a result of these advantages, they are well placed to assist member States to pursue and achieve their objectives of self-reliance and self-sustainment. Hence, they have to defer as much as possible to the wishes of the recipient countries and encourage those countries to do things for themselves. As is often stated, the purpose of aid is to promote economic viability and self-reliance. International agencies should help member States to achieve this objective. Therefore, inter-agency rivalries and "tribal" warfares have to be reduced to the minimum.

This brings me to the all-important question of creating the right international political and economic environment for the implementation of the African Strategy and Plan of Action. For it is important to remind ourselves, as I have already alluded to in the course of this lecture, that no country, no continent can be an island unto itself. Indeed, the fact that all our member States are members of the United Nations and various other international organisations attests to the fact that we accept the interdependence of our world.

Therefore, the environment which the entire world, including their divisions into ideological camps, constitutes to us is very crucial to the successful implementation of the Plan. Indeed, for the foreseeable future, we shall need trade, aid, technical assistance and other components of international relations. Our insistence on self-reliance and self-sustainment does not mean that we do not want to obtain from the external world those goods and services which we need for supplementing our own resources so that we may eventually achieve our own objectives and goals. In fact, the main purpose of such insistence is to indicate clearly that without such approach we cannot benefit effectively from our association with the rest of the world.

In this context, what type of political and economic environment do we want? First and foremost, we will need peaceful environment short of the present military rivalry between the superpowers. Secondly, and as a corollary to the first, we would like to see disarmament pursued vigorously so that the resources released from such activities can be used to assist our development efforts. Thirdly, we would like to see Africa demilitarised and forbidden as the theatre of war among the military powers of the world. In saying this, I am particularly worried about the likelihood of Africa being turned into a theatre of war because of the quest for raw materials. Fourthly, we would like to see the activities of the merchants of the instruments of death, the salesmen of international corporations and even governments which produce military equipment and wares reduced considerably. In this connection, it is a fact that the increasing expenditure on military equipment and wares by African governments derives from two sources: the desire of African governments themselves and the encouragement given to them from abroad. Since the push from the supply side is stronger than that from the demand side, we should like to see the activities of the producers, whether government or international corporations, considerably reduced.

As far as the economic environment is concerned, we should like to see aid and technical assistance being given more in terms of grants. Similarly, since external trade is still of importance to us, we would like to see those obnoxious protectionist measures reduced or removed. Finally, in view of the great involvement of transnational corporations in our economies and the fact that up to now, their practices have left much to be desired, we would like to see their activities and operations properly monitored and controlled by the governments of their countries of origin.

It is in the light of such wishes as I have just expressed that I am personally unhappy about the way things are going in the world today. For instance, look at the way the proposed launching of a series of global negotiations on raw materials, energy, development, money and finance has been handled. At the eleventh Special Session of the General Assembly in August/ September 1980, no agreement could even be reached on the procedures and the agenda. Yet, all sides continue to say that they need one another. To my mind, the whole cause of the present polarisation is to be found in the persistence of the old habits, prejudices and fears, on both sides. I have no doubt that the day we accept that the industrialised economies are no longer as all-powerful as they think they are and that the developing countries are not as helpless and hapless as they give the impression they believe they are, then on that day there will be a meeting of the minds!

It is in this context that one looks with hope to the proposed International Summit of a selected group of eminent Heads of State and Government chosen from both the South and the North to deliberate on these critical issues and explore ways of disengaging from the present impasse. It is hoped that the Eastern European countries and China will participate in the Summit. For it is unrealistic to assume that world economic issues can be discussed and solved without the participation of such a significant section of the world community.

# A CONFLICT OF CULTURES

Elliott P. Skinner and Gwendolyn Mikell

In this chapter, Professors Skinner and Mikell explore whether it is possible to achieve cultural fusion in societies that encompass three distinct cultural legacies. The authors discuss concepts of sex roles and marriage, legal systems, child rearing, and education, identifying areas where conflicting systems nevertheless manage to coexist. Eds.

Africa has gone through such profound and rapid transformations over the past century that its people have had neither the time nor the opportunity to resolve the many contradictions that result from the meeting of three cultural heritages on its soil. Critics, often in ignorance, remark that Africans are attempting to accomplish in one generation what it took Europeans at least a thousand years to do. The implication here is either that the Europeans consciously sat down and planned the development of their societies while the Africans are unable to do so, or that social and cultural change is a slow and complicated process that cannot be rushed. Global developments over the past century leave Africa no choice but to move quickly in the direction of change. But with the process of change there are conflicts that affect nearly all aspects of life.

## THE FOUNDATIONS OF CONFLICT

Although most Africans and Europeans were aware of the contradictions within African societies attempting to adapt to radical change, the power and might of the colonizers tended to mask the difficulties involved. Caught in the midst of changes he could not understand, a Roman Catholic missionary among the Bakongo in Central Africa later complained:

The people are liars and have no character. They pretend to submit to you, then they deceive you.... They accept nothing that comes from us for fear we will take advantage of our gifts.... False cults have never been so numerous; they come to the very doors of the mission. I barely escaped physical violence.... All our troubles come chiefly from men who once had our confidence and are using our teachings to supplant us.... They combine everything in their ceremonies: fetishes, fits of possession, prayers they have stolen from us, gestures copied from the priest's processions that imitate ours. It is disgraceful! They no longer want us as interpreters of God.... You can feel the desire to isolate us, to weaken us. These fanatics still hesitate to destroy us, but only through lack of courage. One can do nothing for them.... God alone can recognize them as his own. In my opinion, not one of them is worth much. (Balandier, 1966:203)

Ironically, this statement concerns the Bakongo, one of the earliest African peoples to accept Roman Catholicism.

While there are no cultures without internal tensions or contradictions, there must be a modicum of fit between the institutions of any society, and a consensus of sorts about the rules which make social life possible and meaningful. Culture functions to provide knowledge and tools by which people adapt to their environment. It furnishes the rules for economic, political, and social life, and it provides a cognitive, symbolic system which enables people to agree about the nature of the universe and their place within it.

Nevertheless, cultures do change. The simple transmission of ideas from one generation to another brings about gradual change. Most fundamental changes occur, however, when societies are conquered and incorporated into larger units. This is inevitably followed by a time of troubles as new patterns work themselves out, and as local groups formulate variants of dominant cultures.

## TIME AND ECONOMICS

Time is a persistent source of conflict in contemporary Africa. Adherents of Africanity, Islam, and Christendom disagree about the nature and use of time and its effect on human conduct and society. Traditionally, Africans recognized a long past, a dynamic present, and a future indistinguishable from the past and present. Islam saw time as an aspect of the transcendence and immanence of Allah. Westerners usually think of an indefinite past, a present, and an infinite future. For those who follow traditional African religions, human existence has a rhythm which nothing could destroy and which should therefore be savored. Conflict ensues when Africans subject time to social relations, when Muslims regard time as subject to the will of God, and Westerners attempt to control time and especially not to waste time.

Differing attitudes toward work and other economic activities also create conflicts in contemporary Africa. Rural Africans who worked on West and Central African plantations or in the mines of South Africa were regarded as the quintessential "target workers" who returned home as soon as they reached their economic goals. These persons have normally worked hard to meet pressing needs, to pay taxes, to buy tools and equipment, or to get money for bride-prices. Europeans, not understanding the unwillingness of Africans to keep working once their goals were reached, called these workers undisciplined.

Traditional communal economies demanded a sexual division of labor and provided social and economic reciprocity for Africans. Therefore, Africans initially had little faith that the Western supply and demand system could provide the insurance to which they were accustomed. Nor did those Africans who planted peanuts in Senegal, cotton in Burkina Faso (Upper Volta), coffee in the Ivory Coast, cocoa in Ghana, and sisal in Tanzania understand or appreciate the ability of impersonal Western commodity exchanges to arbitrarily reduce the prices of crops for which they had worked so hard. Nationalist leaders, as well as Southern and East African workers, considered it unfair that now women bore the brunt of subsistence cultivation on increasingly infertile farms, while the men were paid less than a living wage in far-off towns and mines.

The economic experiences of Africans in colonial and settler societies did not especially endear to them a private enterprise system which discriminated against them and favored whites and strangers in all spheres: housing, education, and preferential compensation for comparable work. Nor did the emerging elite approve of their societies being saddled with one-product economies, whether tied to copper (Zambia), peanuts (Senegal), or cocoa (Ghana). Therefore, with independence, African leaders opted for socialist-type economies out of disenchantment with capitalist approaches, which they mistrusted. Many of these leaders were attracted by the vision of a return to African economic values, reciprocal and communal in theory and humanistic in intent. At loggerheads with Western multinationals in their midst and with those Africans who favored dealing with the world as it was, these persons attempted a return to the source without recognizing that the economies of their countries were, perhaps irrevocably, tied to the global economic system.

## MARRIAGE AS A SOURCE OF CONFLICT

Although Africans attempted to protect and to defend their social systems from alien influences, there were already changing male-female social dynamics within Africanity. The attitudes of African men have always been modified by women's status positions—as daughters, wives, mothers, sisters, mothers-in-law, royal wives, royal sisters, queens, queen-mothers, and so forth. Early matrilineality, whatever the cause for its origin, enhanced the status of women to such an extent that the institution was under attack even before the advent of either Islam or Western Christendom.

The gradual movement of Islam down into western Africa during the colonial period assaulted the traditional independence of women. Nevertheless, Islamic divorce practices, coupled with Muslim men's reluctance to marry divorced women, gave Songhay and other Sudanese women the opportunity to live their lives as they saw fit.

The need of the early European traders, settlers, and administrators for female companionship transformed the status of some African women and made for conflict between these women and African men. The so-called *signares* of 16th and 17th century Senegal, who were often married *à la mode du pays* to transient European traders, possessed numerous domestic slaves, houses, gold and silver jewelry, and splendid clothing. Indisputably they knew how to acquire and enjoy wealth. Other women, such as the Itsekiri of the Rivers area in Nigeria also used their high royal status to facilitate marriage and economic partnerships with European traders. As European dominance progressed, however, African communities were sometimes scandalized by the degradation of these women and the lowered status of their children if they had not gathered sufficient economic resources to protect themselves. In the case of Afrikaner men in South Africa who took Khoi women as wives or concubines, their "colored" progeny derived a status which was later troubling to both blacks and whites in the region.

Christian attitudes towards the bride-price and polygyny created grave conflicts between them and both Muslims and non-Muslims. Convinced that the serious but often good-natured bargaining that accompanied African marriages really involved the sale of wives, missionaries forbade it among their converts and railed against it among others. In rebuttal, Africans insisted that the bride-price, like the European dowry, legitimized marriage, determined the paternity of children, and protected marriages from easy divorce. They accused Christians of striking at the root of the African family. The problem was compounded when young Christians took the missionary view of the bride-price. They incurred the wrath of traditionalist parents, who sometimes took matters into their own hands, negotiating the bride-price without notifying the couple. Later generations of African Christians attempted to recover their Africanity and defy the whites by restoring the bride-price. In contemporary times, the bride-price often compensates for the education of the bride, or provides her with a trousseau or business capital.

The insistence by both Christian and governmental Westerners that emerging African elite groups abandon polygyny created unforeseen difficulties. True, many African women did not accept polygyny; but most, apparently, had learned to deal with it. Men, on the other hand, saw polygyny as the ideal state and were ambivalent about giving it up to enter the world of Europeans. Monogamous men had to deal with the pressure from older relatives to take additional wives and from families to divorce wives who did not conceive. In addition, they had to cope with persisting traditional attitudes of wives who returned to parents in observance of the lactation sexual taboo, paid an interminable visit to their parents, or opted to live with sons and grandchildren. Finally, there was the inclination of both men and women to move toward Africanity as they grew older.

Those men who were attracted by other women and opted to marry them by customary law, with or without the consent of their monogamous spouses, had to face the reality that these women and their offspring were not protected by any laws of inheritance and could be in jeopardy if not supported by extended kin. Facing all African men and women are conflicts between modern legal and customary African and Islamic provisions for support of divorced wives and widows. Powerful elite men sometimes find their property so tied up with families that widows inherit little or nothing.

Emerging as a conflict with not only domestic but also national and global dimensions is the African attitude towards progeny. Improved health and urbanization (among other factors) have increased the population of the continent, leading such global activists as the Club of Rome to suggest that unless Africans practice greater birth control African governments would be forced to apply the principle of triage (which means that the worst off receive little or no help). Independent African states have taken conflicting views on family planning, often reacting to the changing attitudes of the major global actors. Among ordinary Africans, opinions differ as a function of class, education, religion, and often region. Traditionalist and Muslim rural Africans (male and female) still opt for large families, often feeling that fertility is in the hands of God. Moreover, faced with the continuing exodus of children to the urban centers or places of employment, these parents feel that the larger the number of children, the better the chance that one will care for them in old age. Urban dwellers, on the other hand, especially monogamous nuclear families, are beginning to exhibit concern over high fertility. However, they are often too bound by traditional values to seek family planning counsel, or are inhibited from practicing it by traditional structures. Members of the elite generally desire fewer children but may feel that curbing fertility is somehow selfish and "European" (meaning the same thing). In Islamic areas, fear of being labeled "immoral" sometimes prevents women from seeking birth control information. In general, conflicting attitudes of husbands and wives often prevent discussion and thereby effective family planning among African families.

The increasing cost of childrearing, especially in towns, has created something of a problem for families with limited income. This is compounded by such multinational companies as Gerber and Nestle which market powdered milk and nutritional supplements. Eager for their babies to resemble those whose pictures appear on the billboards, poor mothers bought those products, preferring them to breast millk. The combination of unclean water, unsterilized bottles and nipples, lack of refrigeration, and a tendency to overdilute the mixture to save money created a scandal—which led to an international campaign to force the companies to take local conditions into consideration when merchandising their products. Still a sensitive issue is the effect of missionary strictures against naked breasts for mothers who breastfeed their infants on demand. Whereas traditionally breastfeeding was not regarded as erotic, this is no longer the case. Therefore, in elite households, women excuse themselves when the time comes to feed their infants.

## ATTITUDES TOWARD EDUCATION

Book learning, which has been hallowed by Islam and Western Christendom alike as the path to a good life, has been the source of conflict and controversy in Africa. The literati have always challenged the power of established leaders, whether in Pharaonic Egypt, medieval Islamic Sudan, Solomonic Ethiopia, colonial and settler Africa, or apartheid South Africa. In the past, as presently, those Africans who acquired new knowledge often felt that they were good enough to share or usurp power from their erstwhile betters. Paradoxically, while missionaries, administrators, and businessmen wanted Africans to learn "the book," they also insisted that these persons work with their hands—something that educated Europeans did not do. While technicians and craftsmen were needed, whites did not reward them as much as they did clerks and teachers. Therefore, the brightest Africans preferred the book to the tool, thereby continuing a tradition which still haunts Africans bent on "development." In most of Africa, scholarly education became and remains a major source of stratification and conflict.

Traditionalists concede, often with sorrow, that their children, especially the boys, will enter the world of Europeans, even though Africans are now governing most of their own societies. They often assert that having been born in towns their children have lost their Africanity and must be reared as "Europeans." And while these parents know that they cannot do so themselves, they are psychologically prepared for their children to behave in strange, incomprehensible ways. Such parents have been known to give their children "Christian" names to facilitate future school enrollment. While most rural parents still send their children to circumcision lodges and to the houses of older women for clitoridectomy, they, too, are aware that even then the children may come under the influence of Christian and Islamic beliefs. In many cases, the educational aspects of the initiation rituals are ignored. Urban parents may have sons circumcised at birth and avoid clitoridectomy for their daughters, preferring to avoid conflict with modernizing neighbors. However, the continuing social importance of clitoridectomy for marriage is such that some urban parents place their daughters in private, sterile hospitals to have the operation performed.

Despite their suspicion of secular Western education and preference for typically male Koranic schools, many Muslim parents have had to modify their views. Some now even permit daughters to attend Koranic schools. However, since the Muslim elite are generally unable to introduce modern subjects into their schools, they are often forced to send their children either to Christian schools, or (as in francophone Africa) to secular public schools. Concern for the education of daughters has often led such Muslim parents to clamor for single-sex schools, much to the annoyance of Christians who have abandoned the prudery of the early missionaries and accept coeducation as normal. Muslim parents realize that there are few ways to avoid Western Christendom if their children are to be truly educated, since even in highly Islamized areas such as Mauritania the higher study of Islamic law is declining.

Historically, Western-educated Africans have often come into conflict with their rulers, whether traditional hereditary monarchs and chiefs or colonial officers. The first educated men in the Gold Coast (now Ghana) criticized the traditional rulers for appropriating the gold-bearing subsoil and forest lands rather than preserving them. And educated persons there were also the first to attack the colonially supported chiefs of straw for being exploitative. The French attempted to educate the ruling class so that it could serve better and combat the rising of the educated commoners; but they found that the royalty were suspicious of the French schools, and in many instances sent their young slaves to pose as sons. Thus, a considerable number of commoners gained a rudimentary education while the aristocratic families remained tradition-bound and out of touch with the modern world. Sons of royal families in South Africa who were trained by missionaries were sometimes less critical than commoners were of the chieftainship, but education did not make them fond of the Europeans. Many African revolutionaries such as Patrice Lumumba and Jomo Kenyatta were trained by Protestant missionaries, then directed their hostility against colonialism.

The desire for higher education often led rural Africans to migrate to African towns and then to travel abroad to universities, with revolutionary implications for the continent. To their chagrin, budding African scholars frequently found Europeans and Americans more interested in knowing about Africa than in talking about European culture. For the first time in their lives, these African students realized that others thought their culture had value; and this recognition forced them to reevaluate themselves and Africa.

## CULTURAL VALUES AND SELF-IMAGE

Taught by missionaries that the image of God was European and the European culture was superior to all others, Africans had learned to denigrate themselves and all aspects of their traditional culture. Afro-Muslims, long aware of the early conflict between Islam and Christianity and of the Muslims' role in transmitting aspects of Hellenic culture to Western Europe through Spain, were less susceptible to feelings of inferiority in the face of European boasting. Yet they, too, could not escape the fact that Western Christendom was in control. Ironically, those Afro-Muslims such as Fulani, Somali, and North Africans with caucasized physical features adopted many of the European stereotypes about Africans and African culture. Considering themselves physically and spiritually inferior, African Christians consciously and unconsciously took a dim view of their erstwhile "heathen" culture. African art, judged by missionaries to be not only works of the devil but also made in the image of the devil, became anathema to Christians and educated Africans. Thus, from the advent of the Portuguese to the early 20th century there were many veritable *autos-da-fé* in which converts to Christianity burned African sculpture. These rituals had more than a religious aspect; they had an aesthetic aspect as well. Significantly, some African intellectuals were suspicious when they were told that as far as Picasso, Modigliani, and other well-known European artists were concerned, African art, once thought of as disgraceful, had become a liberating force. They voiced their fear that European and American idealized views of the African past, inspired by the great works of art, would divert attention from the duties of the present. On the other hand, many of these same persons have willingly pointed to the African origins of man and civilization as the ultimate rebuttal of the charge that Africans gave little or nothing to the world.

Faced with the need to define themselves, many Africans were led to place both Islam and Western Christendom in a new context, and to critically evaluate their impact on Africa and its people. When this self-discovery was linked to political economic theories about the relationship of colonialism to imperialism and racism, the seeds were planted for philosophies such as *Négritude*, the African personality, and African socialism. These concepts would later be used in the struggle for decolonization of African minds as well as African countries.

**REFERENCE**

Balandier, Georges. 1966. *Ambiguous Africa: Cultures in Collision.* New York: Pantheon.

---

## Reading 8.1

Before they were humbled by the incoming Europeans and the new educated African elite, traditional African nobility expected deference and homage from ordinary people. In the western Sudan this homage took the form of full prostration with the subordinate often picking up dust and covering his head with it. The child of "Essay," the schoolmaster, and "Wild Christian," who had converted to Christianity, Soyinka was being prepared by his chaperones to become a member of the elite—almost a white person. But he grew scornful of prostration. This, however, was never appealing to the traditional nobility which did not wish to be eclipsed by the new elite even when everyone recognized that it would be the "new men" who would free their land from European domination.

## Wole Soyinka, *Aké: The Years of Childhood*

It was understood in Isara that the children of the Headmaster did not prostrate themselves in greeting; our chaperon always saw to that. The children of Headmaster on arrival for Christmas and New Year had to be taken round to every house whose inmates would be mortally offended otherwise. On the streets we met relations, family friends, gnarled and ancient figures of Isara, chiefs, king-makers, cult priests and priestesses, the elders of *osugbo* who pierced one through and through with their eyes, then stood back to await the accustomed homage. We were introduced—the children of Ayo—at long last we were in one place where Essay's name was called as a matter of course—the children of Ayo, just arrived to celebrate *odun*. The elder waited, our chaperon smiled and explained.

'They don't know how to prostrate, please don't take offence.'

Reactions varied. Some were so overawed by these aliens who actually had been heard to converse with their parents in the whiteman's tongue that they quickly denied that they had ever expected such a provincial form of greeting. A smaller number, especially the ancient ones whose skins had acquired the gloss of those dark beaten *etù* [locally woven cloth, much valued] merely drew themselves up higher, snorted and walked away. Later, they would be mollified by the Odemo, the titled head of Isara, to whose ears their complaints might come. Perhaps the fact that we were related to this royal house eased their sense of being slighted, we only observed that when we met the same ancients again, they smiled more indulgently, their frowns eased to amused wrinkles at the strange objects whom their own son of the soil had spawned in some far-off land. And perhaps news of an embarrassing encounter at the palace had spread to them.

After church service one Sunday, our first, I accompanied Essay to the Odemo's palace. When we came into the parlour, a number of the chiefs were already seated, so were some faces I had never seen before, including a heavily-beaded and coralled stranger, in a wrapper of *aso-oke*, who was very clearly not of Isara. He spoke and acted more like a brother-chief to the most senior of the chiefs, even carried himself as if he was the Odemo's equal.

We entered, the Odemo hoisted me on his knees and asked me a number of questions about school. The usual cries went up 'A-ah omo Soyinka, wa nube wa gbowo'[Ah, Son of Soyinka, come over and shake hands.] and they stretched out their hands.

Kabiyesi put me down, I went and shook hands round the assembly. The tall, self-consciously regal man was standing by a cupboard, lazily waving a fan across his face. When I came to him, he looked down on me from his great height and boomed out in so loud a voice that I was rocked backwards on my feet.

'What is this? Omo tani?' [Whose child is this?]

A chorus of voices replied, 'Omo Soyinka' pointing to my father who was already in close conversation with Odemo. The stranger's lip turned up in a sneer; in the same disorientating boom as before he ordered,

'Dòbalè!' [Prostrate yourself!]

The response from the parlor was good-humoured, bantering... of course you don't know, they are these 'ara Egba', the children of Teacher, they don't even know how to prostrate.

The stranger's eyes flashed fire. He looked from me to Essay, to the chiefs, back to me and then to Odemo. 'Why NOT?'

I had recovered from the onslaught of his voice and his truly intimidating presence. In place of it, I felt only a cold resentment of his presence in that place and finally, his choice of Essay as his enemy. I had never given the question of prostration much thought except that, on the red dusty roads of Isara and its frequent dollops of dog and children's faeces, prostration did not seem a very clean form of salutation. I would not, I knew, have minded in the least prostrating to Father, or to the Odemo, or indeed to some of the elders seated in Odemo's reception room or those others who flocked to Father's house to drink their thanks to the gods for our safe arrival. But I would have tried every dodge in the world to avoid prostrating on those streets whose dust stuck to one's clothes, hair, skin, even without dragging oneself on the ground or placing one's nose to a patch of urine, human or canine. To this arrogant stranger however, not even Essay and his Wild Christian could make me prostrate, even if they had a change of mind!

Coming directly from the Sunday service probably brought the response to my head, certainly it was no justification which I had ever thought out before, or heard used in any argument. I heard myself saying, with a sense of simply pointing out the obvious,

'If I don't prostrate myself to God, why should I prostrate to you? You are just a man like my father aren't you?'

There followed the longest silence I had ever heard in an assembly of grown-ups. Odemo broke the silence with a long-drawn whistle ending by swearing: 'O-o-o-o-o-oro baba o!' And turning to Essay, 'E mi su' wo re ko?' [By my Oro ancestors! Did you teach him that?]

My father shook his head, gestured with open hands that he had nothing to do with it. Odemo's voice had made me turn to look at him, then round the room at a surprising identity of expressions on the faces of all the guests. Suddenly confused, I fled from the room and ran all the way back home.

At the end of that vacation, Essay decreed that full prostration should commence, not only in Isara, but in our Aké home.

---

### Reading 8.2

Few traditional African customs have created as much conflict between traditionalists and Western Christians as has clitoridectomy. Practiced in Pharaonic Egypt and throughout the continent from ancient times, the origin of this operation is unknown. Known as female circumcision and performed by women, it often functions as a female ritual of rebellion in which women have appropriated for themselves those practices (such as male circumcision) whose secrets were said to have given men power over them. Significantly, because of the opposition of Europeans to clitoridectomy, the practice became the focus of African reaction to alien domination, especially since the institution attacked was viewed as belonging to the most private and domestic domain of Africanity. Jomo Kenyatta defended clitoridectomy. Nevertheless, many social and cultural changes had eroded the importance of the practice even when Kenyatta was still alive. Dr. Conteh's views of clitoridectomy still reflect those of a person defending an institution of Africanity even though he, too, recognized that this custom, and even that of male circumcision, may be doomed by the passage of time.

---

## J. Sorie Conteh, "Circumcision and Secret Societies," from *West Africa*

It would appear that the UN Conference on Women's Decade which convened in Copenhagen from July 14 gave serious consideration to female circumcision in Africa and other places where it is practiced, an issue referred to as "Taboo subject for Africa" (*West Africa*, July 28). This was not the first time the subject became a topic of concern. While one is aware of the inherent fragility of the subject by reason of its moral content, it is unrealistic to say as some Africans have that "female circumcision is a very sensitive subject and that it should not be discussed beyond the confines of African nations." After all it was colonial anthropologists who first wrote on the subject.

In what follows, I wish to make certain observations, which I hope will highlight aspects of the subject. I am interested in the topic not because it falls within the ambit of my own discipline, but from a more enlightened perspective, a perspective coloured by my thirst for information having roots in my culture. In doing so, I do not wish to tread on the sensibilities of those who are emotionally involved in the issue. I belong to two of the ethnic groups (Mende and Temne) in Sierra Leone that practice female circumcision. It is easy for me to imagine what the reaction of my people would be if told that the practice should stop forthwith. It is an aspect of their culture which has been institutionalised to the extent that it has unquestionably become part and parcel of their existence.

Nevertheless, as a student of social change, I do not believe in the perpetuation of moribund practices with the simplistic reason that it is "our cultural heritage," a penumbra which could be used by dictators to frustrate human endeavour. However, one needs at the same time to make a strong case either for the retention or abolition of any system that has no relevance within the context of modern existence. So far, those who advocate the eradication of female circumcision in Africa and other places have done so in a one dimensional manner, thus treating it out of context.

In a special report in the issue of *People* (volume 6, no. 1, 1979), the subject of female circumcision was given prominence by the Doctors Epelbion (husband and wife). In the same issue, a Nigerian writer, Esther Ogunmodede, gave her opinion on the matter. The gist of the report was that the practice of female circumcision posed continued "dangers of infection, pain and death." Ogunmodede discussed the issue with devastating thoroughness and clarity, addressing herself to the enormous ills which girls suffer as a result of the practice. No one, I believe, needs to dispute this, medically or even commonsensically. I am myself aware of reported cases of death as result of the operation....

It has been in existence for a long time. The practice is widespread among the other ethnic groups: Susu, Fullah, Limba, Kono etc. It is a cultural imperative, so to speak. In fact in Sierra Leone when we talk of female secret societies, by this we comprehend first and foremost female circumcision. There are male secret societies, but these are not readily equated with male circumcision *per se*. These secret societies have succeeded in building around them an aura of esoterism and sanctity.

It is colossal ignorance to assume that female secret societies in Sierra Leone concern themselves exclusively with clitoridectomy. What is not known to the untutored mind is the enormous socio-cultural apparatus associated with female circumcision as an institution. By singularly eradicating the practice, one is setting into motion a chain reaction that will have far-reaching social, cultural and psychological effects. In this respect, those who are prepared to undertake the task should be in a position to conceive of the solutions to the above problems.

Anthropological literature is replete with the raison d'etat for female secret societies where they have been effectively institutionalised. Formerly and even now, young girls were taken to a grove away from town. It was an exclusive female affair; men were forbidden either to enter the grove or see the young initiates during the session. Formerly, the period of initiation lasted about three months, sometimes longer. It becomes clear therefore that it was not a clitoridectomy alone that was involved. Girls were supposed to be taught many skills that stood them in good stead when they assumed their place in society. Female secret societies were considered as educational institutions in traditional societies. Culturally and more significantly, a female non-initiate was not considered an adult, whatever her chronological age. She was a non-woman. Her identity was that of a child. She could not participate in many adult functions. Such cases were rare. It was culturally incomprehensible, out of focus with the logic and ethic of society.

This age-old practice has undergone many changes without legislation. The time for the initiation has been effectively curtailed as a result of the dictates of modern life. Girls now have to go to school. Domestic science is taught in schools etc. Parents everywhere want their children to be adequately prepared to cope with modern existence, so they willingly yield to the dictates of social change. But the fact of clitoridectomy still remains. This is what is at issue....

Let me point out the more crucial problems associated with the eradication of female circumcision. The obvious dimensions fall into four categories, namely, social, cultural, psychological and political. It is important to mention that those who are emotionally involved with the practice of female circumcision and its associated institutional complex are our women folk. The vast majority are rural folk with rural mentality but many of our urbanised women also form part of the number.

Socially, for these people, the initiation of their girls into female secret society—the graduation ceremonies—are events they look forward to with emotional fervour. For some, the occasion is the most socially electrifying event in their entire life. It is an occasion of tremendous social magnitude. During such times, the whole community is mobilised to celebrate the event with pageantry and decorum. Communal cordiality and solidarity assume greater momentum than most other events in the community. It is a time for jubilation. For the young graduates, it is a breakthrough in life, a social metamorphosis. Now, they are entitled to citizenship, they are women entitled to get married and have children. Prior to this they were denied womanhood; marriage or sexual relations were anathema. It was the pride of every parent to witness this festive occasion.

It is in its cultural aspect that the practice has far reaching implications. The secret societies were part of the structure of traditional societies. For instance, the head of the female secret society anywhere in Sierra Leone is a woman who commands tremendous respect among her people. Below her, there are others who also command deference according to their status within the society. By virtue of these secret societies, whether male or female, certain artistic accomplishments have been made, some of which are the pride and treasure of the country. Some of our most beautiful carvings (masks) have been accomplished as a result of these societies. So are people we refer to as traditional artists, our musicians, some of whom had their training while they were initiates of these secret societies. Some of these people have acquired national fame. For these people the system serves as a solid psychological anchor. What are the likely effects on these people if the practice is stopped? For them, it is nothing but an act of cultural assassination in its totality.

The psychological effects are easy to imagine. Their cognitive apparatus will be broken apart if no mechanism exists to replace the void created. This phenomenon is one that is familiar to anthropologists and sociologists.

Politically, it is assumed that UNICEF will "collaborate with governments in the eradication of the practice." There is no denying that governments have the power to do anything.... In this regard we may expect Parliament to pass legislation to abolish female circumcision....

Political expedience militates against the total utilisation of the sovereignty of parliament. In any country the practice exists, an attempt to abolish it demands a shrewd and calculated formula.

One should be alert to the fact that where women themselves resist pressure for the eradication of the practice, they may make the similar proposition that male secret societies be abolished since they are not in tune with modern reality. Indeed, there may be some truth in this. The subject may even be extended to the so-called ethnic marks, if only because they also pose dangers of infection and pain.

Finally, while accepting the reality of female secret societies and female circumcision as part of our cultural heritage, and while aware of the likely, socially, cultural and psychological consequences that will result as a consequence of its eradication, there are other paramount considerations. Culture is dynamic. In this respect, any cultural practice that has detrimental effect on the people, any practice that is out of focus with the reality of contemporary life, should be abandoned in the interest of the people. If we fail to get rid of moribund cultural practices in the name of our cultural heritage, we will be suffering from cultural rigidity, which could give rise to cultural ossification. Consequently, therefore, any claim that African culture can make regarding its vigour and resilience rests squarely on the fact that it can sort out those systems or practices that serve us best within the context of the reality of our present world. The development of any culture should be viewed as an ongoing process and no possibility should be fore-closed in this regard.

Significantly, if we are to make even greater strides, it is necessary that we take a critical stock of our cultural heritage with a view to harmonising it with the well-being of our people. In the final analysis, only those dominant cultural systems and practices that emerge, and that benefit the people which serve them as general principles of action should be accommodated. Our task therefore is to articulate our cultural heritage in desirable directions.

## Reading 8.3

Traditionally, many Africans have viewed cities as dens of iniquity and places of loneliness. Separated from kinsmen upon whom they could rely for help and comfort, African men and women often formed voluntary associations which enabled them to deal with the anonymity of urban life. Whether these were associations of clerks, laborers, market women, or civil servants, these bodies furnished their members with the opportunity to celebrate the institutions of traditional Africanity, while giving priority to developing those skills, roles, and statuses that helped them adapt to the modern world.

## Georges Balandier, *Ambiguous Africa: Cultures in Collision*

In a city which may be called improvised because most of it has been built in a hurry, the material and social conditions of existence can only be precarious. The majority of men are wage earners, but the wage is primarily that of the laborer. Having arrived with the illusion that they might save money, often against the price of a dowry, the young workers soon feel the weight of the cost of living and of usury, both of which are particularly heavy in a society in which everything costs money. The official definition of their salary, based on the 'irreducible needs of the single individual,' is tragically absurd. Here is a list of the household goods allotted in a typical annual budget: '1/3 storm lantern, 1/5 canteen, 2/5 stool or chair, 2/3 bowl or basin, 2/3 saucepan, 2/3 plate, 3/5 napkin and knife, 1/5 table.' This list gives an index of the gap separating dreams from reality!

Since he is underpaid, the urban laborer is naturally exploited by his African landlords and tradesmen, who appropriate as much of his meager salary as they can. He lives in cheaply built rooms almost without furniture, often doubling up with friends in order to reduce the rental. He buys his food from shopkeepers who know how to lure him into debt by a kind of charge account system. And the rate of interest on loans runs from 25 to 35 percent a month! Having brought a certain image of social relations from his village, where food and lodgings are not evaluated in terms of money and where relations of brotherhood and reciprocity still operate, he discovers at his own expense the law of supply and demand and the bondage of paid labor. He begins to feel resentment. He is trapped in the city by his debts and the shame of his failure.

But he suffers even more acutely from the uniformity and comparative solitude of the urban center. He has become an anonymous, uncommitted individual, although he still remains on his guard. He often lives as a bachelor, vaguely connected to some distant relative or group of comrades. He lives isolated among strangers, disoriented by the confusion of customs, the novelty of the practices and temptations. In the absence of a frame of reference he has only one infallible rule: to shift for himself. Indeed, this is what he is advised to do in more expressive language, by the Europeans to whom he confides his anxieties. He is lost, in most cases against his will.

A few energetic men have taken the initiative of forming ethnic associations whose purpose is to counteract this alienation by reviving 'racial brotherhood' and by acting in time of death so as not to leave deceased persons in the hands of strangers. The attempt has not been entirely successful. The educated persons who controlled these new groups remained too remote from the uneducated mass of citizens, too formalistic in their approach. I attended an attempt to revive one of these associations, known as Mbongui after the village where the members of a single 'scattered family' were gathered, which was addressed to the inhabitants of Bacongo. The opening session took place in the assembly room of the Cultural Circle before a sparse audience but in the presence of a representative of the administration. The leader of this undertaking, a post office clerk, was formal in his white suit and had the air of a professor who was more pleased with himself than he was with his audience. In a nervous, droning voice he read a prepared speech to the accompaniment of rattling papers. His auditors sat stiffly, like school children. This academic ritual was ill-calculated to arouse the enthusiasm of men who were disillusioned and who remembered the exciting ceremonies they had once known.

---

### Reading 8.4

Contradictions between different legal codes have posed problems for Africans for many centuries. As recently as the spring of 1985, Egypt, a predominantly Moslem country, struggled over whether to adopt the Sharia, or Islamic law, as state law. Opposition was strong from Egypt's Coptic Christians who comprise about one-eighth of the population. The ambiguities inherent in a legal code that is based on the Sharia as opposed to being the Sharia, are described in the article which follows.

---

## Judith Miller, "Egypt's Assembly Bars Full Islamic Law," from *The New York Times,* May 5, 1985

CAIRO, May 4—The Egyptian Parliament today in effect rejected calls for the imposition of Islamic law in this predominantly Moslem country.

Instead, the 448-seat People's Assembly voted to review Egypt's legal code "gradually and scientifically" to revise provisions that contradict Islamic law.

The vote today was a defeat for Egyptians who have championed the immediate imposition of Islamic law, or Sharia, as it is known.

The 1,300-year-old Islamic legal code prescribes behavior for nearly every human activity. In its harshest form, it provides amputation of hands for theft, stoning for adultery and flogging for other social crimes. It also bans alcohol, interest on bank loans and most modern forms of taxation.

### Code Anathema to Copts

In Egypt, the Moslem Brotherhood and other Islamic fundamentalists have pressed President Hosni Mubarak's Government to make the Islamic code the law of the land.

But Islamic law is anathema to Egypt's Coptic Christians, who are estimated to total 5 to 6 million of Egypt's 48 million people.

Deputies from President Hosni Mubarak's National Democratic Party quietly lobbied in favor of the milder recommendation of Parliament's Committee on Religion and Islamic Message and against proposals favoring immediate adoption of the code.

President Mubarak has often said most of Egypt's laws are based on the Islamic code and therefore do not require extensive revision. But he and other prominent Egyptian officials have been reluctant to oppose the adoption of Islamic law openly.

Twelve deputies spoke in favor of the code in the debate today, which was attended by about 200 deputies, including Sheik Salah Abu Ismael, an influential Moslem who formally proposed adoption of the code.

### Called 'Major Source of Law'

His motion was ruled out of order on procedural grounds by Rifat el-Mahgoub, Speaker of the Parliament and President Mubarak's chief party spokesman.

Ahmed Heikal, another member of the ruling party, said everyone agreed that Islamic law was, as the 1980 Constitution provides, "the major source of law."

The only issue, he said, was how laws inconsistent with it should be changed.

He said he favored revision of the laws "scientifically and gradually," the formulation adopted by the Assembly.

Moslem fundamentalism has been growing in Egypt and elsewhere in the Middle East. Iran, Pakistan and the Sudan have adopted Islamic law.

Moslem fundamentalists were suppressed by President Gamal Abdel Nasser, but his successor, Anwar el-Sadat, generally permitted them to flourish. After militant Moslems assassinated Mr. Sadat in 1981, fundamentalists were jailed and banned again, but President Mubarak's Government has lately granted them greater political freedom.

## Part of Opposition Group

A year ago, the Moslem Brotherhood was permitted to form a coalition with Egypt's leading opposition party, the Wafd. The coalition is the only opposition group that won enough support to be represented in the Parliament.

Parliament also voted today in favor of the religious committee's second recommendation: that religious education be improved and expanded.

Cairo is the home of Al Azhar University, the Moslem world's oldest university, where students rioted last fall over educational conditions and in favor of Moslem law.

Western and other non-Egyptian reporters who tried to cover the Assembly debate today were barred from the hall. Parts of the debate were broadcast tonight on Egyptian television.

---

## Reading 8.5

Now that independence has come to most of their societies, African women are holding their own with men both in offices and in the home. Especially along the west coast of Africa, women rapidly passed from their role as vendors in the markets to owning or controlling trucking businesses. Women such as Mrs. Ondo in Wolfson's piece are traditional in many ways, but have mastered the intricacies of modern business and are at home in the establishments (whether bars or offices) from which they conduct their affairs.

---

## Freda Wolfson, *Pageant of Ghana*

...The 'Paradise'[bar was a] favourite rendezvous of the African timber contractors.... It was principally a bar, although it boasted a reception desk at the foot of a narrow stairway, and a number of upstairs bedrooms. Otherwise its decor was much like that of the 'Happy' or 'Love-All': of cement floor with strips of frayed matting, whitewashed walls decorated with old calendars—worn canvas and wicker chairs around beer-marked tables—a bar counter and a gramophone with a merciless loudspeaker. This whole downstairs portion was social in character and unprivate in construction; it was screened from the main street's thoroughfare only by flimsy sections of battered grey plyboard. This insecure frontage scarcely kept at bay the pavement merchandise of a hardware shop on one side and a furniture maker's on the other.... A guest in the Paradise Bar could, if he wished, purchase an enamel bucket or a curly Victorian-style hat stand, merely by raising his voice and shifting his chair a little. This rarely happened, however, because the bar habitués were in the main busy with matters of far greater import. The casual passer-by would be much mistaken in assuming that the figures lounging around the little tables were merely idling away their time; the ambitious briefcases held on laps or propped against chair legs told a different story—likewise the seriousness of voices absorbed in talk of gainful getting and spending, borrowing and lending, and the cautiousness of fountain pens drawn from breast pockets to conclude yet another 'deal'.

For the town's African business men, as for those out-of-towners intent on making their visits profitable, the 'Paradise' was a useful forum for the exchange of news and views over beer and under cover of the gramophone's comprehensive cacophony. The reception desk trafficked briskly in 'trade' messages; the telephone was constantly busy. Information-seekers who dropped in to reconnoitre could glean much by casual inquiry: who was in town and what doing: who would be likely to enter the bar that day to meet whom, and when; who had just left town and why....

It was hard to say at what stage a 'little man' became, by virtue of ability, persistence and good luck, a 'big'[timber] contractor—or exactly what manner of borderline separated the striving 'little' from the respected 'big'. In the big men, of whom James Ondo was one, the expected qualities were of reliability coupled with a steady, subtle shrewdness—a business attitude progressive and opportunist without hot-headedness. Instead of veering with every wind that blew, they pursued, well-ballasted, a considered course. Their trading was dignified rather than histrionic. When, for instance Mr. James Ondo came into the office in his neat grey suit and polished black shoes we felt him to be of quite a different order from our previous caller, an excitable young up-and-comer who had uttered his exaggerations with theatrical verve while Francis [son of a chief and himself a business man in the making, employed as a clerk in the office], having briefly glanced up to send Bill the silent message 'no good', bent over his figures. But on Mr. Ondo, Francis never presumed to make so much as an eyebrow-flicker of comment, nor indeed on Mrs. Ondo who was her husband's business partner and, some said, even more capable than he. The partnership surprised me at first, for in our past bush experience we had not met anything like it. Mr. Ondo, lean and aquiline of feature, thin and restless of body, well-tailored, direct but ineffusive in manner, might have been, had he a paler skin, any successful business man anywhere—for such was his conservative Western outline of looks and personality. Mrs. Ondo, however, made no concessions whatever to the vogue for European dress and custom. She wrapped her considerable bulk in folds of striped and figured cotton, and her head in West Africa's traditional turban; her large bare feet were thrust into bright shambling slippers. Her appearance beside that of her spare, grey-coloured husband struck a gaudy primitive note, by no means beautiful but utterly self-assured.

As a business woman Mrs. Ondo was formidable; the more so, perhaps, because although she could 'hear' English she did not speak it and only occasionally made pronouncements in her own tongue. Her knowledge of Coast timbers was extensive, and her comprehension of all documentary intricacies as swift and sure as her mathematical and human summing up of potential profit or risk. Here in this middle-aged unsophisticated African wife (who had borne six children and sent one daughter to the London School of Economics) was a fearless first-class mind which, despite little or no formal education, had somehow made itself capable of meeting on equal grounds the minds of trained European business men. Not that she frequently did so directly; she preferred to remain as a power behind the scenes in the sprawling warren-like house which the Ondos shared with four generations of their kinsfolk. James Ondo had his small dark office there, up the steep shallow-grooved steps which ascended from a communal courtyard to a shabbily linoleumed corridor. Although we understood the important—even controlling—part Mrs. Ondo played in her husband's timber concerns, we never found her in that office. Her commercial talents were not for the mechanics of typing or filing, nor even, as a rule, for the niceties of *tête-à-tête* discussion. They lay in the subtle offstage use of her power of memory and large-scale bargaining, and her access to a news grapevine which we imagined to be even more richly productive than Francis'. Mr. Ondo was welcome to his place as company director, influential citizen and signer of documents so long as Mrs. Ondo held the family purse strings.

# AFRICA IN THE WORLD

## Victor T. Le Vine

The majority of this book has focused on the internal workings of Africa. In this chapter, Professor Le Vine looks at the place of Africa in world politics. Among the topics he discusses are several "Back to Africa" movements initiated in the late 19th and early 20th centuries, and Africa's role in the United Nations after independence. Looking at Africa's position in the world today, Professor Le Vine examines the relationships between Africa and the superpowers and the continuing crisis in South Africa. Eds.

One popular image of Africa is that of a huge continental island, distinct and separate, with its people—particularly those south of the Sahara—distanced from the rest of the world by immense and perhaps unbridgeable differences in cultural advancement, political development, and economic growth. This view is largely grounded in ignorance; but it also has been fueled by stubbornly persistent racist attitudes, by survival of the colonial romanticism of the 19th and early 20th centuries, and by the condescension of those who see modern Africa (with the exception of South Africa) as little more than an impoverished, unsuccessful extension of Europe. It hardly need be said that such a view is not only wrong but destructive, because it fails to give credence to an Africa that has always been a part of the world, and which today plays a major role in international affairs.

## LINKS WITH THE WORLD OF THE PAST

The evidence we have strongly suggests not only that Africa was the earliest home of humankind but also that it was the cradle of civilization. In that sense, Africa and the rest of the world have always been inextricably linked. The civilizations of Egypt, Phoenicia, Palestine, Greece, and Rome were not just local phenomena but owed their importance in part to a creative melding of peoples and cultures from southern Europe, the Middle East, and North Africa. Byzantium and the post-Hellenic Christian civilizations of the area were similar blends of African and other Mediterranean cultures, as was the Arab tide which swept over North Africa between the middle of the seventh and eighth centuries. Before emerging from their peninsula, the Arabs of the Hijaz (the western coast of Arabia) for centuries had been in close contact with their African neighbors across the Red Sea and the Gulf of Aden, and also had established commercial contacts with African peoples along the northeastern shores of the continent. These contacts were later to flower into an African-Arab culture based in a series of trading towns and cities along the east coast of Africa. In North Africa, Arab culture, though dominant, eventually took on some of the characteristics of the peoples whom the Arab empire incorporated. That mix is especially noticeable in the Maghreb (northwestern Africa, including today's Morocco, Algeria, and Tunisia), where the distinct Arab-Berber culture has emerged. And, of course, the millions of blacks brought to North Africa and the Middle East as slaves between the eighth and 20th centuries have left an indelible, unmistakable biological and cultural imprint on the Arab world.

In its larger sense, then, the triple heritage represents the continuity of African interaction with the non-African world. The period of Atlantic slave trade (from the beginning of the 15th to the middle of the 19th century) and European colonialism (roughly from the mid 1800s to about 1960) admittedly represents an era during which Africa had no voice in the world save (after 1800) what could be articulated by free blacks living outside the continent, by educated Africans in the colonies, and by sympathetic Europeans and Americans opposed to slavery or the excesses of some of the colonial powers. Although the African voice was weak during this period, Africa's impact on the world was enormous. The biological, cultural, political, social, and economic consequences of the Atlantic slave trade for the Caribbean and for the northern, central, and southern regions of America are visible to this day. During the 19th century it was clear that Africa increasingly became a matter of intense preoccupation for the major European powers. Not only did they compete with one another for access to African resources and places to implant settlers, but (particularly after 1870) territorial dominion in Africa came to be seen as a way of strengthening their positions vis-à-vis each other in Europe itself. The famous "Scramble for Africa" was part of the great 19th century European scramble for an empire, and each European state in a position to do so reached for as much of the continent as it could take before any of its competitors got there. In 1885, at the Congress of Berlin, the European powers, tired of fighting over African footholds, more or less agreed to stay out of each other's hair and peaceably settle conflicting territorial claims. There was no question, however, about the power, prestige, and status that empire conferred: when Germany was defeated in World War I, one of the punishments imposed by the victorious allies was to strip it of its African colonies.

As important as the colonial period was in making Africa an issue in European and world politics, it was finally the African voice that established Africa as an entity in its own right and Africans as full members of the world community of nations. One part of that voice was clearly that of black slaves abroad, whose memories of Africa remained alive in their stories, language, customs, and, frequently, in revolts against their alien masters. Another part, perhaps more important politically, was that of free blacks outside Africa itself, first becoming audible in the early Back to Africa movements that established Sierra Leone and Liberia, and then, after a long pause, gaining strength and influence in the "Black Zionist" movement of Marcus Garvey and the Pan-Africanist movement.

## "BACK TO AFRICA," PAN-AFRICANISM, AND BLACK ZIONISM

In 1787 the first group of black repatriates, popularly known as Creoles, were established in Sierra Leone as the vanguard of what their British abolitionist, philanthropic, and commercial sponsors hoped would become a "National Home for Negroes" in West Africa. These blacks eventually included nearly all of England's "Black Poor," plus others repatriated from Nova Scotia and the Caribbean. All were descendants of African slaves liberated before the British emancipation of 1834, ex-slaves settled in Nova Scotia, and others rescued from transatlantic slave ships following the abolition of the slave trade in 1807.

The success of the Sierra Leone settlement inspired black and white members of the American anti-slavery movement to undertake a similar venture with much the same purposes. Beginning in 1820, a series of settlements involving free American blacks was established east of Sierra Leone along the Guinea coast. By 1847 there were some 3,000 people in the four Liberian settlements; and on July 26 of that year, their representatives met in Monrovia to sign the Declaration of Independence and to adopt a constitution modeled on that of the United States.

Sierra Leone and Liberia's importance to modern Africa can hardly be underestimated. Not only were the two territories evidence of the potential impact of the black diaspora, but along with Dakar, where a French-speaking African elite was being created, they provided the fertile soil from which an educated African class capable of challenging European colonialism on its own premises could grow.

The external African voice, incorporated in what came to be called the "Pan-African movement," was destined to play an even larger part in establishing Africa's legitimate world role, first against the colonial powers, and later, after independence, in the community of free nations. Though Pan-Africanism's slogan was—and still is— "Africa for the Africans" (that is, an assertion of a racial home for blacks), one of its primary themes has always been an attempt to promote an Africa self-consciously united on behalf of its own interests and against foreign domination. These aims were first coherently articulated by an influential Trinidadian lawyer, Henry Sylvester Williams, who organized the first Pan-African congress in London in 1900, and by the distinguished black American sociologist, William E. Burghardt Du Bois. Du Bois helped found the U.S.'s premier civil rights organization, the National Association for the Advancement of Colored People (NAACP), and wrote scholarly and popular books and articles designed to educate Americans on racial issues. Du Bois also organized the second Pan-African congress (Paris, 1919), and was a moving spirit in the subsequent congresses of 1921, 1923, 1927, and 1945. Williams' 1900 congress was held principally to protest the seizure of African lands by Europeans. The 1919 congress, held in Paris with some 57 delegates from French and British colonies in attendance, raised various colonial issues including a demand that the ex-German colonies be placed under the international tutelage of the new League of Nations. The 1921 congress, again held in London, proclaimed the absolute equality of all human races and asserted the equality of rights between blacks and whites. The 1923 congress, held in London and Lisbon, dealt with colonial issues and reaffirmed the declarations of the 1921 meeting. The 1927 congress, held in New York with 208 delegates from 12 countries, not only demanded an African voice in colonial administration, but proclaimed the right of blacks to Africa's lands and resources. The fifth Pan-African congress, held in Manchester, England in 1945, was Du Bois' last and the last held prior to the wave of independence which began in 1957. In all respects, this was the most ambitious and significant of the congresses held up to that point. With the blessings of Clement Atlee's Labor government in Great Britain, and with future African presidents Kwame Nkrumah and Jomo Kenyatta playing important roles, the Manchester congress denounced the colonial territorial division of the continent and demanded the application of the principles of the Atlantic Charter enunciated by Churchill and Roosevelt, including the right to political self-determination.

The Pan-African movement was launched by American and Caribbean blacks, but because of the universality of its message it was able to attract the support of sympathetic whites and the emerging leadership of Africa itself and to blend the external and internal African voices into one. The Pan-African congresses also laid the groundwork for the subsequent congresses and conferences of independent African states, beginning with the Accra (Ghana) conference of April 1958 and culminating with the Addis Ababa conference of 1963, at which the Organization of African Unity was founded. Most important, however, the Pan-African movement asserted and kept alive the right of Africans and Africa to a respected, consequential place in the world.

Finally, in this context, mention must be made of Marcus Garvey and his extraordinary "Black Zionism." Garvey was born in Jamaica in 1887. Soon after World War I he launched a movement popular among black Americans with its main aim the return of all blacks to Africa, the "motherland." A genuinely charismatic figure, Garvey attracted millions of American blacks to his Universal Negro Improvement Association (UNIA) between 1919 and 1921 and collected well over $10 million for his various grandiose but often chimeric projects. He founded his own church, the African Orthodox Church, complete with black angels and a white devil; he created a shipping company, the Black Star Line; he proclaimed a Negro Empire with himself as "Provisional President of Africa" surrounded by a titled black aristocracy; and he sent emissaries to Liberia and Sierra Leone. It was very difficult to be neutral to Garvey. At the time, he inspired both adoration and revulsion. Almost inevitably, vindictive feuding developed between him and the more established black leaders such as Du Bois. Garvey's detractors have contended that he was a charlatan as well as a demagogue, while others argue that he was a victim of crooks who attached themselves to his operations. Whatever the case, by 1923 most of his various schemes had gone bankrupt. In 1925 he was arrested, convicted of fraud, and imprisoned. Two years later, President Calvin Coolidge granted him a pardon, and he was deported back to Jamaica. He died in London in 1940, penniless and almost without friends. Kwame Nkrumah considered Garvey's life and writings to have been the greatest single influence upon his career, and there is little question but that his ideas and activities had an extraordinary impact on blacks abroad and in Africa. His doctrines, by stressing the complete equality of blacks and whites, inevitably led to the idea of the complete liberation of Africa from colonial rule. Despite his personal failure, Garvey was able to lead blacks to take pride in their origins, creating for the first time a sentiment of international solidarity among all those of African descent.

## INDEPENDENT AFRICA AND THE WORLD

The fruit of the Back to Africa and Pan-African movements and of the generations of African leaders nourished by their ideas was the creation of 48 independent African states between 1951 and 1980. That number includes the Indian Ocean island republics of Malagasy, Mauritius, the Comoros, and Seychelles, as well as the Arab states of North Africa. It does not include the Republic of South Africa, which became independent in 1910 and remains at odds with the rest of the continent over its racial politics, or Egypt, Liberia, and Ethiopia, which had already been independent for a long time. In 1984 it seemed for a time as if Namibia (the former South-West Africa, under South African control since the end of World War I) might join the others as an independent state in 1985 or 1986; but by mid-1985, that prospect had faded considerably, because the principals involved in trying to settle the territory's future (the Namibian nationalists, South Africa, Angola, and the five non-African "contact states" led by the United States) still had not come to an agreement.

Since the first wave of independence crested in Africa, the African states have made their weight felt in the world, both collectively and individually. For example, that weight is particularly evident in the United Nations and its allied international organizations. Before the annual fall meeting at the UN, the African caucus, composed of representatives from almost all the African states, meets to discuss the agenda of the General Assembly and the Security Council. Though the African states will vote individually and differently on most issues, they usually act together on so-called Third World, colonial, and African issues, particularly on the latter if they involve South Africa.

Also, since 1967 a fluctuating but sizeable number of African states have voted together to support Arab initiatives having to do with the Arab-Israeli conflict, Palestinians, and condemnation of Israel. (Support of the Arab position on these questions has diminished since Egypt and Israel signed a peace treaty in 1977, and as relations between Israel and a number of African states improved or were formally resumed.) At the United Nations and at such UN-sponsored meetings as the Law of the Sea Conference, the Conference on Trade and Development (UNCTAD), and the conferences on the New International Economic Order (NIEO), African states tend to act together to support the case for a more equitable use and distribution of the world's resources, especially on behalf of the so-called "Least Developed Countries" (LDCs), 11 of which are found in Africa itself.

## AFRICA AND SUPERPOWERS

During the colonial period, such interests as the United States and the Soviet Union had in Africa were either mediated through the colonial powers or concentrated in the few independent states—the United States in Liberia, Ethiopia, and South Africa; and the Soviet Union in Ethiopia. With the advent of independence, however, both superpowers—and within a decade, Communist China—had begun to compete with one another for friends and influence on the continent. That rivalry put the United States and the Soviet Union against each other, on the one hand, and the Russians and the Chinese (in the context of their old rivalry), on the other.

For a time, the Russians were unsure about how to deal with the emerging elites of the new Africa, mainly because these groups of leaders were coming to power through negotiation with the colonial metropoles rather than by revolution, and because most represented bourgeois rather than proletarian or radical elements in their respective countries. Until 1960, the Russians mainly dealt only with the very few Marxist political groups and with those having genuinely revolutionary credentials, such as the Front de Liberation Nationale (FLN) in Algeria, at the time engaged in a bloody guerrilla war against France. When Nikita Krushchev came to power, however, Russian policy changed and a number of African socialist leaders, including Kwame Nkrumah of Ghana, Modibo Keita of Mali, Ahmed Sékou Touré of Guinea, and Gamal Abdel Nasser of Egypt, were warmly embraced. The Russians also tried their hand at more direct involvement, becoming an open ally of the Congo's first prime minister, Patrice Lumumba, and attempting to persuade the new African governments not to become involved with the European Common Market. The latter initiatives failed; but, in general, the Soviet Union's uncompromising stand against colonialism and imperialism, its opposition to capitalist ventures in Africa (especially American ones), and its friendly attitudes to liberation movements, did win many friends in Africa, particularly in the socialist African countries and among African intellectuals.

The year 1960 also marked a turning point for United States involvement in and with Africa. Before 1960, American interests in Africa were those connected with American business activity in the colonies and South Africa; close and long-standing ties to Liberia; missionary and educational activity in the English-speaking territories; and a broad concern about decolonization, self-determination, and progress toward democracy, generally expressed in the United Nations and other international forums. President John Kennedy in effect "rediscovered" Africa for Americans, making the United States an active partisan of African independence through establishing political and economic ties with the new African nations and by sending groups of idealistic Peace Corps volunteers to assist them. Though Kennedy was worried about growing Russian involvement and activity in Africa, it was not until the administration of President Richard Nixon—and the coming the Henry Kissinger to the post of Secretary of State—that the United States and the Soviet Union became open adversaries in Africa. Two key events in 1974 and the collapse of an assumption about southern Africa triggered the change. According to Arthur Gavshon,

> Until the downfall of Portugal's dictatorship in 1974, and, with it, Portugal's empire in Africa, American—and West European—policy had rested on the Henry Kissinger thesis for southern Africa that "white rule is here to stay." White rule not only collapsed in Mozambique and Angola, pulling down with it the structure of a European state system in Portugal, but it also hurried Rhodesia's reincarnation as Zimbabwe, shook the *apartheid* Republic of South Africa, and transformed the entire continent into a theatre of superpower competition. Ever since, Soviet-American rivalries in Africa have intensified, either directly or indirectly, via "surrogates"—modern diplomacy's new catch-all phrase for the other side. (Gavshon, 1981:27–28)

The Portuguese revolution led directly to independence for Angola and Mozambique under avowedly Marxist parties, parties that enjoyed very strong political and military support from the Soviet Union. Indeed, the Popular Movement for the Liberation of Angola (Movimiento Popular de Libertação de Angola, MPLA), which was locked in an armed struggle with two other Angolan factions, could not have won power without the help of some 15,000 Cuban troops ("surrogates") brought in for the purpose. The United States tried to prevent an MPLA victory by giving covert military and financial assistance through the CIA to one of the other factions, the National Union for the Total Independence of Angola (União Nacional para a Independência Total de Angola, UNITA), but, obviously, failed to affect the outcome. Both Mozambique and Angola became independent in 1975. The Cubans remained in Angola to guarantee MPLA rule. By mid-1975, they were still there, double in number and augmented by East German and other east European advisors, unable to defeat UNITA (assisted by the South Africans and still indirectly helped by the United States), but able to prevent a UNITA victory. Angola and Mozambique seemed to confirm Kissinger's—and Nixon's—deepest fears about possible Russian intentions to establish imperial outposts in Africa and to threaten vital Western interests on the continent, including the strategic sea lanes around the Cape of Good Hope. These fears diminished somewhat during the Carter years, but re-emerged during the first term of the Reagan regime. Beginning in 1982, however, some interesting changes had begun to alter the shape of Soviet–U.S. rivalry in southern Africa: Rhodesia, with British (and some American) help, became Zimbabwe under black rule, and the United States promised over $200 million to help the new government of Prime Minister Robert Mugabe with the task of economic recovery from the long guerrilla war. Although the United States has consistently refused to recognize the MPLA government, it drew Angola into the negotiations over a Namibian/South African settlement at the request of a group of U.S. oil multinationals, led by Gulf, who enjoy excellent relations with Angola's Luanda regime. The Mozambiquans, frustrated by the Soviet Union's unwillingness—or inability—to help them out of their political and economic problems, discovered that Washington was willing to provide economic and financial assistance.

In addition to the Portuguese revolution, another event occurred in 1974 that helped draw the line between the United States and the Soviet Union. This was the revolution in Ethiopia that overthrew Emperor Haile Selassie and which, with Russian help, ushered in a self-styled Marxist regime every bit as brutal, and certainly much more dictatorial than the monarchy it replaced. In 1977, the Somalis, who

themselves had been Russian allies before the Soviet Union switched
its support to Ethiopia, invaded the disputed Ogaden region. The
Russians immediately sent Ethiopia over 1,000 military and technical
advisors, enough equipment for an entire armored division, and
approximately 15,000 Cuban troops as well as a constant stream of
military supplies. In 1978, the combined Ethiopian-Cuban-Russian
forces badly mauled the Somalis, who were forced to retreat back into
their own territory. The Cubans and Russians remained in Ethiopia to
help the regime of Colonel Haile Mengistu Mariam fight the old
insurgency in Eritrea (and the newer ones in Tigre and Wollo provinces),
establish Russian bases, and defend the country against the Somalis,
now supported by the United States and its Arabian peninsular allies.
The United States, anxious to provide a counterweight to the Russian
presence in Ethiopia as well as to acquire a strategic position from
which it could check a possible Russian threat to the vital Arabian gulf
area and access to the Red Sea and the Suez Canal, became Somalia's
principal foreign ally. Though the American military presence in
Somalia was already formidable by 1985, the United States was careful
not to give the Somalis enough war materiel to enable them to renew
their war with Ethiopia.

By mid-1985 Ethiopia had come as close to being a Soviet satellite
as any state outside the immediate orbit of the Soviet Union. Rigidly
Marxist in its orientation and Stalinist in its internal structures, Ethiopia
almost by itself managed to keep American fears of Russian mischief-
making alive. Elsewhere on the continent, the Russians were not doing
as well, even in the so-called "Afromarxist" or "Afrocommunist" states
of Benin, Congo (the People's Republic of Congo, whose capital is
Brazzaville), and the Malagasy Republic, not to speak of Angola and
Mozambique. Though these states, because of their ostensible Marxist
orientation, enjoy excellent relations with the Soviet Union, Cuba, and
other Russian allies, they are far from being Russian satellites, or even
Russian allies except when their votes are needed in the United Nations
and other international bodies. Congo, for example, makes a great
show of its dedication to Marxist principles and certainly benefits from
Russian military and technical assistance, yet the government of President Denis Sassou-Nguesso has steadfastly refused to grant the Russians
bases in the country, to cut its close commercial ties with France, or to
do anything about its highly profitable relationships with American
and other Western oil companies who lift and distribute Congo's oil.
The situation in Benin is much the same: despite the Marxism of its
regime and its strong ties to Communist countries, it is with France,

not the Soviet Union, that Benin has its closest economic and political links.

Libya represents a special case. Libya is politically close to the Soviet Union and has long been one of the main Arab recipients of Russian weapons and military assistance. Consequently, when Libya occupied Chad's northern border area (the Auzou strip) in 1975 and began to intervene militarily in Chad's long-standing civil war, alarms began ringing not only in neighboring African capitals, but also in Paris and Washington. The French, whose troops had been asked to leave Chad in 1977, returned in force in 1983. The Libyan (and, by implication, Soviet) threat also caused the United States to offer additional military and economic help to Tunisia and Sudan, both of whose governments had been the objects of pro-Libyan attempted coups, and who now felt further endangered by the Libyan military presence in Chad. It should be added that there is some evidence of Russian impatience with Libya's leader, Colonel Muammar Qaddafi, who tends to pursue his own quixotic designs despite cautionary warnings from Moscow. The most troubling aspect of Libya's Chadian venture, however, is only discussed in the most hushed tones in Washington. The Auzou Strip probably contains uranium, and if there are, in fact, significant deposits and if the Libyans have begun to mine them, Colonel Qaddafi may have moved several steps closer to the "Islamic Bomb" he seeks to acquire.

Despite its status as a world power, Communist China has had only moderate impact on Africa, and this has been mainly in the context of its conflict with the Soviet Union. Unwilling to cede the field completely to the Russians, but limited in their capabilities and resources, the Chinese, after a poor start in 1963, eventually turned to demonstrating how much better and more reliable they were than the Russians in providing economic and technical assistance to Africa. Their crowning achievement was the construction of what became known as the "Tanzam" or Great *Uhuru* (freedom) Railway, linking Dar es Salaam in Tanzania with Lusaka in landlocked Zambia, some 1,200 miles away. The project cost nearly $500 million, took nearly six years (1969–1976) to complete, and involved some 20,000 Chinese and 50,000 African workers. The Tanzam caused Chinese stock in Africa to soar. By 1977, China had almost 21,000 engineers, builders, transportation specialists, doctors, and project technicians at work in various parts of the continent. Polite, unobtrusive, low-paid, and willing to live according to local standards, the Chinese made an excellent impression wherever they went. Besides their behavior, which (perhaps deliberately) contrasted starkly with that of the Russians, Chinese projects were usually models of efficiency and quality performance. Where Chinese assistance was available on a construction project, they were almost invariably selected over U.S., Russian, or European competitors. Sometimes the Chinese could be quite creative on projects they could not handle by themselves. For example, in 1984 a superbly engineered 100-mile-long highway was completed in the most mountainous areas of Rwanda. The Chinese undertook the engineering and, with Rwandan labor, did the actual construction. However, the financing was Italian; the earthmoving and other equipment, Japanese, and the steel and concrete needed for bridges and abutments, Belgian. The credit, it should be added, went to the Chinese. The new highway is universally known in Rwanda as *La Route Chinoise* (Chinese Road).

## AMERICAN FOCUS ON AFRICA

One of the more important consequences of the renewed postwar U.S. interest in Africa was the development of a U.S. African constituency composed of a number of organizations seeking to help shape U.S. policies in and toward Africa. The group includes TransAfrica, the major black U.S. lobby on African and Caribbean affairs; the Protestant-supported Washington Office on Africa; and the American Committee on Africa, based in New York. Other members of the constituency that seek to influence policy through more traditional lobbying techniques and channels—notably the Congressional Black Caucus, The African American Institute just left of center, and the newer African Heritage Foundation on the right—have had varying degrees of access and influence, depending on which political party controls the White House. The African Heritage Studies Association and the African Studies Association have frequently taken positions on African policy matters; and within the House of Representatives, the Subcommittee on Africa of the Committee on Foreign Affairs has become a principal arena for wide-ranging discussions on African policy issues. The subcommittee's Democratic chairmen, Charles Diggs, Steven Solarz, and Howard Wolpe (himself a former Africanist scholar), have been extremely influential in helping to shape U.S. African policy. During the Nixon, Ford, and Reagan administrations, they acted as spokesmen for the "loyal opposition" on African matters.

Perhaps the most interesting and powerful member of the "African Constituency" has been TransAfrica, founded in 1976 and financed by contributions from various domestic black organizations and black private donors. Its executive director, Randall Robinson, frequently testifies before the African-related subcommittees in Congress, and the organization has been able to mobilize liberal sentiment on important African issues. One of its notable activities in 1985 was organizing the continuing anti-apartheid demonstrations in front of the South African embassy in Washington, D.C., during which dozens of prominent protestors, including members of Congress, were arrested.

## SOUTH AFRICA AND THE WORLD

In 1948, as a result of national elections in South Africa, the old struggle between the descendants of the country's English and Dutch settlers shifted decisively in favor of the latter. The Nationalist Party, playing on the fear that white supremacy was being threatened by a rising tide of black assertiveness, gained a majority in South Africa's parliament and, thereby, control of the government. Though Asians (mostly of Indian descent) and mixed-race coloreds (together, about 13 percent of the total population) did vote, blacks, who comprise about 68 percent of the population, were completely disenfranchised, and remain so to this day. (By 1955 both coloreds and Asians had been removed from the electoral rolls. In 1984 they were again permitted to vote, but only for representatives to two segregated and largely powerless "legislative" chambers. Most of them, in protest, boycotted the referendum that endorsed the change.)

Once in power, the Nationalists profoundly altered the social and political face of South Africa by creating a massive legal and institutional structure to ensure perpetuation of white rule. Hendrick F. Verwoerd, the editor of a leading Nationalist paper and later Prime Minister, called for the separation of the races in South Africa by rigid barriers, including restricting the entry of each racial group to particular portions of the country. Segregation in multiracial areas was to be carried into every field. Hitherto, separation had been legally established only in major matters, such as separate schools; and public opinion rather than law had been depended upon to enforce most segregation. The new legal structure now demanded separation in everything. The new policy was labeled *apartheid*, literally, apartness.

Since 1948 South African politics have centered on apartheid and have been dominated by the recurrent and often bitter conflict it has engendered. In the process, the South African government created some ten bantustans (ethnic homelands) of which four were granted nominal independence; and the South African regime became an efficient and brutal police state, periodically smashing the waves of opposition and protest that rose against it. By 1980, the intense, insistent political pressures from within, the mounting political isolation of the country, and a depressed economy had begun to have some effect on the regime, and it began to relax some of the most vexing aspects of the apartheid system. By mid-1985, facing yet another round of bloody internal protest, the regime appeared to have defined its new stance. It was prepared to dismantle part of the country's repressive apartheid apparatus, but intended to hold on to its core: residential segregation and the denial of the vote to the black majority. (See Table 9.1, which summarizes the situation as of mid-1985 prior to the imposition of emergency rule.)

Part of the pressure on South Africa's regime has come from abroad, from an international community which, since 1945, has proclaimed its moral outrage at a regime stubbornly insistent on maintaining a system of racial domination in the face of a world becoming increasingly color-blind. The United Nations has had South Africa on its agenda since 1946, and a stream of condemnatory and denunciatory publications, declarations, resolutions, calls for sanctions and embargoes, and the like, issue from the UN every year. South Africa has been one of the principal preoccupations of the Organization of African Unity since its inception in 1963, and South Africa and apartheid have been condemned by virtually every major and minor international organization worthy of the name. As a result, South Africa has become a "skunk among nations" (as one South African leader put it), denied a seat in the UN, largely ostracized from international cultural and sporting events, condemned from all sides, and even frequently denounced by the leaders of its major international economic partners, Great Britain, France, West Germany, and the United States. In 1984 and 1985, when black protest and discontent in South Africa again erupted in a wave of demonstrations, riots, and even terrorist attacks, the role of foreign (particularly U.S.) investment and companies in South Africa once again became a heated issue in Europe and the United States. College students, liberal organizations, leaders of church groups, concerned members of Congress, and the liberal wing of the Africa lobby combined to attack the Reagan administration's alleged tolerance of the South African government (the policy of "constructive engagement") and its inability to bring the Namibian independence

**TABLE 9.1.   Apartheid: The Situation at Mid-Year 1985**

| What has changed | What remains |
|---|---|
| *Daily discrimination.* So-called "petty apartheid" has been gradually eliminated since 1973. Signs reserving benches, elevators, or entrances to public buildings for one race or the other have practically disappeared. Banks and post offices have largely abolished separate windows. Numerous hotels, restaurants, movie-houses, and cafes catering to "mixed" clientele have been granted formal licenses. However, beaches, hospitals, and above all, public transport (except airplanes), are still not completely desegregated. | *The "Group Areas Act"* of 1950, the real keystone of apartheid, obliges all South Africans to live in the areas exclusively reserved (by government decision) to members of each race. This law has remained intact, despite some local adaptations and exceptions. |
| *Sexual segregation.* In June 1985, the "Mixed Marriage and Immorality Acts" were formally repealed. | *The "Bantu Homelands Citizenship Act,"* which makes each black a citizen of one of the ten bantustans, remains in force. Blacks who live in the black townships are considered migrant laborers, and they may not live there permanently unless they were born there or have lived there without interruption for 15 years. |
| *The "Job Reservation Act"* is in the process of being dismantled for economic reasons—a shortage of qualified workers. Henceforth, theoretically, blacks may take any job hitherto reserved to whites including (in the mines) those involving the use of explosives. Blacks may now join trade unions, but under certain conditions. | *The "Pass Laws,"* which require every black to carry a kind of passport at all times, under the penalty of law (638,000 people were arrested for pass violations in the last ten years), remain in full force, despite the promise to institute a national identity card system for everyone, regardless of race. |
| *The armed forces* are increasingly recruiting blacks and Indians. Non-whites now comprise 50% of the police, 30% of the navy, and 10% of the army. | *The "Bantu Education Act"* and the "University Education Act" have, since 1953, enforced the existence of separate schools and colleges for the races, despite several tolerated exceptions. (Private schools are not covered by the Act.) |
| *Coloreds and Asians,* since 1984, have their own segregated houses of assembly within the national parliament; but the assemblies have little power. | *The right to vote* does not exist for blacks, save for local elections in the segregated areas. The idea of "one man—one vote" is still rejected by most whites, including many liberals. |
| *Sport,* in principle, is becoming "multiracial." However, local resistance (in various towns, provinces, and sports organizations) to such desegregation remains strong and effective. | |

(Adapted from "Afrique du Sud: un apartheid new look," *Jeune Afrique* 1269, May 1, 1985: p. 23.)

negotiations to term. The U.S. protesters demanded, among other sanctions and forms of economic pressure, that the 350 U.S. companies with branches in South Africa disinvest (liquidate their South African assets) and that various U.S. public entities and private institutions (such as university corporations) divest themselves of (sell off) securities in companies and banks doing business in South Africa.

By mid-September 1985, when the wave of violence and black South African protest had reached new heights (and a toll of over 700 blacks killed), the country's main economic partners had begun to react against the mounting repressiveness of President P.W. Botha's regime. The members of the European Economic Community agreed to impose limited economic and cultural sanctions, the French recalled their ambassador to Pretoria and suspended all new French investment in South Africa, and various other countries (including the United States and Canada) recalled their envoys as a sign of their displeasure. Further, a number of large private international banks, led by Chase Manhattan, suspended all loans to South Africa. Earlier, in mid-August, South African officials had signalled that far-reaching changes in the apartheid system were afoot; instead (and to the pained embarrassment of the U.S. government, which had taken South Africans at their word) President Botha, in a defiant speech on August 15, pointedly refused to propose any specific changes in the country's racial policies. The speech spurred the U.S. Congress to agree on a series of economic sanctions against South Africa; and on September 9, President Reagan, in order to avoid Congressional action (and the possible embarrassment of having his veto of the sanctions legislation overturned by Congress), himself imposed a series of relatively mild sanctions by executive order.

Embattled, the object of near-universal opprobrium, and an international pariah to boot, the South African regime nonetheless still holds a number of formidable cards, including a number of political and economic facts of life in South Africa; the frequent, patent gap between the words and deeds of its critics; and the country's strategic economic, political, and military position. South Africa, with a GNP (in 1984) of about $80 billion, is Africa's most highly industrialized country and the only one to have successfully made the transition from an agrarian to a modern industrial economy. Part of its strength derives from its intimate economic links with the industrialized countries of the West, including trade, substantial private foreign capital investment (around $15 billion), and production of several strategic minerals vital to modern industry (including chrome, manganese, antimony, vanadium, gold, platinum, and uranium). South Africa has 80 percent of the world's known reserves of chrome and manganese and dominates the international market for vanadium, antimony, and gold. Moreover, the country's strategic position athwart the vital oil shipping lanes around southern Africa gives it additional leverage in Europe and North America. For all these reasons—plus its zealous anti-communist stance—Western countries are reluctant to put too much pressure on the South African regime, its racist internal policies notwithstanding. Add to this South Africa's economic domination of southern Africa. Zaire, Zambia, Zimbabwe, Mozambique, not to speak of Botswana, Lesotho, and Swaziland, all depend on the South African economy for such necessities as transport for exports and imports, trade, employment, and sometimes, food and technical assistance. South Africa's ability to intimidate those of its neighbors aiding black South African and Namibian liberation movements resulted in what amounted to peace treaties with Angola and Mozambique in 1984, and the imposition of what has been called a *"pax Pretoriana"* in the region.

All this has considerably blunted the force of international pressure on South Africa: none of the many sanctions, embargoes, and condemnations voted by various international bodies have done much damage to South Africa's economy or noticeably affected the regime's determination to preserve the system of white supremacy. Further vitiating the impact of international pressures has been the fact that many of South Africa's most verbally belligerent foes maintain profitable economic relations with it, be it openly or through third parties. For example, South Africa annually does approximately $2 billion worth of (mainly covert) trade with some 41 African states. Most of its oil imports, come indirectly from Arab ports and Arab capital has been invested in such South African multinational companies as the London-Rhodesia Company (Lonrho). China and the Soviet Union continue to trade with it, and France has been the country's prime supplier of advanced military and nuclear technology.

Nonetheless, despite the ambivalence of many of the countries involved in trying to help South African nonwhites change the country's political system, the international anti-apartheid campaign continues to gather force and may even have already forced the regime into moderating some of its more objectionable policies. In the final analysis, however, it will be South Africans themselves—black, white, Asian, and mixed-race—who will ultimately decide the issue.

REFERENCE

Gavshon, Arthur. 1981. *Crisis in Africa, Battleground of East and West*. New York: Penguin Books.

*Reading 9.1*

This speech shows Marcus Garvey at his most eloquent. The second Universal Negro Improvement Association (UNIA) convention, at which the speech was given, was to some extent overshadowed by the mounting scandal over Garvey's shipping line, the Black Star Line. The shipping line's managers were accused of misappropriating the company's funds and of failing to live up to the great promises Garvey had made about the line's future. Within several months of the UNIA convention, the Black Star Line went bankrupt and Garvey was arrested for mail fraud. Although Garvey left troubles and shattered dreams behind him, the impact of his ideas and words outlived and outshone the man himself. The following speech was delivered in Liberty Hall in Harlem during the second international UNIA convention in August of 1921. It is representative of Garvey's lifelong belief in the importance of Africa for black men and women everywhere.

## Marcus Garvey, *Redeeming the African Motherland*

Four years ago, realizing the oppression and the hardships from which we suffered, we organized ourselves into an organization for the purpose of bettering our condition, and founding a government of our own. The four years of organization have brought good results, in that from an obscure, despised race we have grown into a mighty power, a mighty force whose influence is being felt throughout the length and breadth of the world. The Universal Negro Improvement Association existed but in name four years ago, today it is known as the greatest moving force among Negroes. We have accomplished this through unity of effort and unity of purpose, it is a fair demonstration of what we will be able to accomplish in the very near future, when the millions who are outside the pale of the Universal Negro Improvement Association will have linked themselves up with us.

By our success of the last four years we will be able to estimate the grander success of a free and redeemed Africa. In climbing the heights to where we are today, we have had to surmount difficulties, we have had to climb over obstacles, but the obstacles were stepping stones to the future greatness of this Cause we represent. Day by day we are writing a new history, recording new deeds of valor performed by this race of ours. It is true that the world has not yet valued us at our true worth but we are climbing up so fast and with such force that every day the world is changing its attitude towards us. Wheresoever you turn your eyes today you will find the moving influence of the Universal Negro Improvement Association among Negroes from all corners of the globe. We hear among Negroes the cry of "Africa for the Africans." This cry has become a positive, determined one. It is a cry that is raised simultaneously the world over because of the universal oppression that affects the Negro. You who are congregated here tonight as Delegates representing the hundreds of branches of the Universal Negro Improvement Association in different parts of the world will realize that we in New York are positive in this great desire of a free and redeemed Africa. We have established this Liberty Hall as the centre from which we send out the sparks of liberty to the four corners of the globe, and if you have caught the spark in your section, we want you to keep it a-burning for the great Cause we represent.

There was a mad rush among nations everywhere towards national independence. Everywhere we hear the cry of liberty, of freedom, and a demand for democracy. In our corner of the world we are raising the cry for liberty, freedom and democracy. Men who have raised the cry for freedom and liberty in ages past have always made up their minds to die for the realization of the dream. We who are assembled in this Convention as Delegates representing the Negroes of the world give out the same spirit that the fathers of liberty in this country gave out over one hundred years ago. We give out a spirit that knows no compromise, a spirit that refuses to turn back, a spirit that says "Liberty or Death," and in prosecution of this great ideal—the ideal of a free and redeemed Africa—men may scorn, men may spurn us, and may say that we are on the wrong side of life, but let me tell you that way in which you are travelling is just the way all peoples who are free have travelled in the past. If you want Liberty you yourselves must strike the blow. If you must be free you must become so through your own effort, through your own initiative. Those who have discouraged you in the past are those who have enslaved you for centuries and it is not expected that they will admit that you have a right to strike out at this late hour for freedom, liberty and democracy.

At no time in this history of the world, for the last five hundred years, was there ever a serious attempt made to free Negroes. We have been camouflaged into believing that we were made free by Abraham Lincoln. That we were made free by Victoria of England, but up to now we are still slaves, we are industrial slaves, we are social slaves, we are political slaves, and the new Negro desires a freedom that has no boundary, no limit. We desire a freedom that will lift us to the common standard of all men, whether they be white men of Europe or yellow men of Asia, therefore, in our desire to lift ourselves to that standard we shall stop at nothing until there is a free and redeemed Africa.

I understand that just at this time while we are endeavoring to create public opinion and public sentiment in favor of a free Africa, that others of our race are being subsidized to turn the attention of the world toward a different desire on the part of Negroes, but let me tell you that we who make up this Organization know no turning back, we have pledged ourselves even unto the last drop of our sacred blood that Africa must be free. The enemy may argue with you to show you the impossibility of a free and redeemed Africa, but I want you to take as your argument the thirteen colonies of America, that once owed their sovereignty to Great Britain, that sovereignty has been destroyed to make a United States of America. George Washington was not God Almighty. He was a man like any Negro in this building, and if he and his associates were able to make a free America, we too can make a free Africa. Hampden, Gladstone, Pitt and Disraeli were not the representatives of God in the person of Jesus Christ. They were but men, but in their time they worked for the expansion of the British Empire, and today they boast of a British Empire upon which "the sun never sets." As Pitt and Gladstone were able to work for the expansion of the British Empire, so you and I can work for the expansion of a great African Empire. Voltaire and Mirabeau were not Jesus Christs, they were but men like ourselves. They worked and overturned the French Monarchy. They worked for the Democracy which France now enjoys, and if they were able to do that, we are able to work for a democracy in Africa. Lenin and Trotsky were not Jesus Christs, but they were able to overthrow the despotism of Russia, and today they have given to the world a Social Republic, the first of its kind. If Lenin and Trotsky were able to do that for Russia, you and I can do that for Africa. Therefore, let no man, let no power on earth, turn you from this sacred cause of liberty. I prefer to die at this moment rather than not to work for the freedom of Africa. If liberty is good for certain sets of humanity it is good for all. Black men, Colored men, Negroes have as much right to be free as any other race that God Almighty ever created, and we desire freedom that is unfettered, freedom that is unlimited, freedom that will give us a chance and opportunity to rise to the fullest of our ambition and that we cannot get in countries where other men rule and dominate.

We have reached the time when every minute, every second must count for something done, something achieved in the cause of Africa. We need the freedom of Africa now, therefore, we desire the kind of leadership that will give it to us as quickly as possible. You will realize that not only individuals, but governments are using their influence against us. But what do we care about the unrighteous influence of any government? Our cause is based upon righteousness. And anything that is not righteous we have no respect for, because God Almighty is our leader and Jesus Christ our standard bearer. We rely on them for that kind of leadership that will make us free, for it is the same God who inspired the Psalmist to write "Princes shall come out of Egypt and Ethiopia shall stretch out her hands unto God." At this moment methinks I see

Ethiopia stretching forth her hands unto God and methinks I see the Angel of God taking up the standard of the Red, the Black and the Green, and saying "Men of the Negro Race, Men of Ethiopia, follow me." Tonight we are following. We are following 400,000,000 strong. We are following with a determination that we must be free before the wreck of matter, before the crash of worlds.

It falls to our lot to tear off the shackles that bind Mother Africa. Can you do it? You did it in the Revolutionary War. You did it in the Civil War; You did it at the Battles of the Marne and Verdun; You did it in Mesopotamia. You can do it marching up the battle heights of Africa. Let the world know that 400,000,000 Negroes are prepared to die or live as free men. Despise us as much as you care. Ignore us as much as you care. We are coming 400,000,000 strong. We are coming with our woes behind us, with the memory of suffering behind us—woes and suffering of three hundred years—they shall be our inspiration. My bulwark of strength in the conflict of freedom in Africa, will be the three hundred years of persecution and hardship left behind in this Western Hemisphere. The more I remember the suffering of my fore-fathers, the more I remember the lynchings and burnings in the Southern States of America, the more I will fight on even though the battle seems doubtful. Tell me that I must turn back, and I laugh you to scorn. Go on! Go on! Climb ye the heights of liberty and cease not in well doing until you have planted the banner of the Red, the Black and the Green on the hilltops of Africa.

---

## Reading 9.2

The Pan-African congresses, from the first in 1909 to the last in 1945, proceeded from the basic premise that Africans had the unquestioned right to be involved in decisions that affected their social and political future. At first, as the 1919 resolution demonstrates, Africans appealed to the colonial powers for a recognition of Africans' rights and the demand for participation in the colonial state. By 1945, however, colonialism was condemned outright and the appeal was made for the universal right of self-determination asserted by the wartime United Nations in the Atlantic Charter of 1941. The demand was for political freedom, unconditional and irrevocable. The change in tone is dramatic and startling. The 1945 resolution captures not only the prevailing post-war climate of anti-colonialism, but also the militancy of black leaders who recognized that the war had dealt a death-blow to the old colonial empires and now demanded freedom for their own peoples. The 1945 congress was also a tribute to W.E.B. Du Bois, whose long struggle for black dignity and freedom was about to be crowned with success. For all these reasons, the 1945 Pan-African congress represented a turning point for Africa and Africans: it marked the opening of the 15-year conflict which ultimately led to the relatively peaceful emergence of independent Africa.

## Colin Legum, *Pan-Africanism, A Short Political Guide*

### THE PAN-AFRICAN CONGRESS
**Paris, 1919**
**Resolution**

(a) That the Allied and Associated Powers establish a code of law for the international protection of the natives of Africa, similar to the proposed international code for labour.

(b) That the League of Nations establish a permanent Bureau charged with the special duty of overseeing the application of these laws to the political, social and economic welfare of the natives.

(c) The Negroes of the world demand that hereafter the natives of Africa and the people of African descent be governed according to the following principles:

(i) *The Land.* The land and its natural resources shall be held in trust for the natives and at all times they shall have effective ownership of as much land as they can profitably develop.

(ii) *Capital.* The investment of capital and granting of concessions shall be so regulated as to prevent the exploitation of the natives and the exhaustion of the natural wealth of the country. Concessions shall always be limited in time and subject to State control. The growing social needs of the natives must be regarded and the profits taxed for social and material benefits of the natives.

(iii) *Labour.* Slavery and corporal punishment shall be abolished and forced labor except in punishment of crime, and the general conditions of labour shall be prescribed and regulated by the State.

(iv) *Education.* It shall be the right of every native child to learn to read and write his own language, and the language of the trustee nation, at public expense, and to be given technical instruction in some branch of industry. The State shall also educate as large a number of natives as possible in higher technical and cultural training and maintain a corps of native teachers.

(v) *The State.* The natives of Africa must have the right to participate in the Government as fast as their development permits, in conformity with the principle that the Government exists for the natives, and not the natives for the Government. They shall at once be allowed to participate in local and tribal government, according to ancient usage, and this participation shall gradually extend, as education and experience proceed, to the higher offices of states; to the end that, in time, Africa is ruled by consent of the Africans ... whenever it is proven that African natives are not receiving just treatment at the hands of any State or that any State deliberately excludes its civilised citizens or subjects of Negro descent from its body politic and culture, it shall be the duty of the League of Nations to bring the matter to the notice of the civilised world.

## THE PAN-AFRICAN CONGRESS
## Manchester, 1945

The following are some of the principal resolutions passed:

I

To secure equal opportunities for all colonial and coloured people in Great Britain, this Congress demands that discrimination on account of race, creed or colour be made a criminal offence by law.

That all employments and occupations shall be opened to all qualified Africans, and that to bar such applicants because of race, colour or creed shall be deemed an offence against the law.

In connection with the political situation, the Congress observed:

(a) That since the advent of British, French, Belgian and other Europeans in West Africa, there has been regression instead of progress as a result of systematic exploitation by these alien imperialist Powers. The claims of "partnership," "Trusteeship," "guardianship," and the "mandate system," do not serve the political wishes of the people of West Africa.

(b) That the democratic nature of the indigenous institutions of the peoples of West Africa has been crushed by obnoxious and oppressive laws and regulations, and replaced by autocratic systems of government which are inimical to the wishes of the people of West Africa.

(c) That the introduction of pretentious constitutional reforms in West African territories are nothing but spurious attempts on the part of alien imperialist Powers to continue the political enslavement of the peoples.

(d) That the introduction of Indirect Rule is not only an instrument of oppression but also an encroachment on the right of the West African natural rulers.

(e) That the artificial divisions and territorial boundaries created by the imperialist Powers are deliberate steps to obstruct the political unity of the West African peoples.

\* \* \*

III

1. The principles of the Four Freedoms and the Atlantic Charter be put into practice at once.

2. The abolition of land laws which allow Europeans to take land from the Africans. Immediate cessation of any further settlement by Europeans in

Kenya or in any other territory in East Africa. All available land to be distributed to the landless Africans.

3. The right of Africans to develop the economic resources of their country without hindrance.

4. The immediate abolition of all racial and other discriminatory laws at once (the Kipande system in particular) and the system of equal citizenship to be introduced forthwith.

5. Freedom of speech, Press, association and assembly.

6. Revision of the system of taxation and of the civil and criminal codes.

7. Compulsory free and uniform education for all children up to the age of sixteen, with free meals, free books and school equipment.

8. Granting of the franchise, i.e. the right of every man and woman over the age of twenty-one to elect and be elected to the Legislative Council, Provincial Council and all other Divisional and Municipal Councils.

9. A State medical, health and welfare service to be made available to all.

10. Abolition of forced labour, and the introduction of the principle of equal pay for equal work.


## IV
## DECLARATION TO THE COLONIAL POWERS

The delegates believe in peace. How could it be otherwise, when for centuries the African peoples have been the victims of violence and slavery? Yet if the Western world is still determined to rule mankind by force, then Africans, as a last resort, may have to appeal to force in the effort to achieve freedom, even if force destroys them and the world.

We are determined to be free. We want education. We want the right to earn a decent living; the right to express our thoughts and emotions, to adopt and create forms of beauty. We demand for Black Africa autonomy and independence, so far and no further than it is possible in this One World for groups and peoples to rule themselves subject to inevitable world unity and federation.

We are not ashamed to have been an age-long patient people. We continue willingly to sacrifice and strive. But we are unwilling to starve any longer while doing the world's drudgery, in order to support by our poverty and ignorance a false aristocracy and a discarded imperialism.

We condemn the monopoly of capital and the rule of private wealth and industry for private profit alone. We welcome economic democracy as the only real democracy.

Therefore, we shall complain, appeal and arraign. We will make the world listen to the facts of our condition. We will fight in every way we can for freedom, democracy and social betterment.

V

## DECLARATION TO THE COLONIAL PEOPLES

We affirm the right of all colonial peoples to control their own destiny. All colonies must be free from foreign imperialist control, whether political or economic.

The peoples of the colonies must have the right to elect their own Governments, without restrictions from foreign Powers. We say to the peoples of the colonies that they must fight for these ends by all means at their disposal.

The object of imperialist Powers is to exploit. By granting the right to colonial peoples to govern themselves that object is defeated. Therefore, the struggle for political power by colonial and subject peoples is the first step towards, and the necessary prerequisite to, complete social, economic and political emancipation. The Fifth Pan-African Congress therefore calls on the workers and farmers of the Colonies to organise effectively. Colonial workers must be in the front of the battle against imperialism. Your weapons—the strike and the boycott—are invincible.

We also call upon the intellectuals and professional classes of the colonies to awaken to their responsibilities. By fighting for trade union rights, the right to form co-operatives, freedom of the Press, assembly, demonstration and strike, freedom to print and read the literature which is necessary for the education of the masses, you will be using the only means by which your liberties will be won and maintained. Today there is only one road to effective action—the organisation of the masses. And in that organisation the educated colonials must join. Colonial and subject peoples of the world, Unite!

---

## Reading 9.3

Desmond Tutu is the second black South African leader to win the Nobel Peace Prize; the first was Chief Albert John Luthuli, in 1960. Both men were honored for their life-long nonviolent struggle against apartheid, and their awards were clearly intended to symbolize the international community's abhorrence of apartheid and its continuing support for the ideal of a free, multiracial future for South Africa. Yet even moderates such as Tutu show signs of impatience with the regime's intransigence on the basic racial issues, characterizing a relaxation of petty racial restrictions as little more than window dressing. The alternative for many young, impatient South African blacks is violent confrontation, even revolution, a path now favored by the outlawed African National Congress, which launched a campaign of violence in 1982 that has already taken scores of lives. Bishop Tutu reflects the anguish of black leaders who, like himself, see a bloody future for South Africa unless the regime drastically changes its policies.

---

## Bishop Desmond Tutu, "The Question of South Africa," from *Africa Report*

I speak out of a full heart, for I am about to speak about a land that I love deeply and passionately; a beautiful land of rolling hills and gurgling streams, of clear starlit skies, of singing birds, and gamboling lambs; a land God has richly endowed with the good things of the earth, a land rich in mineral deposits of nearly every kind; a land of vast open spaces, enough to accommodate all its inhabitants comfortably; a land capable of feeding itself and other lands on the beleaguered continent of Africa, a veritable breadbasket; a land that could contribute wonderfully to the material and spiritual development and prosperity of all Africa and indeed of the whole world. It is endowed with enough to satisfy the material and spiritual needs of all its peoples.

And so we would expect that such a land, veritably flowing with milk and honey, should be a land where peace and harmony and contentment reigned supreme. Alas, the opposite is the case. For my beloved country is wracked by division, by alienation, by animosity, by separation, by injustice, by avoidable pain and suffering. It is a deeply fragmented society, ridden by fear and anxiety, covered by a pall of despondency and a sense of desperation, split up into hostile, warring factions.

It is a highly volatile land, and its inhabitants sit on a powder-keg with a very short fuse indeed, ready to blow us all up into kingdom-come. There is endemic unrest, like a festering sore that will not heal until not just the symptoms are treated but the root causes are removed.

South African society is deeply polarized. Nothing illustrates this more sharply than the events of the past week. While the black community was in the seventh heaven of delight because of the decision of that committee in Oslo, and while the world was congratulating the recipient of the Nobel Peace Prize, the white government and most white South Africans, very sadly, were seeking to devalue that prize. An event that should have been the occasion of uninhibited joy and thanksgiving revealed a sadly divided society.

Before I came to this country in early September to go on sabbatical, I visited one of the trouble-spots near Johannesburg. I went with members of the Executive Committee of the South African Council of Churches, which had met in emergency session after I had urged Mr. P.W. Botha to meet with church leaders to deal with a rapidly deteriorating situation. As a result of our peace initiative, we did get to meet with two cabinet ministers, demonstrating thereby our concern to carry out our call to be ministers of reconciliation and ambassadors of Christ.

In this black township, we met an old lady who told us that she was looking after her grandchildren and the children of neighbors while they were at work. On the day about which she was speaking, the police had been chasing black schoolchildren in that street, but the children had eluded the police, who then drove down the street past the old lady's house. Her wards were playing in front of the house, in the yard. She was sitting in the kitchen at the back, when her daughter burst in, calling agitatedly for her. She rushed out into the living room. A grandson had fallen just inside the door, dead. The police had shot him in the back. He was six years old. Recently a baby, a few weeks old, became the first white casualty of the current uprisings. Every death is one too many. Those whom the black community has identified as collaborators with a system that oppresses them and denies them the most elementary human rights have met cruel death, which we deplore as much as any others. They have rejected these people operating within the system, whom they have seen as lackies and stooges, despite their titles of town councilors, and so on, under an apparently new dispensation extending the right of local government to the blacks.

Over 100,000 black students are out of school, boycotting—as they did in 1976—what they and the black community perceive as an inferior education designed deliberately for inferiority. An already highly volatile situation has been ignited several times and, as a result, over 80 persons have died. There has been industrial unrest, with the first official strike by black miners taking place, not without its toll of fatalities among the blacks.

Some may be inclined to ask: But why should all this unrest be taking place just when the South African government appears to have embarked on the road of reform, exemplified externally by the signing of the Nkomati accord and internally by the implementation of a new constitution which appears to depart radically from the one it replaces, for it makes room for three chambers: one for whites, one for Coloureds, and one for Indians; a constitution described by many as a significant step forward?

I wish to state here, as I have stated on other occasions, that Mr. P.W. Botha must be commended for his courage in declaring that the future of South Africa could no longer be determined by whites only. That was a very brave thing to do. The tragedy of South Africa is that something with such a considerable potential for resolving the burgeoning crisis of our land should have been vitiated by the exclusion of 73 percent of the population, the overwhelming majority in the land.

By no stretch of the imagination could that kind of constitution be considered to be democratic. The composition of the committees, in the ratio of four whites to two Coloureds to one Indian, demonstrates eloquently what most people had suspected all along—that it was intended to perpetuate the rule of a minority. The fact that the first qualification for membership in the chambers is racial says that this constitution was designed to entrench racism and ethnicity. The most obnoxious features of apartheid would remain untouched and unchanged. The Group Areas Act, the Population Registration Act, separate educational systems for the different race groups; all this and more would remain quite unchanged.

This constitution was seen by the mainline English-speaking churches and the official white opposition as disastrously inadequate, and they called for its rejection in the whites-only referendum last November. The call was not heeded. The blacks overwhelmingly rejected what they regarded as a sham, an instrument in the politics of exclusion. Various groups campaigned for a boycott of the Coloured and Indian elections—campaigned, I might add, against very great odds, by and large peacefully. As we know, the authorities responded with their usual iron-fist tactics, detaining most of the leaders of the United Democratic Front (UDF) and other organizations that had organized the boycott—and we have some of them now holed up in the British Consulate in Durban, causing a diplomatic contretemps.

The current unrest was in very large measure triggered off by the reaction of the authorities to anti-election demonstrations in August. The farcical overall turnout of only about 20 percent says more eloquently than anything else that the Indians and Coloureds have refused to be co-opted as the junior partners of apartheid—the phrase used by Allan Boesak, the founding father of the UDF and president of the World Alliance of Reformed Churches.

But there is little freedom in this land of plenty. There is little freedom to disagree with the determinations of the authorities. There is large-scale unemployment because of the drought and the recession that has hit most of the world's economy. And it is at such a time that the authorities have increased the prices of various foodstuffs and also of rents in black townships—measures designed to hit hardest those least able to afford the additional costs. It is not surprising that all this has exacerbated an already tense and volatile situation.

So the unrest is continuing, in a kind of war of attrition, with the casualties not being large enough at any one time to shock the world sufficiently for it to want to take action against the system that is the root cause of all this agony. We have warned consistently that unrest will be endemic in South Africa until its root cause is removed. And the root cause is apartheid—a vicious, immoral and totally evil, and unchristian system.

People will refer to the Nkomati accord, and we will say that we are glad for the cessation of hostilities anywhere in the world. But we will ask: Why is détente by the South African government only for export? Why is state aggression reserved for the black civilian population? The news today is that the army has cordoned off Sebokeng, a black township, near Sharpeville, and 400 or so persons have been arrested, including the immediate ex-moderator of the Presbyterian Church of Southern Africa and Father Geoff Moselane, an Anglican priest.

As blacks we often run the gauntlet of roadblocks on roads leading into our townships, and these have been manned by the army in what are actually described as routine police operations. When you use the army in this fashion, who is the enemy?

The authorities have not stopped stripping blacks of their South African citizenship. Here I am, 53 years old, a bishop in the church, some would say reasonably responsible; I travel on a document that says of my nationality that it is "undeterminable at present." The South African government is turning us into aliens in the land of our birth. It continues unabated with its vicious policy of forced population removals. It is threatening to remove the people of KwaNgema. It treats carelessly the women in the KTC squatter camp near Cape Town whose flimsy plastic coverings are destroyed every day by the authorities; and the heinous crime of those women is that they want to be with their husbands, with the fathers of their children.

White South Africans are not demons; they are ordinary human beings, scared human beings, many of them; who would not be, if they were outnumbered five to one? Through this lofty body I wish to appeal to my white fellow South Africans to share in building a new society, for blacks are not intent on driving whites into the sea but on claiming only their rightful place in the sun in the land of their birth.

We deplore all forms of violence, the violence of an oppressive and unjust society and the violence of those seeking to overthrow that society, for we believe that violence is not the answer to the crisis of our land.

We dream of a new society that will be truly non-racial, truly democratic, in which people count because they are created in the image of God.

We are committed to work for justice, for peace, and for reconciliation. We ask you, please help us; urge the South African authorities to go to the conference table with the... representatives of all sections of our community. I appeal to this body to act. I appeal in the name of the ordinary, the little people of South Africa. I appeal in the name of the squatters in crossroads and in the KTC camp. I appeal on behalf of the father who has to live in a single-sex hostel as a migrant worker, separated from his family for 11 months of the year. I appeal on behalf of the students who have rejected this travesty of education made available only for blacks. I appeal on behalf of those who are banned arbitrarily, who are banished, who are detained without trial, those imprisoned because they have had a vision of this new South Africa. I appeal on behalf of those who have been exiled from their homes.

I say we will be free, and we ask you: Help us, that this freedom comes for all of us in South Africa, black and white, but that it comes with the least possible violence, that it comes peacefully, that it comes soon.

# PART III

# AFRICA IS ONE:
# THE VIEW FROM THE SAHARA

Ali A. Mazrui

In this chapter, different ways of presenting the interconnected-ness of North Africa and Africa south of the Sahara are discussed. The author uses Egypt as an example of the triple heritage and discusses in detail two key events in 20th century African history that demonstrate Africa's oneness and its influence on other continents: the Algerian Revolution of 1954–1962 and the Suez War of 1956. The author shows how these events influenced the destiny of Charles de Gaulle in France and Harold Macmillan in Great Britain, who in turn presided over the decolonization of Africa. Eds.

Modern usage sometimes seems to assert that the *real* Africa is south of the Sahara, in the areas of the continent's *black* experience. However, institutions such as the Organization of African Unity based in Addis Ababa have grown out of a different concept of Africa, one that encompasses both black Africa and Arab Africa and refuses to recognize the Sahara as a divide. Kwame Nkrumah of Ghana said in 1958, when addressing both black and Arab Africans: "If in the past the Sahara divided us, now it unites us."(Nkrumah, 1960:25) Another bias that requires reconsideration is a tendency in African studies to regard Africa as the passive continent, a recipient of influences rather than a transmitter. Male chauvinists have even sometimes referred to Africa as the female continent par excellence—passive, penetrable, and, formerly, "virgin territory." But this passive interpretation of Africa often depends upon the angle of perception. What looks like an impact upon Africa may sometimes be an influence *from* Africa. In this section, we propose to examine the relationship of North Africa to sub-Saharan Africa and the Western world.

Ironically, the name *Africa* was originally applied only to the northern part of the continent. The name itself could have been derived from *Afriga*, or *Land of the Afrigs*, the name of a Berber (North African) community south of Carthage in ancient times. Another etymological line traces the name to a productive region in what is today Tunisia, and a name that meant *ears of corn.* Both the ancient Greeks and the ancient Romans limited usage of the term *Africa* to Mediterranean Africa, and it has been speculated that the name is related to the Latin *aprica* (sunny) or the Greek *aphrike* (without cold). The ancient Arabs used a word transliterated as *Ifriqiyah* for what is today North Africa.

Culturally, North Africa as a whole is at once the western extension of the Arab world, the southern extension of Europe, and the northern extension of sub-Saharan Africa. An excellent case-study in cultural interconnections would, of course, be Egypt. After all, the Nile Valley produced Africa's first centralized states and Africa's first urban civilization under the pharaohs. They played a part both in shaping Greco-Roman civilization and in influencing parts of the rest of Africa, both north and south of the Sahara. Ancient Egypt had linkages with such black civilizations as Kush, Merue, Axum (in what today is Ethiopia), and others. Rulers of Egypt who were partly sub-Saharan in parentage include the Fatimid ruler al-Mustansir (1036–1094 A.D.) and the great vizier and ruler Abu al-Misk Kafur. A former slave, Kafur died in 968 A.D. after effectively controlling Egypt for 22 years. Between 957 and 960, he retained at his Egyptian court one of the greatest of Arabic poets, Iraqi-born al-Mutanabbi (915–965 A.D.), himself of southern Arabian parentage. Since the 1952 revolution, two out of four Egyptian presidents, Neguib and Sadat, have ad Sudanese blood in their veins.

Egypt also served as the gateway of Islam into Africa, spreading the religion both westwards across the Sahara and southwards along the Nile Valley. In time, Egypt became the major cultural center of the Muslim world as a whole, especially after the establishment of al-Azhar Mosque (later a university) in the tenth century A.D. Muslim Africa looked to Cairo as well as to Mecca. Today, Egypt still serves as a gateway into Africa, with both the Nile and the Suez Canal playing important roles; and the country serves as a great cultural laboratory for the fusion of indigenous, Islamic, and Western cultures.

In modern times, the profound interconnections between Africa, the Western world, and the forces of Islam can be traced in the experiences of two North African wars: the Algerian revolutionary war

(1954–1962) and the Suez conflict of 1956. Not merely landmarks in imperial history, these wars furthered changes in the political map of Africa and also helped to realign the major Western powers.

## ALGERIA AND THE PROCESS OF DECOLONIZATION

The Algerian revolution catalyzed decolonization not only for much of Africa but also for France. In fighting for independence in Algeria, the National Liberation Front undermined the French Fourth Republic, which had sustained a series of unstable governments in Paris since France's liberation in 1945. This created the climate in which General Charles de Gaulle was restored to public life. De Gaulle's regime became a force for decolonization for the African regions colonized by France, and for France itself.

France's need for decolonization was the result of its humiliation in World War II. During the war, Vichy France had to all intents and purposes been a German colony, and it had been liberated by troops from the United States. Postwar France sought to compensate for the erosion of its former greatness by clinging to its old empire, but the French defeat by the Vietnamese at Dien Bien Phu in 1954 added salt to the wound. Meanwhile, French politicians found distasteful the idea that the United States had become a senior partner in the Atlantic community. The United States and Britain were the only nuclear powers in the North Atlantic Treaty Organization, and the special relationship between the United States and Britain appeared to many French people to be leading to Anglo-Saxon hegemony. Many French patriots felt France was sliding into neocolonial status.

Then the Algerian War broke out in 1954. French soldiers, exasperated with the politicians in Paris, blamed the government for their military setbacks in Algeria. A military coup in France was a tempting solution to this impasse. With the left wing in the metropole preparing to confront the troops militarily should they parachute into Paris, there was only one man who could save France from civil war—the founder of the French Resistance, General Charles de Gaulle.

When the nation started clamoring for de Gaulle, he expressed his willingness to serve; but when he left his village for Paris, the politicians tried to bargain with him about terms. The general refused to consider more negotiating tactics and returned to his village. By the end of May 1958, President René Coty renewed the invitation to de Gaulle just in time to save the country from the army's planned seizure of power. The General Assembly quickly gave him the mandate to save the nation. De Gaulle's Fifth Republic was destined to check France's slide toward mediocrity. He brought France into the nuclear age technologically; he refused to allow American nuclear weapons to be stockpiled in France unless they were under French control; he demanded fundamental reform of NATO; and he brought the stability of charismatic leadership to the French political system. But it was not sheer hero-worship which made the politicians invite de Gaulle from self-imposed obscurity to a new national purpose—it was their fear that the war in Algeria was about to spread to France. Charles de Gaulle was an unintended gift to France from the Muslim patriots in the ghettoes of Algiers and the deserts of the Sahara.

Initially, de Gaulle's triumphs seemed to be detrimental to African interests. His obsession with giving France nuclear capability led to the use of the Sahara in Algeria for nuclear tests. In 1958, de Gaulle presented a referendum to the colonies asking them to choose between association with France or total severance of relations. Only Guinea (Conakry), under the leadership of Ahmed Sékou Touré, voted in favor of independence, and thereby lost all direct contact with France. The rest of francophone Africa experienced *colonialism by consent* for a while.

And yet the new self-confidence France was acquiring did help the cause of at least political decolonization after a brief period of gloom. De Gaulle was seeking to bring France back to greatness through means other than colonialism. He wanted France to lead the whole of Europe, and to play an independent role in the grand confrontation between the United States and the Soviet Union. He wanted France to be an autonomous force in the politics of the Middle East, and to forge more viable relationships with her former colonies. Old-style imperialism could be a shackle preventing France from attaining full stature; such had been the consequence of trying to cling to Algeria. The lessons of Algeria resulted in fundamental rethinking in France about the nature of colonialism elsewhere in Africa. The same de Gaulle who had cruelly forced the colonies to choose between France and economic collapse in 1958 was ready to let the whole of Africa attain formal independence two years later. In fact, francophone black Africa gained its formal independence two years before Algeria did.

Ironically, those in black Africa who had suffered most from French colonialism were often the least supportive of Algeria's lonely war for liberation. Influenced by Paris in their foreign policies, most francophone black governments were cautious in their utterances and their votes in the United Nations on the Algerian question. But there were occasions when Islam made a difference. Sympathy for the Algerian freedom fighters tended to be stronger among black African Muslims than among other blacks in Africa. This was not only because the Algerians were fellow Muslims, but also because they were not called "Algerians" at all at that time in the international press—they were usually referred to as "the Muslims." Because of the myth that Algeria was part of France, the term *Algerians* was supposed to apply as much to the white *colons* as to the indigenous Muslim population. And so the supporters of the National Liberation Front acquired the identity of *Muslims* in news coverage—attracting even more clearly the sympathies of Muslims both north and south of the Sahara. Moreover, the most ideologically radical African countries in the 1960s were disproportionately Muslim. The continent was divided between the Casablanca and Monrovia groups of African states. The Casablanca states were the more anti-imperialistic and the more ideologically militant. The majority of them also espoused some kind of socialism in their domestic policies. In this Casablanca group—named after their founding meeting place in the Moroccan city—the only non-Muslim state was Ghana under Kwame Nkrumah. The other countries included Sékou Touré's Guinea (Conakry), Modibo Keita's Mali, Nasser's Egypt, and the government-in-exile of Algeria.

In the final analysis, the Algerian War would have been less likely had France given Islam due status as a religion earlier. There were periods in Algeria's history under French rule when French citizenship could not be combined with acceptance of Islamic law—not even Islamic law on marriage and divorce. Since French citizenship implied a complete rejection of the *Sharia*, it was difficult for most Muslim Algerians to choose France.

Nearly 20 years before the revolution broke out, on May 5, 1935, the Association of Algerian *Ulama*, an organization of Islamic scholars, came into being, dedicated to the restoration of an Algerian nation under a modernized Islam and based on Arab culture. Inspired by the Egyptian Islamic reformer Mohammed Abduh (1849–1905), the movement opposed on the one hand the more medieval educational and social practices of orthodox Islam and on the other the uncritical Gallicization of Algerian lifestyles and tradition. The Algerian Ulama wanted Arabic to be made compulsory in Algerian elementary and secondary schools—something which was anathema to the French administrators at that time. In 1938, the leader of the movement, Shaykh bin Badis, issued a *fatwa* (legal Islamic opinion) against Algerian adoption of European culture at the expense of an Islamic identity. Gallicized Algerian Muslims had opposed the movement, arguing that France and Islam were not incompatible. But French policymakers had not tried very hard to demonstrate cultural compatibility. When the French began insisting that Algeria was a part of France, there were too few converts to the idea among the Muslim population. The stage had been set for *jihad*—a holy war—against the background of the sands of the Sahara.

Algeria did not win independence until 1962. By then, de Gaulle favored ending the war, opposing the French settlers and soldiers who wished to consider Algeria part of France. In 1957, however, Ghana's attainment of independence from Britain fired the imagination of French-speaking Africa, as well as the rest of the continent. In 1960, 17 African countries gained independence, 14 of them French-speaking. Events in France and in the French colonies before long led to the decision to grant independence to virtually all France's colonies in Africa. The Algerian struggle helped permanently change the pace of African history.

## THE SUEZ WAR: A HISTORICAL LANDMARK?

But there was another North African war whose consequences for the history of decolonization were at least as complex as the repercussions of the Algerian revolution: the Suez War of 1956. That war involved the tripartite invasion of Egypt by Israel, France, and Britain, following Egyptian President Gamal Abdel Nasser's nationalization of the Suez Canal. This may have been the first time a Third World government nationalized a resource vital for the Western world and got away with it.

Nasser was clearly not the military victor in that war. The Egyptian army was humiliated by the Israelis in the Sinai, and Port Said was captured by British and French paratroopers relatively easily. But curiously enough, the United States and the Soviet Union both came in on the same side, opposed to the tripartite invasion.

In some ways the war was a turning point in global history, and in other ways it confirmed changes which had already been taking place. For instance, the war confirmed that Britain had been knocked out of the ranks of first-class powers, and confirmed America's role as a superpower. After all, it was American muscle which forced Britain, France, and Israel to pull out of Egypt after their tripartite invasion.

But from the point of view of decolonization, the most important result of the war was the emergence of Harold Macmillan as the new Prime Minister of Great Britain. The failure of the invasion was a humiliation for Britain. Prime Minister Anthony Eden's health broke down completely—and Harold Macmillan assumed supreme governmental authority. From Africa's point of view, Macmillan was cast by history at the beginning of three major processes of change. One was political decolonization, as European powers retreated from direct control of African societies. Macmillan presided over the independence of Ghana, the first black country south of the Sahara to regain sovereignty from colonization. The second process was the gradual acceptance by Western powers of the legitimacy of nonalignment as a cornerstone of the foreign policies of newly independent African and Asian countries. Macmillan's role in the Suez crisis of 1956 was part of the wider crisis of relations between Western powers and the newly emerging developing countries. The third process of change whose initiation coincided with Macmillan's premiership was a new stage of the international rejection of the legitimacy of white minority rule in Southern Africa. Macmillan presided over the dismantling of the Federation of Rhodesia and Nyasaland, and gave the historic "Wind of Change" speech, addressed to the South African Parliament, which demanded fundamental changes in relations between whites and blacks all over the continent.

## AN EMPIRE IS DISMANTLED

The majority of British colonies in Africa south of the Sahara became independent between 1957, the year following Macmillan's succession as Prime Minister, and 1964, the year following his resignation. Of course the forces which resulted in this process of decolonization were not of Macmillan's making. Great social and political forces had been let loose in Africa, especially after the second World War. Much of Africa was no longer willing to collaborate with a European imperial order under Europe's terms. Modern forms of nationalism were sweeping across the continent, demanding self-determination and political sovereignty. But the humbling of Britain at Suez was a major preparation for British acceptance of a reduced role in the world. And Macmillan helped his countrymen in Britain accept this imperial defeat with a sense that though they shrank in size they grew in stature.

Ghana's independence from Britain took place the year following the Suez War and the year before Charles de Gaulle resumed power in France. Preparations for this epoch-making event antedated Macmillan's premiership, but Macmillan's diplomacy was called on to try to defuse the potential conflict between the Union of South Africa as an old dominion and the first black independent member of the Commonwealth—Ghana under the leadership of Kwame Nkrumah.

Macmillan's Tory government was caught up in the contradiction between the old Conservative loyalty to white settlers in Africa and new interest in a multiracial Commonwealth. The most acute examples of this dilemma were Kenya, still under an emergency following the outbreak of the Mau Mau war, and the Federation of Rhodesia and Nyasaland, linking Northern Rhodesia (now Zambia), Nyasaland (now Malawi), and Southern Rhodesia (now Zimbabwe), under the leadership of Sir Roy Welensky and his white settler constituency.

The Tories in England were still outraged by the very image of Jomo Kenyatta in Kenya, whom the Kenya governor appointed by a Tory administration had described as a "leader unto darkness and death." There was strong sympathy for the white settlers of Kenya, who had until then exercised vastly disproportionate influence on Britain. What is more, after Suez, Mombasa was very attractive to Britain as a naval base. But Macmillan's Colonial Secretary, Ian McLloyd, played a critical role in gradually tilting British policy in the direction of accepting black majority rule in Kenya. In 1960 the Mau Mau emergency regulations were lifted, Jomo Kenyatta was suddenly released from detention, and the country moved swiftly towards independence in spite of settler opposition.

Kenneth Kaunda of Northern Rhodesia and Hastings Banda of Nyasaland both led movements demanding the dismantling of the Federation of Rhodesia and Nyasaland. The white settlers of Southern Rhodesia, under Sir Roy Welensky, stood for defense of the Federation, partly because its existence facilitated white hegemony over all three countries. Harold Macmillan was personally involved in the delicate game of balancing the claims of the whites with the aspirations of the blacks. Dismantling the Federation was probably his most difficult task in Africa during his premiership. But he was prime minister long enough to accomplish this and therefore to prepare the way for the independence of Malawi and Zambia.

Inevitably, white settlers in Southern Rhodesia felt betrayed by Britain. Many concluded that Britain had indeed lost its will to rule, and that their survival in Africa therefore depended upon their own resilience as a "bastion of white civilisation." The stage was set for Ian Smith's Unilateral Declaration of Independence two years after the end of Macmillan's premiership. That in turn led to a long crisis of Rhodesia's isolation and subsequent guerilla war. It was nearly a quarter of a century after the Suez War that Zimbabwe's liberation war ended in independence.

## THE CRISIS OF NONALIGNMENT

Macmillan's premiership was also involved in the broad crisis of nonalignment as a new cornerstone of the foreign policies of the newly independent states. And the Suez War remains part and parcel of the origins of nonalignment. Egypt under Gamal Abdel Nasser had presumed to buy arms from the Soviet bloc. The United States, Great Britain, and the World Bank hit back by cancelling a previous agreement to provide funds for the construction of the Aswan Dam. Partly in a pique of nationalistic fervor, Nasser retaliated in turn by nationalizing the Suez Canal, asserting that he would use the revenue from the canal as part of the slow process of building the dam with Egypt's own resources.

Suez was important for the future of nonalignment partly because Nasser successfully asserted the right to purchase arms from the Soviet bloc in the teeth of Western opposition. The use of Soviet personnel to guide ships along the canal upon the withdrawal of Western pilots and the subsequent commitment by the Soviet Union to build the Aswan Dam were also part of the new balance of forces in former colonized territories. Economic and technical assistance were no longer a monopoly of Western powers, and could now be sought from the Soviet Union and its allies.

Nonalignment also received a boost because two of the mightiest former imperial powers had attempted to thwart the option of a former dependency, and had themselves been thwarted by a new world situation involving two superpowers and the growing diplomatic influence of developing countries. The stage was set for new types of relationships between the former imperial powers and their former dependencies.

In September 1960, Macmillan attended a summit meeting of the General Assembly of the United Nations in New York. Macmillan was attempting to engage in a brief exercise in macro-alignment, to relieve tensions between the Soviet Union and the West following the collapse of summit talks scheduled for Geneva that year. But in addition, Macmillan had conversations with some of the leaders of the Muslim and non-Muslim developing countries who were attending the General Assembly. He assured people like Kwame Nkrumah (who was also at the meeting) of Britain's understanding of those newly independent countries that did not want excessive entanglement in alliances with big powers.

Two years later there was another crisis for nonalignment when China invaded India. India had after all been the very axis of the policy of nonalignment. The viability of nonalignment policy was partly based on the assumption that communist countries were not inherently aggressive—any more than Western capitalist countries were. When China attacked India, this premise seemed to many Westerners to have been destroyed.

Britain was India's most important Western friend. But when Harold Macmillan sent arms and other material support to the Indian government, he met with protest from Africa. President Nkrumah of Ghana asked Britain to desist—arguing that outside involvement on the side of India in the Sino-Indian conflict could lead to outside involvement in support of China, with a serious risk of escalating the war. Macmillan wrote Nkrumah expressing surprise at the protest, and asserting that it was surely right for Britain to give support if a Commonwealth country was attacked from outside. A sharp rejoinder came from Accra: the Commonwealth was not a military alliance. It did not imply an obligation on the part of its members to provide collective security in times of crisis. On balance, Nkrumah's interpretation of the Commonwealth was correct; had it been a military alliance, neither Nehru's India nor Nkrumah's Ghana would have applied to join it in the first place.

But whatever the realities concerning Commonwealth obligations, there was no doubt that the Sino-Indian conflict of 1962 created an acute crisis for nonalignment. Could any country be safe without alliance with others? The Western press seemed at times jubilant over India's embarrassment. "We told you so" seemed to be the tone from *The New York Times* to the *Daily Telegraph.*

It took another crisis later that year on the opposite side of the world to revalidate nonalignment—the Cuban missile confrontation. Cuba had allowed the Soviet Union to start constructing a missile base on its territory. United States President John F. Kennedy ignored the government of Cuba itself and issued an ultimatum to the Soviet Union to dismantle its missiles. A blockade around Cuba was declared by Kennedy—with readiness on the part of the United States to board even Russian ships to prevent any further militarization of Cuba as a base. For a time, the world hovered on the brink of nuclear war. Then, Soviet Premier Nikita Khrushchev and Kennedy made an agreement between themselves over the head of Fidel Castro. Agreement to dismantle the base was reached between the superpowers in total disregard of the wishes of the Cuban government. This was a supreme validation of nonalignment. Cuba had clearly violated one of the most basic precepts of nonalignment by accommodating a nuclear base for one of the superpowers. Yet Cuba had now been humiliated even by the superpower that was its own friend.

## THE CRISIS OF DERACIALIZATION

Harold Macmillan presided not only over Ghana's independence in 1957 but also over South Africa's withdrawal from the Commonwealth in 1961. The two events together virtually constituted the end of de facto apartheid within the Commonwealth itself.

There was a time when the British Empire and its Commonwealth were in fact two parts of a segregated society. The independent dominions (Canada, Australia, New Zealand, the Union of South Africa, and the self-governing colony of Rhodesia) were either white or white-dominated. The colonies and other dependencies had, by the outbreak of World War II, become almost entirely nonwhite. This was the stage of the Commonwealth at its most elaborately segregated. A de facto apartheid separated the white heads of government who met annually at the Commonwealth conference from the overwhelmingly nonwhite population of the British Empire.

The first breach of this Commonwealth apartheid came soon after the second World War when the Asian members of the Commonwealth became independent, and India negotiated new terms of membership which did not imply allegiance to the British Queen but merely involved recognition of the Queen as head of the Commonwealth. But 1957 was definitely another stage—involving the accession of a black member of the Commonwealth, Ghana under Kwame Nkrumah. This was a particularly severe test to the principle of apartheid within the Commonwealth. The Prime Minister of the Union of South Africa was for a while reluctant to grace the annual conference in the presence of a black head of government.

In 1960, Macmillan proceeded to visit South Africa itself—the first British prime minister to do so—and to give a speech before the House of Assembly in Cape Town, arguably the best of his political career. He had visited other African countries before he arrived in South Africa. He said to the South African parliament:

> The most striking of all the impressions I have formed since I left London a month ago is of the strength of this African national consciousness. In different places it may take different forms, but it is happening everywhere. The wind of change is blowing through the continent. Whether we like it or not, this growth of national consciousness is a political fact. We must accept it as a fact.

Macmillan then went on to the core of the problem—South Africa's continuing apartheid policy on the one hand, and Britain's new policy of trying to construct a truly multiracial partnership with her former colonies on the other.

> Let me be very frank with you, my friends. What governments and parliaments in the United Kingdom have done since the war in according independence to Pakistan, Ceylon, Malaya, and Ghana, and what they will do for Nigeria and other countries now nearing independence—all this, though we shall take full and sole responsibility for it, we do in the belief that it is the only way to establish the future of the Commonwealth and of the free world on sound foundations.... In countries inhabited by several different races, it has been our aim to find the means by which the community can become more of a community.... It might well be that in trying to do our duty as we see it, we shall sometimes make difficulties for you. If this proves to be so, I shall regret it. But I know that even so you would not ask us to flinch from doing our duty.... As a fellow member of the Commonwealth, it is our earnest desire to give South Africa our support and encouragement, but I hope you won't mind my saying frankly, that there are some aspects of your policies which will make it impossible for us to do this without being false to our own deep convictions about the political destinies of free men.... I think we ought as friends to face together—without seeking to apportion credit or blame—the fact that in the world of today this difference of outlook lies between us. (Legum, 1965:367)

Macmillan's "Wind of Change" speech was an inspiration to many Africans. He had given notice to the government of South Africa that Pretoria could no longer count on the support of London in defense of some of the internal policies of South Africa. Kwame Nkrumah used the phrase *winds of change* in his own address to the United Nations General Assembly in September 1960—but he then went on to argue that this was no soft breeze of adjustment but a hurricane of revolution. Africa, according to Nkrumah, was ready for fundamental change. (United Nations, 1960)

Under pressure from African nationalism and the world community, Macmillan's government dismantled the Federation of Rhodesia and Nyasaland, sparing at least Zambia and Malawi continuing white hegemony. That left Rhodesia still under white domination—a problem that continued to haunt successive British governments until white rule came to an end in 1980.

For South Africa, there seemed to be no alternative but to withdraw from the Commonwealth. Macmillan himself was most anxious to prevent such a withdrawal, and was convinced that South Africa could best be reformed as a member of the Commonwealth, experiencing the challenges of a multi-racial international partnership. But Julius Nyerere of Tanzania threatened not to apply for membership in the Commonwealth if South Africa remained a member. Even Ghana's Kwame Nkrumah threatened withdrawal. The government of South Africa might have prevented the final rupture had they guaranteed a welcome for high commissioners in Pretoria. But South African Prime Minister Hendrik Verwoerd turned out to be unequal even to this minimum challenge.

## CONCLUSION

The two North African wars we have examined were moments of confrontation between Europe and two African peoples—Algerians in one war and Egyptians in the other. As both peoples were Muslims, Islam played a part in the alignments and repercussions. But in the final analysis the linkages which the two wars particularly illustrate are those complex interrelationships that bind the history of North Africa to the history of the continent south of the Sahara.

Kwame Nkrumah was the founding president of the first case of decolonization south of the Sahara—Ghana. He may have been exaggerating when he said in 1958:

The former imperialist powers were fond of talking about "Arab Africa" and "black Africa"; and "Islamic Africa" and "non-Islamic Africa."

.... These were all artificial descriptions which tended to divide us.... Today the *Sahara is a bridge uniting us.* (Nkrumah, 1960:25–33)

He said those words not long after the end of the Suez War and while the Algerian struggle was still going on. Nkrumah was overstating his case, but he certainly did have a case. The thesis was imperialism, the antithesis was liberation, and the synthesis was African oneness.

## REFERENCES

Legum, Colin. 1965 (2nd ed.). *Africa: A Handbook.* London: Anthony Blond.

Nkrumah, Kwame. 1960. *Hands Off Africa!!!* Accra: Ministry of Local Government.

Sampson, Anthony. 1977. *Macmillan: A Study in Ambiguity.* Harmondsworth, Middlesex: Penguin Books.

*United Nations General Assembly, 15th Session, Official Records, 896th Plenary Meeting, Friday 23rd September, 1960.* New York: United Nations.

# PART IV

# THE CULTURAL DIASPORA

## Mbye Cham

In the final part of this reader, we look at the cultural products of Africa—its poetry, music, stories, and art—and their influence outside the African continent. Professor Cham introduces the concept of an African diaspora that continues to develop the African cultural legacy. His essay is followed by examples of African expression from other parts of the world. **Eds.**

The presence of people of African descent in societies outside of Africa is usually thought to be confined to only certain parts of the western hemisphere. Some persons might be surprised to find blacks in such countries as Peru or India. But blacks have been widely dispersed around the world as a result of a constellation of events and forces in history.

History provides many examples of both forced and voluntary movement of large numbers of people from their territories of birth to new geographic areas. There the newcomers formed new settlements, coexisting and interacting in various ways with others in their new environment. War; economic, ethnic, racial, religious, or political persecution; natural disasters; and search for better material gain are among the factors that account for migration. When migration results in the establishment of large stable communities outside the homeland of origin, one begins to refer to these in terms of *diaspora*, a concept derived from and popularized by the historical experience of the Jewish people.

In its application to people of African descent, the concept of the African diaspora refers to the dispersal of African people to other parts of the world and to the life experiences, challenges, and achievements of these people in their new environments. The major vehicle through which the African presence was established around the world was undoubtedly the slave trade, which forcibly transported Africans across the Atlantic Ocean to the Caribbean and North, Central, and South America; across the Red Sea to the Arabian peninsula; across the Indian Ocean to the Indian subcontinent and to other parts of Asia; and across the Mediterranean to Europe and Asia Minor. However, the slave trade was not the only mechanism by which Africans became part of the wider world. Eminent classicists such as Frank Snowden, author of *Blacks in Antiquity: Ethiopians in the Greco-Roman Experience* (1970), have documented the presence and role of people of African descent as intellectuals, scientists, merchants, seamen, diplomats, and religious figures in classical antiquity in the Mediterranean. Ivan Van Sertima's seminal work *They Came Before Columbus* (1976) presents a detailed, comprehensive account of the black presence in Mexico, the Americas, and other parts of the world long before the adventures of Christopher Columbus in the 15th century. Today, new African arrivals from all walks of life continue to join and add new dimensions to already established African diaspora communities in the Western world.

A brief survey of the geographic distribution of the African diaspora will help us to understand its scope. The largest settlements of people of African descent outside of Africa are found in the Americas—the greatest number in Brazil, where more than 70 million Afro-Brazilians are concentrated mainly in the states of Bahia, Rio de Janeiro, Minas Gerais, Pernambuco, and São Paulo. This has moved certain scholars to dub Brazil the largest African country after Nigeria. It is also in Brazil, especially in Bahia, that one finds the most pronounced manifestations of African culture in the diaspora. In the United States one also finds an influential African diaspora community taking a vanguard role in championing diaspora and African values and interests. Other black communities in the Americas are to be found in Colombia, Peru, Uruguay, Venezuela, Suriname, Guyana, Mexico, and Costa Rica. In the Caribbean Islands, people of African descent make up the majority of the various populations; and one finds a vibrant community of Caribbean blacks in Canada and Britain.

The African diaspora settlements in the eastern hemisphere are relatively small when compared to those in the West. Nevertheless, their presence is significant in the Arabian peninsula, with the highest concentration in Saudi Arabia. They are also found in Yemen and in various parts of the Persian Gulf states. In the Indian subcontinent, descendants of Africans brought over as slaves in the 15th century continue to exist in three main communities. These Afro-Indians, known as "Siddis" or "habshis," came mainly from Ethiopia, Kenya, and other parts of East Africa. Looking at the Pacific region, one also encounters African diaspora settlements of various sizes in a number of the island-nations of the region. The most significant of these is Papua New Guinea, where the majority of the population is composed of people of African descent.

Contrary to popular assumptions, dispersal from a cultural core does not always imply discontinuity with the core culture or its total disappearance in the new environment. Cultures are very versatile and durable. Africans brought to the New World arrived with the cultural apparatus of their respective places of origin, and it was this culture that initially provided them with a grammar of values and actions in their new settlements. In contact with other cultural entities in these new places, and interacting with them over time, the original African cultural apparatus began to undergo various adaptations and transformations in response to the demands of the new environments. In the process, it acquired new features that would in time confer on it a measure of relative autonomy as a new culture having a clearly defined relationship to the original core. Whatever its form, this African cultural apparatus continues to be a vital component in the thought and practice of millions of people of African descent in the diaspora, some of whom consciously reject but unconsciously betray its force over them, and many of whom accept its legitimacy and cultivate its potential.

An overview of religious and artistic currents in selected areas of the diaspora will illustrate the nature and extent of African cultural continuities, adaptations, and transformations in the diaspora, as well as underscore the parallels, convergences, or contrasts between the different communities in the diaspora.

Harold Courlander in *A Treasury of Afro-American Folklore* offers the following synoptic account of the persistence and strength of certain African religious concepts and rites in the Caribbean region and South America:

> Cults and rituals of the Dahomeyan, Yoruba, Akan and various Bantu peoples persist in Brazil, Haiti, Cuba, Jamaica, Martinique, Guadeloupe, Trinidad, Grenada, Suriname and other places where Negro communities exist. In some of these cults, African religious ideas are veneered with Christian beliefs, and essentially African deities may have the names of

Christian saints. In the United States numerous eighteenth- and nine-teenth-century chroniclers recorded the existence of African religious activities in Louisiana, though most of these writers failed to grasp the real meanings of what they had observed. (Courlander, 1976:5)

The most distinctive religion with clearly articulated African ancestry and elements in Haiti is *Vodun* (perjoratively referred to by some as *voodoo*), and in Brazil it is *Candomble*. Vodun owes much of its basic cosmology and theology to those of the Fon people of Benin (formerly Dahomey), while Candomble draws substantially on the *orisha* (pantheon of gods) of the Yoruba of Nigeria as well as gods from Angola and the Congo. Devotees of Candomble conduct worship in temples called *terreiro*. Unlike in Yorubaland where one finds separate temples (*ile orisha*—house of the gods) for the various divinities, in Brazil a terreiro usually serves a multiplicity of deities even though it may be dedicated to one particular deity. This form of liturgy enables a follower of Eshu, for example, to carry out his devotion while at the same time acquiring a knowledge of the symbols and ceremonies of the other gods such as Ogum, Shango, and Yemanja. This accounts for the large measure of synthesis that took place between the various cultures from Africa that met in the New World. The Christian veneer of Candomble and of other African-derived religions in the New World was, according to Arthur Ramos in his book *The Negro in Brazil* (1939), merely a mask to hide the real character of Candomble from the menace of an unsympathetic Catholic state, intolerant of "unorthodox cults." In Brazil today, black and white, rich and poor, and Catholics and non-Catholics are all counted among the followers of Candomble, which also continues to inspire and influence the form and substance of contemporary Brazilian art, literature, and film.

In addition to Candomble and the dominant Catholic church, one also finds in Brazil small pockets of Afro-Brazilians who profess the Islamic faith. These are mainly the descendants of Muslim Yoruba from Ilorin, Nigeria. In 1934–1935, these Muslims, known in Brazil as *Males,* were inspired by Fulani *jihads* (holy wars) in West Africa to wage a series of revolts against what they regarded as infidel secular authority, with a view to instituting a Muslim theocracy in Bahia. The legacy of these Males was still in evidence in the latter 1970s when some carnival groups began to adopt names like *Male de Bale* and to re-enact the Male rebellion as part of their performance repertoire for carnival.

Available written and oral documents indicate the existence of settlements of black Muslims in the coastal region of Georgia and South Carolina, especially the off-shore Sea Islands. These islands are inhabited for the most part by people of African descent whose religious and artistic traditions and language, the Gullah dialect, still retain much that is African in origin. On one of these islands, Sapelo Island, an early literate black Muslim resident, Bilali Mohamet or Ben Ali Mohamet, is still remembered. Bilali Mohamet and his descendants may be the forerunners of the more numerous and influential contemporary black Muslims in the United States.

Whether it is Vodun in Haiti, Candomble in Brazil, Akan-influenced *Pocomania* and Ethiopian-inspired *Rastafarianism* in Jamaica, or the comparatively faint echoes of these in many parts of the United States; or whether it is Islam or Christianity imbued with African-derived elements (witness the performance aspects of black Baptist religious ceremonies and the names of churches with "African" in them) in the United States; or whether it is the Efik-derived Abakwa secret society in Cuba, religion in the African diaspora has always been dynamic, functioning as a means of survival in an oppressive environment.

As is the case in many African societies, in many parts of the African diaspora only a very thin line separates religion and artistic expression. Religion not only features as a theme and source of subject matter in artistic expression, it also shapes and influences the form and other technical aspects of this expression. Like religion, the art of the people of African descent in the West maintains a dynamic rapport with the art of the African core areas. This is particularly evident in oral narrative performance, literature, music, dance, art (painting, sculpture), and craft (textile, weaving). Interacting, nourishing, and influencing each other thematically, stylistically, and formally, these forms of artistic expression constitute the vehicles for conveying the African and New World heritage and for imaginatively interpreting and building on that heritage. In fact, it was through the artistic thought and practice of people of African descent in the diaspora, particularly the Afro-Americans, that much of the world became exposed to the real nature and true dimensions of African artistic, philosophical, and other forms of thought and practice.

Oral narrative performances in the different parts of the African diaspora bear close kinship to each other as well as to their African antecedents. The repertoire of trickster narratives found in many parts of the Caribbean features an impressive array of tricksters and their victims. Among these, the most frequently encountered ones are the Akan trickster Ananse, the Yoruba Elegba, and that perennial dupe Bouki (the Wolof word for hyena). The Djuka of Suriname, a diaspora people who have changed little of their original African culture, call a pleasing story "Ananassy tory." (Courlander, 1976:193) In the United States, one encounters the cunning Brer Rabbit whose ingenious tricks on his perennial foil Brer Wolf bear close parallels to those of Ananse and many another African trickster figure. The style, the idiom, the symbols, and even the substance of these narrative performances may vary from place to place and from one individual artist to the other, but there remain a certain ethos and ambience that render them easily recognizable as sharing similar ancestry.

Oral narratives constitute one particular aspect of the spectrum of genres in the oral traditions of the African diaspora. Other forms that are equally vibrant include poetry, proverbs, riddles, and, to a limited extent, the epic. As is the case with oral narratives, there is also a significant measure of thematic and formal parallels between these genres in the diaspora and their homologues in many parts of Africa. Dynamic and versatile, these traditions continue to inform in various ways the creative genius of many a contemporary artist in the diaspora. The poetic originality and strength of Langston Hughes and Sterling Brown, the distinctive storytelling genius of Zora Neal Hurston and Toni Cade Bambara, the linguistic and idiomatic particularity of Claude McKay and Alice Walker, and the inventive poetic rhythm and soul of Jesse Jackson and Muhammad Ali all derive a good deal of their essence from these traditions.

Music is an integral part of these traditions, too. In fact, poetry and song are synonyms in many African languages. The Wolof of Senegambia use the word *woi* to designate both a poem and a song, and this is why the celebrated African poet and former president of Senegal Léopold Senghor argues that a poem is not a poem until it is sung. In the same vein, reference is frequently made to the jazz, blues, or bebop rhythm of the poetry of Langston Hughes. The music of Charlie Parker and John Coltrane is described as being endowed with a certain poetic aura and intensity, and the calaypso from Trinidad is characterized as "oral literature," as in Keith Warner's book *Kaiso! The Calypso as Oral Literature* (1982). The so-called "rap music" currently in vogue in the United States and its Jamaican equivalent "rap reggae" draw substantially from the formal properties of the poetic and other verbal traditions of the diaspora.

Distinctly New World musical creations by people of African descent include jazz, bebop, ragtime, blues, spirituals, calypso, and reggae. The African influence in Cuban and other Latin American music is also quite pronounced. These creations stand in relation to African musical traditions in much the same way as the oral traditions of the diaspora stand in relation to African oral traditions. Such scholars as Amiri Baraka (formerly Leroi Jones) (1963), Melville Herskovits (1941), Eileen Southern (1971), and Keith Warner (1982) have examined and analyzed this relationship, pointing out continuities, changes, and innovations in terms of style, substance, and function. In *Blues People... Negro Music in White America* (1963), Baraka argues that

> Jazz is commonly thought to have begun around the turn of the century, but the musics jazz derived from are much older. Blues is the parent of all legitimate jazz, and it is impossible to say exactly how old the blues is—certainly no older than the presence of the Negroes in the United States. It is a native American music, the product of the black man in this country: or to put it more exactly the way I have come to think about it, blues could not exist if the African captives did not become American captives. (Jones, 1963:17)

In the area of art, one sees similar continuities and transformations. Unlike any other diaspora community, the black people of Suriname have retained a woodcarving tradition with distinctly Akan features. There are only a few other places in the diaspora—principally in the Caribbean—that the African tradition of woodcarving and sculpture flourishes. African art motifs figure prominently, however, in the work of contemporary black American painters and artists like Lois Maillou Jones, Jeff Donaldson, and other adherents of the Afri-Cobra group of artists of the 1960s and 1970s. In an article in *Art Voices* entitled "African Influences in Contemporary Black American Painting," Peter Mark examines the process of cross-fertilization between African and contemporary Afro-American art, focusing particularly on the work of Lois Maillou Jones, whose career, he observes,

> ...forms a link between the Harlem Renaissance and the 1970s.... Her long and distinguished career has been marked by startling stylistic changes. From a post-Impressionist style during the period 1937–51, she has moved through a period of Haitian themes to her present African-influenced work....

Her interest in African art appeared as early as 1937 when she painted *Les Fetiches*. Most striking in this painting are the linear patterns that animate the mask. In her portrayal of carvings from five Central and West African cultures, Lois Jones was deeply impressed by the rhythmic quality of the sculpture. Thirty years later, precisely this aspect of African art would become a dominant element in her own African style. (Mark, 1981:15)

African art influences in the diaspora are also evident in the colors and designs of textiles woven by Afro-Bahians in Brazil, in the quilts of black women's work groups in rural Alabama, and in other areas such as those outlined by Courlander in the passage below:

Throughout the Caribbean, and in Negro communities on the South American mainland, one finds wooden implements and utensils of African design, musical instruments made to an African pattern, and styles of decoration reminiscent of African prototypes. In Suriname is to be found woodcarving that is stylistically related to Ashanti or other Akan traditions. Haitians make wari (munkala) gameboards, and play the game much as it is played in Africa. Haitian ironsmiths forge paraphernalia for cult centers in a tradition that is clearly related to that of the Yoruba. Some of the old ritual objects in the collection of the Museo Nacional in Havana—once used by the Lucumi (Yoruba), Arara (Dahomey) and Mayombe cults and the Abakwa fraternal society—could well have been fabricated on the African continent. They include elaborately carved drums, Shango wands, forged iron bells and costumes representing various spirits. Mortars for pulverizing grain were used throughout Negro America, and wooden grave markers that stood not so long ago in a burial ground in the southeastern United States were astonishingly similar in concept to markers seen in various regions in Africa. (Courlander, 1976:3)

Mention also should be made of continuities and changes in divination practices (*obeah* in the Caribbean and conjuring in the United States) and in such martial arts forms as the Angolan *capoeira* in Brazil.

It is perhaps appropriate to conclude with a summary overview of the impact of the culture of the African diaspora on Africa and Africans. Historically, there has always existed among many people in the diaspora a desire, indeed a resolve, to return physically, psychologically, intellectually, or otherwise to Africa. This is evident in Liberia (returned Afro-Americans), Sierra Leone (Africans returned from England and Nova Scotia), Marcus Garvey's Back to Africa Movement, Pan-Africanism (W.E.B. Du Bois and George Padmore), the Harlem Renaissance, the Haitian Indigenist Movement, the Cuba Negrismo Movement of the 1920s and 1930s, the Frente Negra of Brazil of the same period, and the Black Arts Movement of the 1960s and 1970s in the United States. Underlying the basic thrust of these movements, especially the artistic movements, was the idea of a return to the source, a call on artists of African descent to push the frontiers of art into new areas by creatively engaging the ensemble of their own heritage. The result was a steady outpouring of literary, musical, and other cultural creations which, with the activities of other diaspora intellectuals and activists in other fields, intensified the assaults on Western pretensions to cultural, intellectual, and political hegemony over Africans and people of African descent. It came as no surprise, then, that Kwame Nkrumah would later champion a political culture influenced, to a large extent, by the political and intellectual thought of Pan-Africanists like Du Bois and Padmore, and that Léopold Senghor would name himself the prime promoter of *Négritude*, deriving much of his conceptual vocabulary from, among other sources, Afro-American artistic and intellectual thought. Jacques Hymans in *Léopold Sédar Senghor: An Intellectual Biography* (1971) has documented succinctly Senghor's debt to Afro-America. This is a typical example of a much larger phenomenon of diaspora literary, intellectual, and political influence over Africans. As Alioune Diop, founder of the journal *Presence Africaine*, used to say, "Afro-Americans spoke for us when we could not speak for ourselves."

## REFERENCES

Courlander, Harold. 1976. *A Treasury of Afro-American Folklore*. New York: Crown Publishers.

Herskovits, Melville. 1958. *The Myth of the Negro Past*. New York: Harper and Brothers, 1941.

Hymans, Jacques. 1971. *Léopold Sédar Senghor: An Intellectual Biography*. Edinburgh: University of Edinburgh Press.

Jones, Leroi (Amiri Baraka). 1963. *Blues People...Negro Music in White America*. New York: William Morrow and Co.

Mark, Peter A. 1981. "African Influences in Contemporary Black American Painting." *Art Voices* (Jan./Feb.):15–19.

Ramos, Arthur. 1939. *The Negro in Brazil*. Washington, D.C.: Associated Publishers, Inc.

Snowden, Frank. 1970. *Blacks in Antiquity: Ethiopians in the Greco-Roman Experience*. Cambridge: Harvard University Press.

Southern, Eileen. 1971. *Music of Black America*. New York: Norton.

Van Sertima, Ivan. 1976. *They Came Before Columbus*. New York: Random House.

Warner, Keith Q. 1982. *Kaiso! The Calypso as Oral Literature*. Washington, D.C.: Three Continents Press.

---

## Reading IV.1

Many of the splendid African works of art are housed outside of Africa, mainly in museums and private collections in Germany, France, England, Belgium, and the United States. How did these works find their way to these countries and what has been the impact of their presence in these countries? These are the basic questions which Alain Locke addresses. He discusses in particular the influence of African art on modern European art, especially the manner in which it provided artists such as Picasso and Modigliani with stylistic and other techniques.

---

## Alain Locke, *Negro Art: Past and Present*

The spiritual discovery of Africa began with artists, and was caused by their discovery of the powerful originality and beauty of African art. It was of course known that Africans made curious things with odd shape and strange primitive purposes. The missionaries had saved a few, primarily to show the state of degradation and idolatry from which Christianity was trying to save the poor, benighted heathen. Everyone was singing in Sunday school how "The heathen in his ignorance,—bowed down to wood and stone;" and what we now prize and cherish as African art was pious exhibit A,—at least that small remnant saved from the pious bonfire which had already consumed so much of it. And then, too, traders, colonial officials and soldiers had to have their souvenirs, and museums and private collections gradually began to fill with these tagged and labelled, and eventually dusty, trophies of imperialism. By the turn of the century, twenty years after the great modern imperialistic penetration of the African interior, a scientific interest in things African had sprung up and elaborate museum collections were in the main capitals of the European powers, the *British Museum* at London, the *Trocadero Museum* Paris, the Ethnographic museums of Berlin, Brussels, and Vienna. The Germans especially, interested in their new African colonial ventures, were feverishly collecting materials and, as might be expected, in a more methodical and scientific way. Not only were there great collections being built up at Berlin, but at Hamburg, Bremen, Leipsig, Frankfort, Munich, Dresden and even smaller centers like Cologne, Lubeck and Darmstadt. This was the situation about 1900. But all this was as yet mere trophy collecting and scientific curiosity at best.

Finally two things happened in the next decade to open European eyes to the art values in these African curios which had been almost completely overlooked. In 1897, a British military expedition had sacked and burned the ancient native city of Benin in West Africa as punishment for tribal raids and resistance to colonial penetration of the interior of that region. Although much was destroyed by fire and careless handling, cartloads of cast bronze and carved ivory from the temples and the palaces were carried to England, and accidentally came to the auction block. Discerning critics recognized them to be of extraordinary workmanship in carving and casting, and that the bronze casting especially had been done by an ancient process by which the finest bronze masterpieces have been made. Acting without official orders, a young curator of the Berlin Museum bought up nearly half of this unsuspected art treasure and founded a reputation and a career. For his auction bargain has turned out to be the most prized and valuable collection of African art in existence, the Benin collection of the Berlin Ethnographic Museum, duplicates were traded to form the basis of the famous collection at Vienna, and the young scholar, Felix von Luschan, by a four-volume folio publication on this art and its historical background easily became the outstanding authority of his generation on primitive African art. The British Museum secured its share of this material, and what was sold for little more than its junk value as old bronze and block ivory was secured as a cornerstone treasure of African art in its best classical period, now considered artistically priceless and on the commercial market today actually worth nearly its own weight in gold.

*The Paris Group.*—At about the same time, a group of young painters and art critics in Paris, coming into contact with some fine specimens of native African fetish carvings from the French West Coast colonies, prized them for their fine finish and workmanship and started to study them out of the atmosphere of dusty museum cabinets and glass cases. Their interest was at first purely technical, but as they became more familiar with these odd objects, their representation of forms,—human, animal and in abstract design, was seen not to be a crude attempt at realism, an unsuccessful attempt to copy nature, but a very skillful and reworking of these forms in simplified abstractions and deliberately emphasized symbolisms. For instance, an animal or human form would be purposely distorted to fit into an element of design as a decorative pattern or the anatomy would be distorted to emphasize an idea and convey an impression of terror, strength, ferocity, fertility, virility or any idea or mood of which the object was a symbol or which was back of the particular cult connected with it. It was then realized that a difference of stylistic patterns had stood between us and the correct interpretation of this art. Moreover, it was seen that the breaking down of such conventional barriers was just as necessary for the appreciation of African art as for understanding the arts of the Orient, which until a half generation before this had been similarly misunderstood. As a result, a New Africa was discovered,—the new continent of the black man's mind. With art as a key, the secrets of African civilization were about to be opened and revealed.

---

### Reading IV.2

Léopold Sédar Senghor, the former president of Senegal, was born in the small village of Joal in Senegal. He went on to become the first black African to ever achieve the highest degree in the French educational system—the *doctorat d'etat*—at a time when racist colonial theories about black genetic, cultural, and intellectual inferiority were gaining popularity. He is considered one of the premier African poets writing in a European language—French—and has established himself as the most eminent exponent of *Négritude* which he defines as the sum total of the cultural values of the black world. Although the Négritude movement sprang up in Paris in the 1940s, many of its basic tenets and principles were derived from the intellectual, literary, and political thought of Afro-Americans. The Afro-American's response to racism, the search for new literary models constructed from the black heritage, and the pride in Africa and its traditions all greatly influenced Senghor and his fellow blacks in Paris at the time.

---

## Jacques Louis Hymans, *Léopold Sédar Senghor: An Intellectual Biography*

The reaction of American Negroes to Western culture was similar to that of the French-speaking Blacks. American efforts at integration paralleled French attempts at assimilation, and neither quite made it. It was impossible for either the black American or the black Frenchman to suppress his Africanness. For example, the blending of African tradition and contemporary Western religion is characteristic of American Negro Spirituals with which Senghor became familiar during the 'Negro Revolution' of the twenties and thirties in Paris. With the group behind the *Revue du Monde Noir*, Senghor discovered that 'animism continues to well up in his soul', coming from 'the far reaches of time as a lively spring below the shadow of Eastern religions'. In American Negro music he re-discovered the forgotten lesson of Joal where 'pagan voices' rhymed the Catholic Tantum Ergo.

A passage written by W.E.B. Du Bois in 1903 could easily have come from Senghor's hand:

> 'It is a peculiar sensation, this double consciousness, this sense of always looking at one's self through the eyes of others, of measuring one's soul by the tape of a world that looks on in amused contempt and pity. One ever feels his two-ness—an American, a Negro: two souls, two thoughts, two unreconciled strivings; two warring ideals in one dark body, whose dogged strength alone keeps it from being torn asunder.'

The Negro American influence on Senghor reinforced his consciousness of dualism, previously encountered in Gide and Goethe. Senghor himself has written about the American Negro author, Countee Cullen:

> 'Cullen was from a bourgeois and very religious family.... Remember too that he was a French teacher, having a solid classical culture, translating from time to time Greek tragedies. And here he is, torn between two traditions: the European, rather the American, and the African.'

To fight cultural alienation American Negro writers in 1925 began a movement which they called the 'Negro Renaissance'. This 'Renaissance' was designed to rehabilitate the Negro's past as well as to re-establish pride in a dark skin. An Anthology-Manifesto of 1925 called *The New Negro* declared that the American Negro must 'rebuild his past to build his future'. Alain Locke, a black Professor of Philosophy at Howard University, contributed to *The New Negro*. During the 1930s Locke was also a frequent visitor to Paulette Nardal's salon. Senghor met with him there and at René Maran's house.

The *Néo-Nègre* or *Nègre-Nouveau* movement begun by Senghor, Césaire, and Léon Damas in 1934 borrowed its name from its American Negro predecessor. In fact, the word *négritude* only appeared in 1939. *Néo-Nègre* or *Nègre-Nouveau* was used in place of *négritude* until that term gained popularity after Sartre had analysed it in 1948. However Senghor continued to use *Néo-Nègres* interchangeably with *Militants de la Négritude* after that time.

[Maurice] Barrès had led the way, but it was the Negro poet and novelist from Jamaica, Claude McKay, who finally swept away Senghor's complexes about African civilization. McKay, a member of the New Negro movement in the 1920s, wrote it in his novel *Banjo:* 'To plunge to the roots of our race and to build on our own foundations is not returning to a state of savagery', and concluded: 'it is culture itself'. McKay had helped the French West Indians behind the *Revue du Monde Noir* turn to African history and anthropology. In America for many years the New Negroes had studied the history and characteristics of their race in order to rehabilitate it in the eyes of the world. For this reason Senghor has written that 'Claude McKay can be considered. ..as the veritable inventor of *négritude*...not of the word...but of the values of *négritude*'.

The ideas of American Negroes reinforced Barrès's influence, which itself was inspired by [Frédérick] Mistral's return to Provençal culture. The Negro re-awakening thus extended the ideas of a provencial re-awakening advocated by Barrés and Mistral.

Senghor found many reasons for turning to American Negro writing for inspiration:

'It has been said and repeated that, as long as the Latin elements dominated, "the Frenchman did not have an epic spirit." This meant that for him intoxication was light; intelligence always controlled imagination and instinct. The American Negro has an epic spirit.... As in the Spirituals [there is] no dogma, but rather an absorbed mysticism, a communion with the heroic, with the divine.'

American Negro literature had an accent which 'pierced him right to his intestines'. Senghor found that Negro culture whether in the Americas or in Africa had a common heritage: 'In its diversity, it remained one, characterized in literary and artistic works by the constant, almost obsessive, use of rhythmic images to translate the vital forces which animate the world'. American Negro literature in which nature is 'animated by a human presence' proved to Senghor that this literature had preserved 'the most profound, the eternal trait of the Negro soul'. In 1939 he used this belief to affirm that the Negro quality 'has resisted all attempts at economic slavery and "moral liberation"'.

This discovery helped greatly in the elaboration of his cultural theories. He used this literature to demonstrate the differences between the Negro soul and the white soul. For Senghor it is soul which 'explains Negro religion and society'. The mystical belief that soul was the mainspring of civilizations is an expression of Senghor's 'spiritual determinism' which rejected economic determinism. For Senghor society and religion are determined by the innate qualities of a people rather than by their mode of production.

Césaire also studied the writings of the New Negroes and wrote his *Diplôme d'Etudes Supérieures* on 'The Theme of the South in American Negro Literature'. Paulette Nardal who advocated the study of Negro topics by Parisian black students had been listened to.

The experience of American Negroes served as a model for Blacks from French Colonies. The Senegalese historian Abdoulaye Ly, who frequently saw Senghor during the latter's stay in Paris, has affirmed that, from 1931 on, Senghor only saw the African personality through a transposition of what he knew about American Negroes. In 1947 Senghor's adversaries accused him of confusing American Negroes and Africans: 'Thus Monsieur Senghor...use your energies in more constructive and more disinterested domains. [In doing so] perhaps and doubtlessly you will attain one day the height of those giant American Negroes whom you bear so much affection'. Certain of Senghor's writings seem to justify this criticism: 'What the Negro contributes is the faculty of perceiving the supernatural in the natural, the transcendental sense and the active abandon which accompanies it, the abandon of love. It is as living an element in his ethnic personality as animism. *The study of the American Negro furnishes proof* of it'. Because he was so captivated by American Negroes, he followed them along the path which led towards the rejection of cultural *assimilation* but which simultaneously advocated political integration. He hardly departed from his path until 1958....

The fact that American Negroes exerted such a strong influence on Senghor seems to carry out the predictions of the 'Theses on the Negro Question' which had been adopted in 1922 by the Fourth Congress of the Communist International. The communists held that American Negroes were the *avant-garde* of the black race, that they were the leaders, and that the Communist International, by establishing its influence over them, could indirectly influence all Negro peoples.'History', according to the 'Theses', 'has devolved on American Negroes an important role in the liberation of the entire African race'. It continued: 'For 250 years, they have worked under the American proprietor's whip: they cut the forests, constructed the roads, planted the cotton, placed the railroad ties and sustained the southern aristo-cracy..."Free" Negro muscles, blood and tears helped establish American Capitalism....American Negroes, and above all, North American Negroes [are] at the *avant-garde* of the African struggle against oppression....The Negro movement should be organized in America, as the centre of Negro culture and the centre of the crystallization of Negro protests'.

---

### Readings IV.3 and IV.4

Poetry has been considered among the highest of the human arts because it seeks to get at emotions tugging at the human psyche and soul. To be black either in Africa or America was to be judged inhuman, subhuman, or just above the level of a beast. Therefore, for the persons of African descent to attempt the poetic was to challenge the basic assumption that they were not human and had none of the higher human attributes. The poets of the movement known as *Négritude* added the other dimensions of glorifying Africanity and criticizing Western Christendom and those Africans who succumbed to the ways of whites. Two poems from Négritude poets follow.

# Francis Ernest Kobina Parkes, "Ghana"

### Ghana

Give me black souls,
Let them be black
Or chocolate brown
Or make them the
Color of dust—
Dustlike,
Browner than sand.
But if you can
Please keep them black,
Black.

Give me some drums;
Let them be three
Or maybe four
And make them black—
Dirty and black:
Of wood,
And dried sheepskin,
But if you will
Just make them peal,
Peal.
Peal loud,
Mutter.
Loud,
Louder yet;
Then soft,
Softer still
Let the drums peal.
Let the calabash
Entwined with beads
With blue Aggrey beads
Resound, wildly
Discordant,
Calmly
Melodious.
Let the calabash resound
In tune with the drums.

Mingle with these sounds
The clang
Of wood on tin:
*Kententsekenken*
*Ken-tse ken ken ken*:
Do give me voices
Ordinary
Ghost voices
Voices of women
And the bass
Of men.
(And screaming babes?)

Let there be dancers,
Broad-shouldered Negroes
Stamping the ground
With naked feet
And half-covered
Women
Swaying, to and fro,
In perfect
Rhythm
To *"Tom shikishiki"*
And *"ken,"*
And voices of ghosts
Singing,
Singing!
Let there be
A setting sun above,
Green palms
Around,
A slaughtered fowl
And plenty of
Yams.

And dear Lord,
If the place be
Not too full,
Please
Admit spectators.
They may be
White or
Black.

Admit spectators
That they may
See:
The bleeding fowl,
And yams,
And palms
And dancing ghosts.

Odomankoma,
Do admit spectators
That they may
Hear:
Our native songs,
The clang of wood on tin
The tune of beads
And the pealing drums.

Twerampon, please, please
Admit
Spectators!
That they may
Bask
In the balmy rays
Of the
Evening Sun,
In our lovely
African heaven!

## Gabriel Okara, "....And The Other Immigrant"

My dignity is sewn
Into the lining of a three-piece suit.
Stiff, and with the whiteness which
Out-Europes Europe,
My crisp Van Heusen collar
Cradles an all-wool Tootal tie,
Turning respectful eyes towards
I, Me resplendent in my three-piece suit.
My dignity I rescue
From the shop assistant's levity
From the raucous laugh
Of the unmannered station guard
(Who hasn't learnt his place)
From the familiarity

Of the Cockney taxi man
Who thinks I'll bandy jokes with him,
A mere
Public servant—
One and all,
They wilt at the touch of ice.
My mouth is shaped perpetually
Upon the word "riff-raff."
The stowaway is a crook
The steerage passenger
Beneath my notice
And nomad is
A dirty word.
I do not shrink from conflict, but
I think exposure
To the merest chance of
A slight, an insult of indignity
Mere foolishness.
My victory is the proof
That I can "do without them."
I keep among my kind
For I condemn
All whiteness in a face.
My mind would open to
The niceties of judgment,
To fine distinctions in a thought
If such things did exist.
But only fools can doubt the solve-all
Philosopher's-stone attributes
Of Up-Nasser-Freedom-for-Africa
The height and end of all
So shout with me!
Let pedants tease their pompous heads
While to my repertoire I add
(The sound, if not the spirit of)
Our new-coined intellectuals' slogan—
*Negritude.*
Untouched I float
Upon the crest of an alien, white society,
My weekly dues are met
(Upon my fourth, hire purchase
Three-piece suit)
With proud regularity,
Ensuring round-the-year entombment

Winter or blazing summer,
(And sacrifices are gladly made
Like two square semolina meals a day)
By thinking of the government house.
Senior service car,
And hordes of admiring women awaiting me,
Where the one-eyed man is king.

---

## Reading IV.5

In the first part of this century, Haitians were being urged by one of their compatriots, Jean Price-Mars, to take pride in their Haitian and African heritage. Price-Mars conveyed his ideas in *Ainsi Parle l'Oncle* (1928) (Thus Spoke Uncle) which gives an inventory of the cultural wealth of African civilizations while describing their continuities and potential in Haitian society. The book had a historic impact on intellectuals, artists, and politicians inside and outside of Haiti. Jacques Roumain stands out as one of the highly talented and committed Haitian writers deeply influenced by Price-Mars. In his poetry and fiction, Africa and the beauty and struggles of Haitian peasants are glorified. He speaks of the beauty of the Haitian peasant's vision of heaven as the distant half-remembered Africa (Guinea) from which his forebears were ruthlessly uprooted.

---

## Jacques Roumain, "Guinea"

*Guinea*

It's the long road to Guinea
death takes you down.
Here are the boughs, the trees, the forest.
Listen to the sound of the wind in its long hair
    of eternal night.

It's the long road to Guinea
where your fathers await you without impatience.
Along the way, they talk,
They wait.
This is the hour when the streams rattle
    like beads of bone.

It's the long road to Guinea.
No bright welcome will be made for you
in the dark land of dark men:

Under a smoky sky pierced by the cry of birds
around the eye of the river
    the eyelashes of the trees open on decaying light.
There, there awaits you beside the water a quiet village,
and the hut of your fathers, and the hard ancestral stone
    where your head will rest at last.

*—Translated by Langston Hughes*

---

### Reading IV.6

This poem by Abioseh Nicol was written about the author's return to Africa after many years in England. It came to be a symbol of the desire of many people of African descent to return to Africa. It was popularized in the Americas by the West Indian poet Lindsey Barret who retitled it "Go For Bush," with bush referring to the interior or countryside. Barret gave a number of very successful public readings of the poem to jazz accompaniment.

---

## Abioseh Nicol, "The Meaning of Africa"

Africa, you were once just a name to me
But now you lie before me with sombre green challenge
To that loud faith for freedom (life more abundant)
Which we once professed shouting
Into the silent listening microphone
Or on an alien platform to a sea
Of white perplexed faces troubled
With secret Imperial guilt; shouting
Of you with a vision euphemistic
As you always appear
To your lonely sons on distant shores.

Then the cold sky and continent would disappear
In a grey mental mist.
And in its stead the hibiscus blooms in shameless scarlet

and the bougainvillea in mauve passion
entwines itself around strong branches
the palm trees stand like tall proud moral women
shaking their plaited locks against the
cool suggestive evening breeze;
the short twilight passes;
the white full moon turns its round gladness
towards the swept open space
between the trees; there will be
dancing tonight; and in my brimming heart
plenty of love and laughter.
Oh, I got tired of the cold northern sun
Of white anxious ghost-like faces
Of crouching over heatless fires
In my lonely bedroom.
The only thing I never tired of
was the persistent kindness
Of you too few unafraid
Of my grave dusky strangeness.

So I came back
Sailing down the Guinea Coast.
Loving the sophistication
Of your brave new cities:
Dakar, Accra, Cotonou,
Lagos, Bathurst and Bissau;
Liberia, Freetown, Libreville,
Freedom is really in the mind.

Go up-country, so they said,
To see the real Africa.
For whomsoever you may be,
That is where you come from.
Go for bush, inside the bush,
You will find your hidden heart,
Your mute ancestral spirit.
And so I went, dancing on my way.

Now you lie before me passive
With your unanswering green challenge.
Is this all you are?
This long uneven red road, this occasional succession
Of huddled heaps of four mud walls

And thatched, falling grass roofs
Sometimes ennobled by a thin layer
Of white plaster, and covered with thin
Slanting corrugated zinc.
These patient faces on weather-beaten bodies
Bowing under heavy market loads.
The pedalling cyclist wavers by
On the wrong side of the road,
As if uncertain of his new emancipation.
The squawking chickens, the pregnant she-goats
Lumber awkwardly with fear across the road,
Across the windscreen view of my four-cylinder kit car.
An overladen lorry speeds madly towards me
Full of produce, passengers, with driver leaning
Out into the swirling dust to pilot his
Swinging obsessed vehicle along.
Beside him on the raised seat his first-class
Passenger, clutching and timid; but he drives on
At so, so many miles per hour, peering out with
Bloodshot eyes, unshaved face and dedicated look;
His motto painted on each side: Sunshine Transport,
We get you there quick, quick. The Lord is my Shepherd.

The red dust settles down on the green leaves.

I know you will not make me want, Lord,
Though I have reddened your green pastures
It is only because I have wanted so much
That I have always been found wanting.
From South and East, and from my West
(The sandy desert holds the North)
We look across a vast continent
And blindly call it ours.
You are not a country, Africa,
You are a concept,
Fashioned in our minds, each to each,
To hide our separate fears,
To dream our separate dreams.
Only those within you who know
Their circumscribed plot,
And till it well with steady plough
Can from that harvest then look up
To the vast blue inside,

Of the enamelled bowl of sky
Which covers you and say
'This is my Africa' meaning
'I am content and happy.
I am fulfilled, within,
Without and roundabout
I have gained the little longings
Of my hands, my loins, my heart
And the soul that follows in my shadow.'
I know now that is what you are, Africa:
Happiness, contentment, and fulfillment,
And a small bird singing on a mango tree.

# APPENDICES

## AFRICAN COUNTRIES: BASIC DATA

| Country (Former Name) | Capital | Date of Independence | Colonial Power | Language | Area Square Miles | Population (1983) | GNP/Capita $ 1980 | Change in GNP 1960–1982 |
|---|---|---|---|---|---|---|---|---|
| Algeria | Algiers | 7-3-62 | France | A | 919,595 | 20,330,000 | 1,920 | +70.3% |
| Angola | Luanda | 11-11-75 | Portugal | P | 481,354 | 7,110,000 | 470 | -4.1% |
| Benin (Dahomey) | Porto Novo | 8-1-60 | France | F | 43,484 | 3,910,000 | — | — |
| Botswana (Bechuanaland) | Gabarone | 9-30-66 | Britain | E | 231,805 | 941,027* | 910 | +74.7% |
| Burkina Faso (Upper Volta) | Ouagadougou | 8-5-60 | France | F | 105,869 | 7,290,000 | 190 | +63.2% |
| Burundi | Bujumbura | 7-1-62 | Belgium | F | 10,747 | 4,920,000 | 200 | +60.0% |
| Cameroon | Yaoundé | 1-1-60 | Fr/Brit | F/E | 183,569 | 9,060,000 | 670 | +62.7% |
| Cape Verde Islands | Praia | 7-5-75 | Portugal | P | 1,750 | 296,093# | 300 | -13.3% |
| Central African Republic (Oubangi-Chari) | Bangui | 8-13-60 | France | F | 240,535 | 2,520,000 | 300 | +46.6% |
| Chad | Ndjamena | 8-11-60 | France | F | 495,755 | 4,970,000 | 120 | +33.3% |
| Comoro Islands | Moroni | 7-6-75 | France | F | 719 | 385,000* | 300 | +43.3% |
| Congo | Brazzaville | 8-15-60 | France | F | 132,047 | 1,660,000 | 730 | +53.4% |
| Djibouti | Djibouti | 6-27-77 | France | F | 8,494 | 350,000* | — | — |
| Egypt | Cairo | 2-28-22 | Britain | A | 386,622 | 46,000,000 | 580 | +56.9% |
| Equatorial Guinea | Malabo | 10-12-68 | Spain | S | 10,831 | 380,000 | — | — |
| Ethiopia | Addis Ababa | ancient | — | Am | 471,778 | 33,000,000 | 140 | +35.7% |
| Gabon | Libreville | 8-17-60 | France | F | 103,347 | 1,290,000 | 3,680 | +64.4% |
| The Gambia | Banjul (Bathurst) | 2-18-65 | Britain | E | 4,017 | 695,886 | 344 | +62.2% |

| Country | Capital | Date | Colonial Power | Lang. | Area | Population | Per Capita | Change |
|---|---|---|---|---|---|---|---|---|
| Ghana | Accra | 3-6-57 | Britain | E | 92,100 | 12,830,000 | 420 | +28.6% |
| Guinea | Conakry | 10-2-58 | France | F | 94,926 | 5,410,000 | 290 | +62.1% |
| Guinea-Bissau | Bissau | 9-10-74 | Portugal | P | 13,948 | 826,000 | 160 | −106.3% |
| Ivory Coast | Abidjan | 8-7-60 | France | F | 123,847 | 9,270,000 | 1,150 | +67.0% |
| Kenya | Nairobi | 12-12-63 | Britain | E | 224,961 | 18,750,000 | 420 | +59.5% |
| Lesotho (Basutoland) | Maseru | 10-4-66 | Britain | E | 11,720 | 1,700,000 | 390 | +74.4% |
| Liberia | Monrovia | 7-26-1847 | — | E | 43,000 | 1,900,000 | 520 | +40.4% |
| Libya | Tripoli | 12-24-51 | Italy | A | 679,362 | 3,500,000 | 8,420 | +59.1% |
| Madagascar (Malagasy) | Antananarivo | 6-26-60 | France | F/M | 226,658 | 9,470,000 | 350 | +57.1% |
| Malawi (Nyasaland) | Lilongwe | 7-6-64 | Britain | E | 45,747 | 6,100,000 | 230 | +52.2% |
| Mali | Bamako | 6-20-60 | France | F | 478,767 | 7,490,000 | 190 | +63.2% |
| Mauritania | Nouakchott | 11-28-60 | France | A/F | 397,956 | 1,780,000 | 320 | +37.5% |
| Mauritius | Port Louis | 3-12-68 | Britain | E | 790 | 994,000 | 1,060 | +61.3% |
| Morocco | Rabat | 1956/69 | Fr/Spain | A | 275,117 | 21,000,000 | 860 | +62.8% |
| Mozambique | Maputo | 6-25-75 | Portugal | P | 308,642 | 13,140,000 | 270 | −40.7% |
| Namibia (SW Africa) | Windhoek | — | S. Africa | Af/E | 318,261 | 1,039,800 | 1,200 | — |
| Niger | Niamey | 8-3-60 | France | F | 489,191 | 6,040,000 | 330 | +69.7% |
| Nigeria | Lagos | 10-1-60 | Britain | E | 356,669 | 82,390,000 | 1,010 | +79.2% |
| Réunion | Saint Denis | — | France | F | 969 | 110,000 | — | — |
| Rwanda | Kigali | 7-1-62 | Belgium | F | 10,169 | 5,580,000 | 200 | +65.0% |
| São Tomé and Príncipe | São Tomé | 7-12-75 | Portugal | P | 372 | 100,000 | 490 | +4.1% |
| Senegal | Dakar | 6-20-60 | France | F | 75,750 | 6,180,000 | 450 | +37.8% |
| Seychelles | Victoria | 6-26-76 | Britain | E | 171 | 69,000 | 1,770 | +79.1% |
| Sierra Leone | Freetown | 4-27-61 | Britain | E | 27,669 | 3,470,000 | 270 | +40.7% |
| Somalia | Mogadishu | 7-1-60 | Brit/Ital | S | 246,201 | 3,860,000 | 130 | +38.5% |
| South Africa | Pretoria | 5-31-10** | Britain | Af/E | 471,445 | 26,120,000 | 2,290 | +54.1% |
| Sudan | Khartoum | 1-1-56 | Britain | A | 967,500 | 18,900,000 | 470 | +72.3% |

| Country | Capital | Independence | Language | Area | Population | GNP | Growth |
|---|---|---|---|---|---|---|---|
| Swaziland | Mbabane | 9-6-68 | E | 6,704 | 585,000 | 680 | +51.5% |
| Tanzania (Tanganyika & Zanzibar) | Dar Es Salaam | 12-9-61 (1963) | Sw | 364,900 | 19,730,000 | 260 | +50.0% |
| Togo | Lome | 4-27-60 | F | 21,925 | 2,960,000 | 410 | +56.1% |
| Tunisia | Tunis | 3-20-56 | A | 63,170 | 6,950,000 | 1,310 | +64.9% |
| Uganda | Kampala | 10-9-62 | E | 91,134 | 13,220,000 | 280 | +46.4% |
| Western Sahara (occupied) | Elaaiun | 2-28-75 (disputed) | A | 102,680 | 79,000 | — | — |
| Zaire (Congo) | Kinshasa | 6-30-60 | F | 905,568 | 31,960,000 | 220 | +36.4% |
| Zambia (Northern Rhodesia) | Lusaka | 10-24-64 | E | 290,586 | 6,240,000 | 560 | +23.2% |
| Zimbabwe (Southern Rhodesia) | Harare | 4-18-80† | E | 150,804 | 7,500,000 | 630 | +31.7% |

A = Arabic  Af = Afrikaans  Am = Amharic  E = English  F = French  M = Malagasy  P = Portuguese  S = Spanish  Sw = Swahili

*1981

#1980

^1982

**became Republic of South Africa May 31, 1961

†unilateral declaration of independence 1964

# Chronology of Key Events in African History

**B.C.**

| | |
|---|---|
| c. 2900–2877 | First pyramid constructed at Giza by Pharaoh Cheops. |
| c. 575 | Ethiopia, using iron weapons, becomes the most powerful state of the Middle East and North Africa. |
| c. 350 | Origins of earliest known Iron Age culture south of Sahara (Nok culture of Nigeria). |
| | Early trans-Saharan trade between the Sudan and North Africa by way of Berber middlemen. |
| c. 300 | Egypt, Tunisia, and Algeria become part of the Roman empire. |

**A.D.**

| | |
|---|---|
| c. 400 | First settlements at site of Great Zimbabwe. |
| 640 | Arabs enter Egypt. |
| 646 | Final Arab capture of Alexandria. |
| c. 750 | Ghana empire in West Africa at its height. |
| c. 800 | Swahili East Africa coastal culture in formative period. |
| | First Muslim settlements on east coast off Kenyan seaboard at Lamu. |
| | Earliest southward penetration of Islam from Morocco and Central Maghreb. |
| | Origins of Yoruba and Hausa states in western and northern Nigeria. |
| c. 1040–1050 | Almoravid empire in northwest Africa and southern Spain at its height. |
| c. 1140–1200 | Almohad empire in North Africa. |
| c. 1230–1255 | Mali empire in West Africa at its height under King Sundiata Keita. |
| c. 1280 | Swahili ports engaged in long-distance trade between inland gold and ivory producers. |
| 1331 | Ibn Battuta visits Kilwa and finds it a strong and wealthy trading city. |

| c. 1400 | Wolof empire well established in Senegal. |
|---|---|
| 1443 | First slaves for Portugal taken directly from African peoples south of Morocco; European slave trade begins. |
| 1482 | First Portuguese fort and training post established on Guinea coast at San Jorge da Mina (Elmina). |
| 1493–1528 | Reign of Askia Mohammed I; Songhay empire at its height. |
| 1505 | Portuguese burn Kilwa, continue ravages up the coast; Swahili city ports begin decline. |
| c. 1510 | Spanish colonies in tropical America begin to be supplied with slaves from Africa; the trans-Atlantic slave trade opens. |
| 1507–1543 | Reign of Bakongo King Afonso I. |
| 1517 | Ottoman Turks complete conquest of Egypt. |
| 1575 | Conquistador Paulos Dias de Novais sets up base at Loanda, defeats Bakongo armies, begins Portuguese conquest of Angola. |
| c. 1600 | Niger delta peoples organize themselves into trading states as landward partners of European maritime traders. This develops into large and continuing sale of captives for enslavement in the Americas. |
| 1637 | Dutch take Elmina, end of Portuguese control on Gold Coast. |
| 1652 | First European settlement in South Africa; Dutch establish small settlement at Cape of Good Hope as way station to the East. |
| 1680 | Ashanti (Asante) found strong state in forest of central Ghana. |
| 1787 | Sierra Leone founded. |
| 1798 | Napoleon invades Egypt. |
| | French African communes (Dakar, St. Louis, Goree) granted representation in French parliament. |
| 1804–1811 | Jihad of Fulani reformer Usuman dan Fodio, leads to Fulani hegemony over most of northern Nigeria under Mohammed Bello. |
| 1807 | British ban Atlantic slave trade, followed by United States in 1808, Holland in 1814, and France in 1818. |
| 1821 | Plan developed for freed slave colony at Liberia. |
| 1830 | French begin occupation of Algeria. |
| 1847 | Liberia becomes independent black republic. |

| | |
|---|---|
| 1854 | The French, under Louis Faidherbe, begin conquest of the Senegal basin. |
| c. 1863 | Tucolor empire of al-Hajj Umar at its height. |
| 1869 | Suez Canal opened. |
| 1878 | Cocoa production begun in West Africa; a Ghanaian, Tetteah Quarshie, brings several pods to Ghana from Fernando Po (now Bioko). |
| | Zulus defeat British at Isandhlwana. |
| c. 1880 | Mandinka empire of Samory Toure at its height. |
| c. 1881 | Mohammed Ahmad proclaims himself *Mahdi* in the Sudan; embarks on recovery of indigenous power. |
| 1884–1885 | Berlin Conference of imperialist powers catalyzes colonial partition of Africa. |
| c. 1899 | Anglo-Afrikaner (Boer) War begins. |
| 1910 | Union of South Africa constituted. |
| 1916–1918 | Germany loses African colonies; these are placed under French or British administration by the League of Nations. |
| 1925 | Portuguese complete colonial occupation of inland Angola and Mozambique. |
| 1936 | Italy attacks and conquers Ethiopia. |
| 1941 | Italy evicted from Ethiopia; Emperor Haile Selassie restored to his throne. |
| 1944 | Brazzaville (French Congo) conference of colonial administrators, called by General de Gaulle, lays out plans for reorganization of French empire. |
| 1946 | First French postwar constitution provides for African representation in the French parliament and for elected local (African) legislative assemblies. |
| 1948 | Afrikaner National Party comes to power in South Africa; apartheid system, based on existing system of discrimination, becomes legalized. |
| 1952 | Free Officers overthrow Egyptian King Farouk; Gamal Abdel Nasser becomes president in 1954. |
| 1954 | Algerians begin war of independence. |
| 1955 | Kikuyu peasant uprising in Kenya (Mau Mau) is defeated by British; an estimated 13,000 African lives are lost. |

1956            Suez War; following nationalization of Suez Canal by President Nasser
               of Egypt, Britain, France, and Israel attack Egypt; political pressure by
               the United States ends war before canal is taken.

1957            Ghana becomes independent.

1958            Constitution of Fifth French Republic opens door for independence of
               French African colonies; Guinea votes *"non"* on constitutional refer-
               endum and gains immediate independence.

1960            Seventeen African states become independent.

               Sharpeville massacre in South Africa; 69 blacks killed by police, many
               more wounded.

               Belgian Congo (now Zaire) becomes independent; Prime Minister
               Patrice Lumumba assassinated; Katanga province (now Shaba) secedes,
               and United Nations intervenes to end Katangan revolt and restore
               order.

1961            Tanzania becomes independent; Angolan nationalist uprising signals
               beginning of anti-colonial wars in Portuguese Africa.

1963            Military seizes power in Togo; first post-independence coup in sub-
               Saharan Africa.

               Organization of African Unity (OAU) founded at Addis Ababa.

1965            Rhodesian whites rebel against Britain, declare unilateral independence
               under their own constitution.

1966            Military coup ousts Kwame Nkrumah in Ghana.

               First of four military coups ends civilian rule in Nigeria; Prime Minister
               Tafawa Balewa and other civilian leaders assassinated.

1967–1970       Nigerian civil war due to secession of Ibo-dominated "Biafra" (eastern
               Nigeria).

1967            Spain pulls out of Western Sahara, leaving it to be divided between
               Morocco and Mauritania; guerilla war by Sahroui rebels involves
               Morocco, Mauritania, Algeria, and Libya.

1971            General Idi Amin seizes power in Uganda, begins eight years of brutal
               rule.

1974            Emperor Haile Selassie of Ethiopia deposed in military coup.

1975            Revolution in Portugal, African resistance, lead to independence for
               Angola and Mozambique.

               Libya occupies northern Auzou Strip of Chad.

1976            Violent demonstrations by blacks in Soweto township spark disorders throughout South Africa.

1977–1978       Shaba I and II: invasions of Zairian Shaba (ex-Katanga) Province from Angola repulsed by Mobutu government with Moroccan help.

                Military conflict between Somalia and Ethiopia in Ogaden area; Somalis are repulsed by Ethiopians backed by the Soviet Union and Cuban troops.

1979            Civil War begins in Chad involving Libya and eventually (in 1983) results in de facto partition of country between Libyan-backed and French-backed factions.

                Three tyrants forced out of power: Idi Amin of Uganda toppled after Tanzanian intervention; "Emperor" Bokassa I (Central African Empire/Republic) removed by French intervention; Macias Nguema (Equatorial Guinea) ousted, then executed, after military coup.

1980            Robert Mugabe becomes prime minister of Zimbabwe following collapse of white-led government.

                First military coup in Liberian history removes President Tolbert; Tolbert and various Liberian leaders killed.

1981            Anwar Sadat, successor to Nasser, assassinated in Egypt by Muslim fundamentalists.

                Eritrean secessionist factions enter 20th year of armed resistance to Ethiopian rule.

1983            Nigeria expels over one million "illegal aliens" (most Ghanaians) from neighboring African countries.

1983–1984       South Africa initiates new constitutional arrangements in which coloreds and Indians are given nominal representation in parliament and government; most boycott referendum on new constitution because blacks not given any voice.

1984            Sékou Touré of Guinea dies; shortly thereafter Guinean military takes over in bloodless coup.

1985            (April)   Nineteen blacks shot dead in South Africa during demonstrations attending commemoration of 25th anniversary of Sharpeville massacre; period of general unrest begins.

                (July)   State of emergency proclaimed by South African government following period of unrest and violence; 600 people detained.

# Biographical Index

AFONSO I (NZINGA MBEMBA) (1506–c. 1545). Ruler of the Congo kingdom. He collaborated with the Portuguese to bring Catholicism to the Congo but was unable to prevent his European allies from expanding the slave trade and exploiting his people.

AL-HAJJ MOHAMMED ABDULLAH HASSAN (1864–1920/1921). Somali poet, scholar, religious reformer, and judge, called the "Mad Mullah" by the British. In 1894, during a visit to Mecca, he strove to promote Islamic reforms, and in 1900 declared a *jihad*. The British, with Ethiopian help, defeated his attempt to conquer Somaliland and the Ogaden.

AHMADU BIN HAMMADI BOUBA (SHEHU HAMADU) (1775–1844). Fulani cleric and disciple of Usuman dan Fodio. In 1818 Shehu Hamadu conquered and then ruled a state centered in Macina. His realm extended over much of the area of the medieval empire of Songhay.

AL-HAJJ UMAR (UMAR IBN SAYYID TAL) (c. 1794–1864). Scholar, religious leader, military strategist, and son-in-law of Mohammed Bello (chief architect of the Sokoto caliphate). Umar established a powerful but short-lived (1852–1862) theocratic empire that at one time included Dinguiray, Bure, Segou, Kaarta, and Macina.

ASKIA MOHAMMED (MOHAMMED TURE; ASKIA AL-HAJJ MOHAMMED IBN ABI BAKR TURE) (c. 1443–c. 1538). Askia the Great, the ruler of Songhay at its height (c. 1493–1538). Askia remodeled the Songhay empire along stricter Muslim lines, developed a strong centralized government, and expanded the empire east to the border of Bornu, north to Hausaland, and west to the Atlantic.

AZIKIWE, BENJAMIN NNAMDI (1904– ). First president of Nigeria (1963–1966) and a leader of the country's independence movement. He later became a proponent of Biafra's secession. Known popularly as "Zik," he attended universities in the United States, went to Ghana to edit a newspaper, then returned home to establish the influential *West African Pilot* and help found the National Council of Nigeria and the Cameroons.

BURTON, (SIR) RICHARD FRANCIS (1821–1890). Orientalist scholar, linguist, diplomat, and explorer. Burton became famous for his visit to Mecca disguised as a Muslim. Together with John Hanning Speke, Burton was commissioned by the Royal Geographic Society to find the source of the Nile River, exploring the Lake Tanganyika region in the process.

CABRAL, AMILCAR (1924–1973). Portuguese Guinean nationalist leader and cofounder of the African Party for the Independence of Guinea and Cape Verde (PAIGC), Guinea-Bissau's governing party. Cabral studied agronomy in Lisbon, and in 1956 returned to Portuguese Guinea to help organize the guerilla resistance against Portuguese rule. Widely known as an ideologist of African nationalism, he was assassinated in Conakry in 1973.

CLAPPERTON, HUGH (1878–1927). Scotch explorer. As a lieutenant in the Royal Navy, he headed an expedition from Tripoli across the Sahara to Bornu, then west to Kano and Sokoto, where he was received with full honors by the Sultan Mohammed Bello. Later he undertook another expedition to the source of the Niger River but died in Sokoto before reaching his goal.

CROWTHER, SAMUEL AJAYI (1808–1891). First Anglican bishop of Nigeria. Crowther was a scholar, missionary, and explorer. His journals of the Niger expeditions and his studies of the Yoruba language and traditions established him as a scholar of note.

DU BOIS, WILLIAM EDWARD BURGHARDT (1868–1963). American civil rights activist and leader in the Pan-African movement. Du Bois founded the Niagara Association, which evolved into the National Association for the Advancement of Colored People (NAACP). After attending the First Pan-African Congress (London, 1900), he became the major organizer of the next four, the last of which he co-chaired with Kwame Nkrumah, future President of Ghana. In 1961, at the age of 93, disillusioned with racial conditions in the United States, he joined the Communist Party and moved to Ghana, becoming a Ghanaian citizen.

GARVEY, MARCUS MOZIAH (1887–1940). International black separatist leader. Garvey was founder of the Universal Negro Improvement Association. Born in Jamaica, where he founded the UNIA, Garvey moved to the United States and preached black separateness and the return of blacks to Africa. His ideas influenced a number of prominent black leaders, including Kwame Nkrumah, President of Ghana.

HOUPHOUET-BOIGNY, FELIX (1905–). When the Ivory Coast became fully independent in 1960, Houphouet-Boigny was elected its first president, an office he occupies to this day. Under Houphouet's leadership, the Ivory Coast developed into one of Africa's most prosperous countries.

IBN BATTUTA (MOHAMMED IBN ABDULLAH IBN BATTUTA) (1304–1377). Moroccan scholar, historian and traveler. He wrote detailed chronicles of his journeys through North, East, and West Africa. These writings provide a first-hand account of the political and social structure of a number of 14th-century African kingdoms and empires.

IBN KHALDUN (1332–1382). Arab historian and scholar. Khaldun was best known for his historical writings and his use of a sociological perspective in his books. He also provided descriptions of the development of such western Sudanic kingdoms as Ghana, Sosso, and Mali.

IBN TUMART (c. 1075–c. 1130). Berber leader of the reformist Almohad religious movement and founder of the Almohad empire, which at its height (c. 1140–1200) included most of the North African coastal regions from Morocco to the Egyptian border. The Almohads arose in reaction to the Almoravids, an earlier reformist movement and dynasty, conquering and expanding its domains.

(ABDULLAH) IBN YACINE (d. 1059). Leader and founder of the Almoravid empire and dynasty. The Almoravids began as a Saharan Berber and Sudanese movement of religious reform and expanded into an empire, which at its height (c. 1050–1140) included Morocco, half of Spain, and various Mediterranean islands.

KAUNDA, KENNETH DAVID (1924–). Leader of northern Rhodesia's independence movement and President of Zambia. Kaunda was the son of a Church of Scotland preacher and missionary from Nyasaland. Kaunda was much influenced by Ghandi's teachings about nonviolence, is an admirer of Abraham Lincoln, and professes a form of political humanism.

KENYATTA, JOMO (b. Kamau Ngengi) (1891–1978). Leader of the Kenyan independence movement and Kenya's first president. Kenyatta visited and studied briefly in Moscow, going on to take a postgraduate diploma in anthropology at the London School of Economics. His book *Facing Mount Kenya,* an anthropological study of the Gikuyu people, was widely hailed as a defense of African traditions and culture undermined by colonial rule.

LEO AFRICANUS (GIOVANNI LEONE, b. Al-Hassan Ibn Mohammed Al-Wizaz Al-Fasi) (1493–c. 1552). Spanish Arab traveler and chronicler. He traveled extensively throughout the western Sudan, including Mali, Songhay, and the Hausa states. Later, he was captured by Christian pirates, baptized by Pope Leo X, and renamed Giovanni Leone. The chronicles of his travels were published in Italian and English.

LEOPOLD II (1834–1909). King of Belgium. In 1885, on the basis of explorations carried out at Leopold's request by Henry M. Stanley, Leopold created the Congo Free State, with himself as monarch. The Free State became an immense private concessionary domain for the commercial exploitation of the Congo's natural rubber and mineral wealth. In 1908, international outcry at the brutal treatment of the native Congolese prompted the Belgian government to annex the territory and strip Leopold of his holdings.

LIVINGSTONE, DAVID (1813–1873). Scotch medical missionary and explorer. Livingstone was mainly concerned with expanding missionary activity and developing legitimate trade in the lower Zambezi area in order to put an end to the Arab-Swahili slave trade. He was the first European to visit Victoria Falls. His name is popularly linked with that of Henry M. Stanley who, in 1871, found Livingstone ("Dr. Livingstone, I presume?") after the latter had dropped from sight for a number of months.

LUMUMBA, PATRICE (1925–1961). Congolese nationalist and first Prime Minister of the Congo Republic (now Zaire). Not quite two months after he was named Prime Minister, he was deposed by army chief of staff Joseph Mobutu and in 1961 was murdered under mysterious circumstances.

LUTHULI, ALBERT JOHN (1898–1967). South African black nationalist, Zulu leader, and Nobel laureate. Luthuli joined the African National Congress in 1946 and was elected national president of the (South African) ANC in 1952. Active in the passive resistance campaign of 1952, he was thereafter repeatedly banned (placed under severe social and political restrictions) for his political activities against the racial policies of the government. In 1961, in recognition of his lifelong commitment to nonviolence and his leadership in the cause of black freedom, he was awarded the Nobel Peace Prize.

MALAN, DANIEL FRANÇOIS (1874–1959). Prime Minister of South Africa (1948–1954). Malan was one of the principal architects and ideologues of the country's policies of racial separation (apartheid).

MANDELA, NELSON ROLIHLAHLA (1918–). South African black nationalist leader. Trained as a lawyer, Mandela joined the African National Congress (ANC) in 1944, becoming active in the legal resistance to apartheid and white rule. From 1953–1955 he was under a banning order and later was tried on treason charges. Acquitted in 1961, he resumed his political activities, both within and outside the country. In 1962 he was captured, tried, and condemned to life imprisonment. In 1985 the government offered to grant him his freedom on the condition that he renounce all political activity, but he refused. He remains titular leader of the ANC and a powerful symbol of black resistance.

MANSA MUSA (KANKAN MUSA) (d. 1337). Ruler of the Mali empire at its peak (1312–1337). Under his rule, Mali reached from the Atlantic to what is today Nigeria, including most of the area between the tropical rain forest and the Sahara.

MENELIK II (b. Sahle Mariam) (c. 1844–1913). King of Shoa and Emperor of Ethiopia at the turn of the 20th century. Menelik brought most of Ethiopia under centralized control with Italian help, establishing his capital at Addis Ababa. In 1896 he routed an invading Italian force at Adowa, forcing a new treaty which acknowledged Ethiopia's complete independence.

MOBUTU SESE SEKO (b. Josehp Desiré Mobutu, renamed MOBUTU SESE SEKO KUKLI NGBENDU WA ZA BANGA) (1930– ). President of Zaire (ex-Democratic Republic of the Congo) since seizing power in 1965. Schooled in Zaire, he first served seven years on the Congolese Army, then turned to journalism and politics, joining Patrice Lumumba's Mouvement National Congolais (MNC) and becoming part of the Congolese leadership negotiating the country's independence. Named chief of staff at independence, he staged his first coup not two months later, surrendering power to civilians in 1961 but retaking it in 1965.

MONDLANE, EDUARDO CHIVAMBO (1920–1969). Mozambiquan nationalist leader. Mondlane worked for the UN's Trusteeship Department, then as a lecturer at Syracuse University before accepting the leadership of FRELIMO (Front for the Liberation of Mozambique) in 1962. In 1964 Mondlane and FRELIMO launched a guerilla war against the Portuguese in Mozambique. The war and the revolution in Portugal in 1974 led directly to Mozambiquan independence in 1975. In 1969 he was killed by a parcel bomb allegedly sent by Portuguese agents.

MOHAMMED BELLO (1781–1837). Sultan of Sokoto, chief architect of the Sokoto caliphate, and son of Usuman dan Fodio, whose jihad resulted in Fulani hegemony over an area that today includes northern Nigeria, northern Cameroon, and southern Niger. In 1804 his father gave him command of one of the Fulani armies, and in 1817 Mohammed became Sultan following his father's death.

NASSER, GAMAL ABDEL (1918–1970). Former President of Egypt and Arab nationalist leader. While serving with the Egyptian Army during the 1940s, Nasser established a secret group of revolutionary officers which deposed King Farouk and seized power in 1952. Nasser himself came to power in 1954, becoming president in 1956. His nationalization of the Suez Canal in 1956 precipitated a short-lived Anglo-French-Israeli invasion, and his pan-Arab and nationalist policies became a major political factor in the Middle East.

NKRUMAH, KWAME (Francis Nwia Kofie) (1909–1972). When Ghana became independent in 1957 he was named prime minister and in 1960 was elected Ghana's first president. Widely hailed for his Pan-African and socialist ideas, his policies nonetheless led to his overthrow by the military in 1966. Until his death in 1972, he lived in Guinea as nominal "co-president" to Sékou Touré.

NYERERE, JULIUS KAMBARAGE (1922– ). President of Tanzania until 1985, when he voluntarily stepped down. Nyerere was educated in Uganda at Makerere College and at Edinburgh University. He pursued policies of self-reliance, African socialism, and nonalignment. A political philosopher as well as a scholar of the Swahili language (he translated Shakespeare's *Julius Caesar* into Swahili), he is revered throughout Africa and was nicknamed *mwalimu* (teacher) by his people.

PADMORE, GEORGE (b. Malcolm Nurse) (1903–1959). West Indian nationalist and exponent of Pan-Africanism. He helped organize the fifth Pan-African Congress in 1945 in Manchester, England. At one time an ardent Communist, he later broke with the party, ending his career as special advisor to Ghanaian Kwame Nkrumah.

RHODES, CECIL JOHN (1853–1902). British statesman and capitalist. Rhodes made his fortune in South Africa by monopolizing diamond production. He founded the British South Africa Company and the De Beers Mining Company, today still the world's biggest producer of gem and industrial diamonds. He was prime minister and virtual dictator of Cape Colony (1890–1896) and principal developer of Rhodesia.

SELASSIE, HAILE (b. Tafari Makonner) (1892–1975). Emperor of Ethiopia (1930–1974). He resisted the Italian invasion of 1936, appealing to the League of Nations for help. His dramatic plea was of no avail, and Ethiopia came under Italian rule until 1941 when, with British help, he reconquered his country. In 1963 he hosted the founding meeting of the Organization of African Unity in Addis Ababa. In 1974 he was overthrown by a military coup, dying in captivity in 1975.

SENGHOR, LÉOPOLD SÉDAR (1906– ). Poet, man of letters, philosopher, and first president of Senegal (1960–1981). A leading poet and ideologue of the *Négritude* movement, he was educated at the University of Paris. He helped found several nationalist parties in Senegal and became president of Senegal when the country became independent in 1960. He retired voluntarily in 1981 in favor of his prime minister, Abdou Diouf, but remains active in Senegalese politics.

SHAKA (CHAKA; TSHAKA) (c. 1787–1829). Nearly invincible as a military leader, Shaka expanded Zulu power throughout a major part of Southern Africa. His tactical innovations, his reorganization of the Zulu regiments, and his development of the *assegai* (short stabbing spear) and long shield made the Zulu armies the most effective indigenous fighting force in Africa. Eventually, defeats at the hands of the British and defections within his ranks sapped his power. In 1829 he was assassinated in a plot led by two of his half-brothers.

SPEKE, JOHN HANNING (1827–1864). After serving for years in the British Indian Army, this British explorer was selected with Sir Richard Burton to lead an expedition to find the source of the Nile. Speke correctly surmised that Lake Victoria was the source of the (White) Nile and returned to England before Burton to argue his case. He shot himself on the eve of a debate with Burton.

STANLEY, HENRY MORTON (b. John Rowlands) (1841–1904). Traveler and writer. Stanley helped popularize African explorations to American and British publics. Employed by Belgian King Leopold II, Stanley helped establish Leopold's Congo Free State. His most famous exploit was his successful search for David Livingstone in 1871. In his later years he was elected to the British Parliament, and during his career wrote more than a dozen volumes.

SUNDIATA KEITA (SUNDJATA; MARI-DJATA) (c. 1210–c. 1260). Founder of the Mali empire. During his 25-year reign (according to Arab historian Ibn Khaldun) Sundiata established the base on which the Mande empire of Male was built. Much of Sundiata's story derives from Mande oral tradition, and he became an epic hero in Mande folk history.

SUNNI ALI (ALI BER) (d. 1492). Military leader and founder-king of the Songhay Empire (1464–1492). Though he was a skilled military tactician, much of his success rested on his use of Songhay's navy, which he employed to blockade and then capture such important river ports as Jenne.

SAMORY TOURE (SAMORI TURE) (c. 1830–1900). Creator and ruler of the last and largest 19th-century Mandinka Dyula conquest states of the western Sudan. Before succumbing to the French (in 1898), his two successive empires covered large parts of the Upper Niger area and the interior of what is today the Ivory Coast.

TOURÉ, AHMED SÉKOU (1922–1984). Nationalist leader and first president of Guinea, a post which he held until his death. During his presidency, Touré attempted to bring his own radical version of African socialism to Guinea. The experiment proved economically and politically disastrous, and at the time of his death his regime had become dictatorial and repressive.

USUMAN DAN FODIO (UTHMAN) (1754–1817). Leader of the Fulani Muslim revolution in the Hausa states of northern Nigeria (1804–1812) and founder of the Sokoto Caliphate and dynasty. Initially active as a scholar and itinerent preacher, beginning in 1789 Usuman had a series of visions which led him (in 1804) to call for a jihad against the debased forms of Islam practiced in the Hausa states. His followers not only conquered northern Nigeria but also reached into neighboring areas of Cameroon, Niger, and Mali.

WILLIAMS, HENRY SYLVESTER (1869–1911). Trinidadian barrister who organized the first Pan-African Congress in London in 1900. Active on behalf of a number of West African traditional chiefs, he called the conference principally to publicize the demands of his clients and to protest European seizure of African lands.

# Bibliography

Abd al-Rahum, M. *Imperialism and Nationalism in the Sudan: A Study in Constitutional and Political Development, 1899–1956*. Oxford: Oxford University Press, 1969.

Abir, M. *Ethiopia and the Red Sea: The Rise and Decline of the Solomonic Dynasty and Muslim-European Rivalry in the Region*. London: F. Cass and Co. Ltd., 1980.

Abun Nasr, J.M. *A History of the Maghrib*. 2nd ed. Cambridge: Cambridge University Press, 1975.

Achebe, C. *Things Fall Apart*. London: Heinemann Educational Books, Ltd., 1958.

Adam, H. *Modernizing Racial Domination: South Africa's Political Dynamics*. Berkeley: University of California Press, 1971.

Adamolekun, L. *Sékou Touré's Guinea*. London: Methuen, 1976.

Adamson, A.H. *Sugar Without Slaves: The Political Economy of British Guiana, 1834–1904*. New Haven: Yale University Press, 1972.

Adedeji, A. *After Lagos What?* Monograph, General Series No. 1. Tripoli: African Center for Applied Research, 1983.

Ajayi, J.F.A., and M. Crowder, eds. *History of West Africa*. 2 volumes. London: Longman, 1971, 1974.

Allott, A. *New Essays in African Law*. London: Greenwood Press, 1970.

Austin, D. *Ghana Observed*. Manchester: Manchester University Press, 1978.

Baker, R.W. *Egypt's Uncertain Revolution under Nasser and Sadat*. Cambridge: Harvard University Press, 1978.

Balandier, G. *Ambiguous Africa: Cultures in Collision*. New York: Pantheon Books of Random House, 1966.

Barth, H. *Travels and Discoveries in North and Central Africa... 1849–1855*. London: F. Cass and Co., Ltd., 1965.

Barton, F. *The Press of Africa—Persecution and Perseverance*. London: MacMillan, 1979.

Bauer, P.T. *Dissent on Development*. London: Weidenfeld, 1971.

Bay, E. (ed.) *Women and Work in Africa*. Boulder: Westview Press, 1982.

Bidwell, R. *Morocco Under Colonial Rule*. London: F. Cass and Co., Ltd., 1973.

Blake, J.W. *West Africa: Quest for God, 1454–1578*. London: Curzon Press, 1977.

Brett, E.A. *Colonialism and Underdevelopment in East Africa*. London: Heinemann Educational Books, 1973.

Brown, M. *Madagascar Rediscovered*. London: D. Tunnacliffe, 1978.

Bundy, C. *The Rise and Fall of the South African Peasantry*. London: Heinemann Educational Books, Ltd., 1979.

Carter, G., and P. O'Meara, eds. *Southern Africa in Crisis*. Bloomington: Indiana University Press, 1977.

Cervenka, Z. *The Unfinished Quest for Unity: Africa and the OAU.* London: J. Friedman Publishers, Ltd., 1977.

Chernoff, J.M. *African Rhythm and African Sensibility.* Chicago: University of Chicago Press, 1981.

Chibwe, E.C. *Arab Relations in the New World Order.* London: J. Friedman Publishers, Ltd., 1977.

Chittick, N. "Kilwa: An Islamic Trading City on the East African Coast." *History and Archeology.* Vol. 1. Nairobi: Thames and Hutchinson, 1974.

Clapman, C. *Liberia and Sierra Leone.* Cambridge: Cambridge University Press, 1976.

Clayton, A., and D.C. Savage. *Government and Labour in Kenya, 1895–1963.* London: F. Cass and Co., Ltd., 1974.

Cohen, R. *Labour and Politics in Nigeria, 1945–1971.* London: Heinemann Educational Books, Ltd., 1974.

Cooper, F. *Plantation Slavery on the East Coast of Africa.* New Haven: Yale University Press, 1977.

Crahan, M., and F.W. Knight, eds. *Africa and the Caribbean: The Legacy of a Link.* Baltimore: Johns Hopkins University Press, 1979.

Cronan, D.E. *Marcus Garvey.* Englewood Cliffs, NJ: Prentice-Hall, Inc., 1973.

Crowder, M. *West Africa Under Colonial Rule.* London: Hutchinson, 1968.

Cruise-O'Brien, D.B. *Saints and Politicians: Essays in the Organization of a Senegalese Peasant Society.* Cambridge: Cambridge University Press, 1975.

Curtin, P.D. *The Atlantic Slave Trade: A Census.* Madison: University of Wisconsin Press, 1967.

Curtin, P.D. *Economic Change in Pre-Colonial Africa: Senegambia in the Era of the Slave Trade.* Madison: University of Wisconsin Press, 1975.

Dalby, D., et al. *Drought in Africa.* London: International African Institute, 1977.

Davenport, T.R.H. *South Africa: A Modern History.* London: MacMillan, 1977.

Deng, F.M. *The Dinka of the Sudan.* New York: Holt, Rinehart & Winston, 1972.

Duffy, J. *Portuguese Africa.* Cambridge: Harvard University Press, 1959.

Duigan, P., and L.H. Gann, eds. *Colonialism in Africa, 1870–1960.* 5 volumes. Cambridge: Cambridge University Press, 1965–1975.

Dunn, J., ed. *West African States: Failure and Promise.* Cambridge: Cambridge University Press, 1978.

Economic Commission for Africa. *Survey of Economic and Social Conditions in Africa.* Addis Ababa, 1976.

Elphick, R. *Kraal and Castle: Khoikhoi and the Founding of White South Africa.* New Haven: Yale University Press, 1977.

Emecheta, B. *The Joys of Motherhood.* New York: George Braziller, Inc., 1979.

Evans-Pritchard, E.E. *Nuer Religion.* New York: Oxford at the Clarendon Press, 1940.

Evans-Pritchard, E.E. *Witchcraft, Oracles and Magic among the Azande.* New York: Oxford at the Clarendon Press, 1937.

Fage, J.D., and R. Oliver, eds. *The Cambridge History of Africa*. 8 volumes. Cambridge: Cambridge University Press, 1975.

Falconbridge, A. *Account of the Slave Trade on the Coast of Africa*. New York: AMS Press, Inc., 1973 (first published 1788).

Fraenkel, P. *The Namibians of South West Africa*. London: Minority Rights Group, 1974.

Fraser, I., and H. Cole, eds. *African Art and Leadership*. Madison: University of Wisconsin Press, 1972.

Furness, E.L. *Money and Credit in Developing Africa*. New York: Heinemann Educational Books, Ltd., 1975.

Garlake, P.S. *The Kingdoms of Africa*. Oxford: Oxford University Press, 1979.

Geiss, I. *The Pan-African Movement*. London: Methuen, 1974.

George, S. *How the Other Half Dies: The Real Reason for World Hunger*. London: Penguin, 1976.

Gibb, H.A.R., ed. *Ibn Battuta: Travels in Asia and Africa*. Boston: Routledge and Kegan Paul, Ltd., 1929.

Gide, A. *Travels in the Congo*. New York: Alfred A. Knopf, 1929.

Gifford, P., and W.R. Louis. *France and Britain in Africa: Imperial Rivalry and Colonial Rule*. New Haven: Yale University Press, 1971.

Gosovic, B. *UNCTAD: Conflict and Compromise*. London: Sijthoff, 1972.

Griaule, M. *Conversations with Ogotemmeli: An Introduction to Dogon Religious Ideas*. New York: Oxford University Press, 1965.

Grigg, D.B. *The Agricultural Systems of the World: An Evolutionary Approach*. Cambridge: Cambridge University Press, 1974.

Gugler, J. and W.G. Flanagan. *Urbanization and Social Change in West Africa*. Cambridge: Cambridge University Press, 1978.

Gutkind, P.C.W., et al., eds. *African Labour History*. London: Sage, 1978.

Gutkind, P.C.W. and P. Waterman, eds. *African Social Studies: A Radical Reader*. London: Heinemann Educational Books, Ltd., 1977.

Hafkin, N., and E. Bay (eds.). *Women in Africa: Studies in Social and Economic Change*. Stanford: Stanford University Press, 1976.

Harris, J.R., ed. *The Legacy of Egypt*. Oxford: Oxford University Press, 1971.

Hay, M. (ed.). *African Women: South of the Sahara*. London and New York: Longman, 1984.

Hayward, F., and Clyde R. Ingle, eds. *African Rural Development: The Political Dimension*. East Lansing: Michigan State University African Studies Center, 1972.

Henrikson, T.H. *Mozambique: A History*. London: R. Collings, 1978.

Hermer, C. *The Diary of Maria Tholo*. Johannesburg: Ravan Press, 1980.

Hess, A.C. *The Forgotten Frontier*. Chicago: University of Chicago Press, 1978.

Hopkins, A.G. *An Economic History of West Africa*. London: Longman, 1973.

Hughes, L. *An African Treasury*. New York: Crown Publishing, 1960.

Hymans, J.L. *Léopold Sédar Senghor: An Intellectual Biography.* Edinburgh: Edinburgh University Press, 1971.

Johnson, R.W. *How Long Will South Africa Survive?* London: MacMillan, 1977.

Jones, D. *Aid and Development in South Africa.* London: Croom Helm, Ltd., 1977.

Jones, T. *Ghana. The First Republic.* London: Methuen, 1976.

Kanza, T. *Conflict in the Congo: The Rise and Fall of Lumumba.* Harmondsworth: R. Collings, 1972.

Kapuscinski, R. *The Emperor: Downfall of an Autocrat.* New York: Harcourt Brace Jovanovich, Inc., 1984.

Kaunda, K.D. *Zambia Shall Be Free.* London: Heinemann Educational Books, Ltd., 1962.

Kennedy, E. *The Négritude Poets.* New York: Viking Press, 1975.

Kenyatta, J. *Facing Mount Kenya: The Tribal Life of the Gikuyu.* New York: Vintage Books, 1962.

Khaketla, B.M. *Lesotho 1970: An African Coup Under the Microscope.* London: C. Hurst, 1973.

Killick, T. *Development Economics in Action.* London: Heinemann Educational Books, Ltd., 1978.

Kilson, M.L. and R.I. Rotberg, eds. *The African Diaspora: Interpretative Essays.* Cambridge, Harvard University Press, 1976.

Klein, M., ed. *Peasants in Africa: Historical and Contemporary Perspectives.* London: Sage, 1980.

Knappert, J. *Four Centuries of Swahili Verse.* London: Heinemann Educational Books, Ltd., 1978.

Leakey, R. and R. Lewin. *Originals.* London: MacDonald, 1977.

Legum, C. *Ethiopia: The Fall of Haile Selassie's Empire.* London: R. Collings, Ltd., 1976.

Legum, C. *Pan-Africanism, A Short Political Guide.* New York: Praeger, 1962.

Le Vine, V.T. *The Cameroon Federal Republic.* Ithaca: Cornell University Press, 1971.

Le Vine, V.T. *The Cameroons from Mandate to Independence.* Berkeley: University of California Press, 1964.

Le Vine, V.T., and Timothy W. Luke. *The Arab-African Connection: Political and Economic Realities.* Boulder: Westview Press, 1979.

Lewis, I.M. *The Modern History of Somaliland.* London: Longman, 1965.

Leys, C. *Underdevelopment in Kenya.* London: Heinemann Educational Books, Ltd., 1975.

Liebenow, J.G. *Liberia, the Evolution of Privilege.* Ithaca: Cornell University Press, 1977.

Lienhardt, G. *Divinity and Experience: The Religion of the Dinka.* New York: Oxford at the Clarendon Press, 1961.

Linden, I. *Church and Revolution in Rwanda.* Manchester: Manchester University Press, 1977.

Lipsky, G.A. *Ethiopia: Its People, Its Society, Its Culture.* New Haven: Yale University Press, 1962.

Locke, A. *Negro Art: Past and Present.* Washington, D.C.: Associates in Negro Folk Education, 1936.

Louis, W.R., and J. Strengers. *E.D. Morel's History of the Congo Reform Movement.* Oxford: Oxford University Press, 1968.

Lowenthal, R. *Model or Ally? The Communist Powers and the Developing Countries.* London: Oxford University Press, 1977.

Luckham, R. *The Nigerian Military.* Cambridge: Cambridge University Press, 1971.

Mandela, N. *No Easy Walk to Freedom.* London: Heinemann Educational Books, Ltd., 1965.

Mangat, J.S. *A History of the Asians in East Africa.* Oxford: Oxford University Press, 1969.

Marcum, J.A. *The Angolan Revolution.* Cambridge: Harvard University Press, 1969 and 1978.

Markakis, J. *Ethiopia: Anatomy of a Traditional Polity.* Oxford: Oxford University Press, 1974.

Martin, I. *General Amin.* London: Faber, 1974.

Martin, T. *Race First: The Ideological and Organizational Struggle of Marcus Garvey and the Universal Negro Improvement Association.* Westport: Greenwood Press, 1976.

Mazrui, A.A. *Soldiers and Kinsmen in Uganda.* London: Sage, 1975.

Mazrui, A.A. *Towards a Pax Africana.* London: Weidenfeld and Nicolson, 1967.

Meillassoux, C., ed. *The Development of Indigenous Trade and Markets in West Africa.* London: International African Institute, 1971.

Mondlane, E. *The Struggle for Mozambique.* Harmondsworth: Panaf Books, Ltd., 1969.

Morton, K., and P. Tolloch. *Trade and Developing Countries.* London: Croom Helm, 1978.

Muga, E. *African Response to Western Christian Religion.* Kampala: Literaries Bureau, 1975.

Mutibwa, P.M. *The Malagasy and the Europeans.* London: Longman, 1974.

Mwase, G. (R.I. Rotberg, ed.). *Strike a Blow and Die: A Narrative of Race Relations in Colonial Africa.* Cambridge: Harvard University Press, 1967.

Nketia, J.H.K. *The Music of Africa.* London: Gollanz, 1975.

Nkrumah, K. *Revolutionary Path.* London: Panaf Books, 1973.

Nyerere, J. *Freedom and Socialism: A Selection from Writings and Speeches, 1965–1967.* Oxford: Oxford University Press, 1970.

Obiechina, E. *An African Popular Literature: A Study of Onitsha Market.* Cambridge: Cambridge University Press, 1973.

O'Connor, A.M. *The Geography of Tropical African Development.* 2nd ed. Oxford: Oxford University Press, 1978.

O'Keefe, P., and B. Wisner, eds. *Land Use and Development in Africa.* London: International African Institute, 1978.

Oliver, R., and B.M. Fagan. *Africa in the Iron Age.* Cambridge: Cambridge University Press, 1975.

Olorunsola, V., ed. *The Politics of Cultural Sub-Nationalism in Africa.* New York: Anchor Books, 1972.

Olorunsola, V. *Soldiers and Power: The Development Performance of the Nigerian Military Regime.* Stanford: Hoover Institution Press, 1977.

Ominde, S.H., and C.N. Ejiogu, eds. *Population Growth and Economic Development in Africa.* London: Heinemann Educational Books, Ltd., 1972.

Oppong, C. *Marriage Among a Matrilineal Elite: A Family Study of Ghanaian Senior Civil Servants.* Cambridge: Cambridge University Press, 1974.

Osuntokun, A. *Nigeria in the First World War.* London: Longman, 1979.

Palmer, R. *Land and Racial Domination in Rhodesia.* London: Heinemann Educational Books, Ltd., 1977.

Palmer, R., and N. Parsons, eds. *The Roots of Rural Poverty in Central and Southern Africa.* London: Heinemann Educational Books, Ltd., 1977.

Penrose, E.F., ed. *European Imperialism and the Partition of Africa.* London: F. Cass and Co., Ltd., 1975.

Perrings, C. *Black Mineworkers in Central Africa: Industrial Strategies and the Evolution of an African Proletariat in the Copperbelt, 1911–1941.* London: Heinemann Educational Books, Ltd., 1979.

Phillipson, D.W. *The Later Prehistory of Eastern and Southern Africa.* London: Heinemann Educational Books, Ltd., 1977.

Pratt, C. *The Critical Phase in Tanzania, 1945–1968.* Cambridge: Cambridge University Press, 1976.

Prothero, R.M., ed. *People and Land in Africa South of the Sahara.* New York: Oxford University Press, 1972.

Ranger, T.O. *The Revolt in Southern Rhodesia.* London: Heinemann Educational Books, Ltd., 1967. New ed. 1979.

Richards, A. *Chisungu: A Girls' Initiation Ceremony among the Bemba of Zambia.* New York: Tavistock Publications, 1982.

Riesman, P. *Freedom in Fulani Social Life.* Chicago: University of Chicago Press, 1977.

Robinson, P.T., and E. Skinner, eds. *Transformation and Resiliency in Africa.* Washington, D.C.: Howard University Press, 1983.

Rostow, W.W. *The Stages of Economic Growth.* Cambridge: Cambridge University Press, 1960.

Rotberg, R.I. *The Rise of Nationalism in Central Africa: The Making of Malawi and Zambia, 1873–1964.* Cambridge: Harvard University Press, 1966.

Rotberg, R.I., and A.A. Mazrui, eds. *Protest and Power in Black Africa.* New York: Oxford University Press, 1970.

Rout, L.B. *The African Experience in Spanish America.* Cambridge: Cambridge University Press, 1976.

Rubenson, S. *The Survival of Ethiopian Independence.* London: Heinemann Educational Books, Ltd., 1976.

Sandbrook, R., and R. Cohen, eds. *The Development of an African Working Class.* London: Longman, 1975.

Sanneh, L.O. *The Jakhanke: The History of an Islamic Clerical People of the Sene-gambia.* London: International African Institute, 1979.

Shostak, M. *Nisa: The Life and Words of a !Kung Woman.* Cambridge: Harvard University Press, 1981.

Skinner, E. *The Mossi of the Upper Volta.* Stanford: Stanford University Press, 1964.

Skinner, E., ed. *Peoples and Cultures of Africa.* New York: The Doubleday/Natural History Press, 1973.

Soyinka, W. *Aké: The Years of Childhood.* New York: Random House, 1982.

Soyinka, W. *Myth, Literature, and the African World.* Cambridge: Cambridge University Press, 1976.

Stevens, C. *Food Aid and the Developing World.* London: Croom Helm, Ltd., 1979.

Stevens, C. *The Soviet Union and Black Africa.* London: MacMillan, 1976.

Turner, H.W. *History of an African Independent Church.* 2 volumes. Oxford: Oxford University Press, 1967.

Turner, V. *The Forest of Symbols.* Ithaca: Cornell University Press, 1967.

Turner, V. *Revelation and Divination in Ndembu Ritual.* Ithaca: Cornell University Press, 1975.

Ullendorff, E. *Ethiopia and the Bible.* London: Oxford University Press, 1968.

UNESCO. *The Sahel: Ecological Approaches to Land Use.* Paris: H.M.S.O., 1975.

United Nations. *A Trust Betrayed: Namibia.* New York: 1974.

van Onselen, C. *Chibaro: African Mine Labour in Southern Rhodesia, 1900–1933.* London: Pluto, 1976.

Vansina, J. *Kingdom of the Savanna.* Madison: University of Wisconsin Press, 1966.

Walshe, P. *The Rise of Nationalism in South Africa: The ANC, 1912–1952.* London: C. Hurst, 1970.

Warwick, P., ed. *The South African War.* London: Longman, 1980.

wa Thiong'o, N. *Petals of Blood.* New York: E.P. Dutton, 1977.

Welmers, W.E. *African Language Structures.* Berkeley and Los Angeles: University of California Press, 1973.

White, H.P., and M.B. Gleave. *An Economic Geography of West Africa.* London: G. Bell, 1971.

Williams, G., ed. *Nigeria: Economy and Society.* London: R. Collings, 1976.

Wilson, M., and L. Thompson, eds. *Oxford History of South Africa.* 2 volumes. Oxford: Oxford University Press, 1973.

Wolfson, F. *Pageant of Ghana.* New York: Oxford University Press, 1958.

# *The Africans* Project Team

*SENIOR EDITOR:* Ali A. Mazrui is professor of Political Science at the University of Michigan and research professor at the University of Jos, Nigeria. A native Kenyan, Mazrui earned a B.A. from Manchester University, an M.A. from Columbia University, and a doctorate from Oxford University. He taught at Makerere University in Uganda for ten years and is an editor of UNESCO's projected eight-volume history of Africa. He also has served as president of the African Studies Association in the United States and as host of "Searching for a New Zimbabwe," a BBC *Panorama* production. In 1979, he delivered the BBC Reith Lectures entitled *The African Condition.*

*MANAGING EDITOR:* Toby Kleban Levine, president of Toby Levine Communications, is telecourse director and print managing editor of *The Africans.* She is responsible for the instructional design and print materials for the course. The former director of educational activities at WETA-TV, she served as curriculum director of *From Jumpstreet: A Story of Black Music* and as project manager for *Congress: We the People.* She also developed an adult learning programming service for colleges in the Washington, D.C., area and a marketing/distribution service for WETA-produced programs. She was previously employed as an instructional materials designer at Creative Studies, Inc., in Boston; the Children's Museum of Boston; and Synectics, Inc., in Cambridge, Massachusetts.

*COORDINATING EDITOR:* Tracy Burke Carrier came to the project from Cairo, where she taught English at an Egyptian girls' college. She also worked as an editor and broadcast specialist at Virginia Commonwealth University in Richmond and as an announcer and community affairs director at WRFK-FM, the public radio station in Richmond.

*COORDINATING EDITOR:* Frieda Lindfield Werden is a writer and editor whose experience includes scholarly, trade, and textbook publishing. Recently, she served as series producer for National Public Radio's *Faces, Mirrors, Masks: 20th Century Latin American Fiction*, 13 half-hour sound portraits of writers and their culture. Werden was also associate curator of the Texas Women's History Project (1980–1981) and has produced media projects for the Texas Committee for the Humanities.

323

## Chapter Authors and Coordinators

Christopher Davis-Roberts is assistant professor of Anthropology and Afro-American Studies at the University of Michigan. She conducted field research among the Tabwa of Zaire from 1974 to 1978, studying concepts of illness and therapy. Presently, she is completing work on two manuscripts: one on the Tabwa medical system and another on Tabwa concepts of mind, experience, and self as these develop in the context of coping with illness.

Merrick Posnansky is professor of History and Anthropology and director of the Institute of Archaeology at the University of California/Los Angeles. He is presently undertaking archaeological and ethnographic research in Ghana and Togo. He serves on the editorial boards of the *Journal of African History* and the *West African Journal of Archaeology*. He is former warden of the prehistoric sites at the Royal National Parks of Kenya, curator of the Uganda Museum, assistant director of the British Institute in East Africa, director of African Studies at Makerere University College in Kampala, and professor of Archaeology at the University of Ghana.

Elliott P. Skinner is Franz Boas Professor of Anthropology at Columbia University. The former United States ambassador to Burkina Faso (Upper Volta), Skinner has conducted extensive field work in that region and has published *Strangers in African Societies*; *Roots of Time: A Portrait of African Life and Culture*; and *African Urban Life: The Transformation of Ouagadougou*.

Lamin Sanneh is assistant professor of the History of Religion at Harvard University. He had previously taught at the Universities of Ibadan, Fourah Bay, and Legon in Africa and the University of Aberdeen, Scotland. Sanneh, who was born in the Gambia, is the author of over 30 articles and papers and several books, including *West African Christianity*. He is the co-editor of the *Journal of Religion in Africa*.

Robert I. Rotberg is professor of History and Political Science at Massachusetts Institute of Technology and leads a special Africa Study Group at the Center for International Affairs at Harvard University, where he has also taught. He has been concerned with African problems since the late 1950s, when he was a Rhodes Scholar at Oxford. In addition to his more recent books, *Namibia: Political and Economic Prospects* and *Suffer for the Future: Policy Choices in Southern Africa,* he has published more than a dozen books on African politics and history. He is on the Council of Foreign Relations and is a trustee of the World Peace Foundation of Oberlin College.

Pearl T. Robinson is associate professor of Political Science at Tufts University. A specialist in the politics of rural development, she is the head of Oxfam-America's Overseas Projects Committee. Currently, she is working on a book about traditional authority and the political economy of rural development in Niger. She is co-editor and co-author of *Transformation and Resiliency in Africa* and has published articles on regional development issues in the Sahel, Afro-Arab security relations, and political change in Niger.

Fred M. Hayward is professor of Political Science and academic associate dean for the Social Sciences at the university of Wisconsin at Madison. He is former chairman of the African Studies Program and the Political Science Department at the university. He has taught at the University of Ghana and at Fourah Bay College in Freetown, Sierra Leone, where he was Fulbright Professor in 1980–1981. His published works about Africa include studies on national integration, political participation, civil education, political information, rural politics, elections, and political parties. His field work has been carried out primarily in Ghana, Senegal, Sierra Leone, and Nigeria.

Victor A. Olorunsola is chairman of Political Science at Iowa State University. He is a member of the Council of the American Political Science Association and several other organizations, including the Royal African Society of England. His books include: *State Versus Ethnic Claims: An African Policy Dilemma*; *Soldiers and Power, Societal Reconstruction in Two African States*; and *The Politics of Cultural Sub-Nationalism in Africa*. His numerous articles in journals include several on Nigeria and Ghana.

Gwendolyn Mikell is associate professor of Anthropology in the Department of Sociology at Georgetown University. She sits on the executive committee of the African Studies Program in the School of Foreign Service. She has conducted field work on the Akan of Ghana and has done extensive research on issues regarding women and rural development. She has contributed to and edited articles on African women and development and is currently completing a book, *Cocoa and Chaos*.

Victor T. Le Vine is professor of Political Science at Washington University in St. Louis. He has taught at the University of Ghana and at Yaoundé (Cameroon) University and has conducted research in Ghana, Cameroon, Senegal, Burkina Faso, Niger, Benin, Nigeria, the Central African Republic, and the Congo Peoples' Republic. He has lectured in West, Central, and East Africa. His current projects include a study of petrodollar politics in Cameroon, Gabon, and the Congo, as well as editing an encyclopedic volume on African political parties. His published works include books on Cameroon, a book on bureaucratic corruption in Ghana, a monograph on elite generational conflict in francophone Africa, and a volume on the political economy of Afro-Arab relations.

Mbye Cham is assistant professor in the African Studies and Research Program at Howard University in Washington, D.C. Originally from the Gambia, in West Africa, he studied in Senegal, France, and the United States, specializing in oral and written African literature and film. His publications have appeared in *Présence Africain, Africana Journal, The American Journal of Islamic Studies, A Current Bibliography on African Affairs, The Western Journal of Black Studies, Ufahamu,* and others. He is currently editing a book, *Literature, Film, and Society in Africa.*

## Executive Producers

Charles Hobson, American project director and executive producer is senior vice president—special projects at WETA-TV. Hobson has been project director/executive producer of numerous educational and public television projects, including the 13-part telecourse *From Jumpstreet: A Story of Black Music.*

David Harrison, British project director and executive producer, formerly was deputy editor of the BBC's *Panorama* series. Harrison, who received the British Royal Television Society's Supreme Award for the best documentary of 1979, has been filming in Africa for 12 years.

## Producers

Peter Bate, producer, has filmed in 20 countries in the past ten years, specializing in Middle East issues. Prior to his work on *The Africans*, he produced *Hanging Fire*, a four-part series on Israel; edited film for the BBC; and was a producer on the BBC's *Panorama* series.

Tim Copestake, producer, specializes in the production of current affairs programs at the BBC. He is a graduate of Oxford University and the London International Film School and was film editor of an EMMY award—winning program for *Panorama* about Georgi Markov and the arms trade in South Africa.

## Senior Researcher

Diana Frank is research coordinator for special projects at WETA-TV. She is a graduate of Georgetown University (Phi Beta Kappa) and holds a Ph.D. in linguistics from Cornell University. She also is the author of a novel in Danish, *Et Uaar.*

## Curriculum Advisory Committee

Mbye Cham, Assistant Professor, African Studies and Research Program, Howard University

Christopher Davis-Roberts, Assistant Professor, Center for Afro-American and African Studies and Department of Anthropology, University of Michigan

Jacques Dubois, Director, Special Academic Areas, Prince George's Community College, Maryland

Joseph E. Harris, Professor of History, Howard University

Fred M. Hayward, Professor of Political Science and Academic Associate Dean, University of Wisconsin/Madison

Victor T. Le Vine, Professor of Political Science, Washington University, St. Louis

Merrick Posnansky, Professor of History and Anthropology and Director, Institute of Archaeology, University of California/Los Angeles

Pearl T. Robinson, Associate Professor of Political Science, Tufts University

Robert I. Rotberg, Professor of Political Science and History, Massachusetts Institute of Technology

Elliott P. Skinner, Franz Boas Professor of Anthropology, Columbia University

Colin M. Turnbull, Research Associate, American Museum of Natural History

## Additional Acknowledgments

The project would like to thank the following individuals for their assistance to this project at critical points: Ellen Casey, WETA project coordinator; Carol Gasparach, permissions coordinator; Vernetta Gill, WETA administrative assistant; Caren B. Levine, project assistant; Judith Pickford-Barse, manuscript preparation; Steven Reichert, project assistant; and Emily Stuman, researcher.

# ———— Acknowledgments ————

Grateful acknowledgment is made to the following for permission to reprint previously published material.

## Part I

*African Rhythm and African Sensibility* by John Miller Chernoff, 1981, pp. 155–156. Chicago: The University of Chicago Press, 1981. © 1979 by the University of Chicago. All rights reserved. Published 1979. Phoenix edition 1981. Printed in the United States of America.

*Witchcraft, Oracles and Magic among the Azande* by E.E. Evans-Pritchard, 1937, pp. 69–70. By permission of Oxford University Press.

*Revelation and Divination in Ndembu Ritual* by Victor Turner, 1975, pp. 221–222, 238–239. By permission of Manchester University Press.

*The Forest of Symbols: Aspects of Ndembu Ritual* by Victor Turner, 1967, pp. 101–104. Published by Cornell University Press. First published in *The Proceedings of the American Ethnological Society,* 1964.

*Facing Mount Kenya: The Tribal Life of the Gikuyu* by Jomo Kenyatta, 1962, pp. 102, 190–191, 193, 196–197. Published by Random House, Inc. All rights reserved under International and Pan-American.

*Chisungu: A Girls' Initiation Ceremony among the Bemba of Zambia* by Audrey I. Richards, 1982, pp. 47–51. Tavistock Publications, London. Reprinted by permission.

*Conversations with Ogotemmêli: An Introduction to Dogon Religious Ideas* by Marcel Griaule, 1965, pp. 77, 82–83, 131, 138–139, 141. Published by Oxford University Press. Reprinted by permission of the International African Institute, London.

*Divinity and Experience: The Religion of the Dinka* by Godfrey Lienhardt, 1961, pp. 10–13. By permission of Oxford University Press.

*Freedom in Fulani Social Life: An Introspective Ethnography* by Paul Riesman, translated by Martha Fuller, 1977, pp. 205–206, 223–224. Published by the University of Chicago Press. © 1977 by The University of Chicago. All rights reserved. Published 1977. Printed in the United States of America.

*The Joys of Motherhood* by Buchi Emecheta, 1979, pp. 10–15. © 1979 by Buchi Emecheta, reprinted courtesy of the publisher, George Braziller, Inc.

# Chapter One

*Nisa: The Life and Words of a !Kung Woman* by Marjorie Shostak, 1981, pp. 81–83, 98–99, 242–243. © 1981 by Marjorie Shostak. Reprinted by permission of Harvard University Press.

*Things Fall Apart* by Chinua Achebe, 1958, pp. 19–20, 29, 31–32. © by Chinua Achebe 1958. All rights reserved. First published by William Heinemann, Ltd., 1958. First published in the *African Writers Series* 1962. Reprinted 1962. Reprinted by permission of William Heinemann, Limited.

*The Dinka of the Sudan* by Francis Mading Deng, 1972, pp. 1–3, 5–6. © 1972 by Holt, Rinehart and Winston, Inc. Reprinted by permission of CBS College Publishing.

# Chapter Two

*Facing Mount Kenya: The Tribal Life of the Gikuyu* by Jomo Kenyatta, 1962, pp. 163–185. Published by Random House, Inc. All rights reserved under International and Pan-American Copyright Conventions.

*Ibn Battuta: Travels in Asia and Africa 1325–1354,* translated by H.A.R. Gibb, 1929, pp. 328–330. Reprinted by permission of Augustus M. Kelley, Publishers.

*African Response to Western Christian Religion* by Erasto Muga, 1975, pp. 211–214. Published by The East African Literature Bureau, Kampala, Uganda.

# Chapter Three

"In the Beginning Was God," *The Prayers of African Religion* by John S. Mbiti, 1976, p. 144. By permission of Maryknoll.

Excerpts from "God," *Nuer Religion* by E.E. Evans-Pritchard, 1956, pp. 1–4, 7–9. By permission of Oxford University Press.

Excerpts from "Sacrifice," *Nuer Religion* by E.E. Evans-Pritchard, 1956, pp. 198–208. By permission of Oxford University Press.

# Chapter Four

*An Account of the Slave Trade on the Coast of Africa* by Alexander Falconbridge, 1977, pp. 149–150, 154–155, 159, 161. Originally published in London, 1788; reprinted by AMS Press, New York, 1977.

*Travels and Discoveries in North and Central Africa . . . 1849–1855* by Heinrich Barth, 1965, pp. 510–511, 513–519. Reprinted by permission of Frank Cass and Company, Ltd., London, England.

*Strike a Blow and Die: A Narrative of Race Relations in Colonial Africa* by George W. Mwase (ed. Robert I. Rotberg), 1967, pp. 82–84. Published by Harvard University Press. *Strike a Blow and Die: A Narrative of Race Relations in Colonial Africa* is © 1967 by Robert I. Rotberg and reprinted by permission of the publisher.

*Travels in the Congo* by André Gide, 1957, pp. 64–67, 70–75, 77. © 1929. Renewed 1957 by Alfred A. Knopf, Inc. Reprinted by permission of the publisher.

*Facing Mount Kenya: The Tribal Life of the Gikuyu* by Jomo Kenyatta, 1962, pp. 305–306. Published by Random House, Inc. All rights reserved under International and Pan-American Copyright Conventions.

## Chapter Five

Excerpt from "Traditional Clientage and Political Change in a Hausa Community" by Pearl T. Robinson, *Transformation and Resiliency in Africa* edited by Pearl T. Robinson and Elliott Skinner, 1983, pp. 117–118. Reprinted by permission of Howard University Press.

*The African-Arab Conflict in the Sudan* by Dunstan M. Wai, 1981, pp. 1, 2, 8. By permission of Africana Publishing Company. © 1981 by Dunstan M. Wai.

*Petals of Blood* by Ngugi wa Thiong'o, 1977, pp. 87–88, 91–95. Reprinted by permission of the publisher, E.P. Dutton, a division of New American Library.

*The Emperor: Downfall of an Autocrat* by Ryszard Kapuscinski, 1983, pp. 98–100. © 1978 by Ryszard Kapuscinski; English translation © 1983 by Ryszard Kapuscinski. Reprinted by permission of Harcourt Brace Jovanovich, Inc.

*The Diary of Maria Tholo* by Carol Hermer, 1980, pp. 23–26. © 1980 by Carol Hermer. Reprinted by permission of Ravan Press (PTY), Ltd., Johannesburg.

## Chapter Six

"Gold Coast Seeks Lead in Industry," *The New York Times*, May 15, 1955. © 1955 by The New York Times Company. Reprinted by permission.

"Black Man in a White Court," *No Easy Walk to Freedom: Articles, Speeches and Trial Addresses of Nelson Mandela*, 1973, pp. 125–131. Reprinted by permission of Heinemann Educational Books Ltd.

"The Policy of Self Reliance," *Freedom and Socialism: A Selection from Writings and Speeches 1965–1967* by Julius K. Nyerere, 1970, pp. 235–246. Reprinted by permission of Oxford University Press, East and Central Africa.

*Revolutionary Path* by Kwame Nkrumah, 1973, pp. 185–188. Copyright and all rights reserved, Panaf Books Limited, 243 Regent Street, London W1R 8PN.

## Chapter Seven

"Development and Economic Cooperation: Proposals for Consideration by African Governments," United Nations Economic Commission for Africa, 1977. In *Economic Bulletin for Africa* 11:2 (New York: The United Nations).

"Implementation of the Strategies and the Plan of Action at the International Global Level," *After Lagos What?* by Adebayo Adedeji, 1983, pp. 41–44. Reprinted by permission of The African Centre For Applied Research and Training in Social Development, Libyan Arab Jamahiriya.

## Chapter Eight

*Aké: The Years of Childhood* by Wole Soyinka, 1982, pp. 126–128. © by Wole Soyinka. Reprinted by permission of Random House, Inc.

"Circumcision and Secret Societies" by J. Sorie Conteh, *West Africa,* August 18, 1980, pp. 1541, ff.

*Ambiguous Africa: Cultures in Collision* by Georges Balandier, translated by Helen Weaver, 1966, pp. 186–187. © 1966 by Pantheon Books, a division of Random House, Inc., and Chatto and Windus, Ltd. Reprinted by permission of the publisher.

"Egypt's Assembly Bars Full Islamic Law" by Judith Miller, *The New York Times,* May 5, 1985. © 1985 by The New York Times Company. Reprinted by permission.

*Pageant of Ghana* by Freda Wolfson, 1958, pp. 249–252. By permission of Oxford University Press.

## Chapter Nine

"Redeeming the African Motherland" by Marcus Garvey, *Philosophy and Opinions of Marcus Garvey,* vol. 1, edited by Amy Jacques Garvey, New York: Universal Publishing House, 1923, pp. 71–74.

*Pan-Africanism: A Short Political Guide* by Colin Legum, 1962, pp. 151–155. Published by Frederick A. Praeger Publishers. © by Colin Legum. Reprinted by permission of the author.

"The Question of South Africa" by Bishop Desmond Tutu, *Africa Report,* Jan.–Feb. 1985, pp. 50–52. Originally appeared as a statement to the United Nations Security Council, October 23, 1984.

## Part IV

*Negro Art: Past and Present* by Alain Locke, 1936, pp. 34–37. © 1936 by The Associates in Negro Folk Education, Washington, D.C.

*Léopold Sédar Senghor: An Intellectual Biography* by Jacques Louis Hymans, 1971, pp. 53–55, 58–59. Reprinted by permission of Edinburgh University Press.

"Ghana" from "African Heaven" by Francis Ernest Kobina Parkes, *An African Treasury* edited by Langston Hughes, 1960, pp. 170–172. © 1960 by Langston Hughes. Used by permission of Crown Publishers, Inc.

"...And The Other Immigrant" by Gabriel Okara from *An African Treasury,* edited by Langston Hughes, 1960, pp. 184–186. © 1960 by Langston Hughes. Used by permission of Crown Publishers, Inc.

"Guinea" by Jacques Roumain, translated by Langston Hughes, *Anthology of Contemporary Latin American Poets,* edited by Dudley Fitts, 1942, pp. 21–22. © 1942 by New Directions Publishing Corporation. Reprinted by permission of New Directions Publishing Corporation.

"The Meaning of Africa," *The Truly Married Woman* by Abioseh Nicol, 1965. Published by Oxford University Press. © Abioseh Nicol. Permission obtained through David Higham Associates, Limited.

## Maps

1.1, Physical Features of Africa. Adapted from "Africa" in *Encyclopaedia Britannica,* 15th edition, 1983, 1:186, by permission of Encyclopaedia Britannica, Inc.

1.2, Rainfall Reliability. Courtesy of Merrick Posnansky.

1.3, Vegetation Zones of Africa. From *Africa,* edited by Phyllis M. Martin and Patrick O'Meara, 1977. Reprinted by permission of Indiana University Press.

1.4, Soils. Courtesy of Merrick Posnansky.

1.5, Area of Tsetse Fly Infestation. Courtesy of Merrick Posnansky.

4.1, Eighteenth Century Slave Trade. From *African History in Maps* by Michael Kwamena-Poh, Jon Tosh, Richard Waller, and Michael Tidy, 1982. Longman Group Limited. Reprinted by permission.

4.2, Nineteenth Century Slave Trade. From *African History in Maps* by Michael Kwamena-Poh, Jon Tosh, Richard Waller, and Michael Tidy, 1982. Longman Group Limited. Reprinted by permission.

4.3, Partition of Africa Following the 1884 Berlin Conference. From *The London Times Atlas of World History.* Reprinted by permission.

## Tables

7.1, Sub-Saharan Africa and the World: Basic Data Chart. From *Accelerated Development in Sub-Saharan Africa: An Agenda for Action,* The World Bank, 1981, pp. 2–4. Reprinted by permission of The World Bank.

9.1, Apartheid: The Situation at Mid-Year 1985. From "Afrique du Sud: un apartheid new look," *Jeune Afrique,* May 1, 1985, p. 23.

# Index of Readings
## (By Author)

# INDEX